Deed Abstracts
Belmont County
Ohio

Volumes D, E and F
(1811-1817)

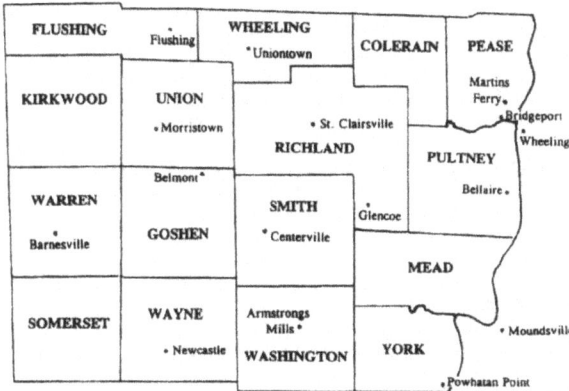

Compiled by
Lorraine Indermill Quillon

HERITAGE BOOKS
2020

HERITAGE BOOKS

AN IMPRINT OF HERITAGE BOOKS, INC.

Books, CDs, and more—Worldwide

For our listing of thousands of titles see our website
at
www.HeritageBooks.com

Published 2020 by
HERITAGE BOOKS, INC.
Publishing Division
5810 Ruatan Street
Berwyn Heights, Md. 20740

International Standard Book Numbers
Paperbound: 978-0-7884-4554-5
Clothbound: 978-0-7884-7330-2

DEDICATION

To my grandpa,
John Phillip Kauffman--

For the memory of sitting in his lap,
being lovingly teased,
and hearing him call all the women in his life "Sis."

I'm sure I will hear him say that again one day.

TABLE OF CONTENTS

<u>Page</u>

LIST OF ILLUSTRATIONS

INTRODUCTION

This volume consists of an index to deeds recorded officially between 1811 and 1817. However, the execution dates may occasionally fall outside that range.

The information is given in the following general order: volume and page of the deed book on which the document appears, date of execution, grantor (and wife) and residence; grantee and residence; amount of consideration offered, land description, history of land, neighbors, if conveyed in fee simple, date by which payments should be completed if done in installments, amount of land involved; the way the grantor(s) signed the document; names of witnesses; name of interviewer (and his office) who conducted the acknowledgment interview (and date of interview if date of document and its approximate recording date are separated by a substantial period of time [a purely subjective evaluation on the compiler's part]); recording data. Some of these elements may be missing in some deeds.

Surnames are placed in all capitals to make them easier to find on the page. Variations in recording of names within the documents and compiler's comments are enclosed within square brackets. The most frequently used spelling within the document is the one which was indexed, unless there was an unusually divergent variation. The only names omitted in the index are those of the U.S. presidents involved with the patenting of land. Please be sure to scan the entire abstract page indicated in the index in order to find any names repeated in subsequent entries on that page.

Dates are entered in standard genealogical order (day, 3-letter month, year). However, if in the original text a month was numbered rather than named (i.e., "the fourth day of the sixth month"), the entry would read as follows: "4 d 6 m" before the year. This will allow for any possibility that the archaic Quaker system of month identification might have been used. Dates recorded subsequently in the affected records may clarify the dating system used.

Abbreviations Used

> BCO = Belmont County, Ohio
> JCO = Jefferson County, Ohio
> S T R = Section [#] Township [#] Range [#]
> J.P. = Justice of the Peace
> CCP = Court of Common Pleas

(Note that although "rood" is often used in the original, it was replaced by the more conventional "rod.")

Names in the index which are obviously the same will be grouped together. References to names which may be related but which were not clearly enough the same will be added after the initial listing.

An honest attempt has been made to report this information exactly as it appears in the original document. However, the reader will need to make allowances for human frailties on the part both of the original recorders and the compiler. Square brackets indicate uncertainty of interpretation or alternate spellings of the entry in the text as well as any additional comments or observations by the compiler. A seeming discrepancy in dates or unusual names is underlined or marked by "[sic]" to show that these items have been rechecked.

It is earnestly hoped that researchers will find this series a useful tool for locating individuals in the Belmont County area during this time period. As with any secondary compilation, its greatest value will be helping to find original records. These originals should always be consulted as the ultimate source of information.

> Lorraine Indermill Quillon
> Charlottesville, Virginia
> March 2007

Deed Abstracts, Belmont County, Ohio
Volume D (Feb 1811 - Sep 1814)

D-1   Indenture, 22 Aug 1805, William WILEY (wife Martha), Peas twp., BCO; Charles IRWIN, same; $145.10, part of S 6 T 6 R 3, NBR: great Road leading to Martin's Ferry, George GIVEN, 22 acres 2 rods 8 perches, conveyed to WILEY by Alexander LATIMORE on 4 Mar 1804, recorded in Book A, p. 304, conveyed to LATIMORE from John JOHNSTON of Washington County on 20 Aug 1802, recorded in Book A, p. 121, fee simple; WIT: Thos. MITCHELL, James GORDON, ack. "same day and year," Thos. MITCHELL, J.P., ent. 20 Feb 1811, rec. 21 same.

D-2   Indenture, 11 Feb 1811, Charles IRWIN (wife Margaret), BCO; George GIVEN, BCO; $180, 30 acres 1 rod 4 poles; his seal, her mark; WIT: Thos. THOMPSON, John HORSEMAN, ack. Thos. THOMPSON, J.P., ent. 20 Feb 1811, rec. 22 same.

D-3   Indenture, 20 Feb 1811, Andrew FENNEFROCK (wife Susanna), BCO; William HUETZ [HULTZ?], BCO; $80, lots #15 and #16 in addition to St. Clairsville as laid out by William MATHERS, conveyed from Sterling JOHNSTON to Samuel STOVER on 26 Dec 1807, as recorded in Book B, p. 214; WIT: Eleazer KINNY, Sterling JOHNSTON, ack. Sterling JOHNSTON, J.P., ent. 21 Feb 1811, rec. 22 same.

D-4   Indenture, 26 Dec 1810, Richard FREEMAN (wife Margery), BCO; Richard CARTER, Ohio County, Virginia; $400, beginning east corner of [NBR:] Thomas THOMPSON's lot, Ezra WILLIAMS; WIT: Elizabeth MORRISON, Sally FLETCHER, ack. 26 Dec 1810, D. MORRISON, J.P., ent. 22 Feb 1811, rec. 23 same.

D-5   Indenture, 22 Feb 1811, David MOORE, Esqr. (wife Isabella), BCO; Joseph GRIFFITH, BCO; $1,100, part of S 28 T 6 R 3, NBR: Frederick AMRINE, 158 acres 1 rod 17 perches, conveyed to MOORE by Jacob ENDLY (wife Mary), on 27 Aug 1808; WIT: Joseph MORRISON, Sterling JOHNSTON, ack. Sterling JOHNSTON, J.P., ent. 22 Feb 1811, rec. 23 same.

D-6   Indenture, 14 Jan 1811, Isaac VORE (wife Eleanor), BCO; Robert WINTER, BCO; $900, lots #84, 1/4 acre, conveyed to VORE by James BARNES (wife Elizabeth) on 11 May 1805; and #91, 1/4 acre, conveyed to VORE by Casper SEVERS (wife Anna) on 20 Aug 1807, fee simple; WIT: Joseph ROBERTS, Sterling JOHNSTON, ack. Sterling JOHNSTON, J.P., ent. 23 Feb 1811, rec. same.

D-8   Indenture, 3 Jan 1811, Bazaleel WELLS (wife Sally), JCO; Daniel McPEAK, BCO; $300, part of S 19 T 7 R 3, border Stump Run, NBR: Thomas BLACKLEDGE, 200 acres; WIT: Andrew BELL, Margt. MARSHALL, ack. JCO, 2 Jan 1811, Andrew BELL, J.P., ent. 23 Feb 1811, rec. 23 same.

D-9   1 Mar 1811, James McCOY (wife Amy), Richland twp., BCO; John LIST, Junr., Wheeling, Ohio County, Virginia; $408, part of SE 1/4 S 30 T 7 R 4, 20 acres, also part of SW corner of S 1/2 S 24 T 7 R 4, 32 acres, total of 52 acres; her name at seal is Ruhamah, WIT: John HINDS, Sterling JOHNSTON, ack. Sterling JOHNSTON, J.P., ent. 1 Mar 1811, rec. same.

D-10   Indenture, 1 Mar 1811, John LIST, Junr., Wheeling, Ohio County, Virginia; David DRAKE, Richland twp., BCO. LIST bound to DRAKE for $288 to be paid by 1 Mar 1815 without interest, securing debt by conveying part of SE 1/4 S 30 T 7 R 4 (20 acres) and part of SW corner of S 1/2 S 24 T 7 R 4 (32 acres), void if debt paid; WIT: John HINDS, Sterling JOHNSTON, ack. Sterling JOHNSTON, J.P., ent. 1 Mar 1811, rec. 2 same; payments made: $40 on 3 Mar 1812, $160 on 15 Nov 1813, and balance 5 Jun 1815 to satisfy mortgage, receipts recorded 20 Jul 1815.

D-12   To all people, James HEDGES, Sheriff, James CALDWELL obtained a judgment against Merchant DEFORD at December term of CCP for $272.49 from 23 May 1808, HEDGES upon a writ of Allias Lavari Facias levied on tract of land, part of S 1 T 6 R 3, 93 1/2 acres, on 15 Aug 1810 sold tract to James CALDWELL for $250, sgn: 27 Nov 1810; WIT: Josiah HEDGES, John BARNES, ack. 27 Nov 1810, Robert GRIFFITH, J.P., ent. 2 Mar 1811, rec. same.

D-13   Indenture, 31 Jul 1810, Mathew SCOTT (wife Elizabeth), BCO; James HUFFMAN, BCO; $150, part of E part of SW 1/4 S 1 T 6 R 3, 66 acres; WIT: :Thos. THOMPSON, George MIERS [his mark], ack. 31 Jul 1810, Thos. THOMPSON, J.P., ent. 4 Mar 1811, rec. same.

D-14   Indenture, 22 d 12 m 1810, Isaac COPPOCK (wife Mary), BCO; William BUNDY, BCO; $360, 81 acres, part of S 13 T 8 R 6; WIT: William PATTERSON, Demsey BOSWELL, ack. John GRIER, J.P., ent. 5 Mar 1811, rec. same.

D-16   Indenture, 31 Dec 1810, Arthur MORRISON (wife Grizzel), BCO; John BOYD, BCO; $320, NE 1/4 S 4 T 8 R 5, Steubenville district, part of land patented to MORRISON on 13 Oct 1807; his seal, her mark; WIT: Robert MORRISON, John FINLEY, ack. 31 Dec 1810, John WILEY, Assoc. Judge, ent. 8 Mar 1811, rec. same.

D-17   James MADISON, President, to all to whom . . . Caleb GREGG, assignee of Stephen McPHERSON, having deposited in the Treasury a certificate and made full payment for SW 1/4 S 4 T 7 R 5, Steubenville district, land granted to GREGG, sgn: 21 Apr 1810, James MADISON, R. SMITH, Secretary of State, ent. 12 Mar 1811, rec. same.

D-17   Indenture, 15 Mar 1811, William W. GAULT, BCO, atty. for Samuel PELLERS of Springfield, Muskingum County, Ohio, by letters dated 15 Aug 1809 recorded in deed office in Book C, p. 315; Samuel ADAMS, Washington County, Pennsylvania; $35, fee simple, lot #35 in Morristown, conveyed to PELLERS by deed dated 15 Jun 1808; WIT: Robert GRIFFITH, William FARIS, ack. Robert GRIFFITH, J.P., ent. 15 Mar 1811, rec. 16 same.

D-18   Indenture, 26 Feb 1811, Eleanor EDWARDS, BCO; John PRICE, BCO; lease 80 acres, part of NW 1/4 S 13 T 10 R 6, dwelling house where Eleanor lives excepted, at decease of her husband John EDWARDS, PRICE to pay $10 every six months plus hay; both mark, WIT: John MOORE, John LEMMENS [his mark], ent. 16 Mar 1811, rec. same.

D-19   Indenture, 15 Mar 1811, Hugh LYONS, BCO; Thomas LYONS, BCO; $30, fee simple, part of S 35 and 36 T 6 R 3, NBR: James HANNAH, 30 acres, reservation of a cole bank during his natural life; WIT: Robert GRIFFITH, Wm. FARIS, Junr., ack. Robert GRIFFITH, J.P., ent. 16 Mar 1811, rec. 18 same.

D-20   Indenture, 25 Feb 1811, Amos JANNEY, BCO; Henry BROWN, BCO; $28, 10 acres, in S 2 T 9 R 5, Steubenville district, fee simple; Amos JANNEY for Joseph JANNEY, WIT: Thos. B. CLARK, Robert LEE, ack. 19 Mar 1811, Sterling JOHNSTON, J.P., ent. 19 Mar 1811, rec. 21 same.

D-21   Indenture, 21 Mar 1811, John FORREST (wife Rachel), BCO; Robert GRAHAM, BCO; $63, NBR: Samuel CRAWFORD, near St. Clairsville, 1/8 acre, conveyed to FORREST by John FRITCH by deed dated 26 Dec 1809, recorded in Book C, p. 127 [or 124?]; his seal, her mark; WIT: Robert GRIFFITH, Henry MITCHELL, ack. Robert GRIFFITH, J.P., ent. 21 Mar 1811, rec. same.

D-22   Indenture, 22 Mar 1811, William DEVLIN (wife Jane), BCO; Isaac HOGE, BCO; $620, NBR: Issaker FOULKS, Evan PHILLIPS, George KELLER, Isaac HOGUE, 80 acres, part of S 23 T 7 R 4, part of land conveyed to DEVLIN and Neal MAHAN by Stephen MILLER, and from MAHAN and wife [not named] to DEVLIN, fee simple; WIT: Solomen WARDELL, Sterling JOHNSTON, ack. Sterling JOHNSTON, J.P., ent. 22 Mar 1811, rec. same.

D-23   Indenture, 22 Mar 1811, Isaac HOGE (wife Elizabeth), BCO; Issacher
FOULKE, BCO; $310, part of S 23 T 7 R 4, NBR: Issacher, Even PHILLIPS, 40
acres, conveyed from William DEVLIN and wife [unnamed] to HOGUE on same
date, fee simple; WIT: Solomon WARDELL, Sterling JOHNSTON; ack. Sterling
JOHNSTON, J.P., ent. 22 Mar 1811, rec. same.

D-24   Indenture, 27 Feb 1811, Jacob COON (wife Barbara), BCO; John
PLOWMAN, BCO; $325, part of NW 1/4 S 14 T 8 R4, patented to COON on 27
Aug 1805, 50 acres, NBR: George LOVE; sgn. Jacob KUHN and Conroe KUHN
[her mark], WIT: David WALLACE, George COON [his mark], ack. 27 Feb 1811,
David WALLACE, J.P., ent. 23 Mar 1811, rec. 25 same.

D-26   Indenture, Know all men, Joseph MERIT [MERRIT], BCO, sell to Wm.
W. FAQUHAR of Knox County, Ohio, for $400, land on which he now resides,
near St. Clairsville, NBR: Moses MOOREHEAD, 5 1/2 acres, $200 plus interest
to be paid to FAQUHAR within 60 days, void if debt paid; sgn: 5 Mar 1811, WIT:
John BROWN, Sterling JOHNSTON, ack. 6 Mar 1811, Sterling JOHNSTON, J.P.
Richland twp., ent. 25 Mar 1811, rec. same.

D-27   Indenture, 25 Mar 1811, Valentine SHEARER (wife Catherine), BCO;
John McMAHAN, BCO; $1,100, NBR: John MAXWELL, Frederick AMERINE,
125 acres 31 perches, part of S 28 T 6 R 3, excepting one acre with benefit of
springs agreeable to agreement between Mordice YARNALL, fee simple,
conveyed to SHEARER by Mordecai YARNALL (wife Phebe) on 6 Oct 1806; his
seal, her mark; WIT: Sterling JOHNSTON, John BROWN, ack. Sterling
JOHNSTON, J.P., ent. 25 Mar 1811, rec. 26 same.

D-28   Indenture, 4 Dec 1810, Frederick OLDFATHER (wife Barbara), Brothers
Valley Township, Somerset County, Pennsylvania, yeoman; Jacob OLDFATHER,
same; land patented to Frederick on 6 Mar 1806, 1/4 S 24 T 6 R 4, 160 acres, for
$480 paid by Jacob all land conveyed by Frederick; his seal [but name written to
appear like "Gundney AULT NORTHS], her mark, WIT: Gabriel KUMMEL,
Jacob KUMMEL, ack. 4 Dec 1810, Somerset County, John KUMMEL, ack. 4 Dec
1810, of Gabriel KIMMEL's signing document, Jacob KIMMEL, WIT: John
KIMMEL.

D-29   To all people, John PATTERSON (wife Geizy), St. Clairsville, BCO;
Thomas McCALL, Washington County, Pennsylvania; on 22 April 1802
PATTERSON and McCALL executed a partnership in trade at St. Clairsville under
title Patterson and McCall, under which title acquired land and houses in St.
Clairsville (an inn lot #24 conveyed by John BLY on 26 Dec 1806, #15 and #23
conveyed by William CONGLETON [wife Nancy] on 9 Jan 1807, #13 containing
1/4 acre conveyed by Joseph McCONNELL [wife Sarah] on 4 Sep 1805, out lot

#10 in land adjoining addition to St. Clairsville containing 11 acres 1 rod 20 perches conveyed by Obadiah JENNINGS on 1 Sep 1806, lot #30 late property of William MATHERS sold by Sheriff Josiah HEDGES on 18 Apr 1805, lot #21 [NBR: John PATTERSON, Samuel SULLIVAN] sold by Samuel SULLIVAN [wife Mary] on 30 Nov 1804, lots #3 and #4 on south side of St. Clairsville conveyed by John G. HAMILTON [wife Nancy] by deed dated 10 Mar 1807), PATTERSON executing deed to John GRIMES, as partnership dissolved by mutual consent, all property quit claimed to McCALL; sgn. 17 Jan 1811, John PATTERSON, Grizey PATTERSON, Thomas McCALL, WIT: Jacob NAGLE, Sterling JOHNSTON, John BUCHANAN, ack. 17 Jan 1811, BCO, of PATTERSONs by Sterling JOHNSTON, J.P., ack. 31 Jan 1811, Washington County, of McCALL by John BUCHANAN, BUCHANAN certified by 6 Feb 1811 by Alexander MURDOCK, Prothonotary, ent. 26 Mar 1811, rec. 29 same.

D-33   Indenture, 26 Jun 1810, George PAULL, BCO; John PATTERSON, BCO; $200, "all that messuage and two lots on south side of St. Clairsville," lots #33 and #34 in addition to St. Clairsville; WIT: Sterling JOHNSTON, John BROWN, ack. 26 Jun 1810, Sterling JOHNSTON, J.P., ent. 26 Mar 1811, rec. 2 Apr same.

D-34   Indenture, 26 Jul 1810, William CONGLETON (wife Nancy), BCO; John PATTERSON, BCO; $15, lot #28 in addition to St. Clairsville; WIT: John C. GILKISON, Sterling JOHNSTON, ack. 27 Jul 1810, Sterling JOHNSTON, ent. 26 Mar 1811, ent. 3 Apr same.

D-34   Indenture, 29 Jan 1811, James PAULL (wife Hannah), Fayette County, Pennsylvania; George PAULL, BCO; $1,600, part of S 6 T 7 R 4, NBR: David HUTCHINSON, 232 acres 1 rod 39 perches; WIT: Jacob STEWART, James PAULL, ack. Fayette County, James PAULL, Junr., James FINLEY, Assoc. Judge, 29 Jan 1811, FINLEY certified 31 Jan 1811 by Richard William LANE, Prothonatary, CCP, ent. 26 Mar 1811, rec. 3 Apr same.

D-36   Indenture, 25 Mar 1811, John PATTERSON (wife Grizzey), BCO; George PAULL, BCO; $126, part of S 5 T 7 R 4, 15 acres 1 rod 30 perches; his seal, her mark, WIT: Robert GRIFFITH, Richard TRUAX, ack. Robert GRIFFITH, J.P., ent. 26 Mar 1811, rec. 3 Apr same.

D-37   Indenture, 25 Mar 1811, Thomas BARR, BCO; George PAULL, BCO; $4, part of S 31 T 7 R 3, small run putting into Indian Wheeling Creek, 93 acres 2 rods; WIT: Sterling JOHNSTON, Robert GRIFFITH, William BROWN, ack. Sterling JOHNSTON, J.P., ent. 26 Mar 1811, rec. 3 Apr same.

D-38   Indenture, 23 Feb 1811, Allen BOND (wife Sarah), BCO; David KINKEAD, BCO; $40, part of S 13 T 8 R 5, Steubenville district, patented to

BOND on 21 Mar 1808, 10 acres, adjoining lands of BOND and KINKEAD; his seal, her mark, WIT: Joseph WRIGHT, James EVANS, [drawing included], ack. 23 Feb 1811, William SMITH, J.P., ent. 30 Mar 1811, rec. 4 Apr same.

D-40   Indenture, William BARCHURST (wife Elizabeth), BCO; Joseph MARSHALL, BCO; $40, lot #114 in St. Clairsville, fee simple; sgn: 1 Apr 1811, his seal [BARCUS], her mark [BARCUS], WIT: Zebulon WARNER, Solomon BENTLEY, ack. Zebulon WARNER, J.P., ent. 2 Apr 1811, rec. 4 same.

D-41   Deed, 31 Dec 1810, Wm. W. FARQUHAR (wife Esther), Knox County, Ohio; Joseph MERRITT, BCO; $600, land adjoining St. Clairsville, NBR: Moses MOOREHEAD, 5 1/2 acres; WIT: Eliza FARQUHAR, James COLVILLE, ack. Knox County, 31 Dec 1810, James COLVILLE, Assoc. Judge, COLVILLE certified by James SMITH at Mt. Vernon in Feb 1811, ent. 3 Apr 1811, rec. 4 same.

D-42   Indenture, 2 Apr 1811, Archibald CRAWFORD (wife Elizabeth), BCO; William WOODS, BCO; $250, 50 acres, part of S 12 T 7 R 4, conveyed from Samuel BROWN (wife Mary) to CRAWFORD on 9 Mar 1808, fee simple; his seal, her mark, WIT: Sterling JOHNSTON, William JOHNSTON, ack. Sterling JOHNSTON, J.P., ent. 3 Apr 1811, rec. 4 same.

D-43   Indenture, 22 Mar 1811, William DIXON (wife Rebeckah), Menallen twp., Fayette County, Pennsylvania; William DIXON, Junr., son of aforesaid, BCO; $50, NW 1/4 S 31 T 8 R 4, 15 acres 9 perches, originally patented to Daniel MERRIT on 27 Aug 1805, conveyed by him and wife Nancy to Moses MERRIT on 1 Oct 1807, Moses and wife Polly conveyed to DIXON on 31 Mar 1810; WIT: Eli HAINES, Daniel JOHNSON, ack. Fayette County, 22 Mar 1811, Daniel JOHNSON, J.P., ack. BCO, Zebulon WARNER, J.P., ent. 6 Apr 1811, rec. 10 same.

D-44   Indenture, 5 Feb 1811, John McWILLIAMS (wife Nancy), BCO; James EAGLESON, BCO. $100 paid by William SMITH on account of James EAGLESON, NE corner of S 25 T 4 R 2, 50 acres 35 perches; his seal, her mark, WIT: Robt. HANNAH, James ALEXANDER, ack. 5 Feb 1811, James ALEXANDER, Assoc. Judge, CCP, ent. 9 Apr 1811, rec. 12 same.

D-46   Indenture, 1 Mar 1811, James ALEXANDER, Senr., BCO; John McWILLIAMS, BCO; $500, land in NE part of S 6 T 5 R 3, Pultney twp., 151 acres 5 perches, in trust for Elizabeth KINKEAD, wife of David KINKEAD, remainder to the eight heirs of James ALEXANDER, Senr., John McWILLIAMS trustee; WIT: Thos. MITCHELL, Wm. WILEY, ack. 1 Mar 1811, Thos. MITCHELL, J.P., ent 9 Apr 1811, rec. 11 same.

D-47   Indenture, 8 Apr 1811, Jacob COON (wife Barbara), BCO; William CLARK, BCO; $381, 61 1/2 acres, part of SW 1/4 S 14 T 8 R 4, patented to COON on 27 Aug 1805, NBR: Jacob COON; his seal, her mark [names appear to be in German and transcriber had difficulty interpreting], WIT: David WALLACE, Alexr. CASSIL, ack. Dd. WALLACE, J.P., ent. 9 Apr 1811, rec. 13 same.

D-48   Indenture, 13 Apr 1811, Jacob COON (wife Barbary), BCO; George LOVE, BCO; $100, part of NW 1/4 S 14 T 8 R 4, patented to COON on 27 Aug 1805, 25 acres, NBR: John PLOWMAN, John COON; his seal, her mark, WIT: Alexr. HAMOND, Robt. HAMOND, ack. David WALLACE, J.P., ent. 15 Apr 1811, rec. 17 same.

D-49   Indenture, 19 Jan 1811, Alexander GRAY (wife Jane), BCO; James GRAY, BCO; $1, part of S 32 T 7 R 3, Steubenville district, patented to Alexander, 100 acres; [witnesses apparently given after ack.], ack. 19 Jan 1811, David MARSHALL, WIT: John NIBLOCK, William GATTON, [ack???]ent. 20 Apr 1811, rec. same.

D-50   Indenture, 1 d 4 m 1811, Joseph PATTERSON (wife Hannah), BCO; William BAILEY, BCO; $200, 80 acres, E 1/2 of SE 1/4 S 13 T 8 R 6; his seal, her mark, WIT: Nathan SIDWELL, Nicolouis [CIPUMGER], ack. 1 d 4 m 1811, John GRIER, J.P., ent. 29 Apr 1811, rec. same.

D-51   Indenture, 20 Mar 1811, James McMILLEN (wife Jane), New Ark twp., Licking County, Ohio; Joseph TILTON, Warren twp., JCO; $1,100, fractional S 15 and 21 T 4 R 2, 80 acres, NBR: Ohio River, Joseph TILTON, John CONNELL; his seal, her mark [Jane A. McMILLEN], WIT: Eddward [HENICK], William O BANON, ack. 20 Mar 1811, Licking County, New Ark twp., William WILSON, President of the fourth circuit of CCP, ent. 30 Apr 1811, rec. same.

D-52   Indenture, 21 Mar 1811, Rice BOGGS (wife Dosha), BCO; William BOGGS, BCO; $400, part of S 14 T 7 R 4, NBR: Rice BOGGS, 36 acres, part of land conveyed to William DUER by Samuel OSGOOD and Walter LIVINGSTON, by DUER to Henry ABORN, by ABORN to Stephen TILLINGHOST, by TILLINGHOST to Nathanaiel SCOT, from SCOT to John JOHNSTON, from JOHNSTON to Rice and William BOGGS, fee simple; WIT: Jos. JOHNSTON, Sterling JOHNSTON, ack. 26 Mar 1811, Sterling JOHNSTON, J.P., ent. 3 May 1811, rec. same.

D-53   Indenture, 21 Mar 1811, William BOGGS, BCO; Rice BOGGS, BCO; $400, part of NE 1/4 S 14 T 7 R 4, 124 acres, part of land conveyed to William DUER by Samuel OSGOOD and Walter LIVINGSTON, from DUER to Henry ABORN, from ABORN to Stephen TILLINGHOST, from TILLINGHOST to

Nathaniel SCOTT, from SCOTT and wife to John JOHNSTON, from JOHNSTON to Rice and William BOGGS on 18 Apr 1803; WIT: Sterling JOHNSTON, Jos. JOHNSTON, ack. 26 Mar 1811, Sterling JOHNSTON, J.P., ent. 3 May 1811, rec. same.

D-54   Indenture, 26 d 12 m 1810, Caleb ENGLE (wife Mercy), BCO; Benjamin COMBS, BCO; [$60 (written in fold of book)], beginning at SW corner of NW 1/4 S 30 T 6 R 4, 12 acres, patented to ENGLE on 29 Dec 1808; [no witnesses given], ack. 26 d 12 m 1810, William SINCLAIR, J.P., ent. 3 May 1811, rec. 4 same.

D-55   Indenture, 22 Mar 1811, John CARTER (wife Mary), BCO, and Josiah UPDEGRAFF (wife Hannah), BCO; John CLARK, Senr., BCO; $150, part of NE 1/4 S 10 T 7 R 4, fee simple, S conveyed to Wm. BOGGS by Bazeliel WELLS by deed dated 13 Jun 18__, conveyed by BOGGS and wife to John CARTER and Josiah UPDEGRAFF by deed dated 13 Mar 1810, NBR: Wheeling Road, 1/2 acre; WIT: John I. WRIGHT, Sterling JOHNSTON, ack. 22 Mar 1811 (CARTERs) and 25 Mar 1811 (UPDEGRAFF), Sterling JOHNSTON, J.P., ent. 4 May 1811, rec. same.

D-57   Indenture, 4 May 1811, John CLARK, Senr., BCO; John HENTHORN, Junr., son of William of Licking County, Ohio; $150, "paid by the said John HENTHORN, Junr., son of William," [then repeated again several more times!], part of NE 1/4 S 10 T 7 R 4, conveyed to CLARK by John CARTER and Josiah UPDEGRAFF on 22 Mar 1811, 1/2 acre, WIT: Zebulon WARNER, Benjamin RUGGLES, ack. Zebulon WARNER, J.P., ent. 4 May 1811, rec. same, 25 May 1813, $100 paid by CLARK to HENTHORN as a first payment of the mortgage, WIT: Wm. FARIS, Junr.

D-58   Indenture, 26 Dec 1810, James WILKINS (wife Lydia), BCO; George ALBEN, St. Clairsville, BCO; $300, E 1/2 of lot #37 and part of lot #38 in St. Clairsville, fee simple; WIT: Sterling JOHNSTON, Jos. JOHNSTON, ack. 7 Feb 1811, Sterling JOHNSTON, J.P., ent. 4 May 1811, rec. same.

D-59   Indenture, 29 Apr 1811, William SPENCER (wife Sarah), BCO; William MOORE [MORE], Loudon County, Virginia; $600, part of SE 1/4 S 7 T 9 R 6, patented to SPENCER on 10 Sep 1806, fee simple; WIT: Henry GILBERT, John MOORE, ack. Henry GILBERT, J.P., ent. 4 May 1811, rec. same.

D-60   Indenture, 14 Feb 1811, Bezeliel WELLS and Elias VAN ARSDALE, two of extrs. of LW&T of Daniel McELHERAN, deceased, of Newark, Essex Cunty, New Jersey; John WALLACE, BCO; McELHERAN by LW&T dated 25 May 1807 empowered extrs. or survivor(s) to dispose in fee simple of his real estate, William HILL in New York City, merchant, Bezeliel WELLS, of Steubenville,

JCO, and Elias VAN ARSDALE, of Newark, Essex County, New Jersey, extrs; $295, NE 1/4 S 1 T 6 R 3, 197 acres, WIT: Philip C. HAY, Thomas WARD [for VAN ARSDALE], J. G. HENING, G. HARTFORD [for WELLS], ack. 17 Apr 1811, JCO, J. G. HENING, J.P., ack. 19 Feb 1811, New Jersey, Thomas WARD, Judge inferior court, WARD certified by Silas CONDIT, ent. 6 May 1811, rec. 7 same.

D-62   Indenture, 4 May 1811, Isaac McALLISTER (wife Mary), BCO; James KELSEY, BCO; $74, part of S 2 T 6 R 3, NBR: John WALLACE, Thomas THOMPSON, James KELSEY, 18 acres 2 8/10 rods; his seal, her mark, WIT: Thos. THOMPSON, Ezra WILLIAMS, ack. Thos. THOMPSON, J.P., ent. 13 May 1811, rec. 14 same.

D-63   Indenture, 15 Feb 1810, Leonard DIVEN (wife Abigal), BCO; Henry BILMAN, BCO; $603, 109 1/2 acres, part of S 2 T 7 R 4, fee simple; both mark, WIT; Sterling JOHNSTON, Valentine AULT, ack. 13 May 1811, Sterling JOHNSTON, J.P., ent. 13 May 1811, rec. 14 same.

D-64   Indenture, 29 d 9 m 1810, William SATTERTHWAITE, Gurnsey County, Ohio; John SMITH, BCO; $110, NBR: Saml. POTTS, 10 1/2 acres, part of land given to William by LW&T of his father William SATTERTHWAITE, part of S 13 T 7 R 3, patented to William, Senr., on 9 d 3 m 1803; sgn: William W. SATTERTHWAITE, WIT: Thomas SATTERTHWAITE, Jesse WHITE, ack. 14 May 1811, Sterling JOHNSTON, J.P., ent. 15 May 1811, ent. same.

D-66   Indenture, 31 Dec 1810, Samuel GREGG, atty. for Josiah HOUGH (wife Pleasant), Loudon County, Virginia; Charles PIDGEON, BCO; $567, SE 1/4 S 1 T 8 R 5, 162 acres, patented to HOUGH on 15 Aug 1808, fee simple; WIT: Robert MORRISON, Enos WEST, ack. 31 Dec 1810, Duncan MORRISON, J.P., ent. 16 May 1811, rec. same.

D-67   Indenture, 15 May 1811, Amos JANNEY, BCO, atty. for Joseph JANNEY, Loudon County, Virginia; William SHAW, BCO; $556, part of S 2 T 9 R 5, Steubenville district, NBR: Robert LEE, 102 1/2 acres, fee simple; WIT: Robert LEE, Nicholas DAVIS, Joseph SHARP, ack. Sterling JOHNSTON, J.P., ent. 16 May 1811, rec. 17 same.

D-68   Indenture, 17 Dec 1810, Daniel McPEAK (wife Elizabeth), BCO; Charles IRWIN, BCO; $114, part of S 12 T __ R 3, 22 acres 3 rods, part of land conveyed to McPEAK by Jonathan TAYLOR (wife Ann) on 1 d 6 m 1810, fee simple; both mark, WIT: Sterling JOHNSTON, Henry STEWART, ack. 22 Dec 1810, Sterling JOHNSTON, J.P., ent. 18 May 1811, rec. same.

D-69   Indenture, 27 Mar 1811, George PAUL; Josiah DILLON (wife Dorothy), Archibald WOODS; on 25 Jul 1809 DILLON by deed of same date conveyed to George PAUL lots #59 and #60 in St. Clairsville so he could raise money required to cover money Samuele SHARP, William SMITH, and Ezer DILLON had to advance for Josiah DILLON as his endorsers to the Bank of Marietta for $2,500, which they were required to do, now PAUL conveys to WOODS the two lots for $2,100; sgn: George PAULL, Josiah DILLON, Dorithy DILLON, WIT: Edw. BRYSON, Saml. DILLON, ack. 27 Mar 1811, Edw. BRYSON, Justice, ent. 21 May 1811, rec. 22 same.

D-71   Indenture, 23 May 1811, Thomas TIPTON (wife Kizia [Kezia]), BCO; Joseph PARISH, Senr., BCO; $300, part of SE 1/4 S 9 T 7 R 4, conveyed to TIPTON by Bazalel WELLS by deed dated 13 Nov 1798, 60 acres; his seal, her mark, WIT: Zebulon WARNER, Samuel ISRAEL, ack. Zebulon WARNER, J.P., ent. 23 May 1811, rec. 25 same.

D-72   Indenture, 16 Apr 1811, Jonathan ELLIS (wife Lydia), Union twp., BCO; George CARR, same; $400, 100 acres, part of SW 1/4 S 3 T 9 R 5, Steubenville district, patented 16 Aug 1807; WIT: James GARRETT, Jane PICKERING [her mark], ack. 16 Apr 1811, Enos PICKERING, Justice, ent. 29 May 1811, rec. same.

D-73   Indenture, 10 May 1811, John NICHOL (wife Ann), Pees twp., BCO; Benjamin VANFOSSEN, Union twp., BCO; $800, SW 1/4 S 25 T 8 R 5, patented to NICHOL, fee simple; his seal, her mark, WIT: Zebulon WARNER, Jeremiah FAIRHURST, ack. Zebulon WARNER, J.P., ent. 29 May 1811, rec. 30 same.

D-74   Indenture, 26 d 12 m 1810, Abraham ENGLE (wife Patience), BCO; Caleb ENGLE, BCO; $430, part of NW 1/4 S 21 T 7 R 4, NBR: James BELLANGE, 43 acres 1 rod 34 poles, part of land that Elijah MARTIN (wife Rebeckah) of Adams County, Ohio, conveyed on 21 Oct 1805 to Abraham ENGLE, as recorded in Book A, p. 468; his seal, her mark; WIT: Samuel ENGLE, Beulah BRADUCK, ack. 26 d 12 m 1810, William SINCLAIR, J.P., ent. 3 Jun 1811, rec. 4 same.

D-76   Indenture, 20 d 11 m 1810, James EDGERTON (wife Sarah), BCO; Isaac HALL, BCO; $300, SW 1/4 S 4 T 6 R 5; WIT: [Nicolous FRYUNNGER (probably German), John GRIER, Senr., ack. 20 d 11 m 1810, John GRIER, J.P., ent. 6 Jun 1811, rec. 7 same.

D-77   Indenture, 22 d 12 m 1810, William BUNDY (wife Sarah), BCO; Richard ENGLISH, BCO; $340, 108 acres, NW 1/4 S 36 T 7 R 6; his seal, her mark; WIT: :William PATTERSON, Demsey BOSWELL, ack. ack. 22 d 12 m 1810, John GRIER, J.P., ent. 6 Jun 1811, rec. 7 same.

D-78   Indenture, 18 Apr 1811, Jacob COON (wife Barbary), BCO; Robert HAMON, BCO; $770, part of NW and SW 1/4 S 14 T 8 R 4, 110 acres, patented to COON on 27 Aug 1805, NBR: John COON, George COON; his seal, her mark, both appear to be German, WIT: David WALLACE, Alexr. CASSIL, ack. 8 Apr 1811, Dd. WALLACE, J.P., ent. 9 Jun 1811, ent. 11 same.

D-79   Indenture, 15 Apr 1811, Jacob WINLIN (wife Margaret), BCO; Ezer [Ezar] DILLON, BCO; $740, part of S 4 T 5 R 4, 70 acres 19 perches; both mark, WIT: Edw. BRYSON, James COLLINS, ack. 15 Apr 1811, Edw. BRYSON, J.P., ent. 18 Jun 1811, rec. same.

D-80   Indenture, 9 d 4 m 1811, Margaret OUTLAND and James EDGERTON, extrs. of William OUTLAND, dec'd; James BROCK, all BCO; $320, SE 1/4 S 18 T 7 R 6; WIT: John GRIER, Senr., Robert GRIER, ack. 9 d 4 m 1811, John GRIER, J.P., ent. 6 Jun 1811, rec. 7 same.

D-81   Know all men, Saml. SPRIGG, BCO, for $1,000, sell to James TAYLOR, Muskindum County, Ohio; lot adjoining commons of St. Clairsville, 7 acres, containing a horsemill and distillery, conveyed to SPRIGG by "Deed Roll" dated 27 Nov 1809; sgn: 7 Feb 1811, WIT: Benj. RUGGLES, Zebulon WARNER, ack. 11 Feb 1811, Zebulon WARNER, Justice, ent. 18 Jun 1811, rec. same.

D-82   Indenture, 15 May 1811, John SMITH (wife Anny [Anna]), JCO; Phineas MARING, BCO; $160, part of S 13 T 7 R 3, conveyed to SMITH by William W. SATTERTHWAITE on 29 d 9 m 1810, fee simple; WIT: Robert WATSON, John WATSON, ack. 18 May 1811, John WATSON, J.P., ent. 22 Jun 1811, rec. same.

D-83   Indenture, 19 Feb 1811, Sterling JOHNSTON (wife Mary), BCO; Eleazer KINNY, BCO; $50, lot #98 in St. Clairsville, fee simple; WIT: Solomon WARDELL, Thomas BARR, ack. 24 Jun 1811, Robert GRIFFITH, J.P., ent. 24 Jun 1811, rec. 25 same.

D-84   Indenture, 24 Jun 1811, Joseph POSEY (wife Susanna), BCO; Isiah ALLEN, BCO; $704, part S 20, T 7 R 4, NBR: Isiah ALLEN [previous purchase of POSEYs], 100 acres 2 rods 20 perches, conveyed to POSEY by John MARTIN on 8 Dec 1806 as recorded in Book B, p. 44, fee simple; [her seal "S. Susana POSY"], WIT: Sterling JOHNSTON, Robert GRIFFITH, ack. Sterling JOHNSTON, J.P., ent. 24 Jun 1811, rec. 25 same.

D-85   Indenture, 22 Jun 1811, Leonard HART, Senr. (wife Jamima), BCO; Margaret HAZLETT, BCO; $62.59, part of land conveyed by William CHAPLINE to HART, part of S 20 T 8 R 5, beginning on commons south of Morristown, 10 acres 1 rod 29 perches; both mark, WIT: Richard FOSTER, James HAZLETT, ack. Duncan MORRISON, J.P., ent. 28 Jun 1811, rec. 29 same.

p.. 86   Indenture, 1 Feb 1811, Samuel McCUNE (wife Sarah), BCO; John McBURNEY, BCO; $200, 50 acres, part of NW 1/4 S 8 T 9 R 5, granted to Samuel McCUNE by patent dated 27 Mar 1809; WIT: John CAMPBELL, John PATTERSON, ack. 1 Feb 1811, John CAMPBELL, J.P., ent. 6 Jul 1811, rec. same.

D-87   Know all men, Peter MANIFOLD, New Town, New York, legally authorized and impowered [sic] by warrant of attorney from David MORRIS (wife Christian) and Elizabeth MERCIER, heirs at law of John D. MERCIER, dec'd, late of State of New York, to sell land in Ohio, two sections unnamed, sold part during lifetime by Jacob [CEONS OR CEOUS?], Daniel McELHERAN and Absolum MARTIN, his attorneys, to Wm. BELL, Danl. HARRIS, and Robert BELL, now MANIFOLD, attorney for heirs of John D. MERCIER, sells to Saml. SPRIGG of BCO balance of two sections, 225 acres for $100, sgn: 6 Feb 1811, David MORRIS, Christiane MORRIS, Elizabeth MERCIER, by Peter MANIFOLD, atty., WIT: Edward G. CARLIN, James SPRIGG, Zac SPRIGG, ack. 25 Jun 1811, BCO, of witnesses to MANIFOLD's signing, Thomas THOMPSON, Justice, ent. 8 Jul 1811, rec. same.

D-88   Indenture, 5 Jul 1811, Samuel GREGG, Senr., (wife Ann), BCO; Samuel GREGG, Junr., BCO; on 1 Oct 1806 patent issued to Samuel Senr., then of Ross County, Ohio, for S 33 T 7 R 4, Steubenville district, now for $60 selling 10 acres 20 poles of said land, NBR: John SPENCER; WIT: William SINCLAIR, Traverse GEORGE, ack. William SINCLAIR, J.P., ent. 8 Jul 1811, rec. 9 same.

D-89   Indenture, 17 Apr 1811, William BROWN (wife Sally), BCO; Samuel ISRAEL, BCO; $300, lot #29 in addition to St. Clairsville, fee simple; WIT: John PATTERSON, Sterling JOHNSTON, ack. 7 Jul 1811, Sterling JOHNSTON, J.P., ent. 12 Jul 1811, rec. 13 same.

D-90   Indenture, 27 Mar 1811, George PAULL, Josiah DILLON (wife Dorothy), and Charles HAMMOND [three parties], whereas on 25 Jul 1809 DILLON conveyed to PAULL property north of commons of St. Clairsville (NBR: William BROWN, John BROWN), 7 acres, also piece of land being part of land whereon Robert THOMPSON now lives, 3 acres, purpose to raise $2,500 or enough to save harm to William SMITH, Samuel SHARP, and Ezer DILLON as Josiah DILLON's endorsers at the Bank of Marietta for the sum of $2,304.45 on 3 Jan 1811, PAULL sold some property to Archibald WOODS of Ohio County, Virginia, for $2,100, of which $204.45 has been paid by WOODS, PAULL now selling to HAMMOND to secure repayment of WOODS money before 3 Jan 1812, overplus to be paid to Samuel SPRIGG for the use of THORNBURGH MILLER & WEBSTER; WIT:

Edw. BRYSON, Saml. DILLON, ack. 27 Mar 1811, Edw. BRYSON, J.P., ent. 19 Jul 1811, rec. 20 same.

D-92   Indenture, 29 May 1811, David LOCKWOOD (wife Rebecca [Rebeckah]), BCO; John DELONG, Gurnsey [sic] County, Ohio; $317, NE 1/4 S 11 T 4 R 3, also 7 acres of a fractional S 5 T 4 R 3 adjoining David HANNAH's line, both in York twp, BCO, fee simple; WIT: William FLETCHER, Levenah LOCKWOOD, ack. 29 May 1811, Samuel DILLE, J.P., ent. 24 Jul 1811, rec. 27 same.

D-93   Indenture, 10 d 2 m 1810, Levi WELLS (wife Margaret), BCO; Horton HOWARD, James RALEY, Samuel POTTS, and Aquila M. [BOLLON] [no location given]; $166.87 1/2, to latter parties as "Trustees appointed by the preparative meeting of Concord to receive and place out at interest a certain Legacy bequeathed by Wm. SATTERTHWAIT for the schooling of certain poor children," SE corner (1/8) of S 9 T 7 R 3, NBR: John LLOYD, Wm. MILHOUS, 80 acres, to be reversed if WELLS pays $166.887 1/2 with interest before 10 d 2 m 1817; his seal, her mark, WIT: Thos. MITCHELL, Nancy MITCHELL, ack. 10 Feb 1810, Thomas MITCHELL, J.P., ent. 27 Jul 1811, rec. same; release recorded in Book H, p. 373.

D-95   Indenture, 11 May 1811, David PARKINS, BCO; Stephen BROCK, BCO; PARKINS executed bonds to Evan JENKINS on 14 Apr 1809 for $225.30, Stephen BROCK bound as surety for that money, now securing payment by conveying part of SW S 24 T 8 R 5, Steubenville district, 77 acres 1 rod 9 perches, void if PARKINS pays to BROCK the $225.30 with interest before 1 Nov 1815; WIT: Enos PICKERING, Thomas BURK, David PICKERING, ent. 31 Jul 1811, rec. 2 Aug same; release in margin of p. 95 dated 10 Jul 1815, WIT: Peter TALLMAN, Nathan PARKINS.

D-97   Indenture, 4 Jul 1811, Ralph HEATH (wife Elizabeth), St. Clairsville, BCO; Peter YARNELL, same; $750, lot #61 in St. Clairsville; WIT: Zebulon WARNER, Jeremiah FAIRHURST, ack. 4 Jul 1811, Zebulon WARNER, J.P., ent. 31 Jul 1811, rec. 2 Aug same.

D-98   Indenture, 10 Aug 1811, George PAULL (wife Elizabeth), BCO; John BAKER, BCO; $748, part of S 31 T 7 R 3, 93 acres 2 rods; WIT: Robert GRIFFITH, William CLARK, ack. Robert GRIFFITH, J.P., ent. 10 Aug 1811, rec. same.

D-99   Indenture, 8 Apr 1811, Jacob COON (wife Barbary), BCO; John COON, BCO; $100, 75 acres, part of NW 1/4 S 14 T 8 R 4, patented to Jacob on 27 Aug 1805, NBR: John PLOWMAN, George LOVE, Jacob COON; his seal, her mark [both appear to be in German], WIT: David WALLACE, Alexr. CASSIL, ack. 8 Apr 1811, Dd. WALLACE, J.P., ent. 10 Aug 1811, rec. 12 same.

D-100   Know all men, Benjamin VANFOSSEN for $200 paid by Wm. NICHOL sells SW 1/4 S 25 T 8 R 5, Benjamin to pay to John NICHOL $200 with interest on or before 28 Aug 1811; sgn: 28 May 1811, WIT: Jeremiah FAIRHURST, James HANNAH, ack. 29 May 1811, Zebulon WARNER, ent. 13 Aug 1811, rec. 17 same; release 8 Mar 1833, WIT: Wm. FARIS, Crawford WELSH.

D-101   Indenture, 21 Jun 1811, Jonathan ELLIS (wife Lydia), Union twp., BCO; Thomas SMITH, BCO; $640, 327 acres in Union twp., N divide of S 3 T 9 R 5, Steubenville district, patented to ELLIS 15 Aug 1807; WIT: John CAMPBELL, John LYLE, ack. 21 Jun 1811, John CAMPBELL, J.P., ent. 19 Aug 1811, rec. same.

D-103   Indenture, 17 Aug 1811, John RUSSELL (wife Anne), BCO; Eleazer EVANS, BCO; $160, S 1/2 S 11 T 7 R 5, Steubenville district, patented 20 Jun 1809; WIT: [she signs "Ann"](???) Jacob GREGG, Joseph WRIGHT, ack. William SMITH, J.P., ent. 19 Aug 1811, rec. 22 same.

D-104   Indenture, 21 May 1811, Samuel LEWIS, "Wheelen," BCO; Robert HENDERSON, same; $450, 90 acres, part of S 20 T 8 R 4, Steubenville district, patented 10 Oct 1806 to Michael JENKINS, conveyed by JENKINS (wife Sarah) to LEWIS on 8 May 1809, recorded in Book C. p. 51; WIT: William CAMPBELL, Mary CAMPBELL, ack. 21 May 1811, John CAMPBELL, J.P., ent. 21 Aug 1811, rec. 22 same.

D-105   Indenture, 17 Aug 1811, Obadiah JENNINGS (wife Ann), Steubenville; George ALBAN, St. Clairsville; $200, lots #9 and #10 in addition to St. Clairsville; WIT: Moses W. KENNEDY, J. G. HENING, ack. JCO, J. G. HENING, J.P., ent. 21 Aug 1811, rec. 22 same.

D-106   Know all men, Peter YARNALL, St. Clairsville, for $750 convey to Ralph HEATH, same, part of lot #61 of St. Clairsville, void if YARNALL pays to HEATH $750 in payments ending 25 Dec 1813, sgn: 4 Jul 1811; both seal, [no witnesses given], ack. 4 Jul 1811, Zebulon WARNER, J.P., ent. 22 Aug 1811, rec. 23 same.

D-107   Indenture, 21 d 8 m 1811, Jonathan TAYLOR (wife Ann), Mount Pleasant, JCO; Benjamin BAILEY, BCO; $220, part of S 12 T 6 R 3, patented to TAYLOR on 10 d 8 m 1807, 110 acres; WIT: Thomas MITCHELL, Hariet MITCHELL, ack. BCO, Thomas MITCHELL, J.P., ent. 23 Aug 1811, rec. same.

D-108   Indenture, 21 Aug 1811, William CONGLETON (wife Nancy), Gurnsey [sic] County, Ohio; John McELROY, BCO; $75, E 1/2 lot #73 in St. Clairsville, 1/8 acre, fee simple; WIT: Sterling JOHNSTON, Frederick AULT, ack. Sterling JOHNSTON, J.P., ent. 24 Aug 1811, rec. same.

D-109   Indenture, 24 Aug 1811, Daniel MERRIT (wife Nancy), BCO; William PARRY, BCO; $55, 11 acres, part of NE 1/4 S 31 T 8 R 4, patented to MERRIT on 27 Aug 1805, NBR: William DIXON; WIT: John CAMPBELL, Mary CAMPBELL, ack. John CAMPBELL, J.P., ent. 24 Aug 1811, rec. 26 same.

D-111   Indenture, 13 May 1811, James SINCLAIR (wife Mary) BCO; John McKINDLEY, BCO; $192.50, 55 acres, part of S 17 T 7 R 5, Steubenville district, patented to SINCLAIR on 6 Jun 1806; his seal ["James SINCLER"], her mark ["Mary SINKLER"], WIT: Traverse GEORGE, Esther GEORGE, ack. 13 May 1811, William SINCLAIR, J.P., ent. 26 Aug 1811, rec. same.

D-112   Indenture, 15 May 1811, Amos JANNEY, BCO, attorney for Joseph JANNEY, Louden [sic] County, Virginia; Robert LEE, BCO; $700, part of S 2 T 9 R 5, Steubenville district, NBR: Andrew WALKER, 134 acres, fee simple; WIT: Nicholas DAVIS, Joseph SHARP, ack. 15 May 1811, Sterling JOHNSTON, J.P., ent. 29 Aug 1811, rec. same.

D-113   Indenture, 29 Aug 1811, Thomas SMITH (wife Martha), BCO; John FAWCETT, BCO; $1,074.50, 163 50/100 acres, part of N divide of S 3 T 9 R 5, patented to Jonathan ELLIS [no date given], conveyed by ELLIS (wife Lydia) to Thomas SMITH on 21 Jun 1811, SMITH; WIT: Robert GRIFFITH, Wm. FARIS, Junr., ack. Robert GRIFFITH, J.P., ent. 29 Aug 1811, rec. 30 same.

D-115   Indenture, 23 Aug 1811, William CONGLETON (wife Nancy), Guernsey County, Ohio; Jacob AULT, BCO; $717, 114 acres, part of S 2 T 7 R 4; WIT: Sterling JOHNSTON, Frederick AULT; following is a notation that an agreement has been reached whereby Thomas ROBERTSON is to have use of as much property as is necessary for his mill dam, ack. Sterling JOHNSTON, J.P., ent. 31 Aug 1811, rec. 3 Sep same.

D-116   Indenture, 7 Jul 1811, Jacob HOULTS (wife Peggy), BCO; John THOMPSON, BCO; $1,200, lots #12, #3, and #11 in St. Clairsville, fee simple; both mark [she is given as "Margat"], WIT: D. MORRISON, William EDGER, ack. 7 Jul 1811, D. MORRISON, J.P., ent. 2 Sep 1811, rec. 3 same.

D-117   Indenture, 5 Apr 1811, Jacob PICKERING and Samuel PICKERING, BCO; Brice HOWARD, BCO; $400, 160 acres, NW 1/4 S 13 T 9 R 6, patented to PICKERINGs, fee simple; sgn: Jacob, Hannah [her mark], Samuel, Phebe

PICKERING, WIT: Sarah TAYLOR, Elizabeth BROWN, Sarah PICKERING [her mark], ack. 5 Apr 1811, Enos PICKERING, J.P., ent. 3 Sep 1811, rec. same.

D-118   Indenture, 15 Sep 1810, Samuel LUCAS (wife Eleanor), BCO; John PRIOR, BCO; $120, part of NE S 28 T 6 R 4, NBR: Samuel LUCAS, patented to LUCAS on 7 Apr 1810; his seal, her mark, WIT: Zebulon WARNER, Abner MOORE, ack. 25 Sep 1810, Zebulon WARNER, J.P.

D-119   Indenture, 17 d 8 m 1811, William BUNDY (wife Sarah), Warren twp., BCO; George STARBUCK, BCO; $400, SW 1/4 S 36 T 6 R 5, 111 acres, fee simple; his seal, lher mark, WIT: David SMITH, Benjamin WATKINS, ack. David SMITH, J.P., ent 4 Sep 1811, rec. 5 same.

D-120   Indenture, 22 d 12 m 1810, Isaac COPPOCK (wife Mary), BCO; William PATTERSON, BCO; $240, 60 acres, part of S 13 T 8 R 6; WIT: [Demsey] BOSWELL, William BUNDY, ack. 22 d 12 m 1810, John GRIER, J.P., ent. 4 Sep 1811, rec. 6 same.

D-121   Indenture, 11 Jul 1811, Rebeckah DODD, BCO; Joseph ARNOLD, BCO; $100, 38 1/2 acres 20 perches, part of S 20 T 8 R 6; her mark, WIT: Joel JUDKINS, Henry BARNES, ack. 11 Jul 1811, Jacob MYERS, J.P., ent. 4 Sep 1811, rec. 6 same.

D-122   Indenture, 4 Sep 1811, Thomas THOMPSON, Esq. (wife Elizabeth), BCO; John LEVINGSTON, late of BCO; $471.15, part of S 2/1 T 6 R 3, 104.7 acres, fee simple; WIT: James KELSEY, Sterling JOHNSTON, ack. Sterling JOHNSTON, J.P., ent. 4 Sep 1811, rec 6 same.

D-124   Indenture, 2 d 9 m 1811, Harmon DAVIS (wife Hannah), BCO: William BUNDY, BCO; $200, 100 acres, part of S 14 T 8 R 6; WIT: David SMITH, Nathan MILLS, ack. David SMITH, J.P., ent. 5 Sep 1811, rec. 6 same.

D-126   Indenture, 13 Jan 1811, James BARGAW, Guernsey County, Ohio; Robert JOHNSTON, same; $30, lot #??? in St. Clairsville, sold by Henry STONER to BARGAW; his mark, WIT: Lloyd TALBOTT, Geo. I. JACKSON, ack. Guernsey County, Ohio, 13 Jan 1811, Lloyd TALBOTT, J.P., ent. 9 Sep 1811, rec. same.

D-127   Indenture, 21 May 1811, Henry CARVER (wife Telitha [Talitha]), Union twp., BCO; John CROSSLEY, same; $140, 70 acres, part of SE 1/4 S 27 T 9 R 5, Steubenville district, patented to CARVER on 23 Jun 1810; his seal, her mark, WIT: Peter TALLMAN, Elenor HORUTH, ack. 21 May 1811, John MERCER, J.P., ent. 14 Sep 1811, rec. same.

D-128   Indenture, 17 Aug 1811, James SINCLAIR (wife Mary), BCO; Hannah FARNLEY, Frederick County, Virginia; whereas SINCLAIR patented S 17 T 7 R 5, Steubenville district, on 6 Jun 1806, now for $366.43 conveying 162 acres 3 rods 18 poles; his seal [SINCLER], her mark [SINKLER], WIT: William SINCLAIR, John GEORGE, David FAWCETT, ack. 17 Aug 1811, William SINCLAIR, J.P., ent. 17 Sep 1811, rec. 18 same.

D-129   Indenture, 25 Mar 1811, Isaac HALL for love and affection for Joseph DOD[???], his son-i-l, and support offered HALL, conveys at his decease and decease of Isaac's wife, NE 1/4 S 31 T 8 R 6; only Isaac HALL seals, WIT: Robert PLUMMER, Harmon DAVIS, ack. 25 Mar 1811, John GRIER, J.P., ent. 18 Sep 1811, rec. 19 same.

D-130   Indenture, 24 Aug 1811, John SPENCER (wife Lydia), BCO; James EATON, BCO; whereas SPENCER patented SE 1/4 S 26 T 7 R 4, Steubenville district, on 31 May 1811, now for $640 conveys 1/4 S; his seal, her mark, WIT: William SINCLAIR, Batteal HARRISON, Alice SINCLAIR, ack. 24 Aug 1811, William SINCLAIR, J.P., ent. 28 Sep 1811, rec. 30 same.

D-131   Indenture, 7 May 1808, William Nicholson JEFFERS, Washington County, Ohio; Henry W. LIVINGSTON, Philip H. LIVINGSTON, and Walter LIVINGSTON, Esqrs., Counties of Collumbia [sic] and Dutchess, New York; $4,032.75, fractional T 1 R 3, on the Ohio River, 5,927 acres, patented to Henry W. LIVINGSTON on 28 Mar 1788, void if JEFFERS pays full sum by 1 May 1810; WIT: James FELAN, ack. New York, 25 May 1811, William W. VAN NESS, Justice of Supreme Court of Judicature, affirmation of James FELAN to JEFFERS' execution of indenture, ent. 7 Oct 1811, rec. 9 same.

D-133   Indenture, 30 d 9 m 1811, David SMITH (wife Judith), Warren twp., BCO; Jacob CREW, same; $44, part of SW 1/4 S 1 T 8 R 6, 8 acres, fee simple; his seal, her mark; WIT: Saml. RING, John COLYAR, ack. same date, Saml. RING, J.P., ent. 7 Oct 1811, rec. 9 same.

D-134   Indenture, 28 d 9 m 1811, John COLYAR (wife Rhoda), Warren twp., BCO; Jacob CREW, same; $550, part of NE 1/4 S 7 T 8 R 6, 92 acres, fee simple; WIT: David SMITH, Isaac WILLIAMS, ack. same date, David SMITH, J.P., ent. 7 Oct 1811, rec. 10 same.

D-135   Indenture, 30 d 9 m 1811, John COLYAR (wife Rhoda), Warren twp., BCO; David SMITH, same; $440, part of NE 1/4 S 7 T 8 R 6, 68 acres, fee simple; WIT: Jacob CREW, Saml. RING, ack. same date, Saml. RING, J.P., ent. 7 Oct [1811], rec. 10 same.

D-136   Indenture, 7 Oct 1811, Joseph ROBERTS (wife Sally), BCO; Lambert POND, BCO; $1,200, 99 acres, part of S 34 T 6 R 3, fee simple; his seal, her mark, WIT: Sterling JOHNSTON, John BROWN, ack. 7 Oct 1811, Sterling JOHNSTON, J.P., ent. 8 Oct 1811, rec. 10 same.

D-138   Indenture, 12 Aug 1811, John PRICE (wife Elizabeth), BCO; John MOORE, BCO; $121, part of NW 1/4 S 13 T 10 R 6, 30 acres 36 perches, by survey made by John ISRAEL, patented by William SMITH, conveyed from SMITH to John MOORE, from MOORE to Thomas WILSON, from WILSON to John EDWARDS, from John EDWARDS to James EDWARDS, from James EDWARDS to John PRICE, fee simple; both mark, WIT: Dorsay WILSON, Thos. WILSON, ack. 12 Aug 1811, Thomas WILSON, J.P., ent. 9 Oct 1811, rec. 10 same.

D-139   Indenture, 11 Sep 1811, David RUBLE (wife Susanah [Susannah]), BCO; David McENTIRE, [no location given]; $200, part of S 20 T 4 R 3, Merriatta [sic] district, NBR: land sold by RUBLE to Nancy NOFFSINGER, 70 acres, plus another tract adjoining above, 25 acres 25 perches; his seal, her mark, WIT: Edw. BRYSON, Ruth WILLIAMSON, ack. 11 Sep 1811, Edw. BRYSON, J.P., ent. 12 Oct 1811, rec. 15 same.

D-140   Know all men, Thomas SMITH [wife Martha] of BCO, for $260 paid by Joseph GRIMES sells 25 acres in S 3 T 9 R 5, Steubenville district, NBR: Jonathan ELLIS, John PATTERSON, originally purchased by SMITH in company with Jonathan ELLIS; sgn: 16 Oct 1811, WIT: Zebulon WARNER, Isaac WILSON, ack. Zebulon WARNER, J.P., ent. 18 Oct 1811, rec. 21 same.

D-141   Indenture, 22 Oct 1811, William GOUGH (wife Rachel), BCO; George ALBAN, BCO; $250, lots #11 (5 acres 20 perches) and out lot #12 (6 3/4 acres) in land laid out by Bazaleel WELLS adjoining addition to St. Clairsville laid off by William MATHERS, conveyed to Jacob HOULTZ by Obediah JENNINGS (wife Ann) on 24 Dec 1807, by HOULTZ (wife Peggy) to GOUGH on 24 Mar 1809, fee simple; both mark, WIT: Sterling JOHNSTON, John BROWN, ack. Sterling JOHNSTON, J.P., ent. 22 Oct 1811, rec. same.

D-142   Know all men, Samuel SULLIVAN (wife Mary), Muskingum County, Ohio, for $300 paid by Robert THOMPSON, BCO, sell lots #21 and #22 in addition to St. Clairsville laid out by William MATHERS, same conveyed from Obediah JENNINGS (wife Ann) to Thomas IRELAND, from IRELAND (wife Sarah) to Samuel SULLIVAN by deed dated 14 Mar 1808, recorded in Book B, p. 261, sgn: 24 Sep 1811; WIT: Christian SPANGLER, Thomas IRELAND, ack. 25 Sep 1811, Muskingum County, Christian SPANGLER, J.P., SPANGLER certified by Abel LEWIS, Clerk, CCP, ent. 23 Oct 1811, rec. same.

D-143   Indenture, 29 Oct 1811, Thomas WHITACRE (wife Ann), BCO; Henry GETINGER [GITINGER], BCO; $800, NE 1/4 S 13 T 8 R 4, 160 acres, patented to David BARTON on 20 Dec 1808, conveyed by BARTON to WHITACRE on 6 Dec 1809, fee simple; WIT: David WALLACE, Samuel LEWIS, ack. David WALLACE, J.P., ent. 2 Nov 1811, rec. same.

D-144   Indenture, 30 Oct 1811, John COON (wife Susanah), BCO; Henry GETTINGER, BCO; $175, 25 acres, part of NE 1/4 S 14 T 8 R 4, patented to Jacob COON on 27 Aug 1805, 75 acres conveyed by Jacob COON to John COON on 18 Apr 1811, NBR: George LOVE; his seal, her mark, [both appear to be German], WIT: David WALLACLE, Henry GITTINGER, ack. David WALLACE, J.P., ent. 2 Nov 1811, rec. 4 same.

D-146   Indenture, 29 Oct 1811, Bazaleel WELLS (wife Sally), JCO; Eli KENNARD, BCO; $390, part of S's 19, 20 T 7 R 3, NBR: James McFADDEN, Mordicai BALDERSON, John CAHEY, IDAN, McPEEK, 142 acres; WIT: [J.] G. HENING, William THOMPSON, ack. JCO, J. G. HENING, J.P., HENING certified Thomas PATTON, Clerk, CCP, ent. 4 Nov 1811, rec. 5 same.

D-147   Indenture, 31 Oct 1811, John COON (wife Susanah), BCO; Philip MORGAN, BCO; $350, 50 acres, part of NW 1/4 S 14 T 8 R 4, patented to Jacob COON on 27 Aug 1805, 75 acres of which conveyed by Jacob to John on 18 Apr 1811, NBR: John PLOWMAN, George LOVE; his seal, her mark [both appear to be German], WIT: David WALLACE, George MORGAN, ack. David WALLACE, J.P., ent. 5 Nov 1811, rec. 6 same.

D-148   Indenture, 6 d 11 m 1811, William SMITH (wife Margaret), BCO; Isaac HARRY, Chester County, Pennsylvania; $500, SW 1/4 S 13 T 10 R 6 patented to William SMITH on 22 Sep 1807, 160 acres; his seal, her mark, WIT: John MOORE, Tamer MOORE, ack. same date, John MOORE, J.P., ent. 7 Nov 1811, rec. same.

p.149   Indenture, 28 Oct 1811, John WOLFORD (wife Catherine), BCO; Joseph GRIFFITH, BCO; $1,170, part of S 28 T 6 R 3, NBR: Frederick AMRINE, 158 acres 1 rod 17 perches; his seal, her mark, WIT: [Nabb] E. POWEL, John CLARK, ack. David MOORE, ent. 9 Nov 1811, rec. same.

D-150   Indenture, 26 Aug 1811, Ralph HEATH (wife Elizabeth), BCO; William ASKEW, BCO; for erecting a frame house on the corner of lot #61 in St. Clairsville [house described in explicit detail], to be like Wm. BROWN's, convey lot #109 in St. Clairsville, conveyed to HEATH by John WOODBURN (wife unnamed) on 13 Jun 1806, fee simple; WIT: Robert GRIFFITH, Wm. FARIS, Junr., ack. 26 Aug 1811, Robert GRIFFITH, J.P., ent. 12 Nov 1811, rec. same.

D-152   Indenture, 7 d 9 m 1811, William SATTERTHWAIT, Muskingum County, Ohio; Joseph W. SATTERTHWAIT, BCO; $280, part of S 13 T 7 R 3, Steubenville district, NBR: Short Creek Road, Samuel POTTS, Thomas SATTERTHWAIT, John SMITH, 41 acres 112 perches; he signs Wm. W. SATTERTHWAIT, WIT: Joseph VANLAW, John VANLAW, ack. 12 Nov 1811, William SINCLAIR, J.P., ent. 12 Nov 1811, rec. same.

D-153   Indenture, 10 Jul 1811, David VANCE, BCO; James JOHNSTON, BCO; $399 or upwards and for indemnifying James against paying money, selling livestock and household goods, void if VANCE pays money within four months; WIT: Sterling JOHNSTON, Jeremiah FAIRHURST, ack. 10 Jul 1811, Sterling JOHNSTON, J.P., ent. 14 Nov 1811, rec. 15 same.

D-154   Indenture, 16 Nov 1811, Joseph SHARP (wife Nancy), BCO; Thomas WHITACRE, BCO; $640, 79 acres 1 rod 5 perches, part of NW 1/4 S 30 T 7 R 4, patented to SHARP on 20 Jun 1809, NBR: Isaac FARMER, James WATTS; his seal, her mark; WIT: John CAMPBELL, Joshua BROWN, ack. John CAMPBELL, ent. 18 Nov 1811, rec. 19 same.

D-155   Indenture, 5 Mar 1811, Mordicai YARNALL (wife Phebe), State of Virginia; William BELL, State of Ohio; 1/4 S 27 T 6 R 3 at $3 per acre; WIT: Henry SMITH, Thos. THOMPSON, ack. 5 Mar 1811, BCO, Thos. THOMPSON, J.P., ent. 22 Nov 1811, rec. 25 same.

D-156   Indenture, 19 Nov 1811, Jacob HOULTS [HOLTS] (wife Peggy), BCO; Philip AULT, BCO; $300, part of S 2 T 7 R 4, 100 acres 3 rods 26 perches, fee simple; both mark, WIT: Sterling JOHNSTON, David VANCE, ack. Sterling JOHNSTON, J.P., ent. 25 Nov 1811, rec. same.

D-157   Indenture, 21 Sep 1811, William EWERS [EWARS] (wife Amy), BCO; Henry BROWN, BCO; $350, 87 1/2 acres, S 2 T 9 R 5, Steubenville district, fee simple; WIT: Jacob GREGG, Amy TRAHERN, ack. 26 Sep 1811, John BOYD, J.P., ent. 26 Nov 1811, rec. 27 same.

D-157   Indenture, 6 d 11 m 1811, Isaac HALL (wife Dinah), BCO; Aaron WOOD [no location given]; $320, SW 1/4 S 4 T 6 R 5, Marietta district; both seal "HALLE," David SMITH, Peter SEARS, ack. David SMITH, J.P., ent. 29 Nov 1811, rec. 30 same.

D-158   Indenture, 29 Jul 1811, Samuel GREGG, BCO, atty. for Jonah HOUGH (wife Pleasant), Loudon County, Virginia; Abner GREGG[???], BCO; $364.50, SW 1/4 S 1 T 8 R 5, 162 acres, patented to HOUGH on 15 Aug 1808, fee simple;

WIT: William SMITH, John GEORGE, ack. 29 Jul 1811, William SMITH, ent. 2 Dec 1811, rec. 4 same.

D-159   Indenture, 18 d 9 m 1811, Knowas DOUDNA (wife Hannah), Warren twp., BCO; Jesse BAILY, same; $480, 1/2 SW 1/4 S 3 T 8 R 6, 80 acres, fee simple; he signs "Knowis," WIT: Henry DOUDNA, David SMITH, ack. same date, David SMITH, J.P., ent. 5 Dec 1811, rec. same.

D-160   Indenture, 26 Nov 1811, James SINCLAIR (wife Mary), BCO; Benjamin ALLEN, BCO; whereas SINCLAIR, then of Loudon County, Virginia, patented S 17 T 7 R 5, Steubenville district, on 6 Jun 1806, now for $360.04 selling 107 acres 3 rods 18 poles, NBR: John McKINDLEY; WIT: William SINCLAIR, Traverce GEORGE, ack. William SINCLAIR, J.P., ent. 6 Dec 1811, rec. same.

D-161   Indenture, 16 Jul 1811, Brice HOWARD, BCO; Joel WILLIAMS, Muskingum County, Ohio; HOWARD on this date stands bound to WILLIAMS for $500, securing payment of $250 by 5 Oct 1812 by conveying 160 acres in S 13 T 9 R 6 on NW 1/4 of section, granted by Jacob PICKERING and Samuel PICKERING out of the original deed to HOWARD, void if bond fully paid; WIT: John WOLF [his mark "S"], Philip HAWKINS [his mark], ack. BCO, Henry GILBERT, J.P., ent. 11 Dec 1811, rec. same; release 29 Oct 1813, WIT: Anthony WILLIAMS, Sarah WILLIAMS, rect. entered 11 Jan 1814.

D-163   Indenture, 11 Dec 1811, John NEFF (wife Sarah), Alegany [sic] County, Maryland; Henry NEFF, BCO; natural love and affection towards their son Henry NEFF and $1, NW 1/4 S 13 T 7 R 4, fee simple; only John signs, WIT: Sterling JOHNSTON, Samuel LEWIS, ack. BCO, Sterling JOHNSTON, J.P., ent. 11 Dec 1811, rec. 12 same.

D-164   Indenture, 7 Dec 1811, John NEFF (wife Sarah), Allegheny County, Maryland; Peter NEFF, same; $100, SW 1/4 S 13 T 7 R 4, 160 acres; only John signs, WIT: Sterling JOHNSTON, Samuel LEWIS, ack. Sterling JOHNSTON, J.P., ent. 11 Dec 1811, rec. 12 same.

D-164   Indenture, 31 Jan 1807, Thomas BROOKS, BCO; Jacob DAVIS, Esqr., BCO; $328.--, to secure payment of $328.--, conveying 164 acres, NE 1/4 S 26 T 3 R 2, plus livestock and personal property, void if paid within nine months, interest omitted; WIT: William DAVIS, Jacob LONG, ack. Pultney twp., BCO, 19 Dec 1807, Michael McCLUNEY, J.P., ent. 16 Dec 1811, rec. same.

D-165   Know all men, Enos BROOMHALL during lifetime (sometime in 1806) sold to Daniel McFERSON a tract in S 13 T 8 R 5, NBR: McMahan's Creek, 50 acres, whereas Joseph[???] WRITE, extr., and Phebe BROOMHALL, extx., presented contract before the August session of CCP, court ordered to make a deed in fee simple; sgn. 18 Dec 1811, Josh. WRIGHT, Phebe BROOMHALL, WIT: John CARTER, Saml. SPRIGG, ack. 17 Dec 1811, Sterling JOHNSTON, J.P., ent. 17 Dec 1811, rec. same.

D-166   Indenture, 18 May 1810, David LOCKWOOD (wife Rebecca [Rebeckah]), BCO; David HANNAH, Beaver County, Pennsylvania; $400, part of Fractional S 5 T 4 R 3, NBR: Ohio River, mouth of Gray's Run, Dilles Bottom, 46 acres 3 rods 34 perches; WIT: Joseph BIGGS, Mary BIGGS [her mark], ack. 9 Jul 1810, Levin OKEY, Js., ent. 17 Dec 1811, rec. 18 same.

D-167   Indenture, 19 Apr 1811, Bazaleel WELLS (wife Sally), JCO; William PICKEN, BCO; $130, part of S 26 T 4 R 2, NBR: James EAGLESON, Francis HARDISTY, 70 acres; WIT: J. G. HENING, Margt. MARSHALL, ack. JCO, 19 Apr 1811, J. G. HENING, J.P., HENING certified by Thomas PATTON, Clk., ent. 19 Dec 1811, rec. same.

D-169   James MADISON, President, patent by John MOORE, BCO, assignee of John McLURE, for NE 1/4 S 32 T 3 R 2, Steubenville district; sgn: 1 Jun 1810, R. SMITH, Secretary of State, ent. 2 Jan 1812, rec. same.

D-169   Indenture, 21 Nov 1811, Garret SNEDEKER, Brook County, Virginia; Jacob SNEDEKER, BCO; good will and affection, 80 acres out of parcel purchased by Garret of Amos JANNEY, Columbiana County, Ohio, attorney for Joseph JANNEY, part of S 2 T 9 R 5, fee simple; WIT: Jacob HOLTZ [his mark], Mikel RICHARDS [his mark], ack. BCO, Wm. DUNN, J.P., ent. 3 Jan 1812, rec. same.

D-170   Indenture, 27 d 9 m 1811, James BROCK (wife Martha), [Wane (Wayne)] twp., BCO; Charles NEWSOME, same; $70, part of SE 1/4 S 18 T 7 R 6, 35 acres, fee simple; WIT: David SMITH, Elijah BAIN, ack. same date, David SMITH, J.P., ent. 4 Jan 1812, rec. same.

D-171   Indenture, 27 d 9 m 1811, James BROCK (wife Martha), [Wane (Wayne)] twp., BCO; Elijah BAINS [BAIN], same; $131, 1/2 SE 1/4 S 18 T 7 R 6, 65 1/2 acres, fee simple; WIT: David SMITH, William BAILEY, ack. same date, David SMITH, J.P., ent. 4 Jan 1812, rec. 6 same.

D-172   Indenture, 6 Jan 1812, Benjamin SCRITCHFIELD, BCO; Michael TRUMP, Fayette County, Pennsylvania; $180, NBR: John WORKMAN, Wm. GIFFEN [and others unnamed], 60 acres, part of SW 1/4 S 2 T 6 R 3, conveyed to SCRITCHFIELD by Bazaleel WELLS and Elias VAN ARSDALE as extrs. of Daniel McELHERRAN on 1 Nov 1809; WIT: Robert GRIFFITH, Wm. FARIS, Junr., ack. Robt. GRIFFITH, J.P., ent. 6 Jan 1812, rec. same.

D-173   Indenture, 16 Mar 1811, Leonard HART, Junr., (wife Mary), BCO; William Weir GAULT, BCO; $80, lot #46 in Morristown laid off by William CHAPLINE, conveyed from CHAPLINE (wife Mary) to HART on 24 Jun 1808, fee simple; both mark [his "LH"], WIT: Robert GRIFFITH, Jacob RODEFER, ack. 16 Mar 1811, Robert GRIFFITH, J.P., ent. 10 Jan 1812, rec. 11 same.

D-174   Indenture, 10 Jan 1812, Wm. W. GAULT (wife Sarah), BCO; Benjamin GASSAWAY, BCO; $80, lot #46 in Morristown [see p. 173 for history], fee simple; WIT: James LANDY, William SCOTT, ack. Duncan MORRISON, ent. 10 Jan 1812, rec. 13 same.

D-175   Indenture, 18 Oct 1811, Izak PROCTER, Baltimore, Baltimore County, Maryland; Sarah PROCTER, same; $5, lot #33 in town of Belmont, conveyed by Joseph WRIGHT (wife Elenor) to PROCTER on 12 Aug 1810 as recorded in Book C, p. 261; WIT: Edward JOHNSON[???], Benj. FOWLER, David WHITEFORD, John HARGROVE, ack. Baltimore County, Maryland, 18 Oct 1811, Edward JOHNSTON, Mayor of Baltimore, ent. 11 Jan 1812, rec. 13 same.

D-176   To all people, Richard HARDESTY (wife Mary), BCO, for love and affection for son Robert HARDESTY, BCO, and other good causes and considerations, land on Wheeling Creek, part of S 23 T 6 R 3, Steubenville district, 55 1/4 acres 25 poles, part of two tracts patented by Robert JOHNSTON of Franklin County, Pennsylvania, conveyed by JOHNSTON to John D. MERCIER, New York State, by MERCIER by Daniel McELHERAN his atty. to Richard HARDESTY, now of BCO, other deeded by Doctor JOHNSTON to Richard HARDESTY, recorded in Washington County, Ohio, under territorial government; sgn: 14 Jan 1812, his mark, wife does not seal, WIT: John PATTERSON, Isaac WILSON, ack. John PATTERSON, Assoc. Judge, ent. 14 Jan 1812, rec. same.

D-177   Indenture, 4 Jan 1812, Joseph MERRIT (wife Mary), BCO; John RODGERS, State of New Jersey; $266.67, land on S side of St. Clairsville, NBR: commons laid out by William MATHERS, Moses MOOREHEAD, 6 acres, void if MERRIT pays RODGERS $266.67 before 1 May 1813; WIT: George THOMPSON, Thomas THOMPSON, ack. 15 Jan 1812, BCO, Robert GRIFFITH, J.P., ent. 15 Jan 1812, rec. same.

D-178   Indenture, 22 Apr 1811, Stephen PERRINE (wife Ann); Peter SNYDER, both of Cross Creek twp., Washington County, Pennsylvania; $200, land on Stillwater, SW 1/4 S 36 T 7 R 5, Steubenville district, patented to PERRINE on 20 Jan 1809; his seal, her mark; WIT: Henry GRAHAM, Thos. ELDER, ack. Washington County, Pennsylvania, 22 Apr 1811, Henry GRAHAM, J.P., GRAHAM certified 7 May 1811 by Alexander MURDOCK, Prothonetory, CCP, ent. 15 Jan 1812, rec. 17 same.

D-179   Indenture, 16 Jan 1812, Thomas TIPTON (wife Kezia), BCO; Jonathan WINTER, BCO; $300, fee simple, part of SE 14 S 9 T 7 R 4, conveyed to TIPTON by Bazaleel WELLS by deed dated 13 Nov 1798, NBR: Joseph PARISH, Eli PLUMER, Alexander BOGGS, 50 acres, free water course reserved by TIPTON; his seal, her mark; WIT: Robert GRIFFITH, Wm. FARIS, Junr., ack. Robert GRIFFITH, J.P., ent. 16 Jan 1812, rec. 17 same.

D-181   Indenture, 20 Nov 1811, Isaac BRODERICK (wife Beulah), Richland twp., BCO; John ELLIOT [ELIOTT], St. Clairsville, Richland twp., BCO; $825, land on which BRODERICKK now lives in Richland twp., part of SW 1/4 S 21 T 7 R 4, NBR: Abram ENGLE, John HAINS, conveyed from Job ENGLE (wife Sarah) To BRODERICK on 12 Sep 1808 as recorded in Book B, p. 510, fee simple; WIT: William JOHNSTON, Sterling JOHNSTON, ack. 9 Nov 1811, Sterling JOHNSTON, J.P., ent. 27 Jan 1812, rec. same.

D-182   Indenture, 28 Jan 1812, Jacob GRUBB (wife Elizabeth), BCO; William FARIS, Junr., BCO; $45, lot #23 in addition to St. Clairsville as laid out by William MATHERS, conveyed by Obediah JENNINGS to Wm. CONGLETON, from CONGLETON to Samuel HAWKINS, and from HAWKINS to GRUBB on 8 May 1807, as recorded in Book B, fee simple; his seal, her mark, WIT: Robert GRIFFITH, Jno. SCATTERDAY, ack. Robert GRIFFITH, J.P., ent. 28 Jan 1812, rec. same.

D-183   Indenture, 26 Aug 1811, William ASKEW (wife Martha), BCO; William FARIS, Senr., and William FARIS, Junr., BCO; $400, lot #109 in St. Clairsville, 1/4 acre, conveyed to Ralph HEATH by John WOODBURN (and wife) on 13 Jun 1806, conveyed by HEATH to ASKEW on 26 Aug 1811, fee simple; WIT: Robert GRIFFITH, Hannah WILSON, ack. 26 Aug 1811, Robert GRIFFITH, J.P., ent. 5 Feb 1812, rec. same.

D-184   Indenture, 10 Feb 1812, John FRITCH, BCO; William MOSLEY, BCO; $200, lot #101 in St. Clairsville, 1/4 acre, conveyed by David NEWALL (wife Sally) to Mary KNOWLS, wife to James KNOWLS, by KNOWLS and wife to Peter MOORE by deed dated 1 Aug 1804, by Isaac MOORE, atty. for Peter MOORE, to John FRITCH by deed dated 6 Feb 1807, fee simple; his mark ["Fo"], WIT: Zebulon WARNER, Wm. FARIS, Junr., ack. Zebulon WARNER, J.P., ent. 10 Feb 1812, rec. 11 same.

D-185   Indenture, 12 Feb 1812, George PAULL, BCO; John WINTER, BCO; $250 [paid by PAULL, and it looks like WINTER is the grantor, especially since the deed history leaves him as the last owner?], lots #1 and #2 in land adjoining addition to St. Clairsville as laid out by Bezaleel WELLS, first one containing 2 acres and 1 perch, second containing 2 acres 6 perches, conveyed by Obediah

JENNINGS, Esqr., to William MOSLEY on 3 Sep 1806, conveyed by MOSLEY to James KNIGHT on 23 Jul 1807, from James KNIGHT (wife Mary) to William MOSLEY on 18 Aug 1807, from Josiah HEDGES, high Sheriff of BCO, to John WINTER on 16 Apr 1808, excluding brick yard; WIT: Benjamin RUGGLES, Josiah HEDGES, ack. Benjamin RUGGLES, President of third circuit of the CCP, ent. 12 Feb 1812, rec. 14 same.

D-187   Know all men, for $350 paid by Andrew WALKER, BCO, convey 87 1/2 acres, part of S 2 T 9 R 5, Steubenville district, sold by William EWERS (wife Amy); sgn: 26 Sep 1811, WIT: Henry BROWN [his mark], Amy TRAKERN [probably TRAHERN], ack. 26 Sep 1811, John BOYD, J.P., ent. 18 Feb 1812, rec. 20 same.

D-188   Indenture, 25 Feb 1812, Amos JANNEY, Stark County, Ohio, atty. for Joseph JANNEY, Louden County, Virginia; John R. NEAL, BCO; $350, part of S 2 T 9 R 5, NBR: William SHAW, 94 acres, fee simple; WIT: Joshua BROWN, James SHARP, John McCASKEY, Henry BROWN, ack. John CAMPBELL, ent. 27 Feb 1812, rec. 29 same.

D-189   Know all men, John LOGUE sold to Henry MITCHELL personal property, sgn: 11 Oct 1811; WIT: Robert GRIFFITH, conditions are that if LOGUE pays two judgments on Robert GRIFFITH's docket in favor of Elijah McNAMAR as soon as they are due, the above agreement to be void, sgn: Jno. LOGUE, Henry MITCHELL.

D-190   Indenture, 6 Oct 1811, Stephen TODD (wife Sibbilla), Warren twp., BCO; Stephen HODGEN, BCO; $21, beginning N of SE corner of S 11 T 8 R 6, 3 1/2 acres, fee simple; WIT: David SMITH, William LAY, ack. 6 Oct 1811, David SMITH, J.P., ent. 7 Mar 1812, rec. 11 same.

D-190   Indenture, 10 Mar 1812, Thomas SMITH (wife Martha), BCO; John PATTERSON, BCO; $554, 138 acres 50/100, NE 1/4 S 3 T 9 R 5, Steubenville district, S patented to Johnathan ELLIS on 15 Aug 1807, Jonathan and wife Lydia conveyed 1/2 to SMITH on 21 Jun 1811; WIT: Zebulon WARNER, James HUGHES, ack. Zebulon WARNER, J.P., ent. 10 Mar 1812, rec. 13 same.

D-192   Indenture, 11 Mar 1812, Elizabeth BEAM, BCO; George BEAM, BCO; $186, part of S 29 T 6 R 3, NBR: [MAXFIELD], School House Run, YARNALL, 57 acres, part of land conveyed to Elizabeth BEAM by M. YARNALL (wife Phebe); her mark, WIT: James HEDGES, Josiah HEDGES, ack. Robert GRIFFITH, J.P., ent. 12 Mar 1812, rec. 13 same.

D-193   Indenture, 24 Dec 1811, Arthur MORRISON (wife Grizzle), BCO; Robert MORRISON, BCO; $360, 120 acres, part of S 1/2 of S 4 T 8 R 5, Steubenville district, NBR: Arthur ERWIN, Arthur MORRISON, patented to Arthur on 13 Oct 1807, fee simple; his seal, her mark, WIT: William MORRISON, John FINLEY, ack. 24 Dec 1811, John BOYD, J.P., ent. 13 Mar 1812, rec. 16 same.

D-194   Indenture, 11 Mar 1812, John CONNELL (wife Elenor), Brooke County, Virginia; James THOMPSON, now of BCO; $376, part of S 31 T 6 R 3, Steubenville district, patented by CONNELL an assignee of David TUNDLE dated 16 Feb 1809; WIT: James HEDGES, Geo. PAULL, ack. BCO, 11 Mar 1812, for John CONNELL, John PATTERSON, Assoc. Judge, ack. JCO, 20 Mar 1812, for Elenor CONNELL, Mordicai BARTLEY, J.P., BARTLEY certified by Thomas PATTON, Clk. CCP, 21 Mar 1812, (ent. 20 Jun 1812, rec. same), ent. [BCO] 13 Mar 1812, rec. same.

D-196   Indenture, 28 Feb 1812, Thomas WILSON (wife Nancy), BCO; John THOMPSON, BCO; $700, SE 1/4 S 18 T 9 R 6, 168 acres, Steubenville district, fee simple; his seal, her mark, WIT: Sterling JOHNSTON, Alexr. JAMESON (for Thos. WILSON), ack. 3 Mar 1812, John MOORE, J.P., ent. 16 Mar 1812, rec. 17 same.

D-197   Indenture, 13 Mar 1812, Bezaleel WELLS (wife Sally), JCO; Jane VANWEY, BCO; $700, part of S 20 T 7 R 3, 200 1/4 acres; WIT: J. G. HENING, Thomas NOLAND, ack. JCO, J. G. HENING, J.P., HENING certified by Thomas PATTON, Clk. CCP.

D-198   Indenture, 14 Mar 1812, William HULSE (wife Elizabeth), BCO; Samuel WILSON, BCO; $50, lots #15 and #16 in addition to St. Clairsville, conveyed by Andrew FENNEFROCK (wife Susanna) to HULSE on 20 Feb 1811, as recorded in Book D, p. 3, fee simple; WIT: Zebulon WARNER, Isaac WILSON, ack. Zebulon WARNER, J.P., ent. 17 Mar 1812, rec. 18 same.

D-199   Indenture, 6 May 1811, John WALLACE (wife Margaret), BCO; Thomas THOMPSON, BCO; $108, part of NE 1/4 S 1 T 6 R 3, conveyed to WALLACE by Elias VAN ARSDALE and Bezeleel WELLS, extrs. of Daniel McELHERAN by deed dated 14 Feb 1811, 27 9/10 acre; WIT: James McKIRK, Samuel CLARK, ack. 6 May 1811, James McKIRK, J.P., ent. 14 Mar 1812, rec. 18 same.

D-201 -Indenture, 2 Mar 1812, Thomas THOMPSON (wife Elizabeth), BCO; Robert THOMPSON, BCO; $1,000, land where Thomas now resides, NBR: CARTER, FREEMAN, no size specification; WIT: Sterling JOHNSTON, William JOHNSTON, ack. 16 Mar 1812, Sterling JOHNSTON, J.P., ent. 17 Mar 1812, rec. 18 same.

D-202 Indenture, 2 Mar 1812, Robert THOMPSON, BCO; Thomas THOMPSON, BCO; Robert bound to Thomas for $1,000, conveying lot in previous entry to secure debt, fee simple, void if paid; WIT: Sterling JOHNSTON, William JOHNSTON, ack. 2 Mar 1812, Sterling JOHNSTON, J.P., ent. 17 Mar 1812, rec. 18 same.

D-203 Indenture, 6 Mar 1812, Peter SNIDER [SNYDER] (wife Catherine), Washington County, Pennsylvania; David SNIDER, BCO; $300, SW 1/4 S 36 T 7 R 5, Steubenville district, patented to Stephen PRYAN on 20 Jan 1809, PRYAN conveyed to SNIDER on 22 Apr 1811; his may be in German, her mark, WIT: Mordicai BARTLEY, John HILL, ack. JCO [?], Mordicai BARTLEY, J.P., ent. 24 Mar 1812, rec. 25 same.

D-204 Ack. BCO, Camm THOMAS testified that he was present to the bargain between Aaron DODD, dec'd., and Joseph ARNOLD when a conveyance for N end of 1/4 S DODD occupied, to be deeded over when patent was obtained, Jacob MYERS, J.P., WIT: Camm THOMAS, ack. BCO, Rebekah DODD of Warren twp., BCO, testifies that Aaron DODD made a will specifying that the S end should be disposed of at the discretion of his extrs., but before his death sold N end himself to ARNOLD, after his death lifted bond and gave him a deed, and destroyed bond believing it to be of no virtue, Jacob MYERS, J.P., WIT: Rebeckah DODD [her mark], 26 Nov 1811. Personally came Joseph DODD, one of heirs of Aaron DODD, witnessing preceding transaction, Jacob MYERS, J.P., 26 Nov 1811, ent. 28 Mar 1812, rec. same.

D-204 23 Mar 1812, Nicholas LUNCEFORD (wife Sarah), Ohio County, Virginia; James BELL [BEALL], same; $200, part of S 28 T 6 R 3, NBR: Jacob ENDLY, 59 1/2 acres 16 poles; both mark, no WIT given, ack. Thos. THOMPSON, J.P., ent. 28 Mar 1812, rec. 31 same.

D-205 Indenture, 16 Oct 1811, John PATTERSON, James CALDWELL, and Samuel SULLIVAN; Jeremiah FAIRHURST; on 25 Jun 1808 Mahlon SMITH, extr. of LW&T of Thomas PLUMMER, sued out of CCP a writ of attachment against Thomas L. JUDGE, an absconding debtor, returnable to the August term of court, writ levied against the E 1/2 lot #16 in St. Clairsville, property of JUDGE; JUDGE present at August term and made default; at December term, PATTERSON, CALDWELL, and SULLIVAN appointed as auditors to adjust accounts of SMITH; auditors reported at April term 1809 JUDGE was found to be indebted to SMITH for $805; December term 1809 ordered auditors to sell E 1/2 lot #16 to highest bidder on second Tuesday of April 1810; for $120.20 auditors sell to FAIRHURST; Robert THOMPSON, W. BROWN, ack. Muskingum County, 26 Dec 1811, for Samuel SULLIVAN, Samuel THOMPSON, J.P., ack. BCO, 1

Apr 1812, for John PATTERSON and James CALDWELL, Zebulon WARNER, J.P.

D-207   Indenture, 2 Apr 1812, Jane VANWEY, BCO; Peter GIBBENS, BCO; $45, part of S 20 T 7 R 3, 1 acre; her mark, WIT: Robert VANCE, ack. Robert VANCE, J.P., ent. 3 Apr 1812, rec. same.

D-208   Indenture, 26 Nov 1811, Joseph SHARP (wife Nancy), BCO; James WATT, BCO; $337, 89 acres 4 perches, part of S 30 T 7 R 4, patented to SHARP on 20 Jun 1809, NBR: John STEWART, Thomas WHITACRE, Isaac FARMER; his seal, her mark, WIT: John CAMPBELL, James SHARP, ack. 26 Nov 1811, John CAMPBELL, J.P., ent. 3 Apr 1812, rec. 7 same.

D-209   Indenture, 2 Apr 1812, Jane VANWEY, BCO; John BELL, BCO; $654, part of S 20 T 7 R 3, 109 acres; her mark, WIT: Robert VANCE, ack. Robert VANCE, J.P., ent. 3 Apr 1812, rec. 7 same.

D-210   Indenture, 31 d 10 m 1811, William HODGIN (wife Agness), Warren twp., BCO; Titas SHOTWELL, same; $400, part of S 8 T 8 R 6, 100 acres, fee simple; his seal, her mark, WIT: David SMITH, Elizabeth NICKOLS, ack. same date, David SMITH, J.P., ent. 4 Apr 1812, rec. 7 same.

D-211   Stephen KINSEY of JCO has made full payment for NE 1/4 S 33 T 9 R 5, Steubenville district, receives patent; sgn: 20 Jan 1812, James MADISON, President, ent. 6 Apr 1812, rec. 7 same.

D-212   Indenture, 12 d 10 m 1811, Jesse DAWSON (wife Elizabeth), BCO; James LISLE [no location given]; $78, part of SE 1/4 S 10 T 6 R 5, Marrieta district, 19 1/2 acres, quit claim; his seal, her mark, WIT: Isaac MOORE, Aaron WOOD, ack. same date, Isaac MOORE, ent. 10 Apr 1812, rec. same.

D-213   Indenture, 12 Oct 1811, Lucius Horatio STOCKTON (wife Elizabeth), Trenton, Huntingdon County, New Jersey; John CLELAND, St. Clairsville, BCO; $979.70, lots #28 and #27 (former NBR: Jacob HOLTZ), in St. Clairsville, each 1/4 acre, plus 4 1/4 acres north of St. Clairsville adjoining commons (curent or former NBR: Josiah DILLON, Bazil ISRAEL, Robert THOMPSON) fee simple; WIT: Richard [IRULAY], ack. New Jersey, 12 Oct 1811, James LINN, Esqr., master of the high court of cancery, ent. 11 Apr 1812, rec. same.

D-215   Know all men, George THOMPSON, for $1,000, sells to Charles HAMMOND and Samuel SPRIGG part of lot #68 in St. Clairsville owned by him, HAMMOND and SPRIGG have endorsed his note discounted at the Bank of Steubenville for $1,000, land given as security; sgn: 28 Dec 1811, WIT: George

FARQUHAR, Robt. GRIFFITH, ack. St. Clairsville, BCO, 10 Jan 1812, Robert GRIFFITH, J.P., ent. 11 Apr 1812, rec. 13 same.

D-216   Indenture, 3 Apr 1812, Arthur MORRISON (wife Grissey [Grizzel]), BCO; James LUNDAY, BCO; $320, NW 1/4 S 4 T 8 R 5, patented to MORRISON on 13 Oct 1807; his seal, her mark, WIT: David LONG, William BOYD, ack. John BOYD, J.P., ent. 11 Apr 1812, rec. 18 same.

D-216   Indenture, 4 Apr 1812, John CONNELL (wife Eleanor), Brook County, Virginia; Samuel CONNELL, BCO; $1,000, NBR: McMahon's Creek, James THOMPSON, 110 acres, part of NE 1/4 S 31 T 6 R 3, patented to John on 16 Feb 1809; only John signs, WIT: James THOMPSON, Jno. HAGIN, Junr., S. CONNELL, ent. 11 Apr 1812, rec. 20 same, ack. JCO, 2 Sep 1813, John BARRETT, J.P., ack. ent. 14 Sep 1813, rec. 16 same.

D-218   Indenture, 28 Oct 1811, Edward MILNER (wife Jane), BCO; Robert MARTIN, BCO; $450, 113 acres, on N side of Edward MILNER's 1/2 S 9 T 8 R 5, Steubenville district, patented to Joshua HATCHER by Thomas JEFFERSON, conveyed to MILNER on 8 Oct 1805 [patent date?], fee simple; his seal, her mark, WIT: Henry ROBERTS, Andrew THOMPSON, ack. 28 Oct 1812 [suspect clerk error], John BOYD, J.P., ent. 14 Apr 1812, rec. 23 same.

D-219   Indenture, 6 Apr 1812, Josiah HEDGES (wife Rebecca [Rebeckah]), BCO; John THOMPSON, BCO; $800, 2 lots of ground N of St. Clairsville, one NBR: Methodist society, total 15 acres 2 rods 10 perches, all of last-mentioned lot and part of first being same which John THOMPSON (wife Sally) conveyed to James BARNES by two special deeds of conveyance dated 7 May 1804, conveyed by BARNES (wife Nancy) to Robert H. JOHNSTON dated 11 Sep 1807, conveyed by JOHNSTON to HEDGES on 2 Nov 1807; WIT: James HUGHES, James HEDGES, ack. John PATTERSON, Assoc. Judge, ent. 14 Apr 1812, rec. 23 same.

D-220   Indenture, 26 Jan 1811, James JOHNSTON, Steubenville, JCO, and Earl SPROAT, Merrietta, Washington County, Ohio; Christian STALEY, Allegheny County, Pennsylvania; $625, NBR: Ohio River, part of fractional T 1 R 3, patented to Henry W. LIVINGSTON, conveyed by him to William N. JEFFERS by deed dated 17 May 1808, by JEFFERS to JOHNSTON and SPROAT on 30 Oct 1809, 125 acres; WIT: Wm. H. SHUTE, [J. MULLINSON], ack. JCO, 26 Jan 1811, James G. HINING, J.P., HINING certified by Thomas PATTON, Clerk, CCP, ent. 21 Apr 1812, rec. 25 same.

D-221   Indenture, 26 Jan 1811, James [James repeated] JOHNSTON, JCO, and Earl SPROAT, Marietta, Washington County, Ohio; Jacob BEAR, Allegheny County, Pennsylvania; $525, 105 acres, part of fractional T 1 R 3, patented to

Henry W. LIVINGSTON, conveyed to William N. JEFFERS by deed dated 7 May 1808, by JEFFERS to JOHNSTON and SPROAT by deed dated 30 Oct 1809; WIT: Wm. W. SHULE or SHUTE, J. [AUTLINSON], ack. JCO, 26 Jan 1811, James G. HENING, J.P., HENING certified by Thomas PATTON, Clerk, CCP, ent. 21 Apr 1812, rec. 25 same.

D-223   Indenture, 28 Mar 1812, William CLARK (wife Christina), BCO; Mary BARTON, BCO; $400, part of SW 1/4 S 14 T 8 R 4, 61 1/2 acres, patented by Jacob COON on 27 Aug 1805; his seal, her mark, WIT: Archibald McELROY, Henry FRUSH, ack. David WALLACE, J.P., ent. 21 Apr 1812, rec. 27 same.

D-224   Indenture, 28 Feb 1812, James SINCLAIR (wife Mary), BCO; Caleb GREGG, BCO; whereas James SINCLAIR, Senr., then of Loudon County, Virginia, patented S 18 T 7 R 5, Steubenville district, on 7 Dec 1811, now for $631 conveying NE 1/4 S to GREGG; his seal, her mark, WIT: William SMITH, Jacob GREGG, Rebecca GREGG, ack. 28 Feb 1812, Wm. SMITH, J.P., ent. 21 Apr 1812, rec. 28 same.

D-225   Indenture, 8 Apr 1812, John DILLE (wife Margaret), BCO; David LAING, late of Fyeatte [sic] County, Pennsylvania; $1,100, NBR: Ohio River, 100 acres, part of S 35 T 1 R 2, patented to John HOPKINS, conveyed by him to Wm. DUER, conveyed by him to Leban BROWNSON, conveyed by him to Absalom MARTIN, conveyed by him to John DILLE; WIT: Levin OKEY, James DAVIS, ack. York twp., BCO, Levin OKEY, J.P., ent. 21 Apr 1812, rec. 29 same.

D-226   Indenture, 20 Apr 1812, James CLARK, BCO; James ALEXANDER, Junr., BCO; $500, S 32 T 4 R 2, originally patented to both of them on 21 Oct 1806, WIT: Thos. MITCHELL, John MITCHELL, ack. Thos. MITCHELL, J.P., ent. 21 Apr 1812, rec. 29 same.

D-227   Indenture, 20 Apr 1812, James ALEXANDER, Junr., (wife Isabell), BCO; John MITCHELL, BCO; $500, W 1/2 S 32 T 4 R 2, land formerly belonging by agreement to James CLARK; WIT: Thos. MITCHELL, James ALEXANDER, ack. Thos. MITCHELL, J.P., ent. 21 Apr 1812, rec. 29 same.

D-228   Indenture, 7 d 3 m 18812, John STANLEY (wife Elizabeth), BCO; Reuben POWEL [POWELL], [no location given]; $360, part of SW 1/4 S 10 T 6 R 5, Marietta district, 60 acres; his seal, her mark, WIT: George HALL, Isaac MOORE, ack. Isaac MOORE, J.P., ent. 22 Apr 1812, rec. 30 same.

D-229   Indenture, 12 Nov 1811, Abijah SANDS (wife Elizabeth), Loudon County, Virginia; Henry LONG, same; $500, NW 1/4 S 8 T 10 R 6, Steubenville district, patented to Thomas HUGHES on 21 Oct 1807, by HUGHES to SANDS by deed dated 28 Jul 1810; [no WIT given], ack. Loudon County, Virginia, 11 Nov 1811 in open court, C. BINNS, Clerk, certified by John LITTLEJOHN, presiding magistrate, ent. 24 Apr 1812, rec. 2 May same.

D-230   Indenture, 12 Sep 1810, Mathew McCALL (wife Nancy), BCO; Alexander McCALL, Pennsylvania [no county given]; for half the original purchase price, W 1/2 S 18 T 8 R 5, Steubenville district, patented to Mathew on 20 May 1806; his seal, her mark, WIT: Jos. SHAPP[???], John CAMPBELL, ack. 12 Sep 1810, John CAMPBELL, J.P., ent. 25 Apr 1812, rec. 2 May same.

D-231   Phineas PRICE gives all that he now possesses to Jonathan WRIGHT and Zephaniah BELL until the judgment which stands against him on Esqr. VANCE's docket is satisfied, ent. 25 Apr 1812, rec. 7 May same.

D-232   To all people, James HEDGES, Sheriff, BCO, at December term 1811, CCP, Jacob DAVIS, Esqr., obtained a judgment against Thomas BROOKS for $328.00 debt and 8.10 interest, levied against NE 1/4 S 26 T 3 R 2, 164 acres, described by said writ of Levera facias as property of BROOKS, advertized for sale on 29 Feb 1812, sold to Jacob DAVIS for $391.00; sgn: 5 Mar 1812, James HEDGES, Sheriff, WIT: Ellzey HEDGES, John BARNES, ack. 5 Mar 1812, John PATTERSON, Assoc. Judge, ent 25 Apr 1812, rec. 2 May same.

D-233   Indenture, 24 Apr 1812, Caleb ENGLE (wife Mercy), BCO; Richard TRUAX, BCO; $1,500, part of S 36 T 6 R 4, 100 acres, fee simple; WIT: Sterling JOHNSTON, Levi PICKERING, ack. Sterling JOHNSTON, J.P., ent. 25 Apr 1812, rec. 2 May same.

D-234   Indenture, 22 d 10 m 1811, Samuel WOOLMAN, Junr. (wife Rebecca), Columbianna [sic] County, Ohio; Samuel WOOLMAN, Senr., same; $2,210, S 19 T 8 R 5, patented to Samuel, Junr.; WIT: David GASKIEL, William HEACOCK, ack. Columbiana County, David GASKIEL, J.P., certified by Reasin BEALL, Clk., Thos. McKNIGHT, ent. 29 Apr 1812, rec. 30 same.

D-235   Indenture, 27 Apr 1812, Robert GREENLEE (wife Mary), BCO; Jonah HOUGH, BCO; $1,000, part of S 34, 35, and 28 T 6 R 3, Steubenville district, 100 acres 2 rods 20 perches, patented to Notley HAYS, from Josiah DILLON (wife Dorothy) and Mordicai YARNALL (wife Phebe), then conveyed from Notley HAYS (wife Salley) to Merchant DEFORD, from DEFORD to GREENLEE, fee simple; WIT: Sterling JOHNSTON, John ELLIOTT, ack. Sterling JOHNSTON, J.P., ent. 29 Apr 1812, rec. 4 May same.

D-236   Indenture, 1 Feb 1812, Joshua WOODROW, Junr. (wife Nancy), Highland County, Ohio; Jonathan ELLIS, BCO; $560, SW 1/4 S 3 T 10 R 6, Steubenville district, patented to WOODROW on 10 Dec 1808; WIT: Allen TRIMBLE, James DANIEL, ack. Highland County, 1 Feb 1812, James DANIEL, J.P., ent. 30 Apr 1812, rec. 6 May same.

D-237   Indenture, 28 Apr 1812, John CONNELL (wife Eleanor), Brook County, Virginia; Robert GRAY, BCO; $302.23, NBR: Indian Wheeling Creek, Barr's Run, 75 acres 89 poles, part of S 31 T 7 R 3, patented to David BARR on 8 May 1806, conveyed to John CONNELL; WIT: Thomas THOMPSON, John BARRETT, ack. JCO, John BARRETT, J.P., certified by Thomas PATTON, Clerk, CCP, ent. 30 Apr 1812, rec. 7 May same.

D-239   Indenture, 24 Apr 1812, Richard TRUAX (wife Mary), BCO; Jonas PICKERING, BCO; $2,025, 101 1/2 acres 24 perches, fee simple, part of S 13 T 8 R 4; his seal, her mark, WIT: Sterling JOHNSTON, Levi PICKERING, ack. Sterling JOHNSTON, J.P., ent. 12 May 1812, rec. 13 same.

D-240   Indenture, 13 May 1812, John McCULLOCK (wife Mary), Ohio County, Virginia, Robert GREENLEE, BCO; $1,000, part of S 22 T 7 R 4, 100 acres, granted to John HOPKINS by Samuel OSGOOD and Walter LIVINGSTON, commissioners of the Board of Treasury on 3 Mar 1789, from HOPKINS to William DUER on 6 Jun 1792, from DUER to William HILL on 7 Mar 1796, from HILL to McCULLOCH on 23 Nov 1796, fee simple; WIT: Jacob NAGLE, Sterling JOHNSTON, ack. Sterling JOHNSTON, J.P., ent. 13 May 1812, rec. 19 same.

D-241   Indenture, 1 Jan 1812, Robert HENDERSON (wife Margaret), Wheeling twp., BCO; John LOVE, BCO; $500, 90 acres, part of S 20 T 8 R 4, Steubenville district, patented to Michael JENKINS on 10 Oct 1806, from JENKINS (wife Sarah) to Samuel LEWIS on 8 May 1809 (recorded in Book C, p. 51), from LEWIS to HENDERSON on 21 May 1811 (recorded in Book D, p. 91); his seal, her mark ["Peggy"], WIT: Benjamin MERIDITH, William DEVLON, ack. 25 Jan 1812, John CAMPBELL, ent. 19 May 1812, rec. 22 same.

D-243   Plat of Woodfield, laid out by Archibald WOODS, Levi BARBER, Benjamin RUGGLES, and George PAULL, on 4 Jun 1812, by Sterling JOHNSTON, J.P., ent. 4 Jun 1812, rec. 5 same.

D-244   Know all men, George PAULL, Josiah DILLON (wife Dorithy), on 7 Mar 1811, executed to Charles HAMMOND a deed of trust on property adjoining St. Clairsville, to sell to raise money, HAMMOND sells to Robert THOMPSON, St. Clairsville, for $100, 3 acres 18 perches; sgn: 19 May 1812, WIT: William BROWN, Nancy HAMMOND, ack. 8 Jun 1812, Sterling JOHNSTON, J.P., ent. 8 Jun 1812, rec. 11 same.

Plat of Woodfield

D-244   Indenture, 27 Apr 1812, Jonah HOUGH, BCO; Robert GREENLEE, BCO; whereas HOUGH is bound to GREENLEE for $250 payable by 1 Apr 1813, sells part of S 34 T 6 R 3, 100 acres 2 rods 20 perches, conveyed on this date by Robert to Jonah, void if $250 paid; WIT: Sterling JOHNSTON, John ELLIOTT, ack. 27 Apr 1812, Sterling JOHNSTON, J.P., ent. 10 Jun 1812, rec. 13 same.

D-246   Indenture, 2 Apr 1812, Jane VANWEY, BCO; Robert McFARLAND, BCO; $200, part of S 20 T 7 R 3, 50 acres; her mark, WIT: Robert VANCE, ack. 2 Apr 1812, Robert VANCE, J.P., ent. 12 Jun 1812, rec. 13 same.

D-246   Indenture, 2 Apr 1812, Jane VANWEY, BCO; Thomas MAJOR, BCO; $360, part of S 20 T 7 R 3, NBR: Mordicai BALDERSON, Robert McFADDEN, James McFADDEN, 40 acres; her mark, WIT: Robert VANCE, ack, Robert VANCE, J.P., ent. 12 Jun 1812, rec. 13 same.

D-247   Indenture, 5 Jun 1812, Robert COGHRON [COUGHRON] (wife Rebeckah), BCO; Stephen MAYERS, Barkley [Berkley?] County, Virginia; $375, part of S 14 T 8 R 4, NBR: George ARMSTRONG, 50 acres, conveyed to COUGHRON aby Peter WYRICK by patent dated 10 Oct 1808, conveyed to WYRICK by Jacob COON on 10 Feb 1808 (recorded Book B, p. 236), fee simple; both mark, wit: David WALLACE, James HANNAH, ack. David WALLACE, J.P., ent. 13 Jun 1812, rec. 15 same.

D-249   Indenture, 17 Jan 1812, Thomas MARQUES (wife Joannah), BCO; William STEPHENSON [no location given]; $320, 80 acres in NE 1/4 S 7 T 9 R 5, patented to MARQUES on 15 Nov 1807; WIT: Arthur MORRISON, William DUNN, ack. 18 Jan 1812, William DUNN, J.P., ent. 19 Jun 1812 rec. 24 same.

D-250   Whereas Peter MANIFOLD of Newtown, New York, executed instrument to Samuel SPRIGG, BCO, dated 6 Feb last, stating he was legally empowered by David MORRIS (wife Christiana), and Elizabeth MERCIER, heirs at law of John D. MERCIER, dec'd, late of New York, John MERCIER was legally seized of [unspecified S T R] but in lifetime sold to Samuel SPRIGG the balance of two sections deducting land sold by attorneys during life time, estimated at 225 acres; sgn: 14 Sep 1811, WIT: Isaac A. VAN HOOK, Jno. L. LAWRANCE, ack. New York, 9 Nov 1811, Brockholst LIVINGSTON, Assoc. Judge, Supreme Court, ent. 23 Jun 1812, rec. 25 same.

D-251   Indenture, 28 d 5 m 1812, Joseph HOLLOWAY (wife Ealeanor [Eleanor]), BCO; Asa HOLLOWAY, Senr. [no location given] $2 per acre, SE 1/4 S 23 T 9 R 5, Steubenville district; WIT: Jacob PICKERING, Jacob BRANSON, ack. 28 May 1812, John MERCER, J.P., ent. 29 Jun 1812, rec. 30 same.

D-252   Indenture, 30 d 5 m 1812, Jacob PICKERING (wife Hannah), BCO; Asa HOLLOWAY, Senr., BCO; $270, part of NW 1/4 S 14 T 9 R 5, NBR: Jacob BRANSON, 90 acres; his seal, her mark, WIT: Stephen BROCK, John TALBOTT [his mar], ack. 15 Jun 1812, John MERCER, J.P., ent. 29 Jun 1812, rec. 30 same.

D-252   Indenture, 29 d 5 m 1812, Jacob PICKERING (wife Hannah), BCO; Jacob BRANSON, BCO; $270, part of NW 1/4 S 14 T 9 R 5, 90 acres, fee simple; his seal, her mark, WIT: Stephen BROCK, John TALBOTT [his mark], ack. 15 Jun 1812, John MERCER, J.P., ent. 29 Jun 1812, rec. 1 Jul same; NOTE following: "There was some errors in this deed the deed which is intended to correct them is recorded in Book O pages 105 & 106."

D-254   Article of an agreement between James McCUNE, Huntingdon County, Morris twp., farmer; and Joseph CULBERSON, JCO; McCUNE sells to CULBERSON 120 acres on N or NE corner of S8 T 9 R 5, $200 to be paid 1 Dec 1803 and remainder to be paid 1 Dec 1805, McCUNE to make a deed when he gets one himself, penal sum of $400; sgn: 22 Aug 1803, McCUNE and CULBERSON both seal, WIT: Jas. McCUNE, [ack.???] ent. 30 Jun 1812, rec. 1 Jul same.

D-254   Indenture, 29 May 1812, Samuel McCUNE (wife Sarah), BCO, and Margaret McCUNE, Licking County, Ohio; Joseph CULBERSON, BCO; $240, 120 acres, part of NE 1/4 S 8 T 8 ["(Township numbered eight)" followed by "Township numbered nine" (?)] R 5, S patented to Samuel McCUNE on 27 Mar 1809, NBR: Samuel McCUNE, fee simple; WIT: John ROBERTSON, William DUNN, ack. 29 May 1812, William DUNN, J.P., [Sarah and Margaret being interviewed apart from their husbands, ent. 30 Jun 1812, rec. 1 Jul same.

D-255   Know all men, Archibald McELROY and Nancy BARTON, admrs. of David BARTON, dec'd, by rule passed in CCP in April term 1812 sell lots #135 and #136 in St. Clairsville, sold at public sale on 30 Jun 1812, Magdaline PIPER bid $65, fee simple; sgn: 2 Jun 1812, WIT: John BROWN, Joseph MORRISON, ack. 17 Jun 1812, Sterling JOHNSTON, J.P., ent. 4 Jul 1812, rec. same.

D-256   Indenture, 1 Feb 1812, John EDWARDS (wife Elenor), BCO; John PRICE, BCO; $400, NW 1/4 S 13 T 10 R 6 except what was previously conveyed to James EDWARDS on 13 Oct 1808 (80 acres), piece being conveyed is also 80 acres, fee simple; his seal, her mark, WIT: John MOORE, Hannah MOORE [her mark], ack. 1 Feb 1812, John MOORE, J.P., ent. 4 Jul 1812, rec. 9 same.

D-257   Indenture, 26 Feb 1812, David VANCE (wife Margret), Coldrain [sic] twp., BCO; William GIFFIN, same; $506, NBR: Wheeling Creek, William DENHAM, 126 acres 2 rods 27 poles, fee simple; WIT: Peter YARNALL, ack.

Robert VANCE, J.P., [no day given] Feb 1812, then a second ack., <u>22</u> Feb 1812, Robert VANCE, J.P., ent. 4 Jul 1812, rec. 7 same.

D-259   Indenture, 22 Feb 1812, William GIFFIN (wife Elizabeth), Colerain twp., BCO; Eleazer KENNEY [KINNEY], same; $315, NBR: Wheeling Creek, William DENHAM, 126 acres, fee simple; his seal, her mark, WIT: Peter YARNALL, Robert VANCE, ack. 22 Feb 1812, Robert VANCE, J.P., ent. 4 Jul 1812, rec. 11 same.

D-260   Indenture, 3 Apr 1812, James LUNDY (wife Ann), BCO; Samuel THOMPSON, BCO; $300, 105 acres 30 perches, part of NW 1/4 S 4 T 8 R 5, patented to Arthur MORRISON on 13 Oct 1807, NBR: Arthur MORRISON; his seal, her mark [names given as LONDY here], WIT: David LONG, William BOYD, ack. [same date as above] John BOYD, J.P., ent. 4 Jul 1812, rec. 11 same.

D-261   Indenture, 27 Jun 1812, Margaret HERVEY, extx. of estate of John HERVEY, dec'd., and James HERVEY, legal owner and also extr. of said estate, both JCO; William SMITH, [Senr.], BCO; $7 per acre, 300 acres, part of S 33 T 4 R 2, NBR: Rev. Mr. ANDERSON, patented to Robt. WOODS of Ohio County, Virginia, on 4 Mar 1802, conveyed by WOODS to Henry HERVEY of Brooke County, Virginia, as recorded in Book A, p. 86, HERVEY conveyed by LW&T to sons James and John HERVEY to be divided equally, John at his decease nominated Margaret and James extx. and extr., they now sell land; his seal, her mark, WIT: David BERRY, Thos. MITCHELL, ack. Thos. MITCHELL, J.P., ent. 10 Jul 1812, rec. 11 same.

D-262   Indenture, 27 Jun 1812, William SMITH, Senr., (wife Phebe), BCO; William McKIM, Chester County, Pennsylvania; $2,400, part of S 33 T 4 R 2, NBR: Rev. Mr. ANDERSON, 300 acres; his seal, her mark, WIT: David BERRY, Thos. MITCHELL, ack. Thos. MITCHELL, J.P., ent. 10 Jul 1812, rec. 16 same.

D-264   Indenture, [no day or month given] 1812, Michael CARROLL (wife Sally), BCO; Robert COUGHRON, BCO; $436, 54 acres 2 rods 10 perches, part of S 12 T 7 R 4, patented to Michael CARROLL on 8 May 1806, NBR: Samuel BROWN, William GRAHAM, Andrew BYERS; WIT: Sterling JOHNSTON, James McCONNELL, ack. 11 Jul 1812, Sterling JOHNSTON, J.P., ent. 11 Jul 1812, rec. 16 same.

D-265   Indenture, 1 Jun 1812, William Weir GAULT (wife Sarah), Washington County, Pennsylvania; Jacob RILEY, Licking County, Ohio; $700, lots #19 and #20 in Morristown, fee simple; WIT: Andrew BELL, Edward BELL, ack. JCO, 1 Jun 1812, Andrew BELL, J.P., certified by Thomas PATTON, Clerk, CCP, ent. 14 Jul 1812, rec. 16 same.

D-266 Indenture, 1 Jun 1812, Wm. W. GAULT (wife Sarah), Washington County, Pennsylvania; Jacob RILEY, Licking County, Ohio; $300, NBR: Abner MURPHY, 28 acres, part of S 20 T 8 R 5, conveyed from William CHAPLAIN (wife Mary) to Leonard HART, Senr., on 25 Jun 1808, from HART (wife Jemima) to Wm. W. GAULT on 23 Aug 1808, fee simple; WIT: Andrew BELL, Edward BELL, ack. JCO, 1 Jun 1812, Andrew BELL, J.P., certified by Thomas PATTON, Clerk, CCP, ent. 14 Jul 1812, rec. 16 same.

D-268 Indenture, 14 May 1812, William FARIS, Junr., BCO; William FARIS, Senr., BCO; on 26 Aug 1811 William Junr. purchased lot #109 in St. Clairsville from William ASKEW, now William Junr. sells this to William Senr. for $227, fee simple; WIT: Allen STEWART, Zebulon WARNER, ack. 14 May 1812, Zebulon WARNER, J.P., ent. 17 Jul 1812, rec. same.

D-269 Indenture, 16 Jul 1812, John CLELAND (wife Margaret), Washington County, Pennsylvania; James HUGHES, St. Clairsville, BCO; $1,050, land adjoining St. Clairsville, lot #28, also #19 and #27, all containing 1/4 acre, also land adjoining containing 4 1/4 acres 9 poles, all of which was conveyed by Lucius Horatio STOCKTON (wife Elizabeth) by deed dated 20 Oct 1811; WIT: Zebulon WARNER, Benjamin RUGGLES, ack. Zebulon WARNER, J.P., ent. 18 Jul 1812, rec. 30 same.

D-270 Indenture, 16 Jul 1812, James HUGHES, St. Clairsville, BCO, doctor; John CLELAND, Washington County, Pennsylvania; $787.50, 1/2 of ES and N parts of lot #28, 1/4 acre, NBR: John THOMPSON, commons, also lots #19 and #27, also 4 1/4 acres 9 poles, all conveyed by Lucius Horatio STOCKTON (wife Elizabeth) to CLELAND, from CLELAND to HUGHES, to be void if HUGHES pays CLELAND $787.50 in installments ending 1 Apr 1815; WIT: Benjamin RUGGLES, Zebulon WARNER, ack. 16 Jul 1812, Zebulon WARNER, J.P., ent. 18 Jul 1812, rec. 31 same; satisfaction of mortgage ack. by CLELAND but without date.

D-272 Indenture, 26 Nov 1811, Joseph SHARP (wife Nancy), BCO; Eli NICHOLS, BCO; $94, 23 1/2 acres, part of NE 1/4 S 30 T 7 R 4, patented to SHARP on 20 Jun 1809, NBR: Wheeling Creek, James WATT, Eli NICHOLS, fee simple; his seal, her mark; WIT: John CAMPBELL, James SHARP, ack. 26 Nov 1811, John CAMPBELL, J.P., ent. 20 Jul 1812, rec. 31 same.

D-273 Indenture, 20 Jul 1812, Joseph TILTON (wife Mary), JCO; William STRINGER, Junr., BCO; $140, part of S 21 T 4 R 2, 40 3/4 acres 2 rods, patented to Archibald WOODS 15 Nov 1799, from WOODS (wife Ann) to Absalom MARTIN on 1 Aug 1801, from MARTIN (wife Caty) to John CONNELL, from CONNELL (wife Eleanor) to Joseph TILTON on 22 Nov 1804; his seal, her mark,

WIT: Thos. MITCHELL, John RICKETT, ack. Thos. MITCHELL, J.P., ent. 22 Jul 1812, rec. 31 same.

D-274   Indenture, 28 Feb 1812, James SINCLAIR (wife Mary), BCO; Solomon Messor McFERSON, William McFERSON, and Joseph McFERSON, heirs of John McFERSON, dec'd, BCO; $473.25 paid by John McFERSON, dec'd, conveying not as joint tenants but as tenants in common, NW 1/4 S 18 T 7 R 5, Steubenville district, patented to SINCLAIR on 7 Dec 1811, fee simple; his seal ["Senr."], her mark; WIT: William SMITH, Jacob GREGG, Esther GREGG, ack. 28 Feb 1812, William SMITH, J.P., ent. 4 Aug 1812, rec. 6 same.

D-275   Know all men, George PAUL and Josiah DILLON (wife Dorotha) on 27 Mar 1812 executed to Charles HAMOND [HAMMOND] a deed of trust on 7 acres to sell, now sells to William GAMBLE, St. Clairsville, BCO, NBR: William BROWN, St. Clairsville commons, John CLELAND; sgn: 22 Apr 1812, WIT: Saml. SPRIGG, Sterling JOHNSTON, ack. 23 Apr 1812, Sterling JOHNSTON, J.P., ent. 4 Aug 1812, rec. 6 same.

D-276   Know all men, Joseph GRIMES, BCO, for $320 paid by Scholey RITE, BCO, conveys NE 1/4 S 9 T 10 R 6, Steubenville district, land patented to GRIMES; sgn: 14 Aug 1812; he seals as does wife Elisabeth GRIMES, WIT: Sterling JOHNSTON, William HOLLOWAY, ack. Sterling JOHNSTON, J.P., ent. 15 Aug 1812, rec. 20 same.

D-277   Indenture, 1 d 1 m 1810, Horton HOWARD (wife Hannah), BCO; Isaac PARKER and Jacob PARKER, JCO; $2,500, [I don't think I've ever seen so many trees!], 240 acres, same which HOWARDs granted to William MILHOUSE in fee on 11 d 6 m 1807, conveyed in fee from MILHOUSE (wife Hannah) on 1 d 9 m 1809 back to HOWARD, also part of S 3 T 7 R 3, 25 acres, same conveyed from Thomas MITCHELL (wife Agnes) by indenture dated 11 Jun 1807 to William MILHOUSE in fee, conveyed by William MILHOUSE (wife Hannah) on 1 d 9 m 1809 to HOWARD, first tract beginning at NE corner of S 9 T 7 R 3, 240 acres, same which HOWARDs granted to MILHOUSE on 11 d 6 m 1809 and again granted to HOWARD in fee, second part of S 3 T 7 R 3, same granted to MILHOUSE by Thomas MITCHELL (wife Agnes) on 11 Jun 1807 in fee, by MILHOUSE (wife Hannah) to HOWARD on 1 d 9 m 1809, originally patented to HOWARD on 22 d 1 m 1806, conveyed to MITCHELL on 18 d 2 m 1806; WIT: Josiah BUNDY, Henry HOWARD, ack. 1 Jan 1810, Thos. MITCHELL, J.P.

D-279   Indenture, 18 Jun 1812, Joseph VANLAW (wife Mary), BCO; John SPENCER, BCO; S 33 T 7 R 4, Steubenville district, patented to Samuel GREGG, then of Ross County, Ohio, on 1 Oct 1806, GREGG to Joseph NICKELSON, NICKELSON to VANLAW, now for $12, 1/2 acre, part of above S, NBR: Joseph

VANLAW; WIT: William SINCLAIR, James BUNTING, ack. 18 Jun 1812, William SINCLAIR, J.P., ent. 24 Aug 1812, rec. 29 same.

D-281   Indenture, 18 Jun 1812, Samuel GREGG (wife Ann), BCO; John SPENCER, BCO; whereas GREGG, then of Ross County, Ohio, patented S 33 T 7 R 4, Steubenville district, on 1 Oct 1806, now for $30 sells 3 acres 237 8/50's poles; WIT: William SINCLAIR, Joseph MERRITT, ack. 18 Jun 1812, William SINCLAIR, J.P., ent. 24 Aug 1812, rec. 29 same.

D-282   Indenture, 11 Mar 1812, John CONNELL (wife Eleanor), Brooke County, Virginia; John BAKER, BCO; $500, part of S 31 T 7 R 3, 86 acres 18 perches; WIT: John PATTERSON, James HEDGES, Jon [sic] HILL, ack. of John, BCO, 11 Mar 1812, John PATTERSON, Assoc. Judge, CCP; ack. of Eleanor, JCO, 20 Mar 1812, Mordecai BARTLEY, J.P., certified 21 Mar 1812, by Thomas PATTON, Clerk, CCP, ent. 24 Aug 1812, rec. 31 same.

D-283   Indenture, 27 Aug 1812, John BELL (wife Hannah), BCO; Joseph GIBBONS, Green County, Pennsylvania; whereas Jain [sic] VANWEY, BCO, on 2 Apr 1812 sold to BELL part of S 20 T 7 R 3, now BELLs for $38.56 sell to GIBBONS, NBR: Petter [sic] GIBBONS, John BELL, 5 acres 15 perches; his seal, her mark, WIT: Thomas MAJOR, ack. Thomas MAJOR, J.P., ent. 27 Aug 1812, rec. 31 same.

D-284   Indenture, 17 Aug 1812, Samuel VAIL, Menallen twp., Fayette County, Pennsylvania; Mathew WOOD, Ohio; whereas VAIL patented NE 1/4 S 27 T 7 R 5, Steubenville district, on 12 Oct 1807, now for $454 sells to WOOD; (wife Agnes VAIL), WIT: Obediah JENNINGS, Saml. ROBERTS, receipt of money WIT: Obediah JENNINGS, Wm. DIXON, ack. Pennsylvania, Sam ROBERTS, president of the Court of Common of the fifth Judicial District in Pennsylvania, 17 Aug 1812, certified by Richard William LANE, prothonotary, CCP, Fayette County, Pennsylvania, for Samuel ROBERTS, Esqr., 18 Aug 1812, ent. 31 Aug 1812, rec. same.

D-286   Indenture, 29 d 8 m 1812, Thomas BUFKIN (wife Ruth), Tuscoraway County, Ohio, yeoman; Jesse FOULKE, BCO; whereas [Jonas] PICKERING patented N 1/2 S 20 T 9 R 5, Steubenville district, on 20 Jul 1810, and on 10 Apr 1810 PICKERING (wife Ruth) conveyed half of land (1/4 S) to BUFKIN, 81 acres, recorded 23 May 1810, now for $486 selling to FOULKE 81 acres, WIT: William [MAUKER], Abraham McWILLIAMS, WIT to receipt of payment, John MERCER, ack. John MERCER, J.P., ent. 31 Aug 1812, rec. 3 Sep 1812.

D-287   Indenture, 3 Sep 1812, James GORDON, BCO; Arthur GILLIS, JCO; $500, NW 1/4 S 31 T 3 R 2, patented to GORDON on 20 Apr 1812, WIT: George

PAULL, Benjamin DESELLEM, ack. George PAULL, J.P., ent. 3 Sep 1812, rec. 9 same.

D-288   Indenture, 12 d 6 m 1812, Isaac HALL (wife Mary), BCO; Joseph DODD, BCO; $320, N 1/2 SE 1/4 S 20 T 8 R 6; WIT: Jas. COX, Henry BARNES, ack. 17 Jun 1812, Jacob MYERS, J.P., ent. 10 Sep 1812, rec. same.

D-290   Indenture, 21 d 9 m 1812, Schooley [Scholey] WRIGHT, BCO; Jonathan TAYLOR, JCO; $300, NE 1/4 S 9 T 10 R 6, conveyed to WRIGHT by Joseph GRIMES (wife Elizabeth) by deed dated 14 d 8 m 1812; WIT: David VANCE, Sterling JOHNSTON, ack. 22 Sep 1812, Sterling JOHNSTON, J.P., ent. 22 Sep 1812, rec. 25 same.

D-291   Indenture, 28 d 5 m 1812, Asa HOLLOWAY, Senr., (wife Margaret), BCO; Jacob PICKERING, Senr., BCO; $2 per acre, NE 1/4 S 27 T 9 R 5; WIT: Jacob BRANSON, Joseph HOLLOWAY, ack. John MERCER, J.P., ent. 22 Sep 1812, rec. 25 same.

D-291   Indenture, 27 Jun 1812, Jesse DAWSON (wife Elizabeth), BCO; Ambrose DANFORD, BCO; $15, part of SE 1/4 S 4 T 6 R 5, Marietta district, NBR: Capteen Creek, [Moves's] run, 5 acres; his seal, her mark, WIT: Oliver INGUM, Elisha HARRIS, ack. Elisha HARRIS, J.P., ent. 25 Sep 1812, rec. same.

D-292   Indenture, 15 d 6 m 1812, William SHARRARD, Warren twp., JCO; Matthew WOOD, Goshen twp., BCO; $563.50, NW 1/4 S 19 T 7 R 5, Steubenville district, 161 acres, fee simple; WIT: David SMITH, Joseph NEWPORT, ack. BCO, same day, David SMITH, J.P., ent. 28 Sep 1812, rec. same.

D-293   Indenture, 24 Sep 1812, Peter GIBBINS [sgn: GIBBENS], BCO; Joseph GIBBINS, Green County, Pennsylvania; $45, part of S 20 T 7 R 3, 1 acre; WIT: Thomas MAJOR, ack. Thomas MAJOR, ent. 27 Sep 1812, rec. 30 same.

D-294   Indenture, 3 Oct 1812, John PICKET [PIGGOTT, PIGGOT] (wife Eleanor), BCO; William McKINDLEY, BCO; PIGGOTT patented SE 1/4 S 29 T 7 R 5, Steubenville district, now for $320 conveying all to McKINDLEY, fee simple; [both sgn: PIGGOTT], WIT: George PAULL, William McFARLAND, ack. George PAULL, J.P., ent. 3 Oct 1812, rec. 7 same.

D-295   Indenture, 1 Jun 1812, Samuel GREGG (wife Ann), BCO; Hannah NICHOLS, wife of Solomon NICHOLS, dec'd, and heirs of Solomon NICHOLAS; $160, to Hannah, and after her death to her heirs, part of S 33 T 7 R 4, Steubenville district, NBR: Joseph NICHOLSON, 78 acres, fee simple; WIT: Abel GREGG,

William SMITH, Hannah GREGG, ack. same day, William SMITH, J.P., ent. 10 Oct 1812.

D-297   Indenture, 6 May 1812, Thomas THOMPSON (wife Elizabeth), BCO; Henry MITCHEL [MITCHELL], BCO; $70, lot #79 in St. Clairsville, 1/4 acre, fee simple; WIT: John McELROY, Sterling JOHNSTON, ack. 12 Oct 1812, Sterling JOHNSTON, J.P., ent. 12 Oct 1812, rec. 14 same.

D-298   Indenture, 6 May 1812, Thomas THOMPSON (wife Elizabeth), BCO; Henry MITCHELL, BCO; $70, lot #8 in St. Clairsville, 1/4 acre, fee simple; WIT: John McELROY, Sterling JOHNSTON, ack. same date, Sterling JOHNSTON, J.P. [and date 6 May 1812 repeated at end of ack.], ent. 12 Oct 1812, rec. 14 same.

D-299   Indenture, 20 d 6 m 1812, Samuel GREGG (wife Ann), BCO; James HOLLOWAY, BCO; whereas Jacob GREGG, then of Loudon County, Virginia, patented S 7 T 8 R 5 on 19 Oct 1808, part conveyed to Samuel by Jacob on 29 Jun 1809, now Samuel for $980 conveys to HOLLOWAY 72 1/4 acres 29 poles; WIT: Rebecca GREGG, Josh. WRIGHT, ack. 20 Jun 1812, William SMITH, J.P., ent. 13 Oct 1812, rec. 14 same.

D-300   Indenture, 2 Oct 1812, John McCULLOCK (wife Mary), Ohio County, Ohio; Thomas TOWNSEND, Washington County, Pennsylvania; whereas on 3 Mar 1789 John HOPKINS patented 640 acres, S 22 T 7 R 4, HOPKINS on 5 Jun 1792 conveyed to William DUER, DUER on 7 Mar 1796 conveyed to William HILL, HILL conveyed to John McCULLOCK on 23 Nov 1796, now McCULLOCKs convey for $1,200 part of S 22 T 7 R 4, 120 acres, fee simple; WIT: David VANCE, Sterling JOHNSTON, ack. Sterling JOHNSTON, J.P., ent. 14 Oct 1812, rec. 17 same.

D-302   Indenture, 14 Oct 1812, Jacob AULT (wife Elizabeth), BCO; William CHAMBERS, BCO; $912, part of S 2 T 7 R 4, 114 acres; both mark, WIT: George FARQUHAR and George THOMPSON (for Jacob), Benjamin RUGGLES, Terzish [Terziah?] RUGGLES (for Elizabeth), WIT of receipt of $200 by Jacob ALT, George THOMPSON, ack. Benjamin RUGGLES, President, CCP, ent. 17 Oct 1812, rec. 21 same.

D-303   Indenture, 26 Oct 1812, Charles HAMMOND, BCO; Michael TERNAN, Baltimore; whereas John THOMPSON (wife Sally) conveyed to HAMMOND the NE 1/4 S 25 T 8 R 4 on 7 Feb 1806 in trust for George PRICE & Co., JENKINS & COCHRAN, and Michael [TEIRNAN], merchants of the City of Baltimore, HAMMOND now conveyes to TIERNAN the 1/4 S; WIT: David VANCE, Sterling JOHNSTON, ack. Sterling JOHNSTON, J.P., ent. 27 Oct 1812, rec. same.

D-304   Indenture, 12 d 6 m 1812, Joseph DODD (wife Anna), BCO; Isaac HALL, BCO; $320, NE 1/4 S 31 T 8 R 6; his seal, her mark, WIT: Henry BARNES, Jas. COX, ack. 17 Jun 1812, Jacob MYERS, J.P., ent. 28 Oct 1812, rec. same.

D-305   Indenture, 28 d 3 m 1812, David MOORE (wife Martha), London Grove twp., Chester County, Pennsylvania; Eli BOOTH, [Octorarahundred, Cecil County, Maryland; $350, NE 1/4 S 3 T 7 R 5, 160 acres, patented to MOORE on 21 Sep 1807; WIT: David MOORE, Junr., Caleb MOORE, same WIT for receipt of money, ack. 3 Apr 1812, Chester County, W. FINNEY, Judge, CCP, FINNEY certified by Jesse JOHN, Prothonotary, CCP, 4 Apr 1812, ent 2 Nov 1812, rec. same.

D-307   Indenture, 2 Nov 1812, John WILEY (wife Margaret), BCO; John MARQUES, BCO; $394.25, 100 acres, part of N 1/2 S 6 T 8 R 5 with a reservation, conveyed to WILEY by Charles CAMPBELL on 9 Mar 1810, [both parties living adjoining to land being conveyed]; WIT: Andrew GARRETT, John BELL, ack. Union twp., BCO, William DUNN, J.P. [no entering data].

D-308   Indenture, 21 Aug 1812, John JARVIS (wife Ruth), BCO; Philip JARVIS, Junr., [no location given]; $160, 71 acres, NE 1/2 of NE 1/4 S 34 T 9 R 6, fee simple; his seal, an "x" in the middle of her name but no other annotation that this is her mark, WIT: John HOLMES, John I. MOORE, ack. John N. SMITH, J.P., ent. 18 Nov 1812, rec. 25 same.

D-309   Know all men, John BROWN, Junr., St. Clairsville, BCO, sell to George PAUL and James CALDWELL, St. Clairsville, BCO, for $250, part of lots #160 and #59, conveyed to BROWN by John LONG (wife Catherine) on 6 Apr 1808, void if BROWN pays $150 with interest by 1 Sep next; sgn: 16 Jun 1812, WIT: W. BROWN, Junr., Ellzey HEDGES, ack. 18 Jun 1812, Sterling JOHNSTON, J.P., ent. 28 Nov 1812, rec. 30 same.

D-310   Indenture, 28 Oct 1812, Abigail MEDCALF, Baltimore, Baltimore County, Maryland; William M. MEDCALF, same; $18, lot #37 in Town of Belmont, conveyed to MEDCALF by Joseph WRIGHT (wife Eleanor) on 31 Jul 1810, recorded in Book C, p. 265); WIT: Fielder ISRAEL, Owen DORSEY, ack. Baltimore County, Maryland, 8 Oct 1812, Owen DORSEY, Tho. W. GRIFFITH, J.P.'s, also Edw. JOHNSON, Mayor of Baltimore, DORSEY and GRIFFITH certified by Wm. GIBSON, Clk., ent. 30 Nov 1812, rec. 3 Dec same.

D-312   Indenture, 28 d 9 m 1812, Horton HOWARD (wife Hannah), BCO; Isaac EDWARDS (person of colour), JCO; $240, S 1/2 of NW 1/4 S 9 T 7 R 5, Steubenville district, patented by HOWARD on 30 Dec 1811; WIT: James

CANARY, Sarah HALL, ack. same date, Thomas MITCHELL, J.P., ent. 30 Nov 1812, rec. 3 Dec same.

D-313   Indenture, 28 d 9 m 1812, Horton HOWARD (wife Hannah), BCO; Miner EDWARDS (a person of colour), JCO; $240, N 1/2 NW 1/4 S 9 T 7 R 5, Steubenville district, patented to HOWARD on 30 Dec 1811; WIT: James CANARY, Sarah HALL, ack. same day, Thomas MITCHELL, Justice, ent. 30 Nov 1812, rec. 3 Dec same.

D-314   Indenture, 29 Aug 1812, Daniel THOMAS (wife Elizabeth), BCO; Joseph THORNBURGH, Robert MILLER, and John S. WEBSTER, Baltimore, Baltimore County, Maryland; $1,120, NE 1/4 S 3 T 5 R 4; his seal, her mark, WIT: Edw. BRYSON, James SPRIGG, ack. 29 Aug 1812, York twp., BCO, Edw. BRYSON, J.P., ent. 7 Dec 1812, rec. same.

D-315   Indenture, 6 Apr 1812, John THOMPSON (wife Sarah), BCO; Josiah HEDGES, BCO; $500, SE 1/4 S 18 T 9 R 6, 168 acres, Steubenville district, patented to Thomas WILLSON, conveyed by WILSON (wife Nancy) on 28 Feb 1812 to John THOMPSON, fee simple; his seal, her mark, WIT: Zebulon WARNER, Jacob NAGLE, ack. 6 Apr 1812, Zebulon WARNER, J.P., ent. 1 Jan 1813, rec. 2 same.

D-316   Indenture, 14 d 6 m 1809, Horton HOWARD (wife Hannah), BCO; Levi WELLS, BCO; $200, S 9 T 7 R 3, NBR: John LLOYD, Wm. MILHOUS, 80 acres; WIT: William BARNES, Thos. MITCHELL, ack. [no date given], Thos. MITCHELL, [no office given], ent. 12 Jan 1813, rec. 14 same.

D-317   Indenture, 20 Jun 1810, Jacob REPLOGAL (wife Elizabeth), Montgomery County, Ohio; Eli NICHOLS, BCO; $2,700, part of SE 1/4 S 30 T 7 R 4, patented to Joseph SHARP on 20 Jun 1809, SHARP to REPLOGAL on 27 Apr 1810, NBR: James McCOY, [???]ROSMAN [ROSSMAN], Jacob GOSSER, McCOY and ROSSMAN had contracts on land which were to expire; his seal, her mark, WIT: Zebulon WARNER, Joshua BROWN, ack. BCO, same date, for Jacob, Zebulon WARNER, J.P., ack. Montgomery County, Ohio, 11 Aug 1810, for Elizabeth, John FOLKERTH, J.P., ent. 20 Jan 1813, rec. 21 same.

D-319   Indenture, 19 Jan 1813, Jeremiah BURRIS (wife Rachel), BCO; Christian BLAZER [BLOZER], BCO; $81, lot near W end of St. Clairsville, NBR: Samuel CRAWFORD, 1/8 acre, plus W 1/2 of lot conveyed from John YOUNG (wife Polly) to John FRITCH, from FRITCH to Henry MITCHELL, from MITCHELL to BURRIS on 26 Jan 1810, fee simple; both mark, WIT: David MOORE, Peter BLAZER, ack. David MOORE, J.P., ent. 29 Jan 1813, rec. 1 Feb same.

D-320   Indenture, 30 Dec 1812, Jesse BROCK (wife Polly), BCO; George Saunderson BROCK, BCO; $2/acre, part of NW 1/4 S 27 T 9 R 5, Steubhenville district, 41 1/4 acres; WIT: Benj. BROCK, John MERCER, Abel PICKERING, ack. 30 Dec 1812, John MERCER, J.P., ent. 29 Jan 1813, rec. 1 Feb same.

D-321   Indenture, 30 Dec 1812, Jacob PICKERING, Senr., (wife Hannah), BCO; Benjamin BROCK, BCO; [no purchase price given], part of NE 1/4 S 27 T 9 R 5, Steubenville district, NBR: Geo. S. BROCK, 8 acres; his seal, her mark, WIT: George S. BROCK, Jesse BROCK, John MERCER, ack. 30 dec 1812, John MERCER, J.P., ent. 29 Jan 1813, rec. 3 Feb same.

D-322   Indenture, 30 Dec 1812, Jesse BROCK (wife Polly), BCO; Sally BROCK, BCO; $2/acre, part of NW 1/4 S 27 T 9 R 5, 41 1/4 acres; WIT: Benjamin BROCK, Abel PICKERING, George S. BROCK, ack. 30 Dec 1812, John MERCER, J.P., ent. 29 Jan 1813, rec. 3 Feb same.

D-322   Indenture, 30 Dec 1812, Jesse BROCK (wife Polly), BCO: Benjamin BROCK, BCO; $2/acre, part of NW 1/4 S 27 T 9 R 5, Steubenville district, 41 1/4 acres; WIT: Abel PICKERING, George S. BROCK, John MERCER, ack. 30 Dec 1812, John MERCER, J.P., ent. 29 Jan 1813, rec. 3 Feb same.

D-323   James MADISON, President, patent to Jonathan SUTTON, assignee of Francis BARKHURST, full payment for S 32 T 6 R 3, Steubenville district; sgn: 20 Apr 1812, James MADISON by Secretary of State James MONROE, ent. 2 Feb 1813, rec. 6 same.

D-324   Indenture, 2 Feb 1813, Jonathan SUTTON (wife Hannah), BCO; Fancy [female] BARCHURST, BCO; $800, land in S 32 T 6 R 3, 384 acres, granted to SUTTON on 20 Apr 1812, fee simple; his seal, her mark, WIT: Wm. FARIS, Junr., John PATTERSON, ack. John PATTERSON, Assoc. Judge, CCP, ent. 2 Feb 1813, rec. 6 same.

D-325   3 Feb 1813, John WINTER, BCO; William HATFIELD, BCO; $350, part of lot #93 in St. Clairsville, fee simple; ;WIT: Sterling JOHNSTON, Ira ROBINSON, ack. Sterling JOHNSTON, J.P., ent. 3 Feb 1813, rec. 8 same.

D-326   Indenture, 8 Jun 1811, John TAYLOR (wife Sarah), JCO; Samuel YOCOM, BCO; $278, land in Goshen twp., NW 1/4 S 33 T 7 R 5, fee simple; WIT: Isaac STRAHL, John WATSON, ack. 8 Jun 1811, John WATSON, J.P., ent. 6 Feb 1813, rec. 8 same.

D-327   Indenture, 8 Oct 1812, Amos VERNON (wife Mary), BCO; Robert VERNON, BCO; $150, W part of SE 1/4 S 34 T 7 R 5, 40 acres; WIT: John

STRAHL, Rebecca STRAHL, ack. 8 Oct 1812, John STRAHL, J.P., ent. 6 Feb 1813, rec. 8 same.

D-328   Indenture, 5 Feb 1813, Samuel YOCUM (wife Rebecca), BCO; Joseph WILLIAMS, Chester County, Pennsylvania; $144.61, land in Goshen twp., W 1/2 NW 1/4 S 33 T 7 R 5; WIT: Jonathan FAWCETT, John STRAHL, ack. John STRAHL, J.P., ent. 6 Feb 1813, rec. 10 same.

D-329   Indenture, 24 Aug 1812, Magdaline PIPER, St. Clairsville, BCO; Isaac SIMMONS, BCO; $60, lot #122 in St. Clairsville, conveyed from Nicholas BOWER (and wife) to John MARTIN on 31 Mar [no year] from MARTIN (and wife) to John THOMPSON, from THOMPSON (and wife) to PIPER on 21 Apr 1807, fee simple; her mark, WIT: Sterling JOHNSTON, David VANCE, ack. 24 Aug 1812, Sterling JOHNSTON, J.P., ent. 6 Feb 1813, rec. 10 same.

D-330   Indenture, 15 d 1 m 1813, Jonathan TAYLOR (wife Ann), Mount Pleasant twp., JCO; Richard CROY, BCO; $640, SW 1/4 S 9 T 8 R 6, patented to TAYLOR on 18 d 3 m 1805, NBR: John GRIER, 160 acres; WIT: Henry HANNAH, Thos. MITCHELL, ack. 15 Jan 1813, Thos. MITCHELL, J.P., ent. 8 Feb 1813, rec. 10 same.

D-331   Indenture, 8 Dec 1812, Hugh GILLILAND (wife Elizabeth), BCO; Hugh FORD, BCO; $200, land in S 25 T 9 R 6, patented to Christopher WINTER, sold to GILLILAND, NBR: Ralph COWGIL, 100 acres, fee simple; WIT: Brice HOWARD, Hugh GILLILAND, Junr., ack. Brice HOWARD, J.P., ent. 10 Feb 1813, rec. 15 same.

D-332   Indenture, 3 Feb 1813, John WINTER, BCO; Ira ROBINSON, BCO; $90, lot #93 in St. Clairsville, NBR: BENTLEY, GILL, fee simple; WIT: Sterling JOHNSTON, William HATFIELD, ack. Sterling JOHNSTON, J.P., ent. 10 Feb 1813, rec. 18 same.

D-333   James MADISON, President, Moses CAMPBELL, assignee of William CHAPLAIN, deposited a certificate of the Register in Steubenville, full payment made for SW 1/4 S 34 T 8 R 5, sgn: 15 Aug 1811, Jas. MONROE, Secretary of State, ent. 10 Feb 1813, rec. 18 same.

D-334   Indenture, 25 Dec 1812, John McFADDEN (wife Nelly), BCO; Andrew DOWNING, BCO; $558.66, part S 14 T 7 R 3, NBR: Josiah BUNDAY, Robert McBRATNEY, 69 acres 3 rods 13 perches; his seal, her mark; WIT: Thomas MAJOR, John CAUGHEY, ack. same date, Thomas MAJOR, J.P., ent. 17 Feb 1813, rec. 22 same.

D-335 Indenture, 17 d 9 m 1812, William DIXON, Junr., BCO; David McMASTERS, JCO; $350, NW 1/4 S 31 T 8 R 4, plus 15 acres 9 perches designated in a deed of conveyance from William DIXON, Senr., to William DIXON, Junr., containing 178 acres, void if $350 paid to Merrick STARR of Mountpleasant Town, JCO, on or before 17 d 9 m 1813; his seal, mark of Jane DIXON, ack. John CAMPBELL, Mary CAMPBELL [her mark], ack. 18 Sep 1812, John CAMPBELL, J.P., ent. 19 Feb 1813, rec. 23 same.

D-336 Indenture, 5 d 12 m 1812, Daniel McPEAK (wife Elizabeth), BCO: Joseph WALTON, BCO; $336, part of S 19 T 7 R 3, NBR: Thomas BLACKLEDGE, 84 acres, part of tract conveyed from Bazaleel WELLS (wife Sally) to McPEAK by deed dated 3 d 1 m 1811; both mark; WIT: Thomas MAJOR, Ely [KERMARD][probably Eli KENNARD], ack. 5 Dec 1812, Thomas MAJOR, J.P., ent. 22 Feb 1813, rec. 23 same.

D-337 To all to whom, at Jan term 1810 in CCP, Michael TIERNAN and Luke TIERNAN gained judgment against Josiah DILLON for $1,596 with interest from 1 Jul 1807, also $18.54 9 mills and $8 attorneys fees, and on 27 Feb 1810 a writ of ferri facias was issued to Marshal of district to levy debt, Marshal levied on part of S 4 T 5 R 4, 60 acres 33 perches, not sold for want of bidders, and at same term Dominick GALT and John THOMAS recovered judgment against Josiah DILLON for $650 with interest from 28 Jun 1807, also $18.54 9 mills and $8 attorneys fee, on 28 Feb 1810 a writ of fieri facias issued to Marshal for levying debt, Marshal levied on part of S 4 T 5 R 4, 60 acres 33 perches, on 24 Feb 1812 a writ of fenditioni exponas issued commanding exposure to sale of mentioned land for both petitioners, James CALDWELL bid $294.67, Lewis CASS, Marshal of Ohio District, conveys to CALDWELL 60 acres 33 perches in S 4 T 5 R 4; sgn: 13 Jan 1813, WIT: Edw. KERRICK, Thos. STEEL, ack. Ross County, James FERGUSON, J.P., ent. 22 Feb 1813, rec. 24 same.

D-339 Indenture, 27 Dec 1812, Sterling JOHNSTON (wife Mary), BCL; William BROWN, BCO; $640, NW 1/4 S 7 T 7 R 4, patented to JOHNSTON on 8 Jun 1812, fee simple; WIT: John PATTERSON, Abner MOORE, ack. 27 Feb 1813, John PATTERSON, Assoc. Judge, CCP., ent. 27 Feb 1813, rec. 1 Mar same.

D-340 Indenture, 23 Feb 1813, James CALDWELL (wife Nancy), St. Clairsville, BCO; Alexander ARMSTRONG, St. Clairsville; $500, lots #91 and #92 in St. Clairsville, sold by CALDWELL to William GOUGH in 1809, from GOUGH to William HATFIELD in 1810, from HATFIELD to ARMSTRONG in 1812, no deed previously made; WIT: William HATFIELD, John PATTERSON, ack. John PATTERSON, Assoc. Judge, CCP, ent. 27 Feb 1813, rec. 3 Mar same.

D-341   Indenture, 8 Feb 1813, William SPENCER (wife Sarah), BCO; Joel ELLIOTT, Frederic [sic] County, Maryland; $640, SW 1/4 S 7 T 9 R 6, Steubenville district; WIT: Israel FRENCH, Humphrey ANDERSON, ack. 8 Feb 1813, John N. SMITH, J.P. for Kirkwood twp., ent. 4 Mar 1813, rec. 8 same.

D-342   Indenture, 19 Feb 1813, Christian ROSE (wife Catherine), Hempfield twp., Westmoreland County, Pennsylvania; Abraham WOTRING, Canton twp., Washington County, Pennsylvania; $150, lots #143 and #144 in St. Clairsville, each 1/4 acre; both mark [name is ROSES here], WIT: Hetty B. YOUNG, John YOUNG, ack. Pennsylvania, 19 Feb 1813, John YOUNG, Esq., President of the tenth district, CCP, YOUNG certified by John MORRISON, Prothonotary, CCP, ent. 4 Mar 1813, rec. 8 same.

D-344   Know all men, William RIDLE, BCO, collector of Township Tax for Union twp., BCO, unable to collect 1812 tax of 12.5 cents against fractional lot #89 in Morristown, a nonresident lot, no one to pay, sold on 31 Dec 1812 to Nelley JAKES [no selling price given, no former owner named], sgn: 12 Feb 1813 [RIDDEL here], WIT: Thos. McWILLIAMS, Robert MORRISON, ack. __ Feb 1813, Duncan MORRISON, J.P., ent. 6 Mar 1813, rec. 9 same.

D-345   Know all men, William RIDLE, BCO, [description p. 344 entry], unable to collect 1812 tax of 7.5 cents against lot #98 in Morristown, a nonresident lot, sold 20 feet of lot to Alexander GASTON on 31 Dec 1812 [no selling price, no former owner named]; sgn: 12 Feb 1813 [RIDDEL here], WIT: Robt. MORRISON, Thos. McWILLIAMS, ack. __ Feb 1813, Duncan MORRISON, J.P., ent. 6 Mar 1813, rec. 10 same.

D-346   Know all men, William RIDLE, BCO [description in p. 344 entry], 7.5 cents tax on lot #41, sold 50 feet on E side to Alexander GASTON; sgn: 12 Feb 1813 [RIDDEL here], WIT: Thos. McWILLIAMS, Robt. MORRISON, ack. __ Feb 1813, Duncan MORRISON, J.P., ent. 6 Mar 1813, rec. 10 same.

D-346   Know all men, William RIDLE, BCO [description p. 344 entry], 7.5 cents tax on lot #66 in Morristown, sold 50 feet on W side to Alexander GASTON; sgn: 11 Feb 1813 [RIDDEL], WIT: Thos. McWILLIAMS, Robt. MORRISON, ack. __ Feb 1813, D. MORRISON, J.P., ent. 6 Mar 1813, rec. 11 same.

D-347   Know all men, William RIDLE, BCO [description p. 344 entry], 7.5 cents tax on lot #97 in Morristown, sold 15 feet of E side to Alexander GASTON; sgn: 6 Feb 1813 [RIDDEL], WIT: Thos. McWILLIAMS, Robt. MORRISON, ack. 6 Feb 1813, Duncan MORRISON, J.P., ent. 6 Mar 1813, rec. 11 same.

D-348 Know all men, William RIDLE, BCO [description p. 344 entry], 7.5 cents on lot #99, sold 11 feet on E side to Alexander GASTON; sgn: 12 Feb 1813 [RIDDEL], WIT: Thos. McWILLIAMS, Robt. MORRISON, ack. __ Feb 1813, Duncan MORRISON, J.P., ent. 6 Mar 1813, rec. 12 same.

D-349 Know all men, William RIDLE, BCO [description p. 344 entry], 7.5 cents on lot #100, sold 24 feet of E side to Alexander GASTON; sgn: 12 Feb 1813 [RIDDEL], WIT: Thos. McWILLIAMS, Robt. MORRISON, ack. __ Feb 1813, Duncan MORRISON, J.P., ent. 6 Mar 1813, rec. 12 same.

D-349 Know all men, William RIDLE, BCO [description p. 344 entry], 7.5 cents on lot #76, sold 25 feet of W side to Alexander GASTON; sgn: 6 Feb 1813 [RIDDEL], WIT: Thos. McWILLIAMS, Robt. MORRISON, ack. __ Feb 1813, Duncan MORRISON, J.P., ent. 6 Mar 1813, rec. 12 same.

D-350 Know all men, William RIDLE, BCO [description p. 344 entry], 7.5 cents on lot #75, sold to Alexander GASTON; sgn: 12 Feb 1813 [RIDDEL], WIT: Thos. McWILLIAMS, Robt. MORRISON, ack. __ Feb 1813, Duncan MORRISON, J.P., ent. 6 Mar 1813, rec. 12 same.

D-351 Indenture, 20 Aug 1812, Leonard HART (wife Jamima), BCO; John MILLER, BCO; $150, lot adjoining Morristown, NBR: Duncan MORRISON, Margret HAZLETT, 14.5 acres 38 perches, entered by William CHAPLAIN, from CHAPLAIN to HART; his mark [LH], her mark, WIT: Mathew GRIMES, Alex. GASTON, ack. 13 Oct 1812, William DUNN, J.P., ent. 10 Mar 1813, rec. 12 same.

D-352 Indenture, 20 Aug 1812, Leonard HART (wife Jamima), BCO; William WAGNER, BCO; $100, lot adjoining Morristown, NBR: Margret HAZLET, 4 3/4 acres 27 perches, entered by William CHAPLAIN, from CHAPLAIN to HART; both mark [see p. 351 entry for details], WIT: Matthew GRIMES, Alex. GASTON, ack. 13 Oct 1812, William DUNN, J.P., ent. 10 Mar 1812, rec. 12 same.

D-353 Know all men, Samuel SPRIGG (wife Amelia) for $250 paid by John GREER, sell part of SE 1/4 S 33 T 6 R 3, 50 acres, sold by Joseph PUMPHREY to Samuel MEEKS, from MEEKS to Jeremiah BURRISS, by BURRISS to Charles HAMMOND in trust, by HAMMOND as trustee for BURRISS to SPRIGG; sgn: 9 Dec 1812, WIT: Sterling JOHNSTON, John THOMPSON, ack. 20 Feb 1813, Sterling JOHNSTON, J.P., ent. 10 Mar 1813, rec. 12 same.

D-353 Indenture, 22 Sep 1812, Joseph WRIGHT, admr., and Phebe BROOMHALL, admx., of Enos BROOMHALL, late of BCO; David KINKADE, Brook County, Virginia; during his lifetime, Enos entered into agreement with David dated 14 Oct 1807 selling 70 acres in S 13 T 7 R 5 for $305, CCP at

September session 1812 ordered WRIGHT and BROOMHALL to make a "good and sufficient title in fee simple;" WIT: Ralph HEATH, Geo. PAULL, ack. 22 Sep 1812, George PAULL, J.P., [no entering data].

D-355 Indenture, 22 Sep 1812, John TAYLOR (wife Sarah), JCO; Isaac ANDERSON, BCO; Benjamin STANTON, late of JCO, patented NW 1/4 S 34 T 7 R 5, Steubenville district, STANTON in LW&T bequeathed TAYLOR the 1/4 S, now for $280 selling to ANDERSON; WIT: John WATSON, Joseph BOOL, ack. JCO, 22 Sep 1812, John WATSON, JLLP., ent. 20 Mar 1813, rec. 22 same.

D-356 Indenture, __ Mar 1812, Alexander McCALL (wife Margaret), Washington County, Pennsylvania; John TRIMBLE, same; $440, 220 acres in S 33 T 8 R 4, Steubenville district, patented to McCALL on 26 Jan 1809; WIT: John WATSON, J. WHITE, ack. 27 Mar 1813, Washington County, John WATSON, J.P., ent. 20 Mar 1813, rec. 24 same.

D-357 Indenture, 24 d 3 m 1813, Jonathan TAYLOR (wife Ann), Mountpleasant twp., JCO; William PATTEN, BCO; $320, part of S 9 T 8 R 6, patented to TAYLOR on 18 d 3 m 1805, NBR: Daniel BALLENGER, 80 acres; WIT: James ALEXANDER, Agnes ALEXANDER, ack. 23 Mar 1813, James ALEXANDER, Judge, CCP, ent. 24 Mar 1813, rec. 26 same.

D-359 Indenture, 27 Mar 1813, William LACY (wife Betsy), BCO; Thomas LECY, Patience LECY, Ruana LECY, Rachel LECY, and Piety LECY, children of William; fee simple, SW 1/4 S 4 T 6 R 4, patented to LECY; [the parents sign LACEY], WIT; Sterling JOHNSTON, Ebenezer PIGGOTT, ack. Sterling JOHNSTON, J.P., ent. 27 Mar 1813, rec. 30 same.

D-360 Indenture, 1 d 10 m 1812, Isaac HALL (wife Mary), BCO: Joseph ALBERTSON, BCO; $285, 47 1/2 acres, part of SE 1/4 S 20 T 8 R 6, NBR: John DOUDNA, Joseph DODD, William BOSWELL; WIT: John HALL, Knowis DOUDNA, ack. [not sure which J.P. as there is no name before "in the presence of us" followed by Jas. COX, Casandria SHANNON], ent. 28 Mar 1813, rec. 3 Apr same.

D-361 Indenture, 29 Mar 1813, Garret HAMMERLY [HAMERLY] (wife Priscilla), St. Clairsville, BCO; William BELL, Richland twp., BCO; $750, lots #53 and #??, each 1/4 acre, void if HAMMERLY pays $750 in installments ending 1 Sep 1816; he signs HAMERLIN, her mark [HAMMERLY], WIT: Geo. PAULL, Ralph HEATH, ack. George PAULL, J.P., ent. 29 Mar 1813, rec. 3 Apr same; mortgage satisfied 19 Aug 1816.

D-362   Indenture, 26 Mar 1813, Jacob RILEY (wife Sarah), Licking County, Ohio; Jacob GRUBB, BCO; $170, loats #1 and #2 in addition to St. Clairsville as laid out by William MATHERS; WIT: James McMILLEN, Jane McMILLEN [her mark], ack. Licking twp., James McMILLEN, J.P., McMILLEN certified by Amos H. CAFFEE, Deputy Clerk, ent. 9 Apr 1813, rec. same.

D-364   Indenture, 17 Apr 1812, Leonard HART (wife Jamima), BCO; Robert MORRISON, BCO; $50, lot #15 in Morristown as laid of by William CHAPLIN; both mark, WIT: Alexander GASTON, Joseph BROWN, ack. __ Apr 1812, William DUNN, J.P., ent. 15 Apr 1813, rec. 16 same.

D-364   Indenture, 20 Aug 1812, Leonard HART (wife Jamima), BCO; Margaret HAZLET [HAZLETT], BCO; $300, land adjoining Morristown, NBR: William WAGNER, John SCOTT, 11 1/4 acres 20 perches, entered by William CHAPLIN, conveyed by him to HART; both mark, WIT: Matthew GRIMES, Alexander GASTON, ack. 13 Apr 1812, William DUNN, J.P., ent. 15 Apr 1813, rec. 17 same.

D-365   Indenture, 26 Jan 1813, Samuel FAUCETT (wife Rachel), BCO; Stephen BROCK, BCO; $475, land in Union twp., 50 acres, part of SW 1/4 S 20 T 9 R 5, Steubenville district, patented to Jonas PICKERING on 20 Jul 1808, from PICKERING (wife Ruth) to FAUCETT on 10 Apr 1810, recorded on 27 Jun 1810 in Book [C], p. 242; WIT: John MERCER, Enos PICKERING, ack. 26 Jan 1813, John MERCER, J.P., ent. 17 Apr 1813, rec. 22 same.

D-367   Indenture, 10 Apr 1813, William FROST (wife Nancy), BCO; John BEVANS, Fayette County, Pennsylvania; $90, lot #149 in St. Clairsville, 1/4 acre, fee simple; [she signs her name "Ann"], WIT: Edward BRYSON, ack. 17 Apr 1813, Edward BRYSON, J.P., ent. 19 Apr 1813, rec. 26 same.

D-368   Indenture, 11 Sep 1807, Moses MOOREHEAD (wife Ann), BCO; Israel UPDEGRAFF, Wheeling, Ohio County, Virginia; $200, lot #120 in St. Clairsville, coneyed to MOOREHEAD by William SMITH (wife Nancy) by deed dated 4 Jul 1807; WIT: Saml. SPRIGG, John PATTERSON, ack. 13 Sep 1807, John PATTERSON, J.P., ent. 27 Apr 1813, rec. 28 same.

D-369   Indenture, 10 Jan 1810, Thomas L. JUDGE, Wheeling, Ohio County, Virginia; Israel UPDEGRAFF, same; $100, lot #6 in St. Clairsville, town laid out by James BARNES, William BROWN, and Notley HAYS [looks like HAGS here], plat entered in record on 31 Jan 1806 in Book A, p. 504 and 505, originally conveyed from James BARNES (wife Nancy) to William FARQUHAR by deed dated 26 Sep 1806, from FARQUHAR to JUDGE on 14 Aug 1807; WIT: Thos. THOMPSON, Ezra WILLIAMS, ack. 10 Jan 1810, Thos. THOMPSON, J.P., ent. 27 Apr 1813, rec. 28 same.

D-371   Indenture, 4 Sep 1812, James WRIGHT, BCO; Jonathan FAWCETT, BCO; $204, 51 acres 3 rods 26 perches, part of SE 1/4 S 32 T 9 R 5, patented to WRIGHT on 15 Aug 1811, NBR: William HAMBLETON; WIT: Enos PICKERING, Abraham ROMINE, ack. 4 Sep 1812, William DUNN, J.P., ent. 27 Apr 1813, rec. 28 same.

D-372   Indenture, 24 Apr 1813, Jonathan FAWCETT (wife Rebeccah), yeoman, Goshen twp., BCO; Samuel FAWCETT, miller, same; whereas SE 1/4 S 32 T 9 R 5 patented to James WRIGHT on 15 Aug 181[looks like 7, but must be a 2], conveyed 51 acres 3 rods 26 perches to Jonathan FAWCETT on 4 Sep 1812, now Jonathan conveys to Samuel for $204, NBR: William HAMBLETON; WIT: Jacob FAWCETT [his mark], Mary FAWCETT [her mark], John MERCER, ack. John MERCER, J.P., ent. 27 Apr 1813, rec. 28 same.

D-373   Indenture, 14 Feb 1811, Bezeleel WELLS and Elias VAN ARSDALE, extrs. LW&T of Daniel McELHERAN, dec'd, of Newark, Essex County, New Jersey; William WORKMAN, Senr., BCO; McELHERAN's will dated 25 May 1807 empowered extrs. to dispose of land in fee simple, appointed WELLS, William HILL of New York City, New York (merchant), (VAN ARSDALE counsellor at law), now for $200 convey to WORKMAN part of fractional T 2 R 3, beginning at SW corner of S 29, 200 acres; WIT for VAN ARSDALE: Phillip C. HAY, Thomas WARD; for WELLS: J. G. HINING, Geo. HARTFORD, ack. Essex County, 19 Feb 1811, Thomas WARD, Judge, Inferior CCP, WARD certified by Silas CONDIT, Clerk; ack. JCO, 17 Apr 1811, J. G. HINING, J.P., ent. 28 Apr 1813, rec. 5 May same.

D-375   Indenture, 21 d 4 m 1813, Richard CROY (wife Ann), BCO; William HODGEN, Joseph MIDDLETON, Herman DAVIS, Richard EDGERTON, and Joseph COX, same, trustees for Stillwater monthly meeting, Society of friends; $40, part of SW 1/4 S 9 T 8 R 6, 10 acres; both mark, WIT: Isaac CLENDENON, Isaac COPPOCK, ack. 21 Apr 1813, Thomas SHANNON, J.P., ent. 29 Apr 1813, rec. 5 May same.

D-376   Indenture, 26 d 4 m 1813, Harmon DAVIS (wife Hannah), Warren twp., BCO; John MIDDLETON, same; $200, beginning at NW corner S 14 T 8 R 6, 100 acres, fee simple; WIT: Carolles JUDKINS, Josiah PENINGTON, ack. 26 Apr 1813, Thomas SHANNON, J.P., ent. 29 Apr 1813, rec. 5 May same.

D-377   Indenture, 13 Dec 1812, John ELLIOTT (wife Rachel), BCO; Mary B. NORRIS, BCO; $200, lot #11 [in St. Clairsville], 1 rod 20 perches, fee simple; WIT: C. HAMMOND, Sterling JOHNSTON, ack. 13 Jan 1813, Sterling JOHNSTON, J.P., ent. 30 Apr 1813, rec. 5 May same.

D-378   Indenture, 1 May 1813, Fancy BARCHUS, BCO; Nathaniel HAYS, Senr., Westmoreland County, Pennsylvania; $200, part of S 32 T 6 R 3, 25 acres, fee simple; her mark, WIT: Sterling JOHNSTON, George BARKHURST, ack. Sterling JOHNSTON, J.P., ent. 1 May 1813, rec. 5 same.

D-379   Indenture, 18 d 11 m 1811, Joseph W. SATTERTHWAITE (wife Ann), BCO; Samuel POTTS, BCO; $295.47, part of S 13 T 7 R 3, Steubenville district, NBR: Thomas SATTERTHWAITE, John WILSON, John SMITH, 42 acres 34 perches, same conveyed by William SATTERTHWAITE of Guernsey County, Ohio, to Joseph W. SATTERTHWAITE on 7 d 9 m 1811, recorded in Book D, p. 132; WIT: William SINCLAIR, James PROSSER, ack. 18 d 11 m 1811, William SINCLAIR, J.P., ent. 10 May 1813, rec. 15 same.

D-381   Indenture, 4 d 6 m 1812, Samuel POTTS (wife Mary), BCO; Jesse PYLE, BCO; $396.12, Colerain twp., part of S 13 T 7 R 3, Steubenville district, NBR: Thomas SATTERTHWAITE, John WILSON, John SMITH, 42 acres 34 perches, same sold by Joseph SATTERTHWAITE (wife Ann) on 18 d 11 m 1811 to POTTS; WIT: Josiah FOX, Thomas MAJOR, ack. 4 d 6 m 1812, Thomas MAJOR, J.P., ent. 10 May 1813, rec. 18 same.

D-382   Indenture, 29 Mar 1813, William BELL (wife Sally), Richland twp., BCO; Garret HAMMERLY, St. Clairsville, BCO; $750, lots #53 and #__ in St. Clairsville, each 1/4 acre; his seal, her mark, WIT: Geo. PAULL, Ralph HEATH, ack. 29 Mar 1813, George PAUL, J.P., ent. 21 May 1813, rec. 22 same.

D-384   Indenture, 19 May 1813, William PHILPOT (wife Ruth), BCO; Ezer DILLON, BCO; $1,300, middle part of S 12 T 7 R 5, Steubenville district, patented 15 Nov 1807, NBR: Samuel SHARP, DILLON, WRIGHT, 211 acres, fee simple; WIT: Joseph TAYLOR, Thomas SHANNON, ack. Thomas SHANNON, J.P., ent. 24 May 1813, rec. 28 same.

D-385   Indenture, 5 Mar 1813, Thomas DUNN, Junr., extr. LW&T Thomas DUNN, Senr., late of Fayette County, Pennsylvania; William DUNN, BCO; LW&T dated 2 Feb 1804, said gave to sons William and James DUNN S 11 T 8 R 5, to be divided between them, appointed his wife Mary DUNN extx., and Thomas DUNN, Junr., and James FINLEY, extrs., divided land so that William got W 1/2 and James got E 1/2, this certifies William's ownership; WIT: John WILEY, Joseph DUNLAP, ack. BCO, 5 Mar 1813, John WILEY, Justice of the Court of Belmont, ent. 25 May 1813, rec. 28 same.

D-386   Indenture, 29 Dec 1812, Arthur GRIMES (wife Nelly), BCO; James GRIMES (their son), BCO; for natural love and affection and $120 S 1/2 NE 1/4 S 7 T 7 R 4, fee simple; his seal, her mark, WIT: Sterling JOHNSTON, David

VANCE, ack. 29 Dec 1812, Sterling JOHNSTON, J.P., ent. 26 May 1813, rec. 29 same.

D-387   Indenture, 15 d 1 m 1813, Jonathan TAYLOR (wife Ann), Mount pleasant twp., JCO; Ananias RANDAL, BCO; $385, , part of S 32 T 9 R 6, patented to TAYLOR on 18 d 3 m 1805, NBR: BRADSHAW, RANDAL, 117 acres; WIT: Henry HANNAH, Thos. MITCHELL, ack. 15 Jan 1813, Thos. MITCHELL, J.P., ent. 26 May 1813, ent. 29 same.

D-388   Indenture, 13 Apr 1812, Sterling JOHNSTON (wife Mary), BCO; Arthur GRIMES, Senr., BCO; $632, NE 1/4 S 7 T 7 R 4, fee simple, patented to JOHNSTON on 1 Oct 1811; WIT: John PATTERSON, Jacob NAGLE, ack. 13 Apr 1812, John PATTERSON, J.P., ent. 29 May 1813, rec. 1 Jun same.

D-389   Indenture, 29 Dec 1812, Arthur GRIMES, Senr., (wife Nelly), BCO; Arthur GRIMES, Junr. (son), BCO; love and affection and $151, N 1/2 NE 1/4 S 7 T 7 R 4, fee simple; his seal, her mark, WIT: Sterling JOHNSTON, David VANCE, ack. 29 Dec 1812, Sterling JOHNSTON, J.P., ent. 29 May 1813, rec. 2 Jun same.

D-390   Know all men, Jonas PICKERING, admr., and Phebe PICKERING, admx., of Samuel PICKERING, BCO, dec'd., in pursuance of rule of CCP at September term 1812 empowering admr. and admx. to convey land Samuel had conveyed during his lifetime on the __ day of January 1810 for $300 to Caleb ENGLE, part of S 13 T 9 R 6, 100 acres; sgn: 2 Oct 1812, by Jonas PICKERING, Phebe PICKERING [her mark], Jacob PICKERING, Hannah PICKERING [her mark], WIT: David VANCE, ack. 2 Oct 1812, Sterling JOHNSTON, J.P., ent. 29 May 1813, rec. 2 Jun same.

D-392   Know all men, Jonas PICKERING, admr., and Phebe PICKERING, admx., of Samuel PICKERING, BCO, dec'd, in pursuance of rule of CCP at September term 1812 allowing admr. and admx. to convey to William SPENCER, BCO, part of S 13 T 9 R 6, 100 acres, land conveyed by Samuel during his lifetime on 27 Mar 1809 for $300, (plus considerations to grantors for their interest in land), now conveyed in fee simple; sgn: 2 Oct 1812, Jonas PICKERING, Pheby PICKERING [her mark], Jacob PICKERING, Hannah PICKERING [her mark], WIT: David VANCE, ack. 2 Oct 1812, Sterling JOHNSTON, J.P., ent. 29 May 1813, rec. 2 Jun same.

D-393   Know all men, Jonas PICKERING, admr., and Phebe PICKERING, admx., of Samuel PICKERING, BCO, dec'd, in pursuance of rule of CCP at September term 1812 allowing admr. and admx. to convey to Jacob PICKERING part of S 13 T 9 R 6 as agreed during Samuel's lifetime; sgn: 2 Oct 1812, his seal, her mark, WIT: David VANCE, ack. 2 Oct 1812, Sterling JOHNSTON, J.P., ent. 29 May 1813, rec. 2 Jun same.

D-394   Indenture, 27 Jan 1813, William BROWN (wife Sally), BCO; Thomas LAWSON, BCO; $300, 80 acres, part of NW 1/4 S 7 T 7 R 4, patented to Sterling JOHNSTON on 8 Jun 1812, conveyed from JOHNSTON (wife Mary) to BROWN on 27 Dec 1812, fee simple; WIT: Samuel ISRAEL, Sterling JOHNSTON, ack. 28 Feb 1813, Sterling JOHNSTON, J.P., ent. 2 Jun 1813, rec. 7 same.

D-395   Indenture 26 May 1813, George GOETZ (wife Sevile [Cevile]), BCO; Elijah JOHNSTON, BCO; $175, 87 1/2 acres on Ohio River, part of fractional S 9 T 3 R 3 patented to GOETZ on 7 Apr 1810; his seal ["GOTZ"], her mark ["GEITZE"], WIT: Edw. BRYSON, John ANDERSON, ack. Edw. BRYSON, J.P., ent. 3 Jun 1813, rec. 7 same.

D-396   Indenture, 5 d 6 m 1813, Caleb ENGLE (wife Mercy), BCO; Richard TRUAX, BCO; $647, begin NE corner S 36 T 6 R 4, conveyed to ENGLE by William CHAPLIN (wife Mary) on 27 Jun 1808, recorded Book B, p. 460; WIT: Mordecai BALDRSTON [sic], Sterling JOHNSTON, ack. 5 Jun 1813, Sterling JOHNSTON, J.P., ent. 5 Jun 1813, rec. 7 same.

D-398   Indenture, 4 Jun 1813, Bazaleel WELLS (wife Sally), JCO; Alexander BOGGS, BCO; $2,300, part of S 8 aT 7 R 4, NBR: Thomas TIPTON, Wm. BOGGS, 254 3/4 acres; WIT: J. G. HINING, Saml. SALMAN, ack. JCO, J. G. HINING, J.P., ent. 7 Jun 1813, rec. same.

D-399   Indenture, 2 d 3 m 1813, Robert WOODS (wife Elizabeth), Ohio County, Virginia; Horton HOWARD, BCO; $245, part of S 19 T 4 R 2, 22 acres 44 perches; WIT: Thos. MITCHELL, Ann PAYLLS, ack. 2 Mar 1813, Thos. MITCHELL, J.P., ent. 7 Jun 1813, rec. same.

D-400   Indenture, 2 d 3 m 1813, Borden STANTON (wife Charlotte), BCO; Horton HOWARD, James RALEY, Stafford MILTON, trustees of society of friends or "people called Quakers, Concord monthly meeting, BCO; [no dollar amount given], part of S 7 T 7 R 3,, patented to STANTON [no date given], 11 acres 16 perches; WIT: Borden STANTON, Junr., Phebe HOPKINS [her mark], ack. 2 Mar 1813, Thos. MITCHELL, J.P., ent. 7 Jun 1813, rec. 8 same.

D-402   Indenture, 8 Jun 1813, Alexander BRATNEY, BCO; Francis HALL, BCO; $120, part of SW 1/4 S 29 T 9 R 6, 60 acres; WIT: Thomas MAJOR, John MAJOR, ack. Thomas MAJOR, J.P., ent. 9 Jun 1813, rec. same.

D-403   Indenture, 7 Jun 1813, William McKINDLEY (wife Tamer), BCO; Andrew McKINDLEY, BCO; William by deed from John PIGGOTT dated 3 Oct 1812 possesses part of SE 1/4 S 29 T 7 R 5, Steubenville district, now for $160, fee simple; his seal, her mark [both "McKINLEY"], WIT: William SMITH, Mary SMITH [her mark], ack. William SMITH, J.P., ent. 9 Jun 1813, rec. 11 same.

D-404   Indenture, 21 d 9 m 1812, Isaac CLENDENON (wife Hannah), BCO; Phillip [Philip] STRAHL, BCO; $362, 100 acres, W part of NW 1/4 S 33 T 7 R 5; WIT: John STRAHL, Rebecca STRAHL, ack. 21 Sep 1812, John STRAHL, J.P., ent. 10 Jun 1813, rec. 11 same.

D-405   Indenture, 29 May 1813, Aaron NEWPORT, Charles ECCLES, and Job DILLON, trustees of "the original surveyed" T 6 R 3, BCO; Samuel SHARPLESS, George SHARPLESS, and John KINSY; on 4 Feb 1813 the General Assembly passed an act to enable the trustees of the original surveyed T 6 R 3 to make a permanent lease for part of the school land in said twp., appointed John THOMPSON, Mahlon SMITH, and Joseph MORRISON disinterested freeholders of BCO and not inhabitants of twp. to affix a valuation on land and on 17 May 1813 set $4.75 per acre, total $969, now conveying 204 acres, from 1 Apr 1813 for 99 years, to be used for a fulling mill, to be revalued every 33 years, annual rent of $59.14 due 1 Apr annually, no waste of live timber, plant 100 apple trees; all sign, WIT: C. HAMMOND, ack. Thos. THOMPSON, ent. 12 Jun 1813, rec. same; receipt of $2,000 ack. 18 Apr 1815 by Saml. SHARPLESS of receipt of $2,000 for his right to land, WIT: Sterling JOHNSTON, ack. 18 Apr 1815, Sterling JOHNSTON, J.P., transfer entered 18 Apr 1815, rec. 19 same.

D-407   Indenture, 12 Jun 1812, William HUTCHISON (wife Jane), JCO; Humphrey ALEXANDER, BCO; $180, part of SW 1/4 S 3 T 8 R 4, NBR: Joseph HENRY, 40 acres, patented to HUTCHISON on 20 Jan 1812, fee simple; his seal, her mark, WIT: Jesse SPARKS, Sterling JOHNSTON, ack. 12 Jun 1813, Sterling JOHNSTON, J.P., ent. 12 Jun 1813, rec. 19 same.

D-408   Indenture, 12 Jun 1813, William HUTCHISON (wife Jane), JCO; Joseph HENRY, BCO; $325, part of SW 1/4 S 3 T 8 R 4, 100 acres, patented to HUTCHISON on 20 Jan 1812, fee simple; his seal, her mark, WIT: Jesse SPARKS, Sterling JOHNSTON, ack. 12 Jun 1813, Sterling JOHNSTON, J.P., ent. 12 Jun 1813, rec. 19 same.

D-410   Indenture, 21 Feb 1813, John PRICE (wife Betsy), BCO; John EDWARDS, [Senr.], BCO; $607, part of NW 1/4 S13 T 10 R 6, 31 1/2 acres; both mark, WIT: John MOORE, Phillip AWBREY, ack. same date, John MOORE, J.P., ent. 19 Jun 1813, rec. same.

D-411 Indenture, 18 Jun 1813, William BOGGS, BCO; Allen STEWART, Joshua HATCHER, and David DRAKE, trustees of original surveyed T 7 R 4; $9, for school house, part of S 8 T 7 R 4, NBR: Wm. and Alexr. BOGGS, Joseph PARISH, 1 acre, free passage for scholars; WIT: Patrick NELLONS, Sterling JOHNSTON, ack. Sterling JOHNSTON, J.P., ent. 19 Jun 1813, rec. 26 same.

D-412 In the name of God (LW&T, Joshua RUSSELL, BCO), appoints Henry JOHNSTON, St. Clairsville, sole heir and extr., also attorney in fact; sgn: 12 Jun 1813, WIT: Sterling JOHNSTON, William BROWN, Robert THOMPSON, ack. Sterling JOHNSTON, J.P., ent. 21 Jun 1813, rec. 26 same.

D-413 Indenture, 9 Jun 1813, John McFADDEN, Senr., (wife Margaret), Cadiz twp., Harrison County, Ohio; William GILLCHRIEST, BCO; $1,076.25, part of NW 1/4 S 9 T 9 R 5, Steubenville district, 153 75/100 acres, patented to Thomas SHARP on 8 May 1806, conveyed by SHARP (wife Jenny) to McFADDEN on 15 Dec 1808, recorded in Book B, p. 552 [crossed out] 477 [written above]; his seal, her mark, WIT: John CAMPBELL, Samuel McFADDEN, ack. 9 Jun 1813, John CAMPBELL, J.P., ent. 21 Jun 1813, rec. 26 same.

D-414 Indenture, 5 Mar 1813, Thomas DUNN, Junr., BCO, acting extr. of LW&T of Thomas DUNN, Senr., late of Fayette County, Pennsylvania, dec'd; James DUNN, BCO; Thomas DUNN, Senr., died possessing S 11 T 8 R 5, made LW&T on 2 Feb 1804, gave two sons James and William above S to be divided, appointed wife Mary DUNN extx., Thomas DUNN, Junr., and James FINLEY, extrs., conveying to James E 1/2 of S 11 T 8 R 5; WIT: John WILEY, Joseph DUNLAP, ack. 5 Mar 1813, John WILEY, Judge of Court, ent. 22 Jun 1813, rec. 25 same.

D-415 Indenture, 29 Mar 1813, John AULT (wife Eve), Richland twp., BCO; John WINTER, St. Clairsville, BCO; $60, part of NE 1/4 S 6 T 6 R 4, Richland twp., patented to AULT on 15 Jan 1810, 22 1/2 acres, fee simple; his seal, her mark, WIT: Sterling JOHNSTON, Charles JORDON, ack. 9 Apr 1811, Robert GRIFFITH, J.P., second ack. 26 Jun 1813, Sterling JOHNSTON, J.P., ent. 26 Jun 1813, rec. 2 Jul same.

D-417 Indenture, 24 Jun 1813, John WINTER, BCO; John BROWN, St. Clairsville, BCO; $200, part of S 6 T 6 R 4, 22 1/2 acres, conveyed by John AULT (wife Eve); WIT: Robt. GRIFFITH, Sterling JOHNSTON, ack. Sterling JOHNSTON, J.P., ent. 26 Jun 1813, rec. 2 Jul same.

D-418 Indenture, 26 Apr 1813, Mahlon SMITH (wife Mary), St. Clairsville, BCO; Nathan PEARCE, BCO; $256.75, land in S 10 T 8 R 5, part of S patented to SMITH on 27 Feb 1812, NBR: Mahlon SMITH, Robert WILLIS, 100 1/2 acres 10 perches, fee simple; WIT: Notley HAYS, Robert VANCE, ack. 26 Apr 1813, Geo. PAULL, J.P., ent. 29 Jun 1813, rec. 3 Jul same.

D-419   Indenture, 24 Jun 1813, John BROWN (wife Elizabeth), BCO; John WINTER, BCO; $200, part of lot #67 in St. Clairsville, conveyed to BROWN by David NEWALL (wife Sally) on 4 Jul 1809, fee simple; his seal, her mark, WIT: Robt. GRIFFITH, Sterling JOHNSTON, ack. Sterling JOHNSTON, J.P., ent. 29 Jun 1813, rec. 3 Jul same.

D-420   Indenture, 21 Jun 1813, Mishael [sic] JENKINS (wife Sarah), BCO; William HOGE, BCO; $400, 126 3/4 acres 32 perches, part of NE 1/4 S 19 T 9 R 5, patented to JENKINS on 13 Jul 1812, NBR: Mishael JENKINS, John VANPELT; WIT: John CAMPBELL, Jonathan CROOKS [his mark], ack. 21 Jun 1813, John CAMPBELL, J.P., ent. 6 Jul 1813, rec. 12 same.

D-421   Indenture, 3 d 7 m 1813, William BUNDY (wife Sarah), BCO; Demsey BONVEL [BOSWELL], BCO; $700, 100 acres, part of S 14 T 8 R 6; his seal, her mark, WIT: Joel JUDKINS, Thomas SHANNON, ack. 3 Jul 1813, Thomas SHANNON, J.P., ent. 10 Jul 1813, rec. 12 same.

D-423   Indenture, 10 Jul 1813, Caleb ENGLE (wife Mercy), BCO; Robert PRIOR, BCO; $100, 22 3/4 acres, part of SE 1/4 S 36 T 6 R 4, conveyed to ENGLE on 27 Jun 1808, NBR: William WILSON, John DUGAN; WIT: Sterling JOHNSTON, John STEWART, ack. Sterling JOHNSTON, J.P., ent. 10 Jul 1813, rec. 17 same.

D-424   Indenture, 10 Jul 1813, Caleb ENGLE (wife Mercy), BCO; Christien HASHMAN, BCO; $60, 12 1/4 acres, part of S 36 T 6 R 4, conveyed to ENGLE by William CHAPLIN on 27 Jun 1808, NBR: Benjamin VEEL, Thomas VANLAW; WIT: Sterling JOHNSTON, John STEWART, ack. Sterling JOHNSTON, J.P., ent. 10 Jul 1813, rec. 17 same.

D-425   Indenture, 10 Jul 1813, Caleb ENGLE (wife Mercy), BCO; Benjamin VEEL and Thomas VANLAW, BCO; $2,550, 100 acres, part of S 36 T 6 R 4, conveyed to ENGLE by William CHAPLIN on 27 Jun 1808, NBR: Robert PRYOR, William WILSON, Richard TRUAX, Christein HASHMAN, Jno. DUGAN; WIT: Sterling JOHNSTON, John STEWART, ack. Sterling JOHNSTON, J.P., ent. 10 Jul 1813, rec. 19 same.

D-426   Indenture, 14 d 6 m 1813, Daniel McPEAK (wife Elizabeth), BCO; David PARRY, BCO; $624, part of S 19 T 7 R 3, NBR: John MAIN, Joseph WALTON, 99 acres, conveyed to McPEAK by Bazaleel WELLS (wife Sally) on 3 d 1 m 1811;

both mark, WIT: Thomas MAJOR, Benjamin MARSHALL, ack. same day, Thomas MAJOR, J.P., ent. 23 Jul 1813, rec. 28 same.

D-428   Indenture, 4 Jun 1813, Bazaleel WELLS (wife Sally), JCO; William BOGGS, BCO; $450, part of S 8 T 7 R 4, NBR: Joseph PARISH, Alexander BOGGS, 50 acres; WIT: J. G. HENING, Saml. SALMON, ack. JCO, 4 Jun 1813, J. G. HENING, J.P., ent. 23 Jul 1813, rec. 28 same.

D-429   Indenture, 21 Apr 1812, Benjamin GASSAWAY (wife Ann), BCO; Jacob DOVENBARGER, BCO; $80, lot #46 in Morristown, laid off by William CHAPLAIN, conveyed by CHAPLAIN (wife Mary) to Leonard HART, Junr., on 24 Jun 1808, from HART (wife Mary) to Wm. W. GAULT on 16 Mar 1811, from GAULT (wife Sarah) to GASSAWAY on 10 Jan 1812, fee simple; WIT: George THOMPSON, Basil ISRAEL, ack. 21 Apr 1812, William DUNN, J.P., ent. 2 Aug 1813, rec. 6 same.

D-430   Indenture, 3 Jul 1813, Robert THOMPSON (wife Margaret), BCO: Mahlon SMITH, BCO; $200, out lot #9 adjoining addition to St. Clairsville, laid out by Bazeleel WELLS, 6 acres 9 perches, conveyed from Jacob HOULTS (wife Margaret) to John THOMPSON and George PAULL on 18 Aug 1809, from THOMPSON and PAULL to Robert THOMPSON on 1 Feb 1810, fee simple; his seal, her mark, WIT: John PATTERSON, Isaac VANPELT, ack. 3 Jul 1813, John PATTERSON, Assoc. Judge, ent. 9 Aug 1813, rec. 13 same.

D-431   Indenture, Nathan PEARCE [PEAIRS in ack.], BCO; Mahlon SMITH, St. Clairsville, BCO; $258, part of S 1/2 of S 10 conveyed to SMITH on 27 Feb 1812, NBR: Mahlon SMITH, Robert WILLIS, 100 1/2 acres 10 perches, void if $258 paid by 1 May 1817; sgn: 27 Apr 1813, WIT: Sterling JOHNSTON, Jeremiah FAIRHURST, ack. 28 Jun 1813, Sterling JOHNSTON, J.P., ent. 9 Aug 1813, rec. 13 same; satisfaction of mortgage on 10 Apr 1817, M. SMITH.

D-432   Indenture, 27 Apr 1813, Jeremiah BURRIS (wife Rachel), Richland twp., BCO; William STRANAHAN, same; $150.95, part of S 33 T 6 R 3, NBR: William McFARLAND, Nicholas PUMPHREY, Jonathan SUTTON, 32 acres 2 rods 38 perches, fee simple; both mark, WIT: Geo. PAULL, John THOMPSON, ack. 27 Apr 1813, Geo. PAULL, J.P., ent. 14 Aug 1813, rec. 20 same.

D-433   Indenture, 28 Jun 1813, Joseph HENDERSON (wife Eliza), Washington County, Pennsylvania; Henry BROWN (wife Peggy), BCO; $100, lot #31 in Morristown, fee simple; Joseph is only one to sign, WIT: Israel BARNES, Saml. WILSON, ack. 29 Jun 1813, Duncan MORRISON, J.P., ent. 16 Aug 1813, rec. 20 same.

D-434   Articles of Agreement, 18 Aug 1813, between John ISRAEL, BCO; William GROVES, BCO; GROVES given permission to erect and keep in repair a mill dam, paid $20; both sign, WIT: John N. SMITH, ack. John MOORE, J.P., ent. 18 Aug 1813, rec. 20 same.

D-434   Indenture, 10 d 7 m 1812, Thomas SATTERTHWAITE (wife Elizabeth), Guernsey County, Ohio; Thomas MITCHEL, BCO; $1,500, two contiguous pieces of land, one in NW corner S 13 T 7 R 3, other in NE 1/4 S 19 T 7, 182 acres, received through LW&T of father William SATTERTHWAITE, excepting piece in SE corner of first tract containing upwards of 13 acres previously sold to John WILSON; his seal, her mark, WIT: James ALEXANDER, Horton HOWARD, ack. [no date given], James ALEXANDER, Assoc. Judge, ent. 26 Aug 1813, rec. same.

D-435   Indenture, 31 May 1813, Jesse WHITE (wife Mary), BCO; James WHITE, BCO; $162, E 1/2 SW 1/4 S 20 T 7 R 5, Steubenville district; WIT: Joseph S. NICHOLSON, Israel WHITE, ack. 31 May 1813, William SMITH, J.P., ent. 26 Aug 1813, rec. 30 same.

D-437   Indenture, 31 May 1813, Cyrus BOYD (wife Jane), BCO; James WHITE, BCO; $150, S side NW 1/4 S 20 T 7 R 5, Steubenville district, 60 acres; WIT: Jesse WHITE, William SMITH, ack. 31 May 1813, William SMITH, J.P., ent. 26 Aug 1813, rec. 30 same.

D-438   Indenture, 17 May 1813, Samuel RING, BCO; Ezer DILLON, BCO; RING bound to DILLON in four written obligations payable, to secure obligations convey part of S 4 T 5 R 4, 70 acres, void if payments totaling $700 made by 1 Apr 1817; WIT: Solomon BENTLEY, William SMITH, ack. William SMITH, J.P.; title assigned by DILLON to William PHILPOT for value received on 19 May 1813, WIT: Thomas SHANNON, Joseph TAYLOR; mortgage satisfied, William PHILPOT, assignee of Ezer DILLON, WIT: Wm. FARIS, Jr., ent. 27 aug 1813, rec. 1 Sep same.

D-439   Indenture, 8 Apr 1813, Jacob GRUBB, BCO; Jacob RILEY, Licking County, Ohio; GRUBB bound to RILEY by writing dated 9 Nov 1810 for $114.10, securing debt by conveying lots #1 and 2 in addition to St. Clairsville, laid out by William MATHERS, along with some personal property, void if debt paid within two months; WIT: William HORNER, Geo. PAULL, ack. Geo. PAULL, J.P.; followed by "I do hereby authorize Geo. PAULL attorney at Law to appear for me & confess judgement against me in favor of Jacob RILEY for one hundred & fourteen dollars and ten cents with interest from the eighth day of April Anno Domini one thousand eight hundred & thirteen also for costs of suit with release of errors & stay of execution until the first day of February next; Witness my hand and seal this eleventh day of June A.D. 1813, Jacob GRUBB."

D-440 Indenture, 1 Sep 1813, William POWELL (wife Jane), BCO; Robert FARNSWORTH, BCO; $300, land in NW 1/4 S 10 T 5 R 4, granted to Jane WARD, wife of William POWELL, by patent dated 7 Aug 1812, 60 acres, fee simple; his seal, her mark, WIT: Edw. BRYSON, Jasper MALLORY, ack. Edw. BRYSON, J.P., ent. 3 Sep 1813, rec. 4 same.

D-442 Know all men, William RIDDLE, BCO, tax collector for Union twp., collected $.075 on Lot #102, a nonresident lot in Morristown, sold part to Samuel WILSON on 31 Dec 1812, sgn: 2 Mar 1813, William RIDDLE, WIT: Israel BARNES, John F. MORRISON, ack. 17 May 1813, Duncan MORRISON, J.P., ent. 3 Sep 1813, rec. 4 same.

D-442 Know all men, William RIDDLE, BCO, [same information as above], Lot #43, $.10, sold to John WAGGONER on 31 Dec 1812, sgn: 2 Mar 1813, WIT: Ashael TOMKINS, Elizabeth MORRISON, ack. 25 May 1813, Duncan MORRISON, J.P., ent. 3 Sep 1813, rec. 4 same.

D-443 Know all men, William RIDDLE [same as item #1 on p. 442], Lot #101, $.075, sold to Samuel WILSON, sgn: 2 Mar 1813, WIT: Israel BARNES, John F. MORRISON, ack. 21 May 1813, Duncan MORRISON, J.P., ent. 3 Sep 1813, rec. 4 same.

D-443 Know all men, William RIDDLE [same as item #1 on p. 442], Lot #83, $.10, sold to William WAGGONER, sgn: 2 Mar 1813, WIT: Israel BARNES, John F. MORRISON, ack. 25 May 1813, Duncan MORRISON, J.P., ent. 4 Sep 1813, rec. 6 same.

D-444 Know all men, William RIDDLE [same as item #1 on p. 442], Lot #85, $.125, sold to William WAGGONER, sgn: 2 Mar 1813, WIT: Israel BARNES, John F. MORRISON, ack. 25 May 1813, Duncan MORRISON, J.P., ent. 4 Sep 1813, rec. 6 same.

D-445 Know all men, William RIDDLE [same as item #1 on p. 442], Lot #78, $.10, sold to William WAGGONER, sgn: 2 Mar 1813, WIT: Israel BARNES, John F. MORRISON, ack. 25 May 1813, Duncan MORRISON, J.P.

D-446 Know all men, William RIDDLE [same as item #1 on p. 442], Lot #81, $.10, sold to William WAGGONER, sgn: 2 Mar 1813, WIT: Israel BARNES, John F. MORRISON, ack. 25 May 1813, Duncan MORRISON, J.P., ent. 4 Sep 1813, rec.. 15 same.

D-446 Know all men, William RIDDLE [same as item #1 on p. 442], Lot #82, $.075, sold to William WAGGONER, sgn: 2 Mar 1813, WIT: Israel BARNES,

John F. MORRISON, ack. 25 May 1813, Duncan MORRISON, J.P., ent. 4 Sep 1813, rec. 15 same.

D-447   Know all men, William RIDDLE [same as item #1 on p. 442], Lot #84, $.10, sold to William WAGGONER, sgn: 1 Sep 1813, WIT: Elizabeth MORRISON, Ashael TOMKINS, ack. 1 Sep 1813, Duncan MORRISON, J.P., ent. 4 Sep 1813, rec. 15 same.

D-448   Know all men, William RIDDLE [same as item #1 on p. 442], Lot #40, $.125, sold to William WAGGONER, sgn: 1 Sep 1813, WIT: Ashael TOMKINS, Elizabeth MORRISON, ack. 1 Sep 1813, Duncan MORRISON, J.P., ent. 4 Sep 1813, rec. 15 same.

D-448   Indenture, __ d 5 m 1813, George SMITH (wife Mary), Maduson [sic] twp., Gurnsey [sic] County, Ohio; Joshua WOOD, Union twp., BCO; $1,000, 104 25/100 acres, part of S 20 T 9 R 5, Steubenville district, patented to Jonas PICKERING on 20 Jul 1808, PICKERING (wife Ruth) sold to SMITH on 10 Apr 1810, recorded in Book C, p. 219; WIT: Abel PICKERING, Samuel SMITH, ack. BCO, 8 May 1813, John MERCER, J.P., ent. 14 Sep 1813, rec. 16 same.

D-450   Indenture, 1 Sep 1813, Eleazer KINNEY (wife Jamima), BCO; J_o. BERRY, BCO; $55, Lot #98 in St. Clairsville; his seal, her mark, WIT: Robert VANCE, Joseph POSELY, ack. Robert VANCE, J.P., ent. 14 Sep 1813, rec. 16 same.

D-451   Indenture, 13 Apr 1813, James DUNN (wife Margaret), BCO; Edmond SPENCER, BCO; $84, 12 acres in SE __ S 11 T 8 R 5, conveyed to James by Thomas DUNN, Junr., on 5 Mar 1813; WIT: William DUNN, Wm. W. GAULT, ack. 13 Apr 1813, William DUNN, J.P., ent. 14 Sep 1813, rec. 17 same.

D-452   Know all men, Samuel SPRIGG (wife Amelia), for $300 sell to Robert WILLSON, Junr., land in NW corner of S 24 T 6 R 3, 227 acres 3 rods 24 poles, NBR: Wheeling Creek, Danl. HARRIS, Wm. [MULLAN], Robert THOMAS, William BELL, formerly belonged to Jno. D. MERCER of New York City which had not been sold by his agents Absalom MARTIN, Jacob CROUS, or Daniel McELHERAN, same tract conveyed to SPRIGG by Peter MANIFOLD, agent and attorney for David MORRIS (wife Christiana) and Elizabeth MORRIS, heirs at law of Jno. D. MERCER by deed dated 6 Feb 1811, and by deed from Peter dated 14 Sep 1811 to Robert WILLSON; WIT: Robert GRIFFITH, Sterling JOHNSTON, ack. of Samuel, 27 Apr 1813, Sterling JOHNSTON, J.P., ent. 14 Sep 1813, rec. 17 same; ack. Ohio County, Virginia, of Amelia, Daniel SMITH, judge of General Court and sole Judge of the Superior Court of Law, sgn: 13 Jan 1815, ent. 16 Jan 1815, rec. 6 Feb same.

D-453   Indenture, 21 Jun 1813, Mishael JENKINS (wife Sarah), BCO; John VANPELT, BCO; $181.25, 55 3/4 acres 17 perches, part of S 19 T 9 R 5, S patented to JENKINS on 30 Jul 1812, NBR: William HOGE; WIT: John CAMPBELL, Nathan CROOKS, ack. 21 Jun 1813, John CAMPBELL, J.P., ent. 17 Sep 1813, rec. 22 same.

D-454   Indenture, 17 Sep 1813, Mishael JENKINS (wife Sarah), BCO; George CARPENTER, BCO; $1,000, 319 acres 3 rods 27 perches, beginning at SW corner of S 19 T 9 R 5; WIT: John CAMPBELL, Samuel MILLS, ack. John CAMPBELL, J.P., ent. 21 Sep 1813, rec. 22 same.

D-455   Indenture, 17 May 1813, Ezer DILLON (wife Elizabeth), BCO; Samuel RING, BCO; $1,200, 70 acres 19 perches, part of S 4 T 5 R 4, fee simple; his seal, her mark, WIT: William SMITH, Solomon BENTLEY, ack. 17 May 1813, William SMITH, J.P., ent. 21 Sep 1813, rec. 25 same.

D-457   Indenture, 28 Jun 1813, Hugh GILLILAND; George HENRY, both BCO; $60, land in SW corner of S 19 T 9 R 6, patented to GILLILAND by James MADISON, 16 acres 113 perches, fee simple; sgn: Hugh GILLILAND and Elizabeth GILLILAND, WIT: Jane HOWARD, Brice HOWARD, ack. 28 Jun 1813, Brice HOWARD, J.P., ent. 4 Oct 1813, rec. 6 same.

D-458   Indenture, 28 d 8 m 1813, Henry DOUDNA (wife Pattey), BCO: William PATTERSON, BCO; $500, 142 acres, part of NW 1/4 S 32 T 7 R 5; his seal, her mark, WIT: Edward THORNBURGH, Henry BARNES, ack. 28 Aug 1813, Thomas SHANNON, J.P., ent. 4 Oct 1813, rec. 8 same.

D-459   Indenture, 30 Aug 1813, George ALBAN (wife Margaret), BCO; John WINTER, BCO; $200, 6 acres, part of Lots #11 and #12 on plan of 15 outlots laid out by Bazaleel WELLS adjoining addition of St. Clairsville laid out by William MATHERS, lots conveyted by William GOUGH (wife Rachel) to ALBAN by deed dated 22 Oct 1811, recorded in Book D, p. 123, fee simple; WIT: Sterling JOHNSTON, Mary JOHNSTON, ack. 13 Aug 1813, Sterling JOHNSTON, J.P., ent. 4 Oct 1813, rec. 11 same.

D-460   Indenture, 8 Oct 1813, George WINROD, BCO; John LARKIN, Senr., Frederick County, Maryland; $500, NE 1/4 S 14 T 10 R 6, Steubenville district, patented to WINROD on 10 Jun 1812, fee simple; WIT: Sterling JOHNSTON, Mosses [sic] HILL, ack. Sterling JOHNSTON, J.P., ent. 8 Oct 1813, rec. 13 same.

D-460   Indenture, 28 Aug 1813, Amos JANNEY, Stark County, Ohio, attorney for Joseph JANNEY, Loudon County, Virginia; Henry BROWN, BCO; $150, part of S 2 T 9 R 5, Steubenville district, NBR: John SMITH (formerly Jacob SNEDEKER), Henry BROWN, 57 acres, fee simple; WIT: James McCLINTICK,

William BUSK, Vanmeter REEVES [his mark], ack. Stark County, Ohio, "thirteeth" Aug 1813, James HEWETT, J.P., ent. 18 Oct 1813, rec. 20 same.

D-462   Patent of James McGREGOR of Hartford County, Maryland, for S 1/2 of S 32 T 3 R 2, Steubenville district, sgn: (Thomas JEFFERSON) 1 Aug 1807, ent. 21 Oct 1813, rec. 23 same.

D-462   Indenture, 23 Oct 1813, Moses MOOREHEAD (wife Ann), BCO; Abraham LASH, BCO; $1,000, SW 1/4 S 8 T 7 R 4, Steubenville district, patented to MOOREHEAD on 3 Jun 1813, fee simple; WIT: Thos. THOMPSON, Sterling JOHNSTON, ack. Sterling JOHNSTON, J.P., ent. 23 Oct 1813, rec. 26 same.

D-463   Indenture, 26 Oct 1813, Richard CROY (wife Nancy), Warren twp., BCO; Joseph ALEXANDER, Westmoreland County, Pennsylvania; $1,800, SW 1/4 S 9 T 8 R 6, 10 acres excepted which CROY had previously sold in NE corner, NBR: John GRIER, 150 acres; both mark, WIT: James B. FEIRLEY [probably FINLEY], William PHILPOT, ack. Wm. C. ANDERSON, J.P., ent. 26 Oct 1813, rec. 27 same.

D-464   Indenture, 26 Oct 1813, Joseph ALEXANDER, Westmoreland County, Pennsylvania; Richard CROY, BCO; ALEXANDER bound in 8 written obligations, secured by conveyance of 150 acres, part of SW 1/4 S 9 T 8 R 6, fee simple, void if payments totaling $1,200 made by 25 May 1822; WIT: James B. FINLEY, William PHILPOT, ack. 26 Oct 1813, Wm. C. ANDERSON, J.P., ent. 26 Oct 1813, rec. 27 same.

D-465   Know all men, William RIDDLE, tax collector for Union twp., to collect tax of $.125 on Lot #61 in Morristown sold to Thomas RIDDLE on 31 Dec 1812, sgn: 2 Nov 1813, WIT: Wm. FARIS, Junr., ack. Duncan MORRISON, J.P., ent. 3 Nov 1813, rec. 4 same.

D-466   Know all men, William RIDDLE [same as p. 465], $.125, Lot #37, sold to Thomas RIDDLE, sgn: 2 Nov 1813, WIT: Wm. FARIS, Junr., ack. Duncan MORRISON, J.P., ent. 3 Nov 1813, rec. 4 same.

D-466   Indenture, 6 Oct 1813, John B. MARTIN (wife Elizabeth), Baltimore, Maryland; Samuel B. MARTIN, same; $500, lot #20 in St. Clairsville, 1/4 acre, deed from John MARTIN (wife Elizabeth) of St. Clairsville to John B. MARTIN of Baltimore dated 27 Aug 1806, recorded in Book A, p. 686, also from another deed from Jess McGEE of St. Clairsville to John MARTIN of same dated 22 Mar 1806, recorded in Book A, p. 639; WIT: Edw. WOODYEAR, ack. Baltimore County, Maryland, 6 Oct 1813, Edwd. WOODYEAR, W. [Y.] PURVIANCE, ack.

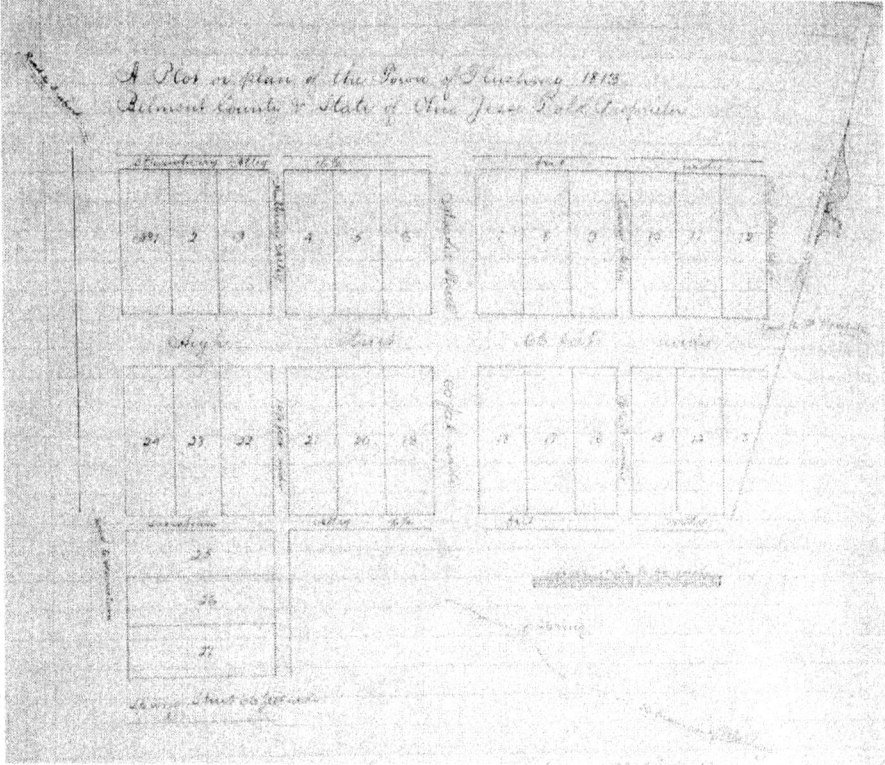

Plat of Flushing

of witnesses by Wm. GIBSON, Clerk of Baltimore "Coty" Court, ent. 4 Nov 1813, rec. 11 same.

D-468   Indenture, 19 Jun 1813, Moses MILLIGAN (wife Mary), BCO; Barnabas CURTIS, BCO; $175, part of S 3 T 9 R 6, 50 acres; his seal, her mark, WIT: John MOORE, William WEST, James EDWARD, ack. 19 Jun 1813, John MOORE, J.P., ent. 4 Nov 1813, rec. 12 same.

D-470   Plat of Flushing, 1813, Jesse FOLK [FOULKE], Proprietor, ack. 9 Nov 1813, laid out on FOULKE's land in S 20 T 9 R 5, Steubenville district, John MERCER, J.P., ent. 9 Nov 1813, rec. 13 same.

D-471   Indenture, 30 Oct 1813, John WISE (wife Jane), BCO; George WISE, BCO; $170, part of NW 1/4 S 32 T 3 R 2, conveyed by Noah LINSLY to John WISE on 4 Dec 1810, 50 acres; his seal, her mark, WIT: George POOLE, John POOLE, ack. 13 Nov 1813, Sterling JOHNSTON, J.P., ent. 13 Nov 1813, rec. 18 same.

D-472   Indenture, 26 May 1813, John ISRAEL (wife Rachel), BCO; Nicholas FLEEHARTY, BCO; 90.55\underline{5}$, 40 acres, part of NE 1/4 S 2 T 9 R 6, fee simple; his seal, her mark, WIT: John N. SMITH, Robert A. DALLIS, ack. 30 Aug 1813, John N. SMITH, J.P., ent. 18 Nov 1813, rec. 19 same.

D-473   Indenture, 17 Nov 1813, James BELL (wife Jane), BCO; Mary HEDGES, JCO; $300, fee simple, part of S 28 T 6 R 3, NBR: Jacob ENDLEY, 59 1/2 acres 16 poles, conveyed to BELL by Nicholas LUNCEFORD (wife Sarah), on 23 Mar 1812, recorded in Book D, p. 138; his seal, her mark, WIT: Sterling JOHNSTON, Wm. PERRINE, ack. 24 Nov 1813, Sterling JOHNSTON, J.P., ent. 24 Nov 1813, rec. 25 same.

D-474   Indenture, 4 Sep 1813, James BARNES (wife Nancy), BCO; John INSKEEP, BCO; $500, parts of lots #45 and #46 in St. Clairsville, fee simple; his seal, lher mark, WIT: James WRIGHT, Sterling JOHNSTON, accompanied by permission to use alley, ack. 4 Sep 1813, Sterling JOHNSTON, J.P., ent. 30 Nov 1813, rec. 2 Dec same.

D-475   Indenture, 26 d 11 m 1813, Jonathan TAYLOR (wife Ann), Mount Pleasant twp., JCO; John BRADSHAW, BCO; $960, part of S 32 T 9 R 6, patented to TAYLOR on 18 d 3 m 1805; WIT: Thos. MITCHELL, Harriet MITCHELL, ack. Thos. MITCHELL, J.P., ent. 30 Nov 1813, rec. 4 Dec same.

D-476   Indenture, 13 Mar 1812, Mahlon SMITH (wife Mary), St. Clairsville, BCO; Henry STEWART, BCO; $44, NBR: Henry STEWART, conveyed to

SMITH by David RUSSELL (wife Hannah) on 27 Oct 1808, lot in St. Clairsville; WIT: Zebulon WARNER, John BROWN, ack. 13 Mar 1812, Zebulon WARNER, J.P., ent. 14 Dec 1813, rec. same.

D-477 Indenture, 9 Mar 1813, Henry STEWART (wife Jennet), JCO; Henry WEST, JCO; [no dollar amount given], lot in St. Clairsville, NBR: Henry STEWART, fee simple; WIT: Robt. PATTERSON, Sarah PATTERSON, ack. JCO, Warren twp., 9 Mar 1813, Robt. PATTERSON, J.P., PATTERSON certified 30 Nov 1813 by Thos. PATTON, Clerk, ent. 14 Dec 1813, rec. same.

D-478 Indenture, 1 Dec 1813, Robert MOORE, Brook [sic] County, Virginia; John SNODGRASS, Ohio County, Virginia; MOORE an assignee of Benjamin MURPHEY by patented 7 Oct 1812 SE 1/4 S 31 T 7 R 3, now for $1,200 sells all to SNODGRASS; WIT: Thomas MAJOR, George ATKINSON, ack. Thomas MAJOR, J.P., ent. 14 Dec 1813, rec. same.

D-479 Indenture, 15 Dec 1813, Henry NEFF (wife Barbary), BCO; Robert WILLIAM and Joseph HARVEY, BCO; $650, land in S 30 T 5 R 3, down Jack's Run, 132 3/4 acres, conveyed to NEFF, assignee of John SHEPHERD by patent dated 23 Jan 1813, fee simple; [looks like the transcriber had trouble with his written name], her mark, WIT: Wm. FARIS, Junr., Goerge BARKHURST, ack. George BARKHURST, J.P., ent. 15 Dec 1813, rec. same.

D-480 Indenture, 15 Dec 1813, Henry NEFF (wife Barbary), BCO; Crawford WELSH, BCO; $400, 50 acres, part of S 30 T 5 R 3, conveyed to NEFF assignee of John SHEPHERD by patent dated 23 Jan 1813; [same trouble with his name-- surname looks like ZRUFF], her mark, WIT: Wm. FARIS, Junr., George BARKHURST, ack. George BARKHURST, J.P., ent. 15 Dec 1813, rec. 20 same.

D-482 Indenture, 26 Jun 1813, Josiah DILLON, BCO; Geo. PAULL, BCO; PAULL bound to DILLON as security for DILLON to John and James ROBERTS for $140, also to McKEON and McCLELLAND for $107, to secure debt conveys salt kettles and three stills with tubs to Geo. PAULL, void if DILLON pays debt within one year; WIT: James CARROTHERS, ent. 20 Dec 1813, rec. same; release 25 Mar 1816, Geo. PAULL.

D-482 Patent to Henry NEFF, Junr., assignee of John SHEPHERD, for S 30 T 5 R 3, Steubenville district, sgn: 23 Jan 1813, James MADISON, Edward TIFFEN, Commissioner, ent. 20 Dec 1813, rec. 24 same.

D-483 By order of CCP sitting as a court of chancery at August term 1813 directed John BROWN, Sheriff, gave notice of sale on 12 Oct 1813 to highest bidder, who was William SHARPLESS, land held by [Enerly, Emrly, Euerly]

BURRIS, part of S 30 T 5 R 3, NBR: Mc. HARVEY; sgn: 18 Dec 1813, WIT: Sterling JOHNSTON, Henry JOHNSTON, ack. Sterling JOHNSTON, J.P., ent. 23 Dec 1813, rec. 25 same.

D-484   Indenture, 11 Dec 1813, Eli BOOTH (wife Mary), BCO; Samuel GILLESPIE, Cecil County, Maryland; $380, NE 1/4 S 13 T 7 R 5, 160 acres, patented to David MOORE on 21 Sep 1807, sold by David (wife Martha) on 28 d 3 m (Mar) 1812 to BOOTH; his seal, her mark, WIT: John PATTERSON, Lambert POND, ack. John PATTERSON, Assoc. Judge, ent. 23 Dec 1813, rec. 27 same.

D-485   Indenture, 29 Dec 1813, Joseph FLORA (wife Rachel), BCO; Phillip SHULTZ, BCO; $500, in S 20 T 6 R 3, NBR: John MAXWELL, 62 acres 3 rods 39 perches, conveyed to FLORA by Mordecai YARNALL (wife Phebe) on 29 Oct 1806, fee simple; his seal, her mark, WIT: Wm. FARIS, Junr., Henry JOHNSTON, ack. Henry JOHNSTON, J.P., ent. 29 Dec 1813, rec. same.

D-486   Indenture, 30 Dec 1813, Ralph HEATH (wife Elizabeth), St. Clairsville, BCO; Ira ROBINSON, same; $500, part of lot #61 in St. Clairsville, NBR: Peter YARNALL, Garret HAMMERLY, conveyed from John PATTERSON (wife Grissey) to HEATH on 31 Oct 1807, fee simple; WIT: Wm. FARIS, Junr., Henry JOHNSTON, ack. Henry JOHNSTON, J.P., ent. 30 Dec 1813, rec. same.

D-487   Indenture, 30 Dec 1813, Ira ROBINSON, St. Clairsville, BCO; Ralph HEATH, same; $300, part of lot #61 in St. Clairsville, NBR: Peter YARNALL, Garret HAMMERLY, void if ROBINSON pays $300 ending 30 Dec 1816; WIT: Wm. FARIS, Junr., Henry JOHNSTON, ack. Henry JOHNSTON, J.P., ent. 30 Dec 1813, rec. same; mortgage recorded satisfied 1 May 1815.

D-488   Indenture, 31 Dec 1813, Ira ROBINSON (wife Judith), St. Clairsville, BCO; Frederick AULT, same; $350, fee simple, part of lot #93 in St. Clairsville, NBR: BENTLEY & GILL[S?], Wm. HATFIELD, conveyed to ROBINSON by John WINTER on 3 Feb 1813, recorded Book D, p. 295; WIT: Wm. FARIS, Junr., Henry JOHNSTON, ack. Henry JOHNSTON, J.P., ent. 31 Dec 1813, rec. same.

D-489   Know all men, Frederick AULT, BCO, bound to Ira ROBINSON for $400, to secure John HINDS and Ira ROBINSON convey to HINDS and ROBINSON in fee simple part of lot #93 in St. Clairsville, NBR: BENTLEY & GILL[S?], Wm. HATFIELD, void if $400 paid into the Bank of Washington; WIT: Wm. FARIS, Junr., Henry JOHNSTON, ack. Henry JOHNSTON, J.P., ent. 1 Jan 1814, rec. 8 same; mortgage recorded satisfied 26 Mar 1817, Ira ROBINSON, admr. for John HINDS, dec'd.

D-490   Indenture, 30 Dec 1813, Thomas BLACKLEDGE (wife Sarah), JCO; Richard JONES, BCO; $160, NBR: Wheeling Creek, part of S 19 T 7 R 3, 36 acres; his seal, her mark, WIT: Thomas MAJOR, Paul PRESTON, ack. Thomas MAJOR, J.P., ent. 1 Jan 1814, rec. 10 same.

D-492   Indenture, 6 Nov 1813, Isaac VORE, Senr. (wife Eleanor), Knox County, Ohio; William PERRINE, BCO; $60, lot #75 in St. Clairsville; WIT: Wm. Z. FARQUHAR, Saml. KRATZER, ack. Saml. KRATZER, J.P., ent. 1 Jan 1814, rec. 10 same.

D-493   Indenture, 1 d 1 m 1814, David SMITH (wife Judith), Warren twp., BCO; Isaac WILLIAMS, same; $260, NW 1/4 S 1 T 8 R 6, Steubenville district, 70 acres, fee simple; his seal, her mark; WIT: John M[c_] LACY, Wm. C. ANDERSON, ack. Wm. C. ANDERSON, J.P., ent. 4 Jan 1814, rec. 11 same.

D-494   Indenture, 1 d 1 m 1814, David SMITH (wife Judith), Warren twp, BCO; Robert BURNET, same; $200, part of NE 1/4 S 7 T 8 R 6, Steubenville district, 50 acres, fee simple; his seal, her mark, WIT: John Mc LACY, Wm. C. ANDERSON, ack. Wm. C. ANDERSON, J.P., ent. 4 Jan 1814, rec. 11 same.

D-495   Indenture, 9 Nov 1813, Christopher HOOVER, BCO; Reese BRANSON, BCO; HOOVER bound in 6 written obligations for $600, secure with lot #40 in St. Clairsville, void if bonds repaid; WIT: Sterling JOHNSTON, William BROWN, ack. 9 Nov 1813, Sterling JOHNSTON, J.P., ent. 5 Jan 1814, rec. 11 same; Isaac BRANSON, admr. of LW&T of Reese BRANSON, dec'd, releases mortgage 11 May 1824, WIT: Wm. FARIS, Jr., Recor_.

D-496   Indenture, 8 Jan 1814, Magdaline PIPER, St. Clairsville, BCO; Enoch DYE, Junr., Washington County, Pennsylvania; $70, fee simple, lots #136 and #135 (#136 conveyed to PIPER by Archibald McELROY and Nancy BARTON, admrs. of David BARTON, dec'd, by deed dated 2 Jun 1812 as recorded in Book D, p. 227; her mark, WIT: Henry JOHNSTON, Samuel CRAWFORD, ack. Henry JOHNSTON, J.P., ent. 8 Jan 1814, rec. 12 same.

D-497   Indenture, 18 d 2 m 1813, Phebe PICKERING, widow of Samuel PICKERING, late of Union twp., BCO, dec'd; Jonas PICKERING, son; Levi PICKERING, son and guardian for Phebe PICKERING and Joshua PICKERING, minor children; Evan JAMES and wife Rebeccah, dau; James CROSIER and wife Mary, dau; Jacob BRANSON, same, yeoman; patent for S 20 T 9 R 5, Steubenville district, to Jonas PICKERING, and Jonas (wife Ruth) sold SE 1/4 S 20 (161 acres) on 10 Apr 1810 to his father, Samuel PICKERING, now dec'd, recorded 20 Aug in Book C, p. 270, Samuel died intestate, Phebe's share divided off by court order held 22 Dec 1812, now parties of first part convey for $65.84 to Jacob BRANSON part of widow's share, NBR: Abel WALKER, Phebe PICKERING, Jonas PICKERING, 13 acres; WIT: John MERCER, Nelson HARDING [his mark], ack. 18 Jul 1813, John MERCER, J.P., ent. 10 Jan 1814, rec. 12 same.

D-498   Indenture, 10 Jan 1814, Caleb ENGLE (wife Mercy), BCO; John PRIOR, BCO; $221, beginning SE corner of NW 1/4 S 28 T 6 R 4, 61 acres; WIT: George THOMPSON, Sterling JOHNSTON, ack. Sterling JOHNSTON, J.P., ent. 10 Jan 1814, rec. 12 same.

D-499   Indenture, 10 Jan 1814, Caleb ENGLE (wife Mercy), BCO; David RANDALL, BCO; $500, beginning SW corner NW 1/4 S 28 T 6 R 4, NBR: John PRIOR, 100 acres; WIT: George THOMPSON, Sterling JOHNSTON, ack. Sterling JOHNSTON, J.P., ent. 10 Jan 1814, rec. 12 same.

D-500   Indenture, 28 Nov 1813, Brice HOWARD, BCO; Jacob BARNETT, BCO; $750, 160 acres, NW 1/4 S 13 T 9 R 6, patented to Jacob and Samuel PICKERING, conveyed to HOWARD, fee simple; sgn: Brice HOWARD, Jane HOWARD, WIT: John N. SMITH, ack. 28 <u>Oct</u> 1813, John N. SMITH, J.P., ent. 11 Jan 1814, rec. 13 same.

D-501   Indenture, 30 Nov 1813, Jesse BATES, BCO; Jacob BARNETT, BCO; by bond executed 30 Nov 1813 BATES bound to BARNETT for $160, securing by conveying 109 acres, SE 1/4 S 20 T 9 R 6, void if $80 paid; WIT: John I. SMITH, John N. SMITH, ack. 20 Dec 1813, John N. SMITH, J.P., ent. 11 Jan 1814, rec. 13 same.

D-502   Indenture, 8 d 10 m 1813, Samuel WOOLMAN (wife Jane), Columbiana County, Ohio; their son Joel WOOLMAN, Philadelphia County, Pennsylvania; $700, SE 1/4 S 19 T 8 R 5, conveyed to Samuel as recorded in Book D, p. 207; WIT: Aaron A. WOOLMAN, George WOOLMAN, ack. 20 Nov 1813, William SINCLAIR, J.P., ent. 12 Jan 1814, rec. 13 same.

D-503   Indenture, 31 Dec 1813, Frances [Francis] BARKHURST, BCO; John SUTTON, BCO; $300, 50 acres, part of SW 1/4 S 32 T 6 R 3, patented to Jonathan SUTTON on 20 Apr 1812, Jonathan conveyed S 1/2 of S 32 on 2 Feb 1813, NBR: Patrick NELLONS; sgn: Fancy BARKHURST [her mark], WIT: John PATTERSON, David NEISWANGER, ack. 31 Dec 1813, John PATTERSON, Assoc. Judge, ent. 12 Jan 1814, rec. 14 same.

D-504   Indenture, 4 Jan 1814, Francis [Frances] BARCHURST, BCO; Nathaniel HAYDEN [HAYDON], Westmoreland County, Pennsylvania; $400, part of S 32 T 6 R 3, NBR: John SUTTON, Patrick NELLANS, 94 acres 3 rods 18 perches, part of S patented to Jonathan SUTTON on 20 Apr 1812, fee simple; sgn: Frances

BARCHUST [her mark], WIT: John PATTERSON, Ezer ELLIS, ack. John PATTERSON, Assoc. Judge, ent. 14 Jan 1814, rec. same.

D-505   Indenture, 4 Feb 1812, Joseph EATTON (wife Jinny), Warren twp., JCO; John EATTON, same. Patent to Joseph on 15 Aug 1807 for S 14 T 8 R 5, Steubenville district, now for $1,000 conveying N 1/2 of S; his seal, her mark ["Jeany"], WIT: John JACKSON, William EATTON, ack. JCO, 5 Feb 1812, John JACKSON, J.P., JACKSON certified 26 Aug 1813 by Thomas PATTON, Clerk, ent. 18 Jan 1814, rec. same.

D-506   Indenture, 4 Feb 1813, Joseph EATTON (wife Jinny), Warren twp., JCO; Joseph EATON, same; patent to Joseph on 15 Aug 1807 for S 14 T 8 R 5, Steubenville district, for $1,000 conveying S 1/2 of S; his seal, her mark ["Jane"], WIT: Jesse MARTIN, John EATTON, ack. JCO, 11 Sep 1813, Jesse MARTIN, J.P., MARTIN certified 8 Dec 1813 by Thos. PATTON, Clerk, ent. 18 Jan 1814, rec. 19 same.

D-508   Know all men, William CONGLETON, Guernsey County, for $30 paid by Moses HILL, BCO, convey 1/2 of land owned in common with Robert JOHNSON, i.e., lot #203 in St. Clairsville, NBR: John BERRY, Joseph MARSHALL, 1/2 of 1/4 acre; sgn: 28 Dec 1813, WIT: A. MARSHALL, D. K. PATRICK, ack. Guernsey County, D. K. PATRICK, J.P., ENT. 18 Jan 1814, rec. 19 same.

D-508   Indenture, 20 Jul 1813, George HARTSHORN (wife Hannah), BCO; Sterling JOHNSTON, BCO; $45, part of lot #97 in St. Clairsville, conveyed to HARTSHORN by Mahlon SMITH (wife Mary) on 23 Jun 1810; WIT: Robert VANCE, David NEISWANGER, ack. 4 Nov 1813, Robert VANCE, J.P., ent. 19 Jan 1814, rec. 22 same.

D-509   Indenture, 26 d 11 m 1813, Jonathan TAYLOR (wife Ann), Mountpleasant twp., JCO; John PICKERING, Pease twp., BCO; $125, land in Pease twp., part of S 12 T 6 R 3, patented to TAYLOR on 10 d 8 m 1807, NBR: Benjamin BAILEY, 61 1/2 acres; WIT: Thos. MITCHELL, Hariet MITCHELL, ack. Thos. MITCHELL, J.P., ent. 22 Jan 1814, rec. 24 same.

D-510   Indenture, 14 d 1 m 1814, John MITCHELL (wife Mary), BCO; Josiah BUNDY and Benjamin BUNDY, BCO; $1,000, part of S 14 T 7 R 3, NBR: Robert McBRATNEY, Francis COOPER, 100 acres, same sold by Bezaleel WELLS (wife Sally) to Charles McMANUS in fee on 13 Aug 1807, as recorded in Book B, p. 170; sgn: [surname looks here like WITCHELL], WIT: John WITCHELL, Junr., Mary KIMBERLY, ack. 14 Jan 1814, Henry JOHNSTON, J.P., ent. 29 Jan 1814, rec. same.

D-511   Indenture, 2 Sep 1813, Enos WEST (wife Margaret), BCO; Isaac CLEVENGER, BCO; $160, part of NW 1/4 S 7 T 10 R 6, 80 acres, fee simple; his seal, her mark, WIT: Otho BARKSHIRE, James MOORE, ack. 2 Sep 1813, John MOORE, J.P., ent. 29 Jan 1814, rec. 2 Feb same.

D-512   Indenture, 29 Sep 1813, Isaac CLEVENGER (wife Catharin), BCO; John EDWARDS, BCO; $80, part of NW 1/4 S 7 T 10 R 6, 40 acres, patented to Enos WEST on 13 Dec 1811, WEST conveyed to CLEVENGER on 2 Sep 1813, fee simple; both mark, WIT: Benjamin [STRAWDET] [his mark], John MOORE, ack. 29 Sep 1813, John MOORE, J.P., ent. 29 Jan 1814, rec. 2 Feb same.

D-513   Indenture, 2 Feb 1814, Allen STEWART (wife Nancy), BCO; James SYMES, BCO; $2,500, NE 1/4 S 15 T 7 R 4, 160 acres, conveyed to Robert and Caleb RUSSEL by Laben BRONSON of New York City by deed dated 21 Jan 1797 as recorded in JCO, and conveyed by Caleb RUSSELL to STEWART by deed dated 8 Nov 1805, recorded in BCO Book A, p. 624, originally conveyed to John HOPKINS by Samuel OSGOOD and Walter LIVINGSTON, commissioners of Board of Treasury of U.S. dated 3 Mar 1789; his seal, her mark, WIT: Sterling JOHNSTON, Joseph MORRISON, ack. 2 Feb 1814, Sterling JOHNSTON, J.P., ent. 2 Feb 1814, rec. 3 same.

D-515   Indenture, 2 Feb 1814, John SNEDAKER (wife Mary), BCO; Allen STEWART, BCO; $1,768, fee simple, part of W 1/2 S 1 T 9 R 5, 221 acres, patented to Garrit SNEDAKER on 10 Sep 1806, from Garrit to John on 12 Aug 1808; his seal, her mark, WIT: Sterling JOHNSTON, David VANCE, ack. Sterling JOHNSTON, J.P., ent. 2 Feb 1814, rec. 8 same.

D-516   Indenture, 15 Jan 1814, Leven OKEY (wife Hester), Monroe County, Ohio; James MARTIN, bco; $1,300, SE 1/4 S 21 T 4 R 3; his seal, her mark; WIT: David RUBLE, Robt. ARMSTRONG, ack. 15 Jan 1814, David RUBLE, J.P., ent. 8 Feb 1814, rec. 9 same.

D-517   Indenture, 4 Jan 1814, Frances BARCHUST, BCO; William McFARLAND, Senr., BCO; $100, part of S 32 T 6 R 3, NBR: Jonathan SUTTON, 32 acres 3 rods 2 perches, patented to Jonathan SUTTON on 20 Apr 1812; her mark, WIT: John PATTERSON, Ezer ELLIS, ack. 4 Jan 1814, John PATTERSON, Assoc. Judge, ent. 9 Feb 1814, rec. same.

D-518   Indenture, 7 Dec 1813, Arthur GILLIS, BCO; Samuel ERWIN, BCO; $250, E 1/2 NW 1/4 S 31 T 3 R 2, conveyed to GILLIS by James GORDON, GORDON patented on 20 Apr 1812; sgn: Arthur and Hanah GILLIS [both mark], WIT: James R. CUNINGHAM, Hanah CUNINGHAM, ack. 24 Dec 1813, John CUNINGHAM, J.P., ent. 10 Feb 1814, rec. 11 same.

D-519   Indenture, 23 Aug 1813, Josiah REEVES (wife Elizabeth); Barney BUCARTUS [BUSCARTUS], [no locations given]; $426, NW 1/4 S 33 T 8 R 5 except 25 acres on north end; his seal, her mark, WIT: G. HAILFORD, J. G. HENING, ack. JCO, 23 Aug 1813, J. G. HENING, J.P., ent. 19 Feb 1814, rec. 21 same.

D-520   Indenture, 8 Jan 1814, Moses NIEL [NEIL] (wife Abigail), Harrison County, Ohio; David BARNES, BCO; $50, lots #99 and #100, formerly owned by Phillip WINDLE; WIT: Andrew McNEELY, Hannah NEIL, ack. Harrison County, 8 Jan 1814, Andrew McNEELY, J.P., McNEELY certified 2 Feb 1814 at Cadiz by Joseph HARRIS, Clerk, ent. 19 Feb 1814, rec. 25 same.

D-521   Indenture, 19 Feb 1814, David BARNES (wife Elizabeth), BCO; William BOOKER, BCO; $200, fee simple, lot #100 (NBR: Widow IRWIN) and #99 (NBR: Widow IRWIN), recorded in Book E, pp. 41-42, conveyed to Moses NEIL, from NEIL to BARNES; his seal, her mark, WIT: Wm. FARIS, Junr., John PATTERSON, ack. John PATTERSON, Assoc. Judge, CCP, ent. 19 Feb 1814, rec. 28 same.

D-522   Indenture, 2 Mar 1808, Richard McKIBBEN (wife Sally), BCO; James MITCHEL, BCO; $1,236, part of S 27 T 4 R 2, NBR: James McCLURE, Joseph SCOT, 154 [acres] 2 rods 6 53/100 perches; WIT: John McELROY, John MITCHEL, ack. 2 Mar 1808, Thos. MITCHEL, ent. 4 Mar 1814, rec. 5 same.

D-523   Indenture, 7 Jul 1811, Mary McKIBBEN, BCO; James MITCHELL, BCO; $500, part of S 27 T 4 R 2, NBR: John McCLURE, James MITCHEL, 50 acres 1 rod 6 perches, ack. 7 Jul 1811, Thos. MITCHEL, J.P., ent. 4 Mar 1814, rec. 5 same.

D-525   Plat of Union Town, by Mr. William DIXON, surveyed by John STEWART, County Surveyor, BCO, ack. of William DIXON (wife Jane) on 26 Apr 1814, Robert LEE, J.P., ent. 7 Mar 1814, recorded 8 same.

D-526   To all People, William THOMAS of BCO for love and affection for son Camm THOMAS, BCO, convey 150 acres in Guernsey County, Ohio, part of NW 1/4 S 1 T 1 R 1, Zanesville district, patented to William on 10 Dec 1806; sgn: 14 Oct 1813, WIT: Wm. C. ANDERSON, George WOOTTON, ack. 14 Oct 1813, Wm. C. ANDERSON, J.P., ent. 9 Mar 1814, rec. same.

D-526   Know all men, William RENNELS, St. Clairsville, BCO, for $90 paid by Moses HILL, BCO, lot #122 in St. Clairsville, conveyed by Nicholas BROWN (unnamed wife) to John MARTIN (unnamed wife), by MARTIN (and wife) to John THOMPSON, from THOMPSON to Magdeline PIPER, from PIPER to Isaac

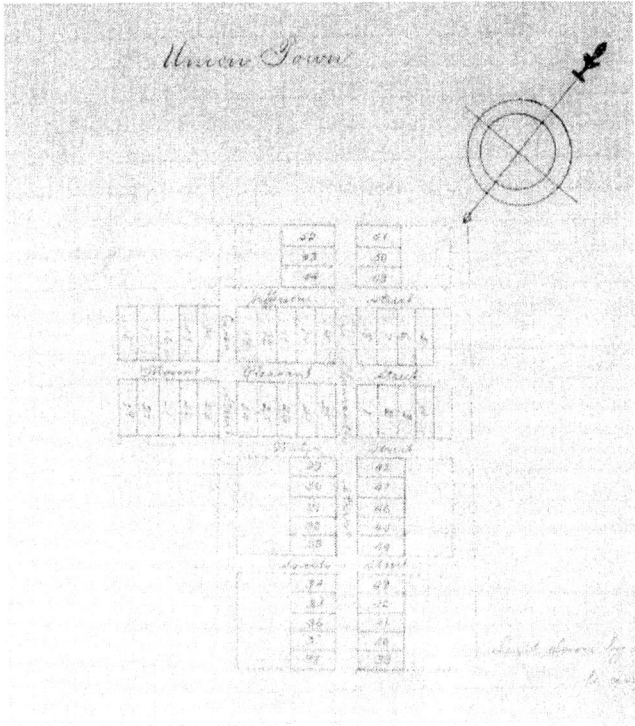

Plat of Union Town

Another Plat of Flushing

SIMMONS (unnamed wife), from SIMMONS to RENNELS; sgn: 9 Feb 1814, "William B. REYNELS," WIT: Sterling JOHNSTON, John BERRY, ack. 17 Feb 1814, Sterling JOHNSTON, J.P., ent. 12 Mar 1814, rec. 14 same.

D-527   Indenture, 1 Mar 1814, William SHAW (wife Elizabeth), BCO; Thomas B. CLARK, BCO; $768.75, part of S 2 T 9 R 5, Steubenville district, NBR: Robert LEE, 102 1/2 acres, fee simple; his seal, her mark, WIT: Robert LEE, William COON, ack. Robert LEE, J.P., ent. 12 Mar 1814, rec. 14 same.

D-528   Indenture, 10 Mar 1814, John SNEDACRE (wife Mary), BCO: Allen STEWART, BCO; $1,792, 224 acres 8 perches, part of W 1/2 of S 1 T 9 R 5, patented to Garret SNEDACRE on 10 Sep 1806, this portion of land conveyed by Garret to John SNEDACREE by deed dated 12 Aug 1808, NBR: Rudolf WELMAN, Nicholas SNEDACRE, fee simple; his seal, her mark [both written SNEDEKER], WIT: John WILEY, Ervin CUTTER [CUTLER], ack. [SNEDDEKER here] John WILEY, Assoc. Judge, 12 Mar 1814 receipt of money WIT by Wm. FARIS, Senr., ent. 12 Mar 1814, rec. 15 same.

D-529   Indenture, 21 Feb 1814, David HANNAH, Columbiana County, Ohio; David LOCKWOOD, BCO; $400, part of fraction S 5 T 4 R 3, NBR: Gray's Run, Dilley's Bottom, 46 acres 3 rods 34 perches; WIT: Joshua B. BREWER, Mahlon LINDLEY, ack. 25 Feb 1814, Valentine SAUERHEBER, J.P., ent. 14 Mar 1814, rec. 15 same.

D-530   "2802" James Madison, President, Charles IRWIN, BCO, payment made for NW 1/4 S 27 T 10 R 7, Steubenville district, letters patent; sgn: 20 Mar 1813, and Edward TIFFIN, Commissioner of the General Land Office, ent. 24 Mar 1814, rec. 25 same.

D-531   Indenture, 9 Nov 1813, Reese [Rees] BRANSON (wife Ruth), BCO; Christopher HOOVER, BCO; $600, lot #40 in St. Clairsville, 1/4 acre, conveyed from William GIFFIN (wife Elizabeth) to BRANSON on 18 Dec 1806, fee simple; WIT: William CRAIG, Sterling JOHNSTON, ack. 14 Nov 1813, Sterling JOHNSTON, J.P., ent. 2 Apr 1814, rec. same.

D-532   Indenture, 1 d 4 m 1814, Joshua WOOD (wife Hannah) and Jesse FOULKE (wife Sarah), BCO; Horton HOWARD, BCO; $160, part of S 20 T 9 R 5, patented to Jonas PICKERING, conveyed by him and wife to George SMITH and Thomas BUFKIN, conveyed by them and wives to WOOD and FOULKE, NBR: FOULKE, near Flushing, about 10 acres; WIT: Robert LEE, Samuel HOLLOWAY, ack. 1 Apr 1814, Robert LEE, Justice, ent. 2 Apr 1814, rec. same.

D-533   Plat of Flushing, laid out on S 20 T 9 R 5, BCO, by Jesse FOULKE and Joshua WOODS; sgn: 1 d 4 m 1814, WIT: Robert LEE, Samuel HOLLOWAY, ack. Joshua WOOD, Jesse FOULKE, and Horton HOWARD, proprietors, Robert LEE, Justice, ent. 2 Apr 1814, rec. same month; on 11 Dec 1815 Robert LEE, J.P., ack. the addition to plat by FOULKE of 24 additional lots, ent. 11 Dec 1815, rec. same day.

D-534   Indenture, 8 d 4 m 1814, John WITCHELL [possibly MITCHELL] (wife Mary), BCO; John N. POWER, , BCO; on 17 Jun 1813 MITCHELL patented W 1/2 of S 14 T 7 R 5, for $182.25 conveying 81 acres of that to POWER, fee simple; WIT: John WITCHELL, Junr., Mary KIMBERLY, ack. 8 Apr 1814, Henry JOHNSTON, J.P., ent. 7 Apr 1814, rec. same.

D-535   Indenture, 22 Mar 1814, Jacob GRUBB (wife Elizabeth), St. Clairsville, BCO; John PATTERSON, same; $140, fee simple, lots #1 and #2 in addition to St. Clairsville laid out by William MATHERS, lots conveyed to GRUBB by Jacob REILY (wife Sarah) on 26 Mar 1813, recorded Book D, p. 325; his seal, her mark, WIT: 22 Mar 1814, Henry JOHNSTON, Anthony WEYER [MEYER?], ack. 22 Mar 1814, Henry JOHNSTON, J.P., ent. 9 Apr 1814, rec. 11 same.

P. 536   Indenture, 4 Apr 1814, Reason PUMPHREY (wife Ann PUMPHREY [note: her surname is consistently repeated]), Brook County, Virginia; Robert McBRIDE, Coshocton County, Ohio; $400, SW 1/4 S 11 T 9 R 6, Steubenville district, patented to PUMPHREY on 30 Jul 1813; WIT: James PATTON, Wm. CHAMBERS, ack. JCO, Joseph McCAUGHEY, J.P., ent 9 Apr 1814, rec. 12 same.

D-537   Indenture, 6 Apr 1814, Isaac ANDERSON (wife Mary), BCO; William LINGO, BCO; $480, NW 1/4 S 34 T 7 R 5; his seal, her mark, WIT: Ezer DILLON, John STRAHL, ack. Wm. SMITH, J.P., ent. 12 Apr 1814, rec. 13 same.

D-538   "2489" James Madison certifies that James GALLOWAY patented SW 1/4 S 35 T 8 R 6, Steubenville district, sgn: 30 Jul 1812, seconded by Edward TIFFIN, Commissioner of the General Land Office, ent. 13 Apr 1814, rec. 15 same.

D-538   Indenture, 14 d 4 m 1814, Nathan UPDEGRAFF (wife Ann), Mount Pleasant twp., JCO; Wilmith [Wilmeth, Wilmoth] JONES, town of Washington, Pennsylvania; $140, lot #41 in St. Clairsville, 1/4 acre, fee simple; WIT: John WATSON, Abner MOORE, ack. JCO, 14 Apr 1814, John WATSON, J.P., ent. 14 Apr 1814, rec. 16 same.

D-539   Indenture, 4 Apr 1814, David RUBLE, Edward BRYSON, and Susannah STOOKEY, admrs. of estate of John DAVIS, BCO; George GAITZE, BCO;

$501.67, NBR: Capteen Creek, part of S 27 T 4 R 3, Meriatta district, NBR: Henry HOOVER, William BROWN, 103 acres, conveyed by RUBLE, BRYSON, and Susannah DAVIS now STOOKEY in care for the heirs of John DAVIS, sold by heirs to satisfy demands against estate; men's seal, her mark, WIT: Valentine SAUERHEBER, [Lynngrif FISBNZ (probably a German name?)], Robrt. GILKINSON, ack. Valentine SAUERHEBER, ent. 14 Apr 1814, rec. 18 same.

D-540   Indenture, 18 d 10 m 1813, John WITCHELL (wife Mary), BCO; Absalom [BRADRICKS], BCO; $284.40, NBR: Wheeling Creek, 31 acres 3 rods 13 perches, part of S 36 T 7 R 4, patented to John EDWARDS, Senr., on 7 d 4 m 1806, from EDWARDS to John PRICE on 28 d 5 m 1806, by PRICE to WITCHELL on 12 d 6 m 1810, fee simple; WIT: John LIST, William MOTT, ack. Henry JOHNSTON, J.P., ent. 18 Apr 1814, rec. same.

D-541   Indenture, 19 Jan 1814, Sterling JOHNSTON (wife Mary), BCO; Patrick NELLONS, BCO; $100, NBR: Robert HOPPER, 36 acres 37 perches, part of S 6 T 7 R 4; WIT: David VANCE, John McELROY, ack. 22 Feb 1814, Robert VANCE, J.P., ent. 23 Apr 1814, rec. 25 same.

D-542   Indenture, 20 Apr 1814, David CAMPBELL (wife Anne [Ann]), Harrison County, Ohio; John LYLE, BCO; $700, land in Wheeling twp., SE 1/4 S 26 T 8 R 4, 171 acres, patented to John CAMPBELL, heirs of John CAMPBELL conveyed by deed dated 1 Nov 1809 to David CAMPBELL, as recorded in Book C, p. 187; WIT: John CAMPBELL, Robert HENDERSON, ack. John CAMPBELL, J.P., ent. 27 Apr 1814, rec. 28 same.

D-543   Indenture, 1 Apr 1814, William DIXON (wife Jane), BCO; John LYLE, BCO; $15, lot #14 in Union, 1/4 acre, fee simple; WIT: Samuel MILLS, John CAMPBELL, ack. 1 Apr 1814, John CAMPBELL, J.P., ent. 27 Apr 1814, rec. 28 same.

D-544   Indenture, 4 Apr 1814, Reasin [Reason] PUMPHREY (wife Ann), Brooke County, Virginia; Joseph MEADLEY, BCO; $400, NW 1/4 S 11 T 9 R 6, patented to PUMPHREY on 30 Jul 1813; WIT: James PATTEN, Wm. CHAMBERS, ack. 4 Apr 1814, JCO, Joseph McCAUGHEY, J.P., ent. 30 Apr 1814, rec. same.

D-545   Indenture, 20 Apr 1814, William PUMPHREY (wife Elizabeth), JCO; John MAJOR, BCO; NW 1/4 S 21 T 7 R 3 patented to PUMPHREY on 30 Jul 1812, now sell for $600, 60 acres; his seal, her mark, WIT: Thomas MAJOR, Wm. BLACKLEDGE, ack. 20 Apr 1814, Thomas MAJOR, J.P., ent. 4 May 1814, rec. 9 same.

D-546 Indenture, 23 Feb 1814, George BROKAW, Senr. (wife Jane), Harrison County, Ohio; George BROKAW, Junr., BCO; George Senr. patented NE 1/4 S 15 T 9 R 5, Steubenville district, on 8 Jun 1812, now sells for $100 and other good causes to George Junr. E 1/2 of NE 1/4 S 15 T 9 R 5; WIT: Robert LEE, Richard COPLEN, ack. 23 Feb 1814, (BCO) Robert LEE, J.P., ent. 5 May 1814, rec. 10 same.

D-547 Indenture, 23 Feb 1814, George BROKAW, Senr. (wife Jane), Harrison County, Ohio; William BROKAW, BCO; George Senr. patented NE 1/4 S 15 T 9 R 5, Steubenville district, on 8 Jun 1812, now sells for $100 W 1/2 NE 1/4 S 15 T 9 R 5; WIT: Robert LEE, Richard COPLEN, ack. 23 Feb 1814, Robert LEE, J.P., ent. 5 May 1814, rec. 10 same.

D-548 Indenture, 2 May 1814, William HULSE (wife Elizabeth), Richland twp., BCO; Joseph GRIFFITH, Abraham AMRINE, John MAXWELL, and Jonah HUFF, trustees for school in district 8, 1 acre at intersecting corner lines on SE corner of S 34 T 6 R 3, [NOTE: repetition of name at end is HUFF instead of HULSE]; his seal, her mark [HULSE here], WIT: Thomas FLANNER, John PATTERSON, ack. John PATTERSON, Assoc. Judge, ent. 11 May 1814, rec. same.

D-549 Indenture, 11 May 1814, David KIRKPATRICK, of Guernsey County, Ohio, guardian for Anne NEWELL, daughter of Benjamin NEWELL, deceased; Garet HAMERLY, BCO; $100, lot #62 in St. Clairsville, 1/4 acre, conveyed to Anne NEWELL by David NEWELL (wife Sally) on 29 Apr 1802, as recorded in Book A, p. 82, fee simple; David KIRKPATRICK, Guardian, WIT: Sterling JOHNSTON, Abraham KINNEY, ack. 11 May 1814, Sterling JOHNSTON, J.P., $60 receipted, ent. 11 May 1814, rec. same.

D-550 Indenture, 13 May 1814, Joseph FERRIL, Ohio County, Virginia; his son James FERRIL, same; for natural love and affection conveys NE 1/4 S 1 T 7 R 4, patented to Joseph on 15 Nov 1812, fee simple; his mark, WIT: James HUGHES, Sterling JOHNSTON, ack. (BCO), Sterling JOHNSTON, J.P., ent. 13 May 1814, rec. same.

D-551 Indenture, 10 Dec 1813, John N. BROCK (wife Martha), BCO; Stephen PARKINS, BCO; $160, W 1/2 SE 1/4 S 30 T 8 R 5, Steubenville district, 62 acres, patented to BROCK on 1 Jan 1812; his seal, her mark, WIT: John MERCER, Nathan PARKINS, ack. 10 <u>Nov</u> 1813, John MERCER, J.P., ent. 16 May 1814, rec. same.

D-552 Indenture, 29 d 1 m 1814, Stephen HODGIN (wife Elizabeth), BCO; Horton HOWARD, BCO; $1,000, part of S 11 T 8 R 6, Steubenville district, NBR:

Stephen TODD, 122 1/4 acres, plus dam privileges on Stillwater Creek; WIT: John N. SMITH, Stephen TODD, ack. 29 Jan 1814, John N. SMITH, J.P., ent. 16 May 1814, rec. 17 same.

D-553   Indenture, 29 d 1 m 1814, James CAMPBEL (wife Ruth), BCO; Horton HOWARD, BCO; $122, part of S 12 T 8 R 6, patented to CAMPBEL on 16 d 8 m 1804, 10 acres; his seal, her mark, WIT: John N. SMITH, Henry HOWARD, ack. 29 Jan 1814, John N. SMITH, J.P.

D-554   Indenture, 15 d 2 m 1814, Samuel EDGERTON (wife Elizabeth), BCO; Jacob NICHOLSON, BCO; $350, W 1/2 of SW 1/4 S 17 T 6 R 5, Marietta district; WIT: Samuel BERRY, Mary BERRY, ack. same as deed, Samuel BERRY, J.P., ent. 16 May 1814, rec. 18 same.

D-555   Indenture, 20 Apr 1814, William PUMPHREY (wife Elizabeth), JCO; Brittain OXLEY, BCO; $700, on waters of Short Creek, beginning at N corner S 21 T 7 R 3, 100 acres, patented by PUMPHREY on 30 Jul 1812; his seal, her mark, WIT: Thomas MAJOR, Wm. BLACKLEDGE, ack. 20 Apr 1814, Thomas MAJOR, J.P., ent. 20 May 1814, rec. 21 same.

D-556   Know all men, Isaac FARMER (wife Mary), Licking County, Ohio; Saml. DAVIS, [feat] County [Fayette?], Pennsylvania; $616.16, 80 acres, NW corner S 30 T 7 R 4; sgn: 11 Apr 1814, his seal, her mark, WIT: Joshua BROWN, Samuel POGUE, ack. Licking County, 11 Apr 1814, Samuel POGUE, J.P., POGUE certified by Stephen McDOUGAL, Clerk, at Newark, ent. 23 May [1814], rec. same.

D-557   Indenture, 24 May 1814, John BROWN, Junr. (wife Elizabeth), BCO; Sarah ROBINSON, BCO; $107, begin SE corner NE 1/4 S 6 T 6 R 4, 22 1/2 acres, part of S conveyed from John WINTER to John BROWN, as recorded in Book D, p. 369; his seal, her mark, WIT: Henry JOHNSTON, Isaac WILSON, ack. Henry JOHNSTON, J.P., receipt for $80 and his note (Levi PICKERING, security), ack. Ira ROBINSON for Wm. ROBINSON, 11 Jul 1815, "Wm. FARIS, Jr. will please to enter satisfaction on the record of the mortgage given by John BROWN, Jur to Sarah ROBINSON he having satisfied the same." Ira ROBINSON for Wm. ROBINSON, ent. 11 Jul 1815, rec. 13 same.

D-558   Indenture, 19 Apr 1814, Abraham DAVIS (wife Abigail), BCO; Joseph TILTON, JCO; $1,400, two fractional lots in S 15 and 21 T 4 R 2, beginning at center of fractional S 15 on Ohio River, NBR: Mr. WOOD[S], 100 acres, originally patented to Archibald WOODS on 15 Nov 1797, 1/2 conveyed to Absalom MARTIN, part of that conveyed by MARTIN to John CONNEL by deed, WIT:

James ALEXANDER, Robert HALL, ack. 19 Apr 1814, James ALEXANDER, Assoc. Judge, ent. 27 May 1814, rec. 28 same.

D-559   Indenture, 6 May 1814, Benoni BRYANT, BCO; Joseph ALEXANDER, BCO; $600, lots #13 and #109 in Barnesville, each 1/4 acre, fee simple; WIT: Thomas SHANNON, James BARNES, ack. 27 May 1814, Thomas SHANNON, J.P.

D-560   Indenture, 1 May 1813, Frances BARKHURST (widow), BCO; Patrick NELLONS, BCO; $607, part of S 32 T 6 R 3, NBR: John SUTTON, Jonathan SUTTON, 101 acres 3 rods 20 perches, fee simple; her mark, WIT: George BARKHURST, Sterling JOHNSTON, ack. same date, Sterling JOHNSTON, J.P., ent. 30 May 1814, rec. 2 Jun same.

D-561   Indenture, 22 Apr 1814, William WORKMAN (wife Phoebe), BCO; David WORKMAN, BCO; $100, 117 acres 2 rods 14 perches, part of 200-acre tract conveyed to WORKMAN by extrs. of estate of Daniel McELHERAN by deed on 14 Feb 1811, part of fractional T 2 R 3; his seal, her mark, no WIT given, ack. 22 Apr 1814, John CUNNINGHAM, J.P., Pultney twp., ent. 2 Jun 1814, rec. 3 same.

D-562   Indenture, 1 Jun 1814, Charles IRWIN (wife Margaret), BCO; George GIVEN, BCO; $220, part of S 6 T 6 R 3, near road leading to Martin's Ferry, NBR: George GIVEN, 72 acres 2 rods 8 perches, conveyed by Charles IRWIN by William WILEY (wife Martha) on 22 Aug 1805; second tract part of S 12 T 6 R 3, 22 acres 3 rods, conveyed from Daniel McPEAK (wife Elizabeth) to Charles IRWIN on 17 Dec 1810, fee simple; WIT: John [HYDE], William GIBSON, ack. 1 Jun 1814, John N. SMITH, J.P., ent. 2 Jun 1814, rec. 3 same.

D-564   Indenture, 19 May 1814, Henry DOUDNA (wife Patty), BCO; James BARNES, BCO; $100, lots #148 and #147 in St. Clairsville, each 1/4 acre; his seal, her mark; WIT: Thomas SHANNON, Josiah PENNINGTON, ack. 20 May 1814, Thomas SHANNON, J.P., ent. 2 Jun 1814, rec. 6 same.

D-565   Indenture, 6 Dec 1813, William ASKEW (wife Martha), St. Clairsville, BCO; George ALBAN, St. Clairsville, BCO; $73, 2 acres of outlot #8 in plan of 15 outlots adjoining addition to St. Clairsville, laid out by William MATHERS, NBR: Michael GROVES, conveyed to ASKEW by Samuel SULLIVAN (wife Mary) on 22 Jan 1810, as recorded in Book C, p. 193; WIT: Henry JOHNSTON, Isaac WILSON, ack. 6 Dec 1813, Henry JOHNSTON, J.P., ent. 3 Jun 1814, rec. 6 same.

D-566   Indenture, 30 d 10 m 1813, William MILLHOUSE (wife Hannah), BCO; Joseph GAMBLE, BCO; Horton HOWARD patented S 8 T 7 R 3, Steubenville district, on 10 Sep 1806, then by deed dated 11 d 6 m 1807 conveyed SW 1/4 S 8 T 7 R 3 to MILHOUSE, now for $85 conveys 6 1/2 acres beginning at NE corner of 1/4 S 8 T 7 R 3; WIT: Thos. MITCHEL, Wm. MILHOUSE, Junr., ack. 30 Oct 1813, Thos. MITCHELL, J.P., ent. 6 Jun 1814, rec. 7 same.

D-567   Indenture, 6 Jun 1814, James BARNES (wife Nancy), BCO; Samuel HILTON, Frederick County, Maryland; $130, lots #58, #90, #59 and #91 in St. Clairsville, each 1/4 acre, fee simple; his seal, her mark, WIT: Thomas SHANNON, Robt. GRIER, ack. Thomas SHANNON, J.P., ent. 7 Jun 1814, rec. same.

D-568   By writ of Fiere facias directed to Sheriff of BCO out of Court of Common Pleas against goods of Robert THOMPSON to satisfy a judgment obtained in favor of Jeremiah FAIRHURST and Thomas THOMPSON, Deputy Sheriff John BROWN held sale on 15 Dec 1813 and sold to John NICHOLS, yeoman, for $333.50 sold lot #49 in St. Clairsville, conveyed from David NEWALL (wife Sally) to Daniel McPEAK, from McPEAK to Job RIDGEWAY, from RIDGEWAY to Josiah DILLON, from DILLON to Jeremiah FAIRHURST, from FAIRHURST to Robert THOMPSON by articles of agreement, sgn: 16 Dec 1813; WIT: Sterling JOHNSTON, William BROWN, ack. 16 Dec 1813, Sterling JOHNSTON, J.P., ent. 8 Jun 1814, rec. same.

D-569   Indenture, 15 Dec 1813, Archibald WOODS (wife Anne), Ohio County, Virginia, and George PAULL, BCO; William SHARPLESS, BCO; $2,720, lots #59 and #60 in St. Clairsville, excepting part of lot on which houses of John and Andrew WHITE now stand; WIT: Thos. THOMPSON, Wm. PERRINE, ack. of Archibald and George on 15 Dec 1813, Thos. THOMPSON, J.P., ack. of Ann directed by Benjamin RUGGLES, Esq., President of Court and signed by Josiah HEDGES, Clerk, 11 Jun 1814; ack. Ohio County, Virginia, of Ann WOODS on 11 Jun 1814, WIT: Geo. MILLER, Joseph CALDWELL, ack. 11 Jun 1814, ent. 13 Jun 1814, rec. same.

D-571   Indenture, 20 Apr 1814, David CAMPBELL (wife Anne), Harrison County, Ohio; Robert HENDERSON, BCO; $1,100, SW 1/4 S 21 T 8 R 4, patented to CAMPBELL on 9 Oct 1812; WIT: John CAMPBELL, John LYLE, ack. 20 Apr 1814, John CAMPBELL, J.P., ent 13 Jun 1814, rec. 15 same

D-571   Know all men, John INSKEEP, BCO, owes Levi PICKERING $300, to be paid in installments by 1 Oct 1816, securing by selling lots #45 and #46 in St. Clairsville, lots conveyed from James BARNES (wife Nancy) to INSKEEP on same date, fee simple, void if payments made; signed by both INSKEEP and PICKERING on 4 Sep 1813, WIT: Sterling JOHNSTON, James BARNES, ack. 4 Sep 1813, Sterling JOHNSTON, J.P., interest in mortgage assigned to John

THOMPSON by PICKERING on 13 Jun 1814, WIT: John BARNES Junr., ent. 13 Jun 1814, rec. 15 same.

D-573   Indenture, 26 Mar 1814, William DIXON (wife Jane), BCO; Samuel MILLS, BCO; lot #1 in Union, 1/4 acre, fee simple; his seal, her mark, WIT: Robert LEE, George KERR, ack. 26 Mar 1814, Robert LEE, J.P., ent. 13 Jun 1814, rec. 15 same.

D-574   Indenture, 13 Jun 1814, James CALDWELL (wife Nancy), BCO; Joel JUDKINS, BCO; $880, SE 1/4 S 15 T 8 R 6; WIT: Henry JOHNSTON, Wm. BOOKER, ack. Henry JOHNSTON, J.P., ent. 13 Jun 1814, rec. 15 same.

D-575   Indenture, 18 May 1814, James WATT (wife Sarah), BCO; Samuel GREGG, BCO; $7, 137 perches, part of S 30 T 7 R 4, S granted to Joseph SHARP on 20 Jun 1809, part conveyed by SHARP to WATT on 26 Nov 1811 for 89 acres 4 perches, 137 perches in that last tract, NBR: James WATT, Wheeling Creek; WIT: William SINCLAIR, James CLEMENTS, ack. 18 May 1814, William SINCLAIR, J.P., ent. 22 Jun 1814, rec. 24 same.

D-576   Indenture, 30 Apr 1814, John THOMPSON (wife Sally); Steel SMITH [no locations given]; $3,000, lot #4 in St. Clairsville, where Zebulon WARNER now lives; WIT: Levi PICKERING, Sterling JOHNSTON, ack. 30 Apr 1814, Sterling JOHNSTON, J.P., ent. 25 Jun 1814, rec. 27 same.

D-577   Indenture, 28 Mar 1814, William DIXON (wife Jane), BCO; Hugh McCASKEY, BCO; $20, lot #10 in Union, 1/4 acre, fee simple; his seal, her mark, WIT: Peter SNEDEKER, Samuel MILLS, ack. 26 Mar 1814, Robert LEE, J.P., ent. 25 Jun 1814, rec. 28 same.

D-577   Indenture, 13 Nov 1813, John GIBSON, Westmoreland County, Pennsylvania; Robert THOMPSON, BCO; GIBSON bound to THOMPSON in two written obligations dated same date for $300 payable by 1 May 1816, for securing payment GIBSON conveys lots #21 and #22 in addition to St. Clairsville, sold by Robert THOMPSON (wife Margaret) on same date sold to GIBSON, fee simple, void if debt paid; John GIBSON, WIT: William BROWN, Sterling JOHNSTON, ack. 13 Nov 1813, Sterling JOHNSTON, J.P., ent. 2 Jul 1814, rec. same.

D-578   Indenture, 19 Jan 1814, Sterling JOHNSTON (wife Mary), BCO; William REYNOLDS, BCO; $60, part of lot #97 in St. Clairsville, conveyed from Mahlon SMITH to George HARTSHORN and from HARTSHORN to JOHNSTON on 20 Jul 1813, fee simple; WIT: William SINCLAIR, David VANCE, ack. 2 Apr 1814, William SINCLAIR, J.P., ent. 2 Jul 1814, rec. 4 same.

D-579   Indenture, 28 May 1814, Jacob SNEDEKER (wife Eleanor), Ohio County, Virginia; John W. SMITH, BCO; $640, 80 acres, part of S 2 T 9 R 5, fee simple; his seal, her mark, WIT: Robert LEE, ack. 7 Jun 1814, Robert LEE, J.P., ent. 4 Jul 1814, rec. 7 same.

D-580   Know all men, Levi PICKERING, St. Clairsville, BCO; Peter YARNAL (wife Lucinda) signed indenture on 8 Jul 1814 for consideration therein conveying in fee simple lot #61 in St. Clairsville, void if PICKERING pays $500 by 8 Jul 1815; sgn: 8 Jul 1814, WIT: John PATTERSON, Ezer ELLIS, ack. John PATTERSON, Assoc. Judge, ent. 8 Jul 1814, rec. 12 same.

D-581   Indenture, 20 Jan 1813, William GILLCHRIST "& fourteen his wife," BCO; George BROKAW, Junr., BCO; $25, 3 acres 20 perches, bounded by NW 1/4 S 9 T 9 R 5, Steubenville district, patented by Thomas SHARP on 8 May 1806, west divide conveyed by SHARP (wife Jenny) by deed dated 15 Dec 1808 to John McFADDEN, Senr., as recorded in Book B, p. 552, 153 acres conveyed by McFADDEN (wife Margaret) to GILLCHRIST; his seal, her mark, WIT: John CAMPBELL, Mary CAMPBELL, ack. 20 Jan 1814, John CAMPBELL, J.P., ent. 8 Jul 1814, rec. 12 same.

D-582   Indenture, 11 Apr 1814, Robert DENT (wife Mary), BCO; Mary B. NORRISS [NORRIS], BCO; $120, land being annexed to St. Clairsville on east end, as recorded in Book A, p. 504, SW corner of lot #10, 22 1/2 perches, fee simple; WIT: Henry JOHNSTON, Isaac BUSKIRK, ack. 11 Apr 1814, Henry JOHNSTON, J.P., ent. 11 Jul 1814, rec. 13 same.

D-583   Indenture, 24 May 1814, William SMITH (wife Rebekah), BCO; John SMITH, BCO; $2,700, SE 1/4 S 18 T 6 R 4, 160 acres, Steubenville district, patented by William on 25 Oct 1813, fee simple; WIT: John PATTERSON, Josiah HEDGES, ack. John PATTERSON, Assoc. Judge, ent. 15 Jul 1814, rec. 16 same.

D-584   Indenture, 31 d 5 m 1814, Benjamin KIRK (wife Elizabeth), cordwainer, Union twp., BCO; Adam KIRK, yeoman, BCO; Benjamin KIRK patented on 22 Dec 1812 SE 1/4 S 15 T 9 R 5, Steubenville district, now for $400 convey 60 acres on south of S; WIT: Samuel PICKERING, ack. Robert LEE, J.P., ent. 16 Jul 1814, rec. 18 same.

D-585   Indenture, 8 Jun 1814, Joseph PATTON (wife Leticia), St. Clairsville, BCO; Henry H. EVANS, BCO; $140, outlot #5 in 15 outlots laid out by Bazaleel WELLS adjoining addition to St. Clairsville, 3 1/2 acres 79 perches; his seal, her mark, WIT: Henry JOHNSTON, David MOORE, ack. 8 Jun 1814, Henry JOHNSTON, J.P., ent. 21 Jul 1814, rec. same.

D-586   Indenture, 2 Jul 1814, Robert THOMPSON (wife Margaret), BCO; Henry H. EVANS, BCO; $150, NBR: now James TAYLOR but formerly Josiah DILLON, William BOGGS, 3 acres 37 perches, same conveyed from David NEWELL to Daniel CHURCH, from CHURCH to William WOODS, from WOODS to THOMPSON; his seal, her mark, WIT: Henry JOHNSTON, Julian SIMS, ack. Henry JOHNSTON, J.P., ent. 21 Jul 1814, rec. same.

D-587   Know all men, Samuel GILL and Solomon BENTLEY in partnership on 5 Sep 1809 purchased of Ezer DILLON (wife Elizabeth) lot #85 in St. Clairsville, now Samuel GILL (wife Eleanor) for $450 convey their interest in lot; sgn: 19 Jul 1814, WIT: Abner MOORE, Sterling JOHNSTON, ack. Sterling JOHNSTON, J.P., ent. 21 Jul 1814, rec. 22 same.

D-588   Indenture, 25 d 2 m 1814, Jacob GREGG (wife Mary), BCO; Noah JOHNSTON, BCO; Jacob GREGG, then of Louden County, Virginia, patented S 7 T 8 R 5, Stenbenville district, on 19 Oct 1808, now convey 160 acres, part of S 7 T 8 R 5, for $600 to Noah JOHNSTON, NBR: William EWERS; WIT: Rebekah GREGG, Wm. SMITH, ack. 25 Feb 1814, Wm. SMITH, J.P., ent. 26 Jul 1814, rec. 29 same.

D-589   Indenture, 18 Jan 1814, Zacheus BIGGS (wife Eliza), Hambleton [Hamilton] County, Ohio; David LOCKWOOD, BCO; $400, SW 1/4 S 20 T 5 R 3; WIT: Michael STOOPS, Sarah PAINTER, ack. 1 Feb 1814, Hamilton County, Ohio, Michael DOBOTT, J.P.

D-590   Indenture, 1 Jul 1814, James McCRARON (wife Bridget), Warren twp., BCO; Andrew McCRARON, BCO; $160, E 1/2 NW 1/4 S 35 T 8 R 6, 67 1/2 acres, fee simple; his seal, her mark, WIT: Wm. C. ANDERSON, James GALLOWAY, ack. 20 Jul 1814, Wm. C. ANDERSON, J.P.

D-591   Indenture, 9 Jul 1814, Joseph WRIGHT (wife Eleanor), BCO; Jacob SWINEHEART, BCO; $40, lots #60 and #61 in town of Belmont each containing 28 rods; WIT: John VANLAW, Nathan PUSEY, ack. 20 Jul 1814, Wm. SMITH, J.P., ent. 28 Jul 1814, rec. 2 Aug same.

D-592   Indenture, 7 d 7 m 1814, John WITCHELL (wife Mary), Richland twp., BCO; John LIST, Wheeling twp., BCO; $440, land in Richland twp. on NW corner of S 1/2 S 24 T 7 R 4, NBR: William McWILLIAMS "and others," 40 acres, same conveyed by Archibald McELROY (wife Sally) to Philip ROSEMAN on 22 Jan 1805, as recorded in Book A, p. 389, part of SE 1/4 of S 30 T 7 R 4 which was patented to Joseph SHARP on 20 Jun 1809, conveyed by SHARP to Jacob REPLOGAL by deed dated 27 Apr 1810, 10 acres conveyed by REPLOGAL,

NBR: James McCOY, John WITCHELL; WIT: Henry JOHNSTON, John WITCHELL, Junr., ack. 7 Jul 1814, Henry JOHNSTON, J.P.

D-593   Ralph HEATH, BCO, patents NE 1/4 S 29 T 7 R 5, Steubenville district, dated 10 Mar 1807, ent. 30 Jul 1814, rec. 4 Aug same.

D-594   Indenture, 7 Apr 1814, Ralph HEATH (wife Elizabeth), BCO; George ADAMS, BCO; $320, NE 1/4 S 29 T __ R 5, Steubenville district, patented 10 Mar 1807; WIT: Ezer ELLIS, John PATTERSON, ack. 7 Apr 1814, John PATTERSON, Assoc. Judge, ent. 30 Jul 1814, rec. 4 Aug same.

D-595   Indenture, 19 Feb 1814, Robert BELL (wife Sarah), BCO; Nathaniel BELL, BCO; $360, part of NW 1/4 S 26 T 8 R 5, patented to Robert BELL, NBR: William WOOD, COLWELL; both mark, WIT: Saml. WILEY, Robert GASTON, ack. Duncan MORRISON, J.P., ent. 1 Aug 1814, rec. 5 same.

D-596   John MILLHORNE [possibly MILLHOUSE?], assignee of Levi PICKERING, patents NW 1/4 S 6 T 9 R 6, Steubenville district; sgn: 1 Jan 1812, ent. 3 Aug 1814, rec. 6 same.

D-596   Indenture, 4 Feb 1814, Isaac MERRIT, BCO; Abraham ENGLE, BCO; MERRIT owes ENGLE 4400, secures payment by selling 82 acres, part of S 27 T 7 R 4, NBR: James BALDRAGE, conveyed to MERRIT by ENGLE on 29 Nov 1813, void if debt paid by 1 Jan 1821; WIT: John BROWN, Sterling JOHNSTON, ack. 4 Mar 1814, Sterling JOHNSTON, J.P., ent. 4 Aug [1814], rec. 8 same.

D-597   Indenture, 8 Nov 1813, William WAGGONER (wife Ann), BCO; John C. AYERS, BCO; $100, lot #90 in Morristown as laid off by William CHAPLIN; his seal, her mark, WIT: Henry BROWN, Jacob [DOWENBERIGER] [DOVENBERGER?], ack. 8 Nov 1813, Duncan MORRISON, J.P., ent. 6 Aug 1814, rec. 8 same.

D-598   Indenture, 8 Nov 1813, William WAGGONER (wife Ann), BCO; John C. AYERS, BCO; $100, lot adjoining Morristown, NBR: Margaret HAZLET, 4 3/4 acres 27 perches, part of land entered by William CHAPLIN and conveyed by him to Leonard HART, conveyed to HART to WAGGONER; his seal, her mark, WIT: Jacob DOVERBERGER [DOVENBERGER?], Henry BROWN, ack. 8 Nov 1813, Duncan MORRISON, J.P., ent. 6 Aug 1814, rec. 8 same.

D-599   Indenture, 8 Jul 1814, Peter YARNALL (wife Lucinda), St. Clairsville, BCO; Levi PICKERING, same; $2,000, lot #61 in St. Clairsville, fee simple; WIT: John PATTERSON, William SHARPLESS, ack. 8 Jul 1814, John PATTERSON, Assoc. Judge, ent. 8 Aug 1814, recorded same.

D-599   Indenture, 18 Feb 1814, Robert BELL (wife Sarah), BCO; Samuel WILEY, BCO; $100, part of NW 1/4 S 26 T 8 R 5, patented to BELL, 20 acres; both mark, WIT: Robert GASTON, Elizabeth MORRISON, ack. Duncan MORRISON, J.P., ent. 10 Aug [1814], recorded 12 same.

D-600   Indenture, 11 Aug 1814, William DIXSON [DIXON] (wife Jane), BCO; David ARMITAGE, Harrison County, Ohio; $20, lot #3 in Union, 1/4 acre, fee simple; WIT: Robert LEE, Robert ROBINSON, ack. Robert LEE, J.P., ent. 13 Aug 1814, rec. 15 same.

D-601   Indenture, 19 May 1814, George SNIDER (wife Barbara), BCO; Aaron SMITH, BCO; SNIDER, assignee of Yosht [ZUKE] patented on 20 Mar 1813 the SW 1/4 S 26 T 7 R 4, Steubenville district, now for $240 conveys 60 acres, fee simple; his seal, her mark, WIT: William SINCLAIR, [Rachel] WILKINSON, ack. 19 May 1814, William SINCLAIR, J.P., ent. 13 Aug 1814, rec. 16 same.

D-602   Indenture, 18 d 2 m 1814, Jacob PICKERING [Senr.] (wife Hannah), BCO; Jacob BARNET, BCO; for $2.75 per acre, beginning at SW corner of S 13 T 9 R 6; WIT: Andrew GARRET, William PARRY, ack. 18 Feb 1814, William DUNN, J.P., ent. 15 Aug 1814, rec. 18 same.

D-603   Indenture, 17 d 2 m 1814, Caleb ENGLE (wife Mercy), BCO; Jacob BARNET, BCO; $4/acre, part of [SW] 1/4 S 13 T 9 R 6, NBR: Jacob BARNET; WIT: William SINCLAIR, Levi PICKERING, ack. 17 Feb 1814, William SINCLAIR, J.P., ent. 15 Aug 1814, rec. 18 same.

D-604   Indenture, 23 Sep 1813, Samuel FAWCETT (wife Rachel), miller, Union twp., BCO; Jacob VANPELT, yeoman, BCO; SE 1/4 S 32 T 9 R 5 patented to James WRIGHT on 15 Aug 1811, WRIGHT granted 51 acres 3 rods 26 perches to Jonathan FAWCETT on 4 Sep 1812, Jonathan conveyed to Samuel on 24 Apr 1813, now Samuel and Rachel for $250, NBR: William HAMBLETON; WIT: John MERCER, Richard MERCER, ack. same date, John MERCER, J.P., ent. 27 aug 1814, rec. 30 same.

D-605   Indenture, 27 Apr 1814, John STANLY (wife Elizabeth), BCO; Tobias MOORE, BCO; $100, part of NW 1/4 S 18 T 6 R 5, Marietta district; his seal, her mark, WIT: George KOON, Jeremiah COOK, ack. same date [name given here as STANLEY] Samuel BERRY, Justice, ent. 27 aug 1814, rec. 31 same.

D-606   Indenture, 27 Apr 1814, John STANLEY (wife Elizabeth), BCO; Mary CAHOON, BCO; $214, part of NW 1/4 S 18 T 6 R 5, Marietta district; his seal, her mark, WIT: George KOON, Jeremiah COOK, ack. same date, Samuel BERRY, Justice, ent. 27 Aug 1814, rec. 31 same.

D-607   Indenture, 20 Jun 1814, James BARNES (wife Nancy), BCO; Camm THOMAS, BCO; $40, lots #35 and #67 in Barnesville, each 1/4 acre, fee simple; his seal, her mark, WIT: Thomas SHANNON, Joel JUDKINS, ack. 20 Jun 1814, Thomas SHANNON, J.P.

D-608   Indenture, 7 Jul 1814, Peter WYRICK (wife Catharine), BCO; Hugh [PIEARCE], BCO; $92, 23 acres 2 rods 27 perches, part of S 14 T 8 R 4, S granted to Jacob COON on 27 Aug 1805, COON conveyed E 1/2 of S to WYRICK on 10 Feb 1808, NBR: James HUNTSMAN, Stephen [MARES]; names signed in what appears to be German script[?], his seal, her mark, WIT: David WALLACE, George ARMSTRONG, ack. 7 Jul 1814, David WALLACE, J.P., Hugh[???] PIERCE comes on 23 Aug 1814 to make his wife Sarah PIERCE sole heir??? of all Real and personal property, before Henry JOHNSTON, J.P., ent. 30 Aug 1814, rec. 8 Sep 1814.

D-609   Indenture, 19 Mar 1814, William DIXON (wife Jane), BCO; Francis SMITH, BCO; $19.55, lot #16 in Union, 1/4 acre; his seal, her mark, WIT: Peter SNEDIKER, George KERR, ack. 19 Mar 1814, Robert LEE, J.P., ent. 2 Sep 1814, rec. 8 same.

D-610   Indenture, 24 Aug 1814, David DRAKE (wife Margaret), BCO; Joshua HATCHER, extr., and Jane NICOLES, now Jane GREG, extx., of Eli NICOLES, dec'd, of BCO; $60, part of NE 1/4 S 29 T 7 R 4, granted to DRAKE on 19 aug 1812, 21 acres 3 rods 32 perches, NBR: Wheeling Creek; his seal, her mark, WIT: John LIST, Henry JOHNSTON, ack. 24 Aug 1814, Henry JOHNSTON, J.P., ent. 3 Sep 1814, rec. 12 same.

D-611   Indenture, 3 Aug 1814, John CARTER (wife Mary), St. Clairsville, BCO; James DOBBINS, late of Mountholly, Burlington County, New Jersey; $1,019.13, land in Union twp., part of SW 1/4 S 15 T 8 R 5, Steubenville district, NBR: Levi PITMAN, Jacob HOLTZ, 101 acres 3 rods 26 poles; WIT: Henry JOHNSTON, [Elam] PATTERSON, ack. 3 Aug 1814, Henry JOHNSTON, J.P., ent. 7 Sep 1814, rec. 12 same.

D-612   Indenture, 3 Aug 1814, Jacob HOLTZ (wife Margaret), BCO; James DOBBINS, late of Mountholly, Burlington, New Jersey; $331.44, in Union twp., part of NW 1/4 S 15 T 8 R 5, Steubenville district, NBR: Levi PITMAN, 33 acres 23 poles; both mark, WIT: Catharine BEARD, Henry ROBERTS, ack. 29 Aug 1814, William DUNN, J.P., ent. 7 Sep 1814, rec. 12 same.

D-613   Indenture, 6 May 1814, David SNYDER, BCO; John ELLIOT [ELLIOTT], BCO; $63.21 1/2, 25 acres 6 rods, agreeable to Robert PLUMMER's survey, SW 1/4 S 36 T 7 R 5, west side of 1/4 S; signed SNIDER, WIT: Wm.

COULSON, Thomas SHANNON, ack. 6 May 1814, Thomas SHANNON, J.P., ent. 8 Sep 1814, rec. 14 same.

D-614   Indenture, 19 d 7 m 1814, James BARNES (wife Nancy), BCO; Joel JUDKINS, BCO; $60, lot #3 near Barnesville, on waters of Stillwater, NBR: Joseph TAYLOR, 5 acres; his seal, her mark, WIT: Thomas SHANNON, Samuel BARNES, ack. 19 Jul 1814, Thomas SHANNON, J.P., ent. 8 Sep 1814, rec. 14 same.

D-615   Indenture, 4 d 6 m 1814, Demsey BOSWELL (wife Mary), BCO; John [MICHEM, MICHENS], BCO; $1,000, 40 acres, part of S 14 T 8 R 6, also 20 1/4 acres, part of S 13 T 8 R 6; his seal, her mark, WIT: Thomas SHANNON, John STEWART, ack. 21 Jun 1814, Thomas SHANNON, J.P., ent. 10 Sep 1814, rec. 15 same.

D-617   Indenture, 29 Aug 1814, George ATKINSON (wife Sarah), formerly the wife of and now the legal representative of Isaac IRWIN, deceased), BCO; William BOOKER, BCO; $75, lots #107, #115, #123 in St. Clairsville, total of 3/4 acre, fee simple; his seal, her mark, WIT: Thomas MAJOR, Brittian OXLEY, ack. same date, Thomas MAJOR, J.P., ent. 12 Sep 1814, rec. 19 same.

D-618   Indenture, 29 Aug 1814, George ATKINSON (wife Sarah); William BOOKER, BCO; $160, NBR: John LONG, near run now the property of James CALDWELL and near SE corner of CALDWELL's lot, Allen STEWART now the property of David NISWANGER, William MATHERS now the property of Michael GROVES, 5 acres, fee simple; his seal, her mark, WIT: Thomas MAJOR, Brittain OXLEY, ack. same date, Thomas MAJOR, J.P., ent. 12 Sep 1814, rec. 19 same.

J. M. BECKETT, Recorder of County, certifies correct copy of Deed Book Vol. D, as ordered by County Commissioners at Spring Session 1889, sgn: 1 Apr 1890.

End of Vol. D.

4 plats

Deed Abstracts, Belmont County, Ohio
Volume E (Sep 1814 - Oct 1815)

E-1   Indenture, 22 Jan 1813, Thomas LAWSON (wife Mary), BCO; William BROWN, BCO, $100, lot #31 in St. Clairsville, conveyed by William VANCE (wife Mary) on 28 Sep 1804; fee simple; his seal, her mark, WIT: Samuel ISRAEL, Sterling JOHNSTON; ack. 22 Feb 1813, Sterling JOHNSTON, J.P., entered 15 Sep 1814, recorded 21 same, $.59.

E-2   Indenture, 8 d 6 m 1814, John PIGGOTT, Union twp, BCO (wife Sarah) and Nathan PIGGOTT, Peas twp, BCO; Ebenezer PIGGOTT, Union twp; John PIGGOTT, late of Loudon Co., Virginia, dec'd. died seized of lots or 1/4 S's in Ohio granted by United States, not having disposed of said lands by LW&T, John and Nathan each entitled to 1/4 part thereof as heirs at law; $100, 1/4 part of NW 1/4 S 26 T 9 R 5, Steubenville district, patent bearing date 3 Aug 1810, (metes and bounds description), 41 1/2 acres (second entry 81 1/2 acres); WIT: Robert LEE, Jesse FOULKE; ack. 8 Jun 1814 Robert LEE, J.P., ent. 17 Sep 1814, rec. 21 same, .87 1/2.

E-3   Indenture, 14 Sep 1814, Abner BURRIS (wife Margaret [Marget]), JCO; William ASKEW, St. Clairsville, BCO; $180, out lot on south side of St. Clairsville #13 in plan of 15 out lots laid out by Bazaleel WELLS, 5 acres 3 rods 30 perches, conveyed from William ROBINSON by deed dated 28 Oct 1809, recorded Book C, p. 136, fee simple; [signature looks like BURROW], WIT: Robert LEE, ack. Robert LEE, ent. 17 Sep 1814, rec. 21 same.

E-4   Indenture, 23 Jul 1814, Reuben POWELL (wife Doris), BCO; John ADAMS, BCO; $320, SE 1/4 S 11 T 5 R 4, Marietta district; both mark, WIT: Moses WOODS, James POWELL, ack. Isaac MOORE, J.P., ent. 17 Sep 1814, rec. 21 same.

E-5   Indenture, 15 Aug 1814, Henry WOLGAMOTE, Coshockton Co., Ohio; Daniel CONNER, BCO; $180, S 3 T 9 R 6, Steubenville district, patent fully paid, NBR: William GROVES, Moses MILLIGAN, Robert MORRISON, and others, 50 acres, fee simple; WIT: James DALLAS, James MORRISON, ack. D. [MORRSAN], ent. 17 Sep 1814, rec. 21 same.

E-6   Indenture, 19 Aug 1814, Allen STEWART and William IRWIN, admrs. of Isaac IRWIN, deceased; George ATKINSON (wife Sarah, formerly wife of Isaac IRWIN deceased; NBR: John LONG (now property of James CALDWELL near run and near SE corner of LONG's), Allen STEWART (now property of

David NEISWANGER), Wm. MATHERS (now property of Michael GROVES), 5 acres, fee simple; [signed William IRWIN, Jun.], WIT: Henry JOHNSTON, Henry HOSHIER [his mark], ack. Henry JOHNSTON, J.P., for Allen STEWART, Thos. MITCHELL, J.P., for William IRWIN, ent. 17 Sep 1814, rec. 21 same.

E-8   Indenture, 18 Mar 1814, William PIGGOTT (wife Mary), of Loudon County, Virginia; Ebenezer PIGGOTT, BCO; John PIGGOTT, dec'd., late of Loudon County died seized of land in Ohio not disposed of in his LW&T, William PIGGOTT therefore entitled to 1/4 part as heir at law, $100, 1/4 of NW 1/4 S 26 T 9 R 5, Steubenville district, granted to John PIGGOTT, dec'd, by patent dated 3 Aug 1810; [WIT seem to be missing], ack. Loudon Co., Virginia, Charles BINNS, Clerk of Court; verified by Stacey TAYLOR, 18 Mar 1814, ent. 17 Sep 1814, rec. 21 same.

E-9   Indenture, 5 Sep 1814, William BOOKER (wife Patience), BCO; Henry H. EVANS, BCO; $175; NBR: James CALDWELL, David NISWANGER, Michael GROVES, 5 acres, fee simple; WIT: Samuel BOOKER, Henry JOHNSTON, ack. Henry JOHNSTON, J.P., ent. 17 Sep 1814, rec. 22 same.

E-10   Indenture, 14 Sep 1814, William CONGLETON (wife Nancy), Guernsey County, Ohio; Peter KREMER [KRAMER]; $325, lot #81 in St. Clairsville, 1/4 acre; WIT: David FULTON, Sterling JOHNSTON, ack. Sterling JOHNSTON, J.P., entered 17 Sep 1814, rec. 21 same.

E-11   Indenture, 11 May 1814, Alexander GRAY, BCO; William FORGUSON [FERGUSON], BCO; $612, part of S 32 T 7 R 3, granted to Alexander GRAY by patent dated 27 Aug 1807, 102 acres, NBR: David MARSHAL, Alexander GRAY, his mark, WIT: Thomas MAJOR, John MAJOR, Jun.; ack. Thomas MAJOR, J.P., ent. 17 Sep 1814, rec. 21 same.

E-12   Whereas Josiah HEDGES, 22 Apr 1812, judgment of court against Jeremiah BURRIS, BCO, for $293.37, writ of feiri facias issued to county sheriff, goods in that amount to be surrendered, 160 acres put up for sale, part of W 1/2 S 25 T 6 R 3 and SW 1/4 S 19 T 6 R 3 (prior claims of James CALDWELL for ____ hundred and ____ dollars and ____ cents, and John SHEPHERD [SHEPPARD] and Richard SIMMS for ____ hundred and ____ dollars and ____ cents, on 11 Aug property went up for sale in St. Clairsville, John CARTIER [CARTER] was highest bidder at $420, sold by John BROWN, deputy sheriff, 180 acres, W 1/2 S 25 T 6 R 3 and SW 1/4 S 19 T 6 R 3, sgn. 13 Aug 1814 by John BROWN, Deputy Sheriff; WIT: Moses [PUL], ack. John PATTERSON, Esq., assoc judge, ent. 21 Sep 1814, rec. 26 same.

E-13 Indenture, 4 Apr 1814, John ARNEAL (wife Marget); William COWEN, both BCO; $658, part of S 2 T 9 R 5, Steubenville district, NBR: Jacob SNEDEKER, William SHAW, 94 acres, fee simple; his seal, her mark, ack. 11 May 1814, WIT: Robert LEE, ack. Robert LEE, J.P., ent. 21 Sep 1814, rec. 27 same.

E-14 Indenture, 15 Sep 1814, John LIST, BCO; Hugh M. COY, BCO; $200, Richland twp., BCO; $200, Richland twp., NW corner of S 1/2 of S 24, T 7 R 4, NBR: William H. WILLIAMS, 40 acres (same sold by Archibald McELROY [wife Sally] sold by indenture dated 22 Jan 1805, recorded in Book A, p. 389, granted to Philip ROSEMAN [in fee], by ROSEMAN to John MITCHELL on 2 Jun 1809, by MITCHEL to John LIST on 7 d 7 m 1814; another tract in BCO, part of SE 1/4 S 30 T 7 R 4, granted to Joseph SHARP by patent dated 20 Jun 1809, by SHARP to Jacob REPROGAL by deed dated 27 Apr 1810, above 10 acres NBR: James McCOY and MITCHEL, sale void if payment of $200 within two years with interest according to bond dated same; in effect if not paid; WIT: James HEWEY, William FARIS, Sen., ack. 29 Sep 1814, Henry JOHNSTON, J.P., ent. 21 Sep 1814, rec. 28 same. [Note in margin indicates mortgage paid off.]

E-16 Indenture, 30 Jun 1814, Jonas PICKERING (wife Ruth), BCO; John GILSON [GIBSON], state of Pennsylvania; $4,000, 101 acres, part of S 13 T 8 R 4, granted to David BARTON by patent dated 20 Dec 1808, by BARTON and wife [unnamed] by indenture dated 26 May 1810 to Richard TRUAX, by TRUAX and wife [unnamed] by indenture dated 24 Apr 1812 to PICKERING, recorded 13 May 1812, Book D, p. 311; WIT: Jon WEBSTER, Robert LEE, ack. Robert LEE, J.P., ent. [15] Sep, rec. 29 same.

E-17 Indenture, 20 Jun 1814, Joseph MERRITT, BCO; Valentine AULT and William BROWN, BCO; AULT and BROWN to become endorsers for MERRITT at Bank of Wheeling in Virginia for $300, to secure which conveys to them 5 acres 60 perches where he now lives, bought of William FORQUHAR, adjacent to public commons of St. Clairsville, NBR: Moses MOORHEAD, void if MERRITT pays $300 with interest; WIT: Wm. PAINE, Sterling JOHNSTON, ack. 20 Jul 1814, Sterling JOHNSTON, ent. 15 Sep 1814, rec. 29 same.

E-18 Indenture, 15 d 9 m 1814, Sarah FARQUHAR of [Chestnut] County, Pennsylvania, widow and relict of William FARQUHAR late of Wheeling, State of Virginia, deceased; Benjamin FARQUHAR and Amos FARQUHAR, two of late husband's brothers; $700, all real and mixed estate of deceased husband, either in Maryland, Virginia, or Ohio; WIT: Igns. [LEITERER]; ack. 16 Sep 1814, York County, Ignatius LEITNER, J.P.; LEITNER certified by William BARBER, prothonotary of Court of Common Pleas, 16 Sep 1814, ent. 4 Oct 1814, rec. same.

E-19   Indenture, 1 d 10 m 1814, Morton HOWARD (wife Hannah), BCO; William WELCH, BCO; $202.50, all of part of NW 1/4 S 18 T 8 R 6 not included in following described tract containing 50 acres lying in NE corner of said 1/4 S; WIT: Thos. MITCHELL, James [KELVY] [his mark], ack. Thos. MITCHELL, Justice, receipt of money certified same day by Morton HOWARD, ent. 4 Oct 1814, rec. same.

E-20   Indenture, 30 May 1814, George WADDELL (wife Lydia), BCO; James WADDELL, BCO; $163, SW part of SE 1/4 S 17 T 9 R 6, 81 1/2 acres, Steubenville district, 1/8 part granted to George WADDELL by patent dated 20 Mar 1809; his seal, her mark; WIT: Thomas DUNN, ack. Thomas DUNN, J.P., ent. 4 Oct 1814, rec. 6 same.

E-21   Indenture, 13 Aug 1814, Robert PRIOR (wife Jemima), BCO; Samuel WRIGHT, BCO; $150, 22 3/4 acres, part of SE 1/4 S 36 T 6 R 4, conveyed to PRIOR by deed dated 10 Jul 1813, NBR: William WILSON, John DUNGAN; [her seal Jemimeh], WIT: Henry JOHNSTON, John PRIOR, Senior; ack. 19 Aug 1814 of Robert LEE who ack. signing deed, ent. 4 Oct 1814, rec. 6 same.

E-22   Indenture, 28 Apr 1814, James CALDWELL (wife Nancy), St. Clairsville, BCO; Ralph HEATH, same; $300, SW 1/4 S 22 T 8 R 6, Steubenville district, patent to CALDWELL dated 10 May 1811; WIT: John PATTERSON, Wm. BROWN, Junr.; ack. John PATTERSON, Assoc. Judge, ent. 4 Oct 1814, rec. 5 same.

E-24   Indenture, 7 Oct 1814, William DIXON (wife Jane); Caleb DILWORTH; $2,148, NW 1/4 S 31 T 8 R [4], 163 acres, 3 rods, 34 perches, NBR: William McWILLIAMS, Daniel MERRET, 15 acres 9 perches, for this land a patent granted to Daniel MERRITT on 27 Aug 1805, Daniel and Nancy conveyed to Moses MERRITT on 1 Oct 1807, Moses and wife Polly conveyed to DIXON on 1 Mar 1810; his seal, her mark; WIT: Wm. WEBB, Robert LEE; ack. Robert LEE, J.P., ent. 8 Oct 1814, rec. 12 same.

E-25   Indenture, 14 Oct 1814, William McWILLIAMS (wife Polly) BCO; Caleb DILWORTH, Jefferson County, Ohio; $1,640, 163 acres, 3 rods, 34 perches, SW 1/4 S 31 T 8 R 4, patent granted to Daniel MERRITT dated 27 Aug 1805, conveyed to William McWILLIAMS by indenture dated 27 Oct 1807; his seal, her mark; WIT: John STEWART, Daniel MERRITT; ack. Robert LEE, J.P., ent. 17 Oct 1814, rec. 3 Nov same.

E-26   Indenture, 3 Oct 1814, David ARMENTAGE [ARMITAGE], Harrison County, Ohio; William DIXON, BCO; $20, lot #3 in Union, 1/4 acre, sale recorded

Book D, p. 466, fee simple; WIT: Robert LEE, Elisabeth [COEN], ack. Robert LEE, J.P., ent. 17 Oct 1814, rec. 3 Nov same.

E-27   Indenture, 10 Oct 1814, John LILLE [LYLE] (wife Isabella), BCO; William DIXON, BCO; $20, lot #14 in Union, 1/4 acre, sale recorded Book D, p. 466, fee simple, his seal, her mark; WIT: John CAMPBELL, David LYLE; ack. John CAMPBELL, J.P., ent. 17 Oct 1814, rec. 4 Nov same.

E-28   Indenture, 5 Oct 1814, Samuel MILLS, BCO; William DIXON, BCO; $30, lot #1 in Union, 1/4 acre, recorded in Book D, p. 466, fee simple; his seal, WIT: John CAMPBELL, Eli NICHOLS, ack. John CAMPBELL, J.P., ent. 17 Oct 1814, rec. 4 Nov same.

E-29   Indenture, 27 Sep 1814, Hugh McCASKEY (wife Rebeckah), BCO; William DIXON, BCO; $20, lot #[Tenn] in Union, 1/4 acre, recorded Book D, p. 66, fee simple, his seal, her mark; WIT: John CAMPBELL, ack. John CAMPBELL, J.P., ent. 17 Oct 1814, rec. 4 Nov same.

E-30   Indenture, 8 Oct 1814, Francis SMITH (wife Mary), BCO; William DIXON, BCO; $19.59, lot #16 in Union, 1/4 acre, fee simple; his seal, her mark; WIT: John CAMPBELL, Samuel MILLS, ack. John CAMPBELL, JP, ent. 17 Oct 1814, rec. 4 Nov.

E-31   Indenture, 18 May 1814, John THOMPSON (wife Sally), BCO; George [SAUCERMAN], BCO; $70, part of N 1/2 S 12 T 6 R 4, 35 acres; [she signs her name as Sarah], WIT: Notley HAYS, ack. 30 May 1814, Sterling JOHNSTON, JP, ent. 21 Oct 1814, rec. 7 Nov.

E-33   Indenture, 5 d 3 m 1814, John MITCHELL (wife Mary), BCO; William RITCHIE, BCO; $284.40, beginning NW corner of S 1/2 S 36 T 7 R 4, 31 acres 3 rods and 13 perches, land granted to John EDWARDS, Senr., by patent dated 7 Apr 1806, from EDWARDS to John PRICE on 38 May 1806, fee simple; WIT: John LIST, Mary KIMBERLY, ack. 5 Mar 1814, Henry JOHNSTON, JP, ent. 31 Oct 1814, rec. 7 Nov.

E-34   Indenture, 23 Oct 1814, Geo. S. BROCK (wife Catharine), BCO: Benjamin BROCK, BCO; $165, Steubenville district, NW 1/4 S 27 T 9 R 5, 41 1/4 acres; his seal, her mark, WIT: Robert LEE, Mary LEE, ack. Robert LEE, ent. 31 Oct 1814, rec. 7 Nov.

E-35   Indenture, 13 Jul 1814, Robert VERNON (wife Deborah), BCO; Garret ACKERSON, BCO; $230, W part of SE 1/4 S 34 T 7 R 5, 40 acres; WIT: Simon HARY, Mary WHITE, ack. James WHITE, JP, ent. 31 Oct 1814, rec. 8 Nov.

E-36   Indenture, 27 Sep 1814, Bezaleel WELLS (wife Sally), JCO; Moses MEDCALF, BCO; $670, part of S 20 t 7 R 3, NBR: Eli KENNARD, 142 acres; WIT: Alex. SUTHERLAND, Joseph DUNLAP, ack. JCO, Alex. SUTHERLAND, JP, Thomas PATTON, Clerk of Court of Common Pleas, certifies SUTHERLAND, ent. 1 Nov 1814, rec. 8 same.

E-37   Indenture, 4 Jul 1814, Nathan SIDWELL (wife Rebekah), Warren twp., BCO; Abraham ACKERSON, BCO; $600, SE 1/4 S 5 T 8 R 6; his seal, her mark, WIT: Joel JUDKINS, John GILL, ack. Thomas SHANNON, JP; ent. 31 Oct 1814, rec. 8 Nov same.

E-38   Indenture, 22 Oct 1814, Jacob LOY (wife Christina), BCO; Elisabeth HOOVER, BCO; $150, beginning NE corner James JOHNSTON's land, corners with land formerly belonging to David VANCE and Robert HOPPER, three acres, conveyed from James JOHNSTON and (wife [Jany]) to Charles FRYMAN on 25 Mar 1805, from FRYMAN (wife Mary) to LOY on 28 Aug 1806; his seal, her mark, no WIT, ack. Sterling JOHNSTON, JP, ent. 1 Nov 1814, rec. 8 same.

E-39   Indenture, 1 Oct 1814, John BELL (wife Hannah), BCO; Levi KENNARD, BCO; whereas Jane VANWEY of BCO on 2 Apr 1812 by indenture sold to BELL a tract of land, part of S 20 T 7 R 3, for [Teen] dollars sell to KENNARD part of S 20 T 7 R 3, NBR: Joseph GIBBON (or GIBBONS), Moses MEDCALF, 103 acres "one hundred .. forty five perches"; his seal, her mark, WIT: Thomas MAJOR, James CAVEN, ack. Thomas MAJOR, JP, ent. 2 Nov 1814, rec. 9 same.

E-41   Indenture, 18 Nov 1814, Conrad NEFF (wife Elisabeth), BCO; Jacob NEFF, <u>Alegany</u> County, Maryland; for 75 acres of land conveyed by Jacob, convey to Jacob part of S 20 T 6 R 3, 76 acres, granted to Conrad by patent dated 7 Jan 1808, fee simple; his seal, her mark, WIT: Sterling JOHNSTON, David MOORE, ack. Sterling JOHNSTON, JP, ent. 18 Nov, rec. same.

E-42   Know all people, Zaccheus BIGGS (wife Eliza) of Brook County, Virginia, for $1,000 paid by David CREAMER [CREMER] of Baltimore County, Maryland, SE 1/4 S 32 T 5 R 3 and SE 1/4 S 27 T 5 R 3, Steubenville district, sgn: 20 Apr 1812, WIT: Joseph DORSEY, J. G. HINING, ack. JCO, 21 Apr 1812, J. G. HINING, JP, ent. 18 Nov 1814, rec. 21 same.

E-43   Indenture, 19 May 1814, James BARNES (wife Nancy), BCO; Henry DOUDNA, BCO; $40, lots #24 and #120, each 1/4 acre, fee simple; his seal, her mark, WIT: Josiah PENNINGTON, Thomas SHANNON, ack. 20 May 1814, Thomas SHANNON, JP, ent. 22 Nov 1814, rec. same.

E-44   Indenture, 19 Nov 1814, Johnathan [Jonathan] MILLER (wife Sarah), BCO; William HENDERSON, Junior, BCO; $480, part of S 23 T 7 R 4, NBR: George KELLAR, 60 acres, part of S granted to John HOPKINS by Samuel OSGOOD and Walter LIVINGSTONE by patent dated 3 Mar 1789; WIT: Sterling JOHNSTON, John LIST, ack. Sterling JOHNSTON, JP.

E-46   Indenture, 19 Nov 1814, Johnathan [Jonathan] MILLER (wife Sarah), BCO; William HENDERSON, Junior, BCO; $480, parcel of land in T 7 R 4, NBR: George KELLAR, Joseph IRWIN, 60 acres, part of NE 1/4 S 24, granted to John HOPKINS by Samuel OSGOOD and Walter LIVINGSTON, commissioners of the board of treasury of the United States by patent dated 3 Mar 1789, sold by George MILLER, attorney for Stephen MILLER to William DEVLIN and Neal MAHON on 4 Sep 1800, fee simple; WIT: Sterling JOHNSTON, John LIST, ack. Sterling JOHNSTON, JP, ent. 22 Nov 1814, rec. 24 same.

E-47   Indenture, 19 Nov 1814, William HENDERSON, Junior, BCO; Jonathan MILLER, BCO; $960, land in S 23, T 7 R 4, NBR: George KELLAR, 60 acres, Joseph [ERWIN], 60 acres, void if HENDERSON pays MILLER $560 according to bond of same date; WIT: Sterling JOHNSTON, John LIST, ack. JOHNSTON, ent. 22 Nov 1814, rec. 25 same.

E-49   Indenture, 12 d 9 m 1814, Amos FARQUHAR of York town Pennsylvania, Allen FARQUHAR and Jonah FARQUHAR of Frederick County, Maryland, and James FARQUHAR of Loudon County, Virginia, heirs and representatives of William FARQUHAR late of Wheeling, Virginia, deceased; Benjamin FARQUHAR of Clinton County, Ohio; $3,000, 400 acres, conveyed to William by Josiah UPDEGRAFF by deed [undated here]; WIT: Belt BREASHEAR, Ezra [MARITZ, MANTZ], ack. Frederick Co., Maryland, Belt BREASHEAR and Ezra [MARITZ, MANTZ], JPs, certified 12 Sep 1814 by William RITCHIE, Clerk, Frederick County Court, ent. 22 Nov 1814, rec. 20 same.

E-50   Indenture, 29 Nov 1813, Abraham ENGLE, BCO; Isaac MERRITT [MERIT], BCO; $492, NBR: James BALANGER, 82 acres, S 27 T 7 R 4, part of tract conveyed to ENGLE [by] George MILLER, attorney for Stephen MILLER on 12 Nov 1802, fee simple; WIT: Sterling JOHNSTON, William BROWN, ack. Sterling JOHNSTON, ent. 22 Nov 1814, rec. 30 same.

E-51   Indenture, 21 Apr 1814, Alice CLOYD (widow and relict of James CLOYD, deceased), BCO; Joseph JOHNSTON, BCO; $643, W 1/2 lot #16 in St. Clairsville, 1/8 acre; WIT: John BERRY, Sterling JOHNSTON, ack. JOHNSTON, ent. 26 Nov 1814, rec. 3 Dec same.

E-52   Indenture, 30 Nov 1814, Jonathan ELLIS (wife Lydia), BCO; John
BEATY, Loudon County, Virginia; $640, SW 1/4 S 3 T 10 R 6, Steubenville
district, granted to Joshua WOODRAM, Junior, by patent dated 10 Dec 1808; WIT:
[Is] GRIMES, Joseph DOUGLASS, ack. Robert LEE, JP, ent. 3 Dec 1814, rec.
same.

E-53   Indenture, 2 Dec 1814, Rees BRANSON (wife Ruth), Flushing, BCO;
Joseph DOUGLASS, Loudon County, Virginia; $300, lots #21, 41, and 42, out lot
#1 in Flushing, NBR: Mary FAWCETT, Grace BAIRS, 2 acres; WIT: Robert LEE,
James BEALY, ack. Robert LEE, JP, ent. 3 Dec 1814, rec. same.

E-54   Indenture, 22 Apr 1814, Joseph JOHNSTON (wife Ann), BCO; John
NICHOLS, BCO; $700, W 1/2 lot #16 in St. Clairsville, 1/8 acre, conveyed from
Alice CLOYD to JOHNSTON on 21 Apr 1814; his seal, her mark, WIT: Sterling
JOHNSTON, Wm. PERINE, ack. Sterling JOHNSTON, JP, ent. 3 Dec 1814, rec.
same.

E-56   Indenture, 25 Nov 1814, Wm. FARIS, Senr., BCO; Ira ROBINSON,
BCO; $200, lot #109 in St. Clairsville, where Wm. FARIS, Senr., now lives;
ROBINSON stands bound in a written obligation with FARIS to Wm. BOOKER
for $200, payable 1 Apr 1815, this void if repayment is made; WIT: Wm. FARIS,
Junr., Wm. BOOKER, ack. Henry JOHNSTON, JP, ent. 3 Dec 1814, rec. 6 same.

E-57   Indenture, 1 d 8 m 1814, Isaac PARKER (wife Sarah) and Jacob PARKER
(wife Faith), of Jefferson and Harrison Counties, Ohio; Emmor BAILEY, BCO;
$6,797.50, NBR: Merrick STARR, 194 3/4 acres and 40 perches, part of S 3 T 7
R 3; 25 acres, part of tracts of land conveyed by Horton HOWARD and Thomas
MITCHELL to William MILLHOUSE, by MILLHOUSE to HOWARD again, by
HOWARD (wife Hannah) to PARKERs by deed dated 1 d 1 m 1810; WIT: Henry
LEWIS, Abner MOORE, ent. 5 Dec 1814, rec. 7 same, ack. 1 Aug 1814, JCO, John
WATSON, JP, WATSON certified by Thos. PATTON, Clk.

E-58   Know all men, Josiah UPDEGRAFF (wife Eliza), then of Wheeling,
Virginia; Benjamin FARQUAR (wife Rachel) of Clinton County, Ohio, Amos
FARQUAR (wife Mary) of York County, Pennsylvania, Allen FARQUAR (wife
Mary) of Frederick County, Maryland, Jonah FARQUHAR (wife Elisabeth), of
Frederick County, Maryland, and James FARQUAR of Loudon County, Virginia,
Benjamin, Amos, Allen, Jonah, and James are brothers and heirs at law of William
FARQUAR late of Wheeling, Ohio County, Virginia, $1, sell to John CARTER of
St. Clairsville lots conveyed to UPDEGRAFF, FARQUAR and CARTER by
KENNEDY and CALHOON of Baltimore, to John CARTER; Josiah
UPDEGRAFF (wife Eliza) agree with John CARTER, sgn. 1 Sep 1814; WIT: Ezra
MANTZ, Belt BRASHEAR, ack. 12 Sep 1814, Frederick County, Maryland, of

Benjamin, Amos, Allen, Jonah, and James FARQUAR, by Ezra MANTZ and Belk BRASHEAR, certified by William RITCHIE, Clerk, ent. 5 Dec 1814, rec. 7 same; ack. Belmont Co., Ohio, 22 Nov 1814, Sterling JOHNSTON, JP.

E-60   Indenture, 28 d 11 m 1814, Jesse FOULKE, one of the proprietors of Flushing in BCO (wife Sarah); Rees BRANSON, same town; $119, lots #21, 41, 42, 40, and out lot #1 in Flushing, NBR: Mary FAWCETT, Grace BAIRS, 2 acres; WIT: Robert LEE, Enos PICKERING, B.S., ent. 5 Dec 1814, rec. 9 same, ack. 28 Nov 1814, Robert LEE, JP.

E-6???   Indenture, 8 Oct 1814, Robert BELL (wife Mary), Colerain twp., BCO; Abner BARTON, late of Chester County, Pennsylvania, now Colerain twp., BCO; $2,500, plantation where Robert and Mary now reside, 100 acres, part of S 24 T 6 R 3, granted to Robert JOHNSTON by patent dated 17 Apr 1788, recorded in patent book A, folio 52, JOHNSTON conveyed to Obediah HARDESTY by deed dated 31 Jan 1794, HARDESTY conveyed to Henry LINGO by deed dated 7 Mar 1796, recorded in JCO Book A, folio 119; LINGO (wife Rebecca) conveyed to BELL by deed dated 13 Oct 1800 (recorded BCO Book A, folio first); his seal, her mark, WIT: Thomas MAJOR, Samuel POTTS, certification of receipt of $2,500 by Robert BELL, WIT: Thomas MAJOR, ack. Thomas MAJOR, JP, ent. 6 Dec 1814, rec. 9 same.

E-64   Indenture, 1 d 12 m 1814, Samuel POTTS (wife Mary), BCO; Job RIDGEWAY, BCO; $1,000, S 13 T 7 R 3, NBR: late Joseph SATTERTHEWAIT, late Samuel POTTS but now Josiah UPDEGRAFF, land late Joseph SATTERTHEWAIT, land late Thomas SATTERTHEWAIT, 96 acres 1 rod 6 perches, part of tract devised to William SATTERTHEWAIT, Junr., by the LW&T of his father William SATTERTHEWAIT, deceased, conveyed by William SATTERTHEWAIT, Junr., to POTTS by deed dated 24 d 6 m 1809, recorded Book C, p. 116; WIT: David MOORE, Sterling JOHNSTON, receipt of $1,000 ack. by Samuel POTTS, ack. 6 Dec 1814, Sterling JOHNSTON, JP, ent. 7 Dec 1814, rec. 10 same.

E-65   Indenture, 14 Jul 1814, Joshua HATCHER, extr., and Jane NICHOLS (now Jane GREG), extx of Eli NICHOLS deceased of BCO; James HAWTHORN, BCO; $80.50, part of SE 1/4 S 30 T 7 R 4, granted to Joseph SHARP by patent dated 20 Jun 1809, SHARP conveys 1/4 S to Jacob REPROGAL by deed dated 27 Apr 1810, REPLOGAL conveyed to Eli NICHOLS deceased by deed dated 20 Jun 1810, NBR: road leading from St. Clairsville to Flushing meeting house, James WATT; WIT: William SINCLAIR, Alice SINCLAIR, ack. William SINCLAIR, JP, ent. 9 Dec 1814, rec. 10 same.

E-67   Indenture, 7 d 6 m 1814, Ebenezer PIGGOT (wife Lydia), Union twp., BCO, and Nathan PIGGOT, Peas twp., BCO; John PIGGOT, Union twp., BCO; John PIGGOT late of Loudon County, Virginia, dec'd, died seized of lots or 1/4 Ss in BCO, not disposed of in his will so Ebenezer PIGGOT and Nathan PIGGOT entitled to 1/4 as heirs at law and William PIGGOT (wife Mary), one of heirs at law residing in Loudon County, Virginia, by indenture dated 18 Mar 1814 conveyed their 1/4 part to Ebenezer PIGGOT; Ebenezer PIGGOT (wife Lydia) and Nathan PIGGOTT for $100 each from John PIGGOT, 1/2 NW 1/4 S 26 T 9 R 5, Steubenville district, 83 acres, 1/4 S land granted to John PIGGOT, dec'd, by patent dated 3 Aug 1810; Ebenezer and Nathan seal, Lydia's mark, WIT: Jesse FOULKE, Robert LEE, ack. 8 Jun 1814, Robert LEE, JP, ent. 9 Dec 1814, rec. 12 same.

E-68   Indenture, 8 jun 1814, Ebenezer PIGGOT (wife Lydia), Union twp., BCO, and Nathan PIGGOTT, Peas twp., BCO; John PIGGOTT, Union twp., BCO; [same history as preceding], $100 each, SE 1/4 S 2 T 10 R 6, Steubenville district, granted to John PIGGOTT of Loudon deceased by patent dated 18 Jul 1812; Ebenezer and Nathan seal, Lydia's mark; WIT: Jesse FOULKE, Robert LEE, ack. Robert LEE, JP, receipt for $200 certified, ent. 9 Dec 1814, rec. 12 same.

E-70   Indenture, 18 Mar 1814, William PIGGOTT (wife Mary), Loudon County, Virginia; John PIGGOTT, BCO; [same history as preceding], $100, 1/4 part of SE 1/4 S 2 T 10 R 6, Steubenville district; no WIT, ack. Loudon Co., Virginia, Charles BINNS, clerk, William and Mary appeared in open court; Stacy TAYLOR certifies BINNS attestation, ent. 9 Dec [1814], rec. 12 same.

E-71   Know all men, Isaac VORE of Mount Vernon, Knox Co., Ohio, and Mahlon SMITH of St. Clairsville, BCO, $1 paid by George THOMPSON of St. Clairsville, lot #68 in St. Clairsville, conveyed by Josiah HEDGES, Sheriff, by judgement against William MATHERS to VORE and SMITH by indenture dated 17 Apr 1807, sgn: 5 Aug 1814; seals: Isaac VORE, Eleanor VORE, Mahlon SMITH, Mary SMITH, WIT: (VOREs) Samuel KRATZER, John JOHNSTON; (SMITHs) Saml. SPRIGG, Lewis [NEILE], ack. (VOREs) Knox Co., Ohio, 5 Aug 1814, Saml. KRATZER, Assoc. Judge; ack. (SMITHs), BCO, 23 Nov 1814, John PATTERSON, Assoc. Judge, ent. 10 Dec 1814, rec. 13 same.

E-72   Know all men, David MOORE (Sheriff, BCO) by writ of Fecia Facius issued out of Court of Common Pleas at St. Clairsville, 18 Oct 1814 on judgment rendered in court at suit of president, directors, and company of bank of Steubenville, to seize enough property of George THOMPSON, Charles HAMMOND, and Samuel SPRIGG sum of $770.80 damages with interest from 23 Jun Jun 1814, plus $8.15 costs, sale at public vendue, purchased by John INSKEEP of St. Clairsville for $1,080, sold half lot #68 in St. Clairsville, sgn: 24 Nov 1814,

WIT: John M. GOODENOW, James ALEXANDER, ack. James ALEXANDER, Assoc. Judge, ent. 10 Dec 1814, rec. 13 same.

E-74   Indenture, 25 Nov 1814, George THOMPSON, Samuel SPRIGG, and Charles HAMMOND [no location given]; John INSKEEP, BCO, $1,080, E 1/2 lot #68, fee simple; WIT: Geo. PAULL, Sterling JOHNSTON, ack. Sterling JOHNSTON, JP, ent. 10 Dec 1814, rec. 13 same.

E-75   Indenture, 27 May 1813, Stephen MILLER, city, county, and state of New York, merchant, by George MILLER, his attorney, by virtue of power granted to George in a letter of Attorney bearing date 15 Jan 1807, ack. before Daniel D. TOMPKINS, one of the Justices of the supreme court of state of New York; John DILLIE, BCO; $880, S 36 T 1 R 2, NBR: David LOCKWOOD, 440 acres plus surplus after deducting 200 acres on N side of S to belong to DILLIE; Stephen MILLER by atty. George MILLER, WIT: Valentine SAUERHEBER, James DAVIS, ack. BCO, York twp., Valentine SAUERHEBER, ent. 14 Dec 1814, rec. same.

E-76   Indenture, 12 Dec 1814, John DILLIE (wife Margaret), BCO; John THOMPSON, BCO; $8,000, 238 1/4 acres, whole of S 29 and part of S 35, T 1, R 2, NBR: land sold by DILLIE to David LANCE, conveyed by Absolem MARTIN to DILLIE on 16 Sep 1796; another piece of land, NBR: David LOCKWOOD, 440 acres, surplus after 200 acres on south side of section to belong to John THOMPSON, conveyed to George MILLER by Stephen MILLER by deed dated 15 Nov 1811, last tract conveyed to DILLIE by George MILLER attorney for Stephen MILLER of New York on 27 May 1813, fraction of S 36 T 1 R 2, 61 1/2 acres, fee simple; his seal, her mark, WIT: Andw. WHITE, Sterling JOHNSTON, ack. 14 Dec 1814, Sterling JOHNSTON, JP, ent. 14 Dec 1814, rec. same.

E-78   Know all men, John THOMPSON, BCO, owing to John DILLIE, BCO, $4,000, to be paid four years and four months from the date hereof (12 Apr 1819), to secure payment conveys 238 1/4 acres S 20 and part of S 35 T 1 R 2, NBR: land DILLIE sold to David LANCE, stones marked L.D. and S.D., stone marked I.D., also 440 acres, NBR: David LOCKWOOD, void if $4,000 paid on or before 12 Apr 1819, sgn: 12 Dec 1814, WIT: David LOCKWOOD, Sterling JOHNSTON, ack. Sterling JOHNSTON, JP, ent. 14 Dec 1814, rec. same; released 5 May 1817, John DILLE, WIT: Wm. FARIS [Junr.] Recorder.

E-79   Indenture, 18 Aug 1814, Wm. C. ANDERSON (wife Agnes), Warren twp., BCO; Robert MAKMSON, JCO; $400, E 1/2 SE S 29 R 6 T 8, 81 acres, fee simple; his seal, her mark, WIT: John N. SMITH, John J. SMITH, ack. John N. SMITH, JP, ent. 17 Dec 1814, rec. 19 same.

E-80   Indenture, 18 Jul 1813, Abraham DEVER (wife Elizabeth), BCO; Levi PICKERING, BCO; $1,100, part of S 13 T 9 R 5, 110 acres, fee simple; his seal, her mark, WIT: John MERCER, Peter TALLMAN, ack. John MERCER, JP, ent. 17 Dec 1814, rec. 20 same.

E-81   Indenture, 26 Oct 1814, John VANPELT (wife Mary), BCO; Darling CONROW, BCO; $180, 50 acres, S 13 T 9 R 5, plus 11 acres 2 rods 5 perches in S 19 T 9 R 5, totaling 61 acres 2 rods 5 poles, NBR: (second piece) George CARPENTER, John VANPELT, fee simple; his seal, her mark; WIT: Peter TALLMAN, Alexander HARAH, ack. William DUNN, JP, WIT: 21 Dec 1814, rec. same.

E-82   Indenture, 9 Sep 1814, John GILSON, West Mooreland County, Pennsylvania; Jonas PICKERING, BCO; GILSON bound to PICKERING for $2,400 in three bonds dated same to be repaid beginning 1 Jan 1815 to 1 Jan 1817, secured by 101 acres 104 perches, part of S 13 T 8 R 4, same granted by Jonas PICKERING (wife Ruth) conveyed to GILSON on 30 Jun 1814, void if payments made, WIT: Sterling JOHNSTON, William SMITH, ack. Sterling JOHNSTON, JP, ent. 21 Dec 1814, rec. 22 same; mortgage satisfied 21 Jan 1818 by Aaron LYLE of Washington County, [Pennsylvania].

E-84   Indenture, 23 Aug 1814, James FURGUSON, BCO; David DRAKE, BCO; $514, 139 1/4 acres 7 perches, part of NE 1/4 S 29 T 7 R 4, granted to David DRAKE by patent dated 19 Aug 1812, void if FURGASON pays $514 on schedule, beginning 15 May 1815 and ending 1819; WIT: John LIST, Hugh McCOY, ent. 21 Dec 1814, rec. 23 same; David DRAKE ack. mortgage satisfied 8 Jul 1818, WIT: Wm. FARIS, Junr., Recorder.

E-86   Indenture, George MILLER, Senr. (wife Hannah); Thomas MILLER, part of NW 1/4 S 28 T 9 R 6, BCO, 20 acres, NBR: Francis HALL, Thomas's dowry, sgn: 8 Oct 1814; WIT: John N. SMITH, Samuel O. DUNN, ack. John N. SMITH, ent. 23 Dec 1814, rec. 26 same.

E-87   Indenture, 8 Oct 1814, George MILLER, Junr., BCO; George MILLER, Senr., BCO; $320, NW 1/4 S 28 T 9 R 6; WIT: John N. SMITH, Thomas MILLER, Samuel DUNN, ack. John N. SMITH, ent. 23 Dec 1814, rec. 27 same.

E-88   Know all men, Joseph JOHNSTON, BCO; bound to Alice CLOYD, extx, and Loyd TALBERT, extr., of James CLOYD, deceased, in two written obligations dated 23 Apr 1814, $125 each payable at sundry times, also a judgment before H. JOHNSTON, Esqr., conveying lot #49 in St. Clairsville, void if debts repaid; sgn: 22 Apr 1814, WIT: Wm. PERRINE, Sterling JOHNSTON, ack. Sterling

JOHNSTON, JP; TALBOTT, extr. of Jas. CLOYD, dec'd, ack. satisfaction of mortgage [sadly, undated].

E-89   Indenture, 28 Dec 1814, Moses MOOREHEAD (wife Anne), BCO; George PAULL, BCO; $6,000, five lots totaling 78 1/2 acres, adjoining public common on south side of St. Clairsville, part of S 4 T 7 R 4, granted to Bazaleel WELLS by U.S., by WELLS to David NEWELL and James E. NEWELL and Abraham LASH (with wives Sally, Elisabeth, and Mary) conveyed to Michael GROVES, James CALDWELL, and Moses MOOREHEAD; James CALDWELL and Michael GROVES conveyed their parts of land to MOOREHEAD; Abraham LASH (wife Mary) on 26 Sep 1808 by deed to 60 acres, Michael GROVES (wife Elisabeth), 23 May 1805 by deed to 10 acres 6 perches, James CALDWELL on 26 Oct 1803 by deed to 3 1/2 acres and 25 perches, James E. NEWELL (wife Elizabeth) on 28 Nov 1805 by deed to 3 1/2 acres, David NEWELL (wife Sally) on 25 Feb 1804 by deed to 2 acres 1 rod and 11 perches, totaling 78 1/2 acres; beginning at MOOREHEAD's sheep pen, fee simple; WIT: Elisabeth MOOREHEAD, Sterling JOHNSTON, ack. Sterling JOHNSTON, JP, ent. 27 Dec [1814], rec. 28 same; George PAULL states 4-5 acres of land belonged to a FOULKE, got $200 back from MOOREHEAD because of taking of land, sgn: 21 Feb 1821, WIT: Wm. BAGGS, ent. 21 Feb 1821.

E-91   Indenture, 24 Aug 1814, David DRAKE (wife Margaret), BCO; James FORGUSON, BCO; $1,114, 139 1/4 acres 7 perches, part of NE 1/4 S 29 T 7 R 4, granted to David DRAKE by patent dated 19 Aug 1812; his seal, her mark, WIT: John LIST, Henry JOHNSTON, ack. 24 Aug 1814, Henry JOHNSTON, JP, ent. 3 Jan 1815, rec. same.

E-93   Indenture, 28 Dec 1814, Geo. PAULL, BCO; Moses MOREHEAD, BCO; PAULL sold 78 1/2 acres whereon MOREHEAD now lives, same conveyed to Abraham LASH and wife, David NEWELL and wife, James E. NEWELL and wife, Michael GROVES and wife, and James CALDWELL to MOOREHEAD; PAULL indebted to MOREHEAD, $3,000 (balance of purchase money), void if paid by 1 Dec 1817, without interest, WIT: Elisabeth MOOREHEAD, Sterling JOHNSTON, mortgage satisfied by 19 Oct 1816, WIT: C. HAMMOND, ack. date of indenture, Sterling JOHNSTON, JP, ent. 7 Jan 1815, rec. 11 same.

E-94   Indenture, 31 Dec 1814, Micheal CARROLL (wife Sally), BCO; David McCLELAND, BCO, $162, part of S 12 T 7 R 4, 81 acres 20 perches, fee simple; WIT: David VANCE, Sterling JOHNSTON, ack. 10 Jan 1815, Sterling JOHNSTON, JP, ent. 14 Jan 1815, rec. 20 same; "This Deed was given for two acres and 1/3 more than the amount in the tract for which Michael CARROLL has paid the original price with interest thereon, Nov. 24th 1852, David McCLELAND, the above receipt entered for recording Sept. 5, 1833, and recorded the same day.

E-95   Indenture, 13 Jan 1815, John THOMPSON (wife Sally), BCO; John WINTER, BCO; $3,000, three lots in St. Clairsville, #12, 13, and 11, granted and conveyed to THOMPSON by Jacob HOLTZ (wife Margaret), 7 Jul 1811, recorded Book D, p. 707; fee simple; wife seals as Sarah, WIT: Joseph MARTIN, Sterling JOHNSTON, ack. Sterling JOHNSTON, JP, ent. 18 Jan 1815, rec. 20 same.

E-97   Know all men, Thomas PERKINS, BCO, for love, goodwill, and affection towards loving and dutiful son Samuel PERKINS, BCO, convey NE 1/4 S 17 T 9 R 6, son to have possession after death of father, sgn [his mark]: 18 Jan 1815, WIT: Henry JOHNSTON, Stephen WILSON, Wm. FARIS, Junr., ack. Henry JOHNSTON, JP, ent. 18 Jan 1815, rec. 21 same.

E-98   Indenture, 20 Jan 1815, John INSKEEP [wife Mary] of St. Clairsville, BCO; John HINDS, same; $100, fee simple, lot #96 in St. Clairsville, NBR: John HINDS' line, same conveyed to James CALDWELL by David NEWALL on 28 Sep 1803, CALDWELL and wife to INSKEEP on 4 Apr 1809, fee simple; WIT: Henry JOHNSTON, Ira ROBINSON, ack. Henry JOHNSTON, JP, ent. 20 Jan 1815, rec. 21 same.

E-99   Indenture, 26 Dec 1814, Jacob NEFF (wife Margaret), Alegany County, Maryland; Conrad NEFF, BCO; for 76 acres, part of S 20 T 6 R 3, conveyed by Conrad NEFF (wife Elizabeth), granted to Jacob by patent dated 1 Oct 1806, fee simple; his seal, her mark, WIT; Jno. SCOTT, Chas. [F.] BRODHOG, ack. Allegany County, Maryland, Jno. SCOTT and Chas. F. BRODHOG, JPs; John SCOTT and Charles F. BRODHOG certified by Hanson BRISCOE, Clk., ent. 21 Jan 1815, rec. 23 same.

E-100   Indenture, 12 Aug 1814, Jacob RILEY (wife Sally), Licking County, Ohio; Abraham KINNEY, BCO; $200, part of S 20 T 8 R 5, NBR: Abner MURPHY, 28 1/2 acres some perches, conveyed from William CHAPLAIN (wife Mary) to Leonard HART, Senr., 25 Jun 1808, from HART, Senr., (wife Jemima) to William WGAULT, 23 Aug 1808, from WGAULT (wife Sarah) to RILEY, 1 Jun 1812; his seal, her mark, WIT: David JOHNSTON, Silas WINCHEL, ent. 28 Jan 1814 [probably 15], rec. 25 same, ack. Licking County, Ohio, Silas WINCHEL, JP, Stephen McDOUGAL, Clerk of CCP, certifies WINCHEL, sgn: 14 Jan 1815.

E-102   Indenture, 12 Aug 1814, Jacob RILEY (wife Sally), Licking County, Ohio; Abraham KINNEY, BCO; $1,000, lots #19 and 20 laid out by William CHAPLAIN, conveyed from CHAPLAIN (wife Mary) to William WGAULT 27 Jun 1808, from WGAULT (wife Sarah) to RILEY on 1 Jun 1812; his seal, her mark; WIT: David JOHNSTON, Silas WINCHEL, ack. Licking Co., Ohio, Silas

WINCHEL, JP; WINCHEL certified 14 Jan 1815, by Stephen McDOUGAL, Clk., ent. 23 Jan 1815, rec. 25 same.

E-103   Whereas register of land office at Steubenville on 9 Oct 1811 granted certificate to Abraham SNYDER of BCO certifying entitlement to a patent for SE 1/4 S 26 T 9 R 6, SNYDER conveys certificate to John BEARD for $100, sgn: 13 Sep 1814, his seal "Iabrajam TWNNURE," WIT: Isaac MERRITT, Sterling JOHNSTON, ack. 30 Sep 1814, Sterling JOHNSTON, JP, ent. 4 Feb 1815, rec. 7 same.

E-104   Indenture, 16 Jan 1815, Robert WILSON, Junr., (wife Ruth), BCO; Abner BARTON, BCO; $1,000, NW corner S 24 T 6 R 3, NBR: HARRIS on Wheeling Creek, McMILLIN, Robert THOMAS, Robert BELL, 227 acres 3 rods and 24 perches, same land conveyed to Samuel SPRIGG by Peter [HANIFOLD or HARRIFOLD], agent for heirs of John D. MERCIER by deed dated 6 Feb 1811, conveyed by SPRIGG (wife Amelia) to WILSON by deed dated 27 Apr 1813, fee simple; WIT: Robert WILSON, Sterling JOHNSTON, ack. Sterling JOHNSTON, JP, ent. 6 Feb 1815, rec. 9 same.

E-105   Indenture, 5 Jan 1815, Samuel IDEN (wife Elisabeth), Bucks County, Pennsylvania, yeoman; Abner BARTON, Colerain twp., BCO, yeoman; $2,763, Steubenville district, part of S 19 T 7 R 3, NBR: Thomas BLACKLEDGE, Thomas SATTERTHWAIT, 307, same conveyed by Bazaleel WELLS (wife Sally) to IDEN on 7 May 1810, recorded Book C, p. 227; WIT: Wm. WATTS, A. CHAPMAN, money received, WIT: Owen DEWEES, Jesse PYLE; ack. 7th District of Pennsylvania, Robert SMITH, Presiding Judge; Bucks Co., Pennsylvania, William WATTS certified Robert SMITH, prothonotary of Bucks Co., Pennsylvania, ent. 6 Feb 1815, rec. 15 same.

E-107   Know all men, Abraham KINNEY, Richland, BCO, for $300 conveyed to Jacob RILEY of Granville, Licking Co., Ohio, part of S 20 T 8 R 5, NBR: Abner MURPHEY, 28 1/2 acres some perches; also lots 19 and 20 in Morristown, BCO, fee simple; sgn: 12 Aug 1814 at Granville, void if KINNEY pays off notes, WIT: David JOHNSON, Silas WINCHEL, ack. Licking County, Ohio, Silas WINCHEL, JP, ent. 10 Feb 1815, rec same.

E-109   Know all men, William SHARPLESS, BCO, for $7,000 convey to Andrew PATTERSON, NW 1/2 S 9 T 6 R 3, 160 acres, same granted to Robert GIFFEN by patent dated 1806, deeded to SHARPLESS by deed dated 20 Jun 1810, wife Ann; sgn: 13 Sep 1813, WIT: John NICHOL, Thos. THOMPSON, ack. Thos. THOMPSON, JP, ent. 10 Feb 1815, rec. 20 same.

E-110   Indenture, , 24 Jan 1815, James WILKINS (wife Lydia), BCO; Joseph BAKER, BCO; $585, land on Wheeling Creek, NBR: William GIFFEN (land sold by David VANCE), S 36 T 6 R 3, 65 acres 2 rods 12 perches, conveyed to WILKINS by David VANCE (wife Margaret) on 13 Apr 1809, fee simple; WIT: David VANCE, Sterling JOHNSTON, ack. 9 Feb 1815, Sterling JOHNSTON, JP, ent. 10 Feb 1815, rec. 25 same.

E-111   Indenture, 1 Dec 1814, Joseph TAYLOR (wife Mary), BCO: James RIGGS, BCO; $1,600, lots #47, 48, and 80, each 1/4 acre, in Barnesville, fee simple; WIT: James BARNES, Jno. BEVAN, ack. John BEVAN, ent. 16 Feb 1815, rec. 28 same.

E-112   Indenture, 23 Jan 1815, John MECHEM (wife Sally), BCO; James RIGGS, BCO; part of S 14 T 8 R 6, 40 acres; also 20 1/4 acres, part of S 13 T 8 R 6; WIT: John BEVAN, Thomas SHANNON, ent. 16 Feb 1815, rec. 28 same, ack. John BEVAN, JP.

E-113   Indenture, 25 Apr 1814, Peter WYRICK (wife Catharine), BCO; James HUNTSMAN, BCO; $200, 100 acres, SE 1/4 S 14 T 8 R 4, granted to Jacob KUHN by patent dated 27 Aug 1805, KUHN conveyed to WYRICK E 1/2 of section by deed dated 9 Feb 1808 with reserve of 50 acres in NE 1/4 of section, his seal [but looks foreign], her mark [also foreign appearnance], ack. David WALLACE, JP, ent. 17 Feb 1815, rec. 1 Mar same year.

E-115   To all who shall see these presents, Mary Ann KINNARD, Washington County, Tennessee, selling lot #73 on main street in St. Clairsville, lately in the occupation of her aunt Mrs. Sarah ROBINSON, deceased, profits from sale to be deposited in the Union Bank of Maryland at the city of Baltimore, sgn: 3 Nov 1814, WIT: John PATTON, John KENNEDY, ack. Washington Co., Tennessee, John PATTON, justice of the court; PATTON certified by Jas. SERVICE, Clk, by his Dept. Jno. C. HARRIS, ent. 27 Feb 1815, rec. 2 Mar same.

E-116   Indenture, 12 d 1 m 1815, Jacob GREGG (wife Mary), BCO; Samuel GREGG, Junr., BCO; land granted to Samuel GREGG, Senr., then of Ross Co., Ohio, for S 33 T 7 R 4, Steubenville district, by patent dated 1 Oct 1806, part of which has been conveyed to Jacob GREGG by deed dated 20 Jun 1810, $240, 69 acres 9 poles, part of same section, NBR: Joseph VANLAW, Joseph GRIFFITH, Samuel GREGG, Junr.; WIT: William SINCLAIR, James GEAGE, ack. 12 Jan 1815, William SINCLAIR, JP, ent. 4 Mar 1815, rec. 6 same.

E-117   Indenture, 22 Feb 1815, Samson ROBSON, Harrison Co., Ohio; Hugh PARKS, BCO; $560, art of S 18 T 6 R 3, NBR: Flat run, Hugh PARK, 56 acres;

WIT: Thomas MAJOR, John WHITE, ROBSON verifies receipt of money on 22 Feb 1815, ack. Thomas MAJOR, JP, ent. 6 Mar 1815, rec. 7 same.

E-118   Indenture, 24 Dec 1814, Joseph EATON, Junr., JCO; John PERRY, Senr., BCO; $654, SW 1/4 S 14 T 8 R 5, 163 1/2 acres 3 perches; WIT: John EATON, John F. MORRISON, ack. Duncan MORRISON, JP, ent. 6 Mar 1815, rec. 7 same.

E-119   Indenture, 25 Aug 1812, Notley HAYS (wife Sally), BCO; Thomas SMITH, BCO; $1,200, part of S 34 T 6 R 3, 100 acres; his seal, her mark, WIT: Sterling JOHNSTON, George SHARP, ack. Sterling JOHNSTON, JP, ent. 7 Mar 1815, rec. 8 same.

E-120   Indenture, 14 Dec 1814, Robert WATSON (wife Rachel), Hartford County, Maryland; Joseph COX, BCO; $400, N 1/2 SW 1/4 S 21 T 8 R 6, Steubenville district, WIT: Wm. WALLACE, Andrew WALLACE, receipt of payment by Robert WATSON, WIT: Alexr. WALLACE, ack. York Co., Pennsylvania, Alexr. WALLACE, WALLACE certified 21 Dec 1814, by Wm. BARBER, Prothonotary, ent. 7 Mar 1815, rec. 9 same.

E-122   Indenture, 16 Jan 1815, Robert VERNON (wife Deborah), BCO; Mahlon PATTON, BCO; $228.37 1/2, E side NW 1/4 S 26 T 7 R 5, 101 1/2 acres; WIT: Mary WHITE, Isaac PATTON, James WHITE, JP, ent. 9 Mar 1815, rec. 20 same.

E-123   Indenture, 20 d 9 m 1814, Stephen HODGIN (wife Elisabeth), BCO; Sarah MILHOUS, admx. to estate of her husband Robert MILHOUS, deceased, BCO; $200 paid by Robert MILHOUS in his lifetime, $800 paid by Sarah MILHOUS, admx., part of S 11 T 8 R 6, granted to HODGIN by patent [no date given], NBR: Stephen TODD, 83 acres 34/100; WIT: Henry HOWARD, John PURVIES, ack. 11 Feb 1815, John BEVAN, receipt of $1,000 acknowledged, ent. 9 Mar 1815, rec. 10 same.

E-124   Indenture, 20 Dec 1809, Stephen HODGIN (wife Elisabeth), Warren twp., BCO; Henry WILLIAMS, same; $160, 80 acres beginning NE corner S 11 T 8 R 6, fee simple; WIT: John GIVEN, Amas DAVIS, ack. John GIVEN, ent. 9 Mar 1815, ent. 11 same.

E-125   Know all persons, George WILLIAMS, BCO, in consideration that William WILLIAMS and Daniel WILLIAMS, two eldest sons heirs of his estate until he can make a proper will, sgn: 8 Mar 1815 [his mark], WIT: George BARKHURST, Haddick WARREN, ent. 9 Mar 1815, rec. 13 same.

E-125   James MADISON, President of the U.S., Know ye that Jacob HOLTZ, assignee of James CALDWELL, having deposited in the treasury a certificate of the register of land office at Steubenville, full payment for NW 1/4 S 15 T 8 R 5, Steubenville district, sgn: at Washington, 12 Dec 1812, Edward [TIFFIN], commissioner of the general land office, ent. 10 Mar 1815, rec. 13 same.

E-126   Indenture, 4 Mar 1815, James BARNES (wife Nancy), BCO; William PHILPOT, BCO; $104.60, lots #51 and 83 and 60 and 92 in Barnesville, each 1/4 acre, also one out lot on north side of town containing 2 acres 8 rods, agreeable to Carolus JUDKINS' survey, NBR: James B. FINLEY; WIT: Jno. BEVAN, Zacheriah BARNES, ack. John BEVAN, JP, ent. 10 Mar 1815, rec. 14 same.

E-127   Indenture, 28 d 11 m 1814, Rees BRANSON (wife Ruth), Flushing, BCO; Isaac BRANSON, BCO, and Jesse FOULKE, Flushing, BCO; BRANSON bound to the company of the Ohio Bank for $400, Isaac BRANSON and Jesse FOULKE endorsed as security, for additional $1 Rees conveys SW 1/4 S 27 T 9 R 5, patented to Rees BRANSON on 1 Feb 1814, void if debt paid to Ohio Bank; WIT: Robert LEE, [Enas] PICKERING, ack. 28 Nov 1814, Robert LEE, JP, ent. 10 Mar 1815, rec. 15 same.

E-128   Indenture, 21 Nov 1814, David MOORE, Sheriff of BCO; John EATON, BCO; at April term 1813 Simon MONTAGUE recovered judgment in Court of Common Pleas against Jacob DOVENBARGER for debt of $66.50 plus $9.19 costs of suit, mortgage on lots #51, 44, and 45 and lot known as school house lot in Morristown, lot #51 for $16.33, 21 Nov 1814 in Morristown a public auction was held, EATON bid $16.33, therefore lot #51 conveyed to EATON; sgn. David MOORE, Sheriff, WIT: Robert GRIFFITH, ack. D. MORRISON, JP, ent. 14 Mar 1815, rec. 20 same.

E-130   Indenture, 9 d 2 m 1815, Jacob PARKER (wife Rhoda), JCO, Solomon COLES, BCO; $21.25, par tof NE corner of NW 1/4 S 21 T 8 R 6, Steubenville district, fee simple; WIT: Benejah PARKER, John WATSON, ack. 9 Feb 1815, JCO, John WATSON, JP, ent. 14 Mar 1815, rec. 20 same.

E-131   Indenture, 7 Mar 1815, William HATFIELD (wife Nancy), St. Clairsville, BCO; Lewis SUTTON, same; $300, fee simple, part of lot #93 in St. Clairsville, NBR: Ira ROBINSON, plat in Book A, p. 31; his seal, her mark, WIT: William SINCLAIR, Wm. FARIS, Junr., ack. William SINCLAIR, JP, ent. 18 Mar 1815, rec. 31 same.

E-132   Indenture, 10 Oct 1814, Mahlon SMITH (wife Mary), St. Clairsville, BCO; Robert WILLIS, BCO; $640 paid to William MERADAY, receipt ack. by Mahlon and Mary SMITH, N 1/2 S 10 T 8 R 5 conveyed to SMITH by patent dated 27 Feb 1812, WILLIS now lives on that land, fee simple; WIT: Lewis [NEILL,

WEILL], Bushrod RUST, ack. 23 Nov 1814, John PATTERSON, Assoc. Judge, ent. 18 Mar 1815, rec. 21 same.

E-133   Indenture, 16 Mar 1815, Demsey BOSWELL (wife Mary), BCO; William PHILPOT, bco; $553.12 1/2, 44 S 142 acres, 142 2/10 perches, part of S 14 T 8 R 6; his seal, her mark, WIT: John BEVAN, Benjamin HALL, ack. John BEVAN, JP, ent. 20 Mar 1815, rec. 22 same.

E-134   Indenture, 21 Mar 1815, James BARNES (wife Nancy), BCO; Thomas PLUMMER, BCO; $120, lots #6 and 102, each 1/4 acre; his seal, her mark, WIT; John BEVAN, Jas. M. RA[VEN], ack. John BEVAN, JP, ent. 20 Mar 1815, rec. 22 same.

E-135   Indenture, [no date], George LIMLEY (wife Catharine), BCO; James BROWN, BCO; $200, 99 acres 3 rods, 14 perches, part of S 14 T 4 R 3, granted to George LIMLEY by patent dated 10 Feb 1807, NBR: Peter LIMLEY, Capteen Creek; his seal, her mark, WIT: Obed. RIDER, Henry B. REYNOLDS, ack. 21 Jan 1815, James SMITH, JP, ent. 21 Mar 1815, rec. 22 same.

E-136   Indenture, 26 Nov 1814, Joseph SHARP (wife Nancy), BCO; George SHARP (BCO; $320, SE 1/4 S 33 T 8 R 4, granted to Joseph SHARP by patent [undated]; his seal, her mark, WIT: John CAMPBELL, Mathew McCALL, ack. John CAMPBELL, JP, ent. 21 Mar 1815, rec. 23 same.

E-13???? Indenture, 23 Mar 1813, Richard SATTERTHWAITE (wife Rebecca), Philadelphia, Pennsylvania; Joseph W. SATTERTHWAITE, BCO; $25, S 13 T 7 R 3, north side of Samuel POTTS, SATTERTHWAITE, two acres 5 poles, WIT: Joseph GIBBONS, Samuel HAINS, ack. Pennsylvania, 24 Mar 1815, William TILGHMAN, chief justice of the supream court of Pennsylvania, TILGHMAN certified by Joseph BARNES, Prothnotary of supreme court of the eastern district of Pennsylvania, sgn: at Philadelphia 24 Mar 1813, ent. 22 Mar 1815, rec. 23 same.

E-139   Indenture, 28 Mar 1815, Abner MURPHY (wife Sarah), BCO; John LACOCK and Alexander REYNOLDS, admrs. of estate of John HUSTON, deceased, late of Washington Co., Pennsylvania, for legal heirs of John HUSTON, deceased; in lifetime of HUSTON he purchased of MURPHY 153 acres 3 rods and 28 perches in NE 1/4 S 32 T 8 R 5, Steubenville district, for $1,230, granted to Abner MURPHEY by patent dated 15 Dec 1811; his seal, her mark, WIT: Sterling JOHNSTON, Wm. PERRINE, ack. Sterling JOHNSTON, JP, ent. 28 Mar 1815, rec. 31 same.

E-141   Indenture, 29 Mar 1815, David NEISWANGER (wife Mary), Richland twp., BCO; William PERRINE, same place; $130, lot #67 in St. Clairsville, previously sold to PERRINE and John BROWN, 52 1/2 feet, conveyed under authority of a certain deed of Indenture executed by Charles HAMMOND 11 Dec 1807, fee simple; his seal, her mark, WIT: Abner MOORE, Henry JOHNSTON, ack. Henry JOHNSTON, JP, ent. 31 Mar 1815, rec. 10 Apr same.

E-142   Indenture, 21 Jan 1815, David MARSHALL (wife Anne), BCO; James GRAHAM, BCO; $459, land in Colerain twp., BCO, part of S 32 T 7 R 3, Steubenville district, granted to Alexander GRAY by patent dated 27 Aug 1807, GRAY conveyed to MARSHALL 124 acres 1 rod 22 perches by deed dated 24 Mar 1810, MARSHALL conveys to GRAHAM 52 acres 3 rods and 38 perches, NBR: William FORGUSON near Barr's run, John GRAY, fee simple; WIT: David WALLACE, John GRAY, ack. David WALLACE, JP, ent. 7 Apr 1815, rec. 10 same.

E-144   Indenture, 29 Mar 1815, William PATTERSON (wife Elizabeth [Elisabeth]), BCO; Robert MILLS, BCO; "full payment," W 1/2 NW 1/4 S 20 T 8 R 6, Warren twp., BCO, 85 acres; his seal, her mark, WIT: John BEVAN, Thos. PLUMMER, ack. of William PATTON and Elisabeth PATTON [but signatures are PATTERSON] by John BEVAN, ent. 7 Apr 1815, rec. 10 same.

E-146   Indenture, 4 Apr 1815, John McFADDEN (wife Margaret), Cadiz twp., Harrison Co., Ohio; Walker CARPENTER, BCO; $1,230, 153 75/100 acres, SW 1/4 S 9 T 9 R 5, Steubenville district, granted to Thomas SHARP by patent dated 8 May 1806, conveyed by SHARP (wife Jennie) to McFADDEN by deed dated 15 Dec 1808, recorded Lib. B, p. 552; WIT: Jonas PICKERING, Samuel PICKERING, ack. Robert LEE, JP, ent. 7 Apr 1815, rec. 11 same.

E-147   Indenture, 8 Apr 1815, John McNABB (wife Sarah), BCO; William CAMPBELL, BCO; $2,000, part of S 14 T 7 R 4, 120 acres, conveyed to McNABBs on 25 Jan 1806, fee simple; his seal, her mark, WIT: Rue BOGGS, Sterling JOHNSTON, ack. Sterling JOHNSTON, JP, ent. 8 Apr 1815, rec. 11 same.

E-149   Indenture, John DILLE (wife Margaret), BCO; A. [Ami, but looks like Arni] MUSSARD, BCO; $1,500 paid in installments, void if payments made without default, sgn: 1 Apr 1815; his seal, her mark, WIT: David WILLIAMS, Valentine LAUERHEBER, payment of $500 received from John THOMPSON in behalf of the DILLEs on 6 Nov 1816, John DILLE paid $500 on 28 May 1817, rec. 2 Jun 1818, ack. Valentine SAUERHEBER, JP for York twp., BCO, ent. 7 Apr 1815, rec. 13 same; received from D. GOBLE the last payment in full, Wheeling, 12 Feb 1818, WIT: Thos. [TONNER].

E-150   Indenture, 15 Apr 1815, William COEN [COWEN] (wife Sarah), BCO; Isaac BOWER, Lancaster Co., Pennsylvania; $732, part of S 2 T 9 R 5,

Steubenville district, , NBR: Jacob SNEDEKER, William SHAW, 94 acres, fee simple; WIT: John KENNEY, John M. BURNERS, John HARDING, ack. Robert LEE, JP, ent. 15 Apr 1815, rec. 17 same.

E-151   Indenture, 15 Apr 1815, Isaac BOWER, BCO; John KENNEY, Columbiana Co., Ohio; $728.50, part of S 2 T 9 R 5, Steubenville district, NBR: Jacob SNEDEKER, William SHAW, 94 acres, fee simple, void if BOWER pays $400 plus interest to KENNEY within four years; WIT: John LIST, John CARTER, ack. Henry JOHNSTON, JP, ent. 15 Apr 1815, rec. 17 of same.

E-153   Indenture, 8 Apr 1815, George McNABB, Junior, BCO; William CAMPBLE [CAMPBEL], BCO; $1,100, part of S 14 T 7 R 4, NBR: John McNABB, 114 acres, conveyed to John McNABB, Junr., by George McNABB, Senior, (wife Martha) on 25 Jan 1806, recorded Book A, p. 512, fee simple; WIT: George ALLAN, Sterling JOHNSTON, ack. Sterling JOHNSTON, JP, ent. 15 Apr 1815, rec. 19 Apr 1815.

E-154   Indenture, 4 Feb 1815, Abraham ACKERSON (wife Darke); Abraham BLAUVELT, all of Warren twp., BCO; love and consideration, BLAUVELT is ACKERSONs' grandson, ACKERSONs conveyed to BLAUVELT SW 1/4 S 5 T 8 R 6, 50 acres, NBR: Nathan SIDWELL; his seal, her mark, WIT: J. E. NEWALL, Jno. BEVAN, ack. 17 Feb 1815, John BEVAN, JP, ent. 17 Apr 1815, rec. 22 same.

E-156   Indenture, 12 d 11 m 1814, Joseph WRIGHT (wife Eleanor), BCO; Nathan PUSEY, BCO; $23, lot #41 in town of Belmont, 28 rods, plat recorded in Book B, p. 288; WIT: John DILLON, Ezer DILLON, ack. 7 Dec 1814, Wm. SMITH, JP, ent. 15 Apr 1815, rec. 19 same.

E-157   Indenture, 28 Oct 1814, John LYLE (wife Isabella), BCO; John LOVE, BCO; $408, land in Wheeling twp., BCO, part of SW 1/4 S 20 T 8 R 4, NBR: James CAMPBELL, 46 acres 2 rods 6 perches, part of conveyance from David CAMPBELL to LYLE recorded in Book D, p. 48; WIT: John CAMPBELL, David LYLE, ack. 26 Dec 1814, John CAMPBELL, ent. 15 Apr 1815, rec. 22 same.

E-158   Indenture, 1 Dec 1814, James BARNS (wife Nancy), BCO; Joseph TAYLOR, BCO; $70, lots #47, 48, 80 in Barnesville, each 1/4 acre, for $60 one out lot #2 containing 5 acres, conveyed to TAYLOR by general warrante deed in fee simple; his seal, her mark, WIT: Jno. BEVAN, James RIGGS, ack. Jno. BEVAN, JP, ent. 15 Apr 1815, rec. 22 same.

E-160   Indenture, 17 d 3 m 1815, Daniel FRAZIER (wife Nelly), BCO; George COPE, JCO; $900, NW 1/4 S 1 T 7 R 3, NBR: BERRY, MELTON, 67 acres, part of land granted to Borden STANTON by patent dated 20 Dec 1808; WIT: James

STEER, Thos. MITCHELL, ack. Thomas MITCHELL, JP, ent. 17 Apr 1815, rec. 24 Apr.

E-161   Indenture, 28 d 10 m 1813, Borden STANTON (wife Charlotte), BCO; James STEER, BCO; $2,600, part of S 7 T 7 R 3, granted to STANTON by patent dated 27 d 8 m 1805, NBR: Horton HOWARD, Thomas EVANS, David BERRY, 635 acres; WIT: Jonathan TAYLOR, Ruth STEER, ack. 22 Mar 1815, Thomas MITCHELL, Justice, ent. 17 Apr 1815, rec. 26 same.

E-163   Know all men, Aaron HOLLOWAY and Benjamin FICKLEN, both of Stafford Co., Virginia, are bound to William WRIGHT, BCO, for $586.80, presents sealed and dated 13 Jun 1806, HOLLIWAY sold WRIGHT 1/4 S, purchased by HOLLOWAY on 25 May 1805 the northernmost 1/2 S 32 T 9 R 5, Steubenville district, 147 20/100 acres, void if HOLLOWAY makes a deed before 25 May 1810; WIT: R. [CURTCHI], Asa HOLLOWAY, Betsey McDANIEL, [no ack.], ent. 27 Apr 1815, rec. same.

E-164   Indenture, 12 Apr 1_15, John WINTER, BCO; Robert WINTER, BCO; $1,600, part of lot #17 in St. Clairsville, conveyed to WINTER by James WILKINS (wife Lydia) on 13 Jun 1808, part of out lots #11 and 12, 3 acres, laid out by Bazaleel WELLS adjoining addition laid out by Wm. MATHERS, two lots conveyed by William GOUGH (wife Racheal), to George ALBAN by deed dated 22 Oct 1811, recorded in Book D, p. 123, fee simple; WIT: William ASKEW, Henry JOHNSTON, ack. Henry JOHNSTON, JP, ent. 17 Apr 1815, rec. 28 same.

E-166   Indenture, 13 Mar 1815, Christopher CARROTHERS, BCO; Philip LAWRANCE, <u>Harrson</u> Co., Ohio; $400, 50 acres, part of SW 1/4 S 9 T 8 R 4, S granted to Adam SEEBERT (though it looks like it could be LEEBERT) by patent dated 28 Dec 1807, SEEBERT conveyed to CARRUTHERS (wife Ruth) by deed dated 29 Dec 1810; his seal, her mark, WIT: John WILSON, Samuel STEEN, receipt for $400 sgn: 30 Mar 1815 by CARROTHERS, ack. David WALLACE, ent. 17 Apr 1815, rec. 28 same.

E-167   Indenture, 17 Apr 1815, James JOHNSTON (wife Jenny [Jennie]), BCO; James WILKINS, BCO; $2,000, part of S 5 T 7 R 4, 110 acres, following reductions: two acres conveyed to Sterling JOHNSTON now in possession of Zachariah HAYS for John NORRIS, 3 acres conveyed to Jacob LOY, both conveyances made by James JOHNSTON, 110 acres conveyed to JOHNSTON by David VANCE (wife Margaret) on 4 Jan 1800, fee simple; wife signs "Jane JOHNSTON"; WIT: John PATTERSON for Jas., Sterling JOHNSTON, ack. 19 Apr 1815, Sterling JOHNSTON, JP, ent. 22 Apr 1815, rec. 29 same.

E-168   Indenture, 18 Apr 1815, George SHARPLESS (BCO); Samuel SHARPLESS, BCO; $2,000, two tracts, one beginning SW corner S 17 T 6 R 3, NBR: John BELL, 164 acres, conveyed to Isaac HILL by Francis [FONNSONE–TOWNSEND?] on 2 Oct 1806, from HILL to George SHARPLESS on 18 Feb 1808; other piece beginning in (NBR:) Aaron NEWPORT's line, George SHARPLESS, Jacob LUST, 33 acres, conveyed to George SHARPLESS by Frances TOWNSEND (wife Minah or Menah), 26 Mar 1810, part of S 17 T 6 R 3, fee simple; WIT: Jacob NAGLE, Sterling JOHNSTON, ack. Sterling JOHNSTON, JP, ent. 29 Apr 1815, rec. 5 May 1815.

E-170   Indenture, 2 Jul 1814, John BEVANS (wife Margaret), of Redstone twp., Fayette Co., Pennsylvania; James THOMPSON, Menallen twp., Fayette Co., Pennsylvania; $130, lot #149 in St. Clairsville, conveyed to BEVAN by William FROST (wife Nancy) on 10 Apr 1813, recorded Book D, p. 328, fee simple; [she signs Marget], WIT: Benjamin ROBERTS, Catharine ROBERTS, ack. 2 Jul 1814, Fayette Co., Benjamin ROBERTS, JP, receipt of $130, ack. 11 Apr 1815, Samuel ROBERTS, president court of common pleas of fifth judicial district, Richard William LANE, prothonotary, certifies Samuel ROBERTS 11 Apr 1815, ent. 22 Apr 1815, rec. 5 May 1815.

E-172   Samuel COLLINS of Washington Co. [Ohio], having deposited in the general land office a certificate of the register of the land office at Marietta, full payment made for NE 1/4 S 35 T 5 R 5, Marietta district, granted to James COLLINS, sgn: 30 May 1814 by James MADISON, Edward TIFFIN, Commissioner of the general land office; power of attorney given to John COLLINS, Senr., of same county [Washington] to sell land in BCO, the NE 1/4 S 32 T 5 R 5, sgn: 20 Aug 1814, WIT: Henry COLLINS, James ROSS, ack. Anthony SHEETS, JP, Levi BARBER, clerk of CCP, certifies SHEETS, sgn: 26 Aug 1814, ent. 29 Apr 1815, rec. 5 May same.

E-173   Know all men, James COLLINS late of Grandview twp., Washington Co., Ohio, $200, convey to David KIRKBRIDE of BCO NW 1/4 S 32 T 5 R 5 conveyed to "said" Samuel COLLINS by patent dated 20 May 1814, James signed [with mark] on 15 Feb 1814 by his attorney John COLLINS, Senr., WIT: Martin SHEETS, Samuel RIGGS [his mark], ack. 16 Feb 1815 via John COLLINS, Senr., in Washington Co., Ohio, Anthony SHEETS, JP, ent. 29 Apr 1815, rec. 5 May.

E-174   Indenture, 3 May 1815, James CALDWELL (wife Nancy), BCO; Vachell HALL, BCO; HALL purchased of Jeremiah BURRIS and George MEYERS 100 acres, part of W 1/2 S 25 T 6 R 3, legal title of land rested in CALDWELL, in consideration of the premises of James CALDWELL (wife Nancy), ack. 4 May 1815, Sterling JOHNSTON, JP, ent. 4 May 1815, rec. same.

E-176   Indenture, 10 d 11 m 1814, Joseph WRIGHT (wife Eleanor), BCO; Martha SHARP, BCO; $.50, lot #125 in town of Belmont, plat in Book B, p. 288; WIT: Calwalder EVANS, Phebe BROOMHALL, ack. 29 d 4 m 1815, Wm. SMITH, JP, ent. 29 Apr 1815, rec. 16 May.

E-177   Indenture, 14 Mar 1815, Noah ZANE (wife Mary [L.]), Ohio Co., Virginia; John ALLEN, BCO; $840, SE 1/4 S 15 T 6 R 3 except 20 acres of 1/4 S as a right angled triangle in NW corner of S; WIT: Ebenezer ZANE, Mother SCOTT, Richd. McCLURE, Charles D. KNOX, ack. 13 Mar 1813, Ohio Co., Virginia, Joseph CALDWELL, Saml. McCLURE, ack. [again?] 13 Mar 1815, Wm. CHAPLIN, Jr., Clk. of the county court, ent. 10 May 1815, rec. 16 same.

E-178   Indenture, 15 May 1815, John GILSON, Westmoreland Co., Pennsylvania; Robert THOMPSON, BCO; $300, two pieces of land in addition to St. Clairsville, as laid out by William MATHERS, lots #21 and 22, conveyed by Samuel SULLIVAN (wife Mary) to THOMPSON on 24 Sep 1811, fee simple; WIT: John HINDS, John LIST, ack. Henry JOHNSTON, JP, ent. 15 May 1815, rec. same.

E-180   Know all men, John HAFLING, BCO, by virtue of a power vested in me as collector of the township tax for Union twp., for year 1813 collected $.075 on lot #41 in Morris Town, non resident lot, no one paid, sold 24 feet of W side of lot 31 Dec 1813 to Alexander GASTON, sgn: 31 Dec 1814, WIT: William DUNN, ack. William DUNN, JP, ent. 10 May 1815, rec. 17 same.

E-180   Know all men, John HAFLING [HEFLING], BCO, same as above for lot #66 in Morris Town, sold 31 Dec 1813 to Alexander GASTON, 24 feet on E side of lot, sgn: 31 Dec 1814, WIT: William DUNN, ack. William DUNN, JP, ent. 10 Ma 1815, rec. 17 same.

E-181   Know all men, John HEFFLING, same basic pattern as preceding, lot #76 in Morris Town, to Alexander GASTON, sgn: 31 Dec 1814, WIT: William DUNN, ack. Wm. DUNN, JP, ent. 10 May 1815, rec. 17 same.

E-182   Know all men, John HEFFLING, same basic pattern as preceding, lot # not given, to Alexander GASTON; sgn: 31 Dec 1814, WIT: William DUNN, ack. William DUNN, JP, ent. 10 May 1815, rec. 17 same.

E-183   Indenture, 22 d 11 m 1813, Joseph WILLIAMS, [Uwehlaw] twp., Chester Co., Pennsylvania, "Taylor" [tailor] (wife Mary); Richard KENNY, East [Caln] twp., same county and state, House Carpenter; $150, land in Goshen twp., W 1/2 NW 1/2 S 33 T 7 R 5, conveyed to WILLIAMS by Samuel YOCOM (wife Rebecca) by deed dated 5 Feb 1813, recorded Book D, p. 291; WIT: Catharine

RALSTON, John RALSTON, receipt of $150, WIT: Joseph [HOUBRY], ack. 22 Nov 1813, Chester Co., Pennsylvania, John RALSTON, judge of CCP, ent. 18 May 1815, rec. same.

E-185 Know all men, John HEFFLING, BCO, tax collector, lot #98 in Morristown (see pp. 180-182 for pattern), Alexander GASTON, 31 Dec 1813, sgn. 31 Dec 1814, WIT: William DUNN, ack. William DUNN, JP, ent. 10 May 1815, rec. 17 same.

E-185 Know all men, John HEFFLING, lot #99 in Morris-town, 31 Dec 1813, Alexander GASTON, sgn: 31 Dec 1814, WIT: William DUNN, ack. William DUNN, JP, ent. 10 May 1815, rec. 17 same.

E-186 Know all men, same as above, lot #100, remainder the same.

E-187 Indenture, 18 Mar 1815, William BROWN (wife Sally), BCO; John McELROY, BCO; $244.50, land at E end of St. Clairsville, NBR: John HINDS, Notley HAYS, 6 acres 19 perches, fee simple; WIT: Sterling JOHNSTON, Jacob NAGLE, ack. 19 May 1815, Sterling JOHNSTON, JP, ent. 16 May 1815, rec. 29 same.

E-189 Indenture, 6 May 1815, Henry WEST (wife Mary), JCO; James PATTERSON, same; $40, part of lot #97 conveyed by Henry STEWART to H. WEST, fee simple; WIT: Thos. MITCHELL, Harriet MITCHELL, ack. Thos. MITCHELL, JP, ent. 16 May 1815, rec. 29 same.

E-190 Know all men, George THOMPSON executed to Charles HAMMOND and Samuel SPRIGG a deed of trust on E 1/2 lot #68 in St. Clairsville to secure Charles and Samuel who were George's endorsers in the bank of Steubenville, debt paid, now release to John INSKEEP of St. Clairsville all claim to the lot, sgn: 22 Mar 1815, WIT: John CARTER, John LIST, ack. Henry JOHNSTON, JP of Richland twp., ent. 16 May 1815, rec. 29 same.

E-191 Indenture, 16 May 1815, Richard KENNEY, Chester Co., Pennsylvania; James BARNES, BCO; $1,050, NE 1/4 S 26 T 7 R 5, Steubenville district; WIT: John BEVAN, William PHILPOT, ack. BCO, John BEVAN, JP, ent. 19 May 1815, rec. 29 same.

E-192 Indenture, 27 May 1815, William BUNDY (wife Sarah), BCO; Thomas MARSHALL, Deleware Co., Pennsylvania; $2,200, 81 acres beginning at SW corner NW 1/4 S 13 T 8 R 6, 10 acres 159 perches beginning at NW corner of SE 1/4 S 19 T 8 R 6, 26 acres 94 perches beginning NW corner 1/4 S last mentioned; his seal, her mark, WIT: John BEVAN, Josiah PENINGTON, receipt of $2,200,

WIT: Jno. BEVAN, Josiah PENNINGTON, ack. John BEVAN, JP, ent. 28 May 1815, rec. 29 same.

E-193   Indenture, 29 Mar 1815, William PATTERSON (wife Elisabeth [Elizabeth]), BCO; Josiah PENNINGTON, BCO; $158, part of NW 1/4 S 20 T 8 R 6, NBR: Joseph ARNOLD, 39 1/2 acres 32 perches; his seal, her mark, WIT: John BEVAN, Thomas PLUMMER, ack. John BEVAN, JP, ent. 19 May 1815, rec. 29 same.

E-195   Indenture, 17 Dec 1814, Henry STANTON (Clary), BCO; James BARNS, BCO; $320, N 1/2 NW 1/4 S 7 T 8 R 6; WIT: James RIGGS, John BEVAN, ack. Jno. BEVAN, JP, ent. 29 May 1815, rec. 30 same.

E-196   Indenture, 29 Mar 1814, Samuel MITCHELL (wife Mary), BCO; Samuel ROBISON [ROBINSON], BCO; $750, part of S 27 T 7 R 4, 30 acres; WIT: Wm. SINCLAIR, Abm. HATCHER, ack. William SINCLAIR, JP, ent. 29 May 1815, rec. 31 same.

E-197   Indenture, 22 d 12 m 1815, Henry CARVER (wife Tabitha) Harrison Co., Ohio; William KIRK, BCO; SE 1/4 S 27 T 9 R 5, Steubenville district, granted to CARVER by patent dated 23 Jun 1810, $735 convey 98 acres, part of 1/4 S 27; WIT: Robert LEE, Mary LEE [perhaps her mark?], ack. 22 Apr 1815, Robert LEE, JP, ent. 31 May 1815, recorded same.

E-199   Indenture, 3 d 6 m 1815, Robert McBRATNEY (wife Jane), Colerain twp., BCO; Josiah BUNDY, BCO; $3,000, part of S 14 T 7 R 3, conveyed to McBRATNEY from Bazaleel WELLS (wife Sally), by deed dated 23 [d] 11 m 1807, NBR: Josiah BUNDY (other lot), Andrew [DOWNING],100 acres; his seal, her mark, WIT: Jonathan TAYLOR, Mavers MEDCALF, ack. 3 Jun 1815, Thomas MAJOR, JP, ent. 5 Jun 1815, rec. 6 same.

E-200   Indenture, 7 Jun 1815, Jacob LASH, Senior, (wife Elizabeth), BCO; Jacob LASH, Junior, BCO; $35, part of S 17 T 6 R 3, NBR: Jacob LASH, Senior, Jacob LASH, Junior, fee simple; his seal, her mark, WIT: Jacob NAGAL, Sterling JOHNSTON, ack. Sterling JOHNSTON, JP.

E-201   Indenture, 3 d 6 m 1815, Josiah BUNDY, Colerain twp., BCO; Robert McBRATNEY, same place; $2,000, part of S 14 T 7 R 3, conveyed to McBRATNEY by Bazaleel WELLS (wife Sally) by deed dated same as this, NBR: Andrew DOWNING, void if BUNDY pays $2,000 with interest; WIT: Jonathan TAYLOR, Thomas MAJOR, ack. Thomas MAJOR, JP, ent. 6 Jun 1815, rec. same day.

E-203   Indenture, 29 d 5 m 1815, Joseph COX (wife Elizabeth), BCO; Thomas MARSHALL, Deleware Co., Pennsylvania; $1,500, E 1/2 S 33 T 6 R 5, Marietta district; WIT: Saml. BERRY, ack. Saml. BERRY, ent. 8 Jun 1815, rec. same.

E-204   Indenture, 29 Mar 1815, Thomas KENNARD and Anthony KENNARD, BCO; Alexander YOUNG, KENNARDs bound to YOUNG for $875 to be repaid in six annual payments through April 1821, to secure debt the KENNARDs convey 187 acres 1 rod 38 perches, part of S 18 T 7 R 4, void if debt repaid; WIT: Thomas SMITH, Sterling JOHNSTON, ack. Sterling JOHNSTON, JP, ent. 7 Jun 1815, rec. same; John BARNES WIT payments in 1816 and 1817, mortgage satisfied 3 Apr 1819, WIT: Wm. FARIS, Jr.

E-206   Indenture, 29 d 5 m 1815, Joseph COX (wife Elizabeth), BCO; Thomas MARSHALL, Deleware Co., Pennsylvania; $1,500, NW 1/4 S 29 T 6 R 5, Marietta district, except for 5 acres bounded and held by a deed of sale to James EGERTON; WIT: Saml. BERRY, ack. Saml. BERRY, Justice, ent. 8 Jun 1815, rec. same.

E-207   Indenture, 26 May 1815, James RIGGS (wife Eliza), BCO; William BUNDY, BCO; $20, part of S 14 T 8 R 6, 1 3/4 acres 34 perches; WIT: John BEVAN, Rachel HICKS, ack. John BEVAN, ent. 8 Jun 1815, rec. 9 same.

E-208   Indenture, 7 d 6 m 1815, Eli KENNARD (wife Catharine), Colerain twp., BCO; William KENNARD, same place; $119, part of S 20 T 7 R 3, 21 acres 2 rods 34 poles; his seal ["Ely"], her mark ["Katharine"], WIT: Thomas MAJOR, Joseph KENNARD, ack. 17 Jun 1815, Thomas MAJOR, JP, ent. 10 Jun 1815, rec. 12 same.

E-209   Indenture, 7 d 6 m 1815, Eli KENNARD (wife Katharine), Colerain twp., BCO; Joseph KENARD, same place; $285, part of S 20 T 7 R 3, conveyed to Eli KENNARD by Bazaleel WELLS (wife Sally) by deed dated 29 d 10 m 1811, NBR: Mordecai BALDERSTON, 44 acres 1 rod 25 poles; his seal, her mark, WIT: Thomas MAJOR, William KINNARD, ack. 7 Jun 1815, Thomas MAJOR, JP, ent. 10 Jun 1815, rec. 12 same.

E-210   Indenture, Henry BROWN (wife Margaret [Margret, Margrit]), 22 Dec 1814; Alexander MORRISON (wife Martha), both BCO; $100, lot #[31], fee simple; WIT: Robt. McBRIDE, Abner MOORE, ack. D. MORRISON, JP, ent. 13 Jun 1815, rec. 15 same.

E-211   Indenture, 1 Nov 1814, James BARNES (wife Nancy), BCO; Carolus JUDKINS, BCO; $80, lots #43, 75, 63 and 95 in Barnesville, each 1/4 acre, fee simple; his seal, her mark, WIT: John BEVAN, Joel JUDKINS, ack. 1 Dec 1814, John BEVAN, JP, ent. 13 Jun 1815, rec. 15 same.

E-212   Whereas, John THOMPSON (wife Sally) by indenture dated 7 Feb 1806 conveyed to Charles HAMMOND NW 1/4 S 25 T 8 R 4 for use and benefit of George PRICE and Company, JENKINS and COCHRAN and Michael [TIERNAN or FURNAN] & Company, all residents of Baltimore (recorded Book A, p. [513], on 13 Feb 1806, signed Sterling JOHNSTON, recorder; HAMMOND conveyed to Michael [TIERNAN] on 26 Oct 1812; now [TIERNAN] for $1,500 conveys to Hugh THOMPSON of Marietta twp., Fayette Co., Pennsylvania; sgn: 1 Nov 1814, WIT: Henry LANE, Alexander McLEAN; ack. Union Town, Fayette Co., 1 Nov 1814, Jonathan ROWLAND, ent. 14 Jun [1815], rec. 16.

E-213   Indenture, 21 Nov 1814, Samuel YOCOM [YOCUM] (wife Rebecca), BCO; Ephriam THOMAS, Allegheny County, Pennsylvania; $461.50, Goshen twp., E 1/2 NW 1/4 S 33 T 7 R 5, 71 acres, fee simple; WIT: Wm. B. ANDERSON, Joseph ALEXANDER, ack. (BCO), J. W. [or M.] ANDERSON, JP, ent. 16 Jun 1815, rec. same.

E-214   Indenture, ___ day of 1813, George LUMLEY (wife Catharine), BCO; Peter LUMLEY, BCO; $416, 208 1/4 acres, part of S 14 T 4 R 3, granted to George LUMLEY by patent dated 10 Feb 1807, NBR: James BROWN; his seal, her mark, WIT: Obed RIDER, Mary SMITH [her mark], ack. [wife's name given as Catrine], 21 Jan 1815, James SMITH, JP, ent. 17 Jun 1815, rec. 19 same.

E-216   Indenture, 20 Feb 1814, Joseph NICHOLSON, BCO; James SINCLAIR [SIN CLAIR], BCO; $50, lot #22, 1/4 acre, fee simple; John J. NICHOLSON, WIT: Harriott BARNS, Jno. BEVAN, ack. 20 Jan 1815, John BEVAN, JP, ent. 18 Jun 1815, rec. 19 same.

E-217   Know all men, Robert RUSSELL, Loudon Co., Virginia, for natural love and affection for son John RUSSELL and $1, SE 1/4 S 8 T 10 R 6 where W. HOWELL now lives, sgn: 13 Feb 1815, [no WITs], ack. 16 Feb 1815, Virginia, certified to county court of [Batimore] in state of Ohio, C. BINNS, C. L. C., Hugh DOUGLASS, president justice of court of Loudoun Co., certifies Charles BINNS, Clerk, ent. 17 Jun [1815], rec. 19 same.

E-218   Know all men, Robert RUSSELL, Loudon Co., Virginia, natural love and affection for son Charles RUSSELL, Loudon County, Virginia, and $1, SW 1/4 S 14 T 10 R 6, settled upon and for several years past occupied by Mr. STODLERS, sgn: 13 Feb 1815, [no WITs], ack. 16 Feb 1815, Virginia, Charles BINNS, clerk, Loudon Co., Hugh DOUGLAS certifies BINNS, ent. 17 Jun [1815], rec. 19 same.

E-219   Indenture, 25 May 1815, Alexander NELANS [NELONS] (wife Rachel), Fyate Co., Pennsylvania; Thomas THOMPSON, BCO; $120, part of S 5 T 6 R 3 beginning at SW corner, NBR: Andrew SCOTT, THOMSON, 25 acres; his seal, her mark, WIT: Jno. LEYBURN, Micheal SAWERS, receipt of $120, WIT: Jno. LEYBURN, Micheal SAWERS, ack. Fayette Co., Pennsylvania, Micheal SAWERS, JP, ent. 17 jun 1815, rec. 19 same.

E-220   Indenture, 2 Mar 1815, William PERRY (wife Jane), BCO; Caleb DILWORTH, JCO; $176, 11 acres, part of NE 1/4 S 31 T 8 R 4, granted to Daniel MERRITT by patent dated 27 Aug 1805, NBR: Caleb DILWORTH, fee simple; his seal, her mark, WIT: John CAMPBELL, Willm. DIXON, ack. John CAMPBELL, JP, ent. 17 Jun 1815, rec. 20 same.

E-221   Indenture, 1 Apr 1815, Ami MUSSARD, BCO; John DILLE (wife Margaret), BCO; $5,000, 200 acres, part of S 35 T 1 R 2, beginning SW corner on bank of Ohio River, granted to John HOPKINS, conveyed by him to William DUNN, conveyed by him to Laban BRONSON, conveyed by him to Absolom MARTIN, conveyed by him to Henry SMITH (40 acres to Martin SHUE, who conveyed to James SMITH, remaining 160 acres conveyed by Henry SMITH to James SMITH, by James SMITH [wife Mary] to MUSSARD), now from MUSSARD to John DILLE and wife Margrit, by patent registered in Book A in treasure office and by deeds recorded in the recorder's office at Marietta and St. Clairsville; WIT: Samuel SPRIGGS, David WILLIAMS, ack. Valentine SAUERHEBER, JP of York twp., ent. 17 Jun 1815, rec. 20 same.

E-223   Indenture, 21 Jan 1815, Henry BROWN (wife Margret), BCO; John W. [William] SMITH, BCO; $152.50, 20 acres, S 2 T 9 R 5, Steubenville district, fee simple; both mark, WIT: Wm. DIXON, James WILKINSON, ack. Robert LEE, JP, ent. 20 Jun 1815, rec. 22 same.

E-224   Indenture, 22 d 6 m 1815, James BARNES (wife Nancy), BCO; Thomas MARSHALL, Delaware Co., Pennsylvania; $40, lot #4 and #100 in Barnesville; his seal, her mark, WIT: John BEVANS, Elizabeth BARNES, ack. 22 Jun 1815, John BEVAN, JP, ent. 3 Jul 1815, rec. same.

E-225   Indenture, 26 May 1815, William BUNDY (wife Sarah), BCO; James RIGGS, BCO; $20, part of S 13 T 8 R 6, 1 3/4 acres 34 perches; his seal, her mark, WIT: John BEVAN, Rachel HICKS, ack. John BEVAN, JP, ent. 4 Jul 1815, rec. same.

E-226   James MADISON, President, Know ye that Josiah JENKINS of Loudon Co., Virginia, deposited in the treasury a certificate of the register of the land office at Steubenville, made full payment for SW 1/4 S 1 T 10 R 6, Steubenville district, sgn: 22 Aug 1810, by R. SMITH, Sec. of State, ent. 13 Jul [1815], rec. 15 same.

E-226   Indenture, 12 Aug 1808, James EDGERTON (wife Sarah) and George STARBUCK (wife Elizabeth), BCO; Robert GILKISON, BCO; $320, part of s 4 T 5 R 4, Marietta district, 160 acres; WIT: Isaac MOORE, Joseph COX, ack. Isaac MOORE, JP, ent. 13 Jul 1814, rec. 15 same.

E-228   Indenture, 3 May 1815, Robert CARNS (wife Agness), Guernsey Co., Ohio; Isabel IRWIN [ERWIN], BCO; $70, lot #39 in St. Clairsville, fee simple; his seal, her mark, WIT: Abraham CLEMINTS, Andrew DAHERTY, ack. Guernsey Co., Ohio, Peter UMSTOL, JP, ent. 13 Jul 1815, rec. 15 same.

E-229   Indenture, 17 Dec 1814, Samuel BARBER, Harrison Co., Ohio, and Isaac PARKER, JCO, extrs. James RATIKIN, deceased, Ohio; Benjamin ALLEN, BCO; $493 paid to RATIKIN during his lifetime, by CCP order dated 13 Apr last [1814], extrs convey remainder of NE 1/4 S 24 T 7 R 5, NBR: William SMITH, Caleb GREG, 155 acres; [signatures look like Samuel BARBER and Isaac BARBER, but a correction written in to the left stating Isaac PARKER], WIT: Joseph LACOSHE, John MORRISON, ack. D. MORRISON, Justice, ent. 13 Jul 1815, rec. 15 same.

E-230   Indenture, 24 Dec 1814, Joseph EATON, Junior, JCO; John PERRY, Junior, BCO; $654, SE 1/4 S 14 T 8 R 5, 163 1/2 acres 3 perches, WIT: John F. MORRISON, John EATON, ack. Duncan MORRISON, JP, ent. 13 Jul 1815, rec. 15 same.

E-231   Indenture, 6 Jan 1815, Arthur GILLIS, BCO; James GORDON, BCO; whereas the honourable executive council of commonwealth of Pennsylvania for consideration of services rendered by GILLIS [muttross] in the late army of the united states, deed dated 13 Jan 1787 under the hand of Benjamin FRANKLIN, Esq., president of said council granted part of the donation lands promised the troops of said state and described: lying in the county of west-moreland in the first district of the donation lands, by lot #110, by lot #122, lot #133, lot #120, 200 acres, GILLIS for $100 conveys to James GORDON [this land lies in Pennsylvania; above instrument not completed].

E-232   Indenture, 18 Jul 1815, Wm. FARIS, Jr., St. Clairsville, BCO; John BROWN, Jr., BCO; $60, addition to St. Clairsville, #23, conveyed by Obediah JENNINGS to William CONGLETON, by CONGLETON to Samuel HAWKINS, by HAWKINS to Jacob GRUBB, by GRUBB to Wm. FARIS, Jr., fee simple; WIT: Jeremiah HAYS, Henry JOHNSTON, ack. Henry JOHNSTON, JP, ent. 21 Jul 1815, rec. same.

E-233   Indenture, 3 d 8 m 1815, Joseph STUBBS (wife Zillpah), BCO; Thomas MARSHALL, Deleware Co., Pennsylvania; $2,475 [or $2,575], part of NE and SE 1/4 S 3 T 8 R 6, 256 acres 44 perches; his seal, her mark, WIT: Daniel WILSON, Hugh WILSON, ack. James WHITE, JP, ent. 4 Aug 1815, rec. 5 same.

E-235   Indenture, 27 May 1815, Stacy BEVAN (wife Lydia), BCO; Samuel BEVAN, BCO; $800, SE 1/4 S 3 T 10 R 6 and part of NE 1/4 S 2, T 10 R 6, Steubenville district, Evan JENKINS, William DUNN, ack. William DUNN, JP, ent. 4 Aug 1815, rec. 5 same.

E-236   Indenture, 27 [d] 3 m 1815, Jacob PICKERING, Senr., (wife Hannah), BCO; Joseph HOLLIWAY, BCO; part of S 14 T 9 R 5, 109 acres 1 rod 27 poles, NBR: Asa HOLLIWAY, $500, fee simple; his seal, her mark, WIT: Robert HOLLAWAY, William DUNN, ack. 27 Mar 1815, William DUNN, JP, ent. 4 Aug 1815, rec. 5 same.

E-237   Indenture, 13 Jul 1815, John BROWN, Junr., (wife Elizabeth), BCO; John CLITHERS, BCO; $125, fee simple, part of S 6 T 6 R 4, 22 1/2 acres, conveyed from John WINTER to John BROWN, Junr., by deed dated 24 Jun 1813, recorded in Book D, p. 369; his seal, her mark, WIT: John INSKEEP, Junr., Henry JOHNSTON, ack. Henry JOHNSTON, JP, ent. 9 Aug 1815, rec. same.

E-239   Indenture, 18 Mar 1815, John SNODGRASS (wife Rebeckah), Ohio Co., Virginia; Archibald MAJOR, BCO; Robert MOORE assignee of Benjamin MURPHY by patent dated 7 Oct 1812 SE 1/4 S 21 T 7 R 3, MOORE made deed dated 1 Dec 1813 granted SE 1/4 S to John SNODGRASS, now $1,600 to convey; his seal, her mark, WIT: Thomas MAJOR, George ATKINSON, ack. Thomas MAJOR, JP, ent. 10 Aug 1815, rec. same.

E-240   Indenture, 23 d 4 m 1814, Joseph WALTON, BCO; Paul PRESTON, BCO; $546, part S 19 T 7 R 3, NBR: Thomas BLACKLEDGE, 84 acres, conveyed to WALTON from Daniel McPEAK (wife Elizabeth) by deed dated 5 d 12 m 1812; WIT: Thomas MAJOR, Jane MAJOR, ack. 23 Apr 1814, Thomas MAJOR, JP, ENT. 16 Aug 1815, rec. 19 same.

E-241   Indenture, 28 d 7 m (July) 1815, Isaac PARKER (wife Sarah), JCO, and Jacob PARKER (wife Faith), Harrison Co., Ohio; Samuel SHAW, JCO; $900, NE corner of S 9 T 7 R 3, NBR: Merick STARR, Emmor BAILEY, 45 1/8 acres, fee simple; WIT: Charles CHAPMAN, [Jf.] HALL, William CARROTHERS, John WATSON, ack. 28 Jul 1815, Harrison Co., Ohio (for Jacob), Charles CHAPMAN, JP, William TINGLEY certifies CHAPMAN; ack. JCO (Jacob), 29 Jul 1815, John WATSON, JP, 1 Aug 1815 Thos. PATTON certifies WATSON, ent. 16 Aug 1815, rec. 19 same.

E-243   Indenture, 12 d 8 m 1815, Samuel EDGERTON (wife Elizabeth), BCO; Martha BROCK, widow of James BROCK, late of BCO, and extx. of LW&T and Jesse BAILEY, extr., BCO; bond by them given to James BROCK for N 1/2 NE 1/4 S 34 T 6 R 5, Marietta district; WIT: John BEVAN, Elijah BAIN, ack. 12 Aug 1815, John BEVAN, JP, ent 18 Aug 1815, rec. 22 same.

E-244   Indenture, 5 d 8 m 1815, William PATTERSON (wife Elizabeth), BCO; Silas PATTERSON, BCO; $30, NW 1/4 S 32 T 7 R 5, excepting 1 1/2 acres sold to Isaac PATTON on the east line; his seal, her mark, WIT: John BEVAN, John I. MOORE, ack. 5 Aug 1815, John BEVAN, JP, ent. 18 Aug 1815, rec. 22 same.

E-246   Indenture, 27 May 1815, Horton HOWARD (wife Hannah), BCO; John HYDE, BCO; $400, NW 1/4 S 30 T 8 R 6; WIT: William DUNN, Agness DUNN, ack. William DUNN, JP, ent. 19 Aug 1815, rec. 22 same.

E-247   Indenture, 19 d 4 m 1815, William BUNDY (wife Sarah), BCO; Richard EDGERTON, BCO; $225, part of SE 1/4 S 19 T 8 R 6, 99 3/4 acres 39 perches; his seal, her mark; WIT: John BEVAN, John WILSON, ack. 22 Apr 1815, John BEVAN, ent. 19 Aug 1815, rec. 22.

E-249   Indenture, 4 Jul 1815, Noble TAYLOR (wife Elizabeth), BCO; Robert MOORE, BCO; $183, part of S 32 T 8 R 5, 61 acres 15 poles, fee simple; WIT: Robert GRIFFITH, John MORRISON, ack. D. MORRISON, JP, ent. 19 Jul 1815, rec. 23 same.

E-250   Indenture, 27 d 6 m 1815, John MITCHELL (wife Mary), Richland twp., BCO; John PORTER; $4,000, part of S 10 T 7 R 4, Steubenville district, NBR: William BOGGS, David McWILLIAMS, 166 acres, same parcel which Alexander BOGGS (wife Hannah) on 23 d 9 m 1808 [conveyed to Ezekiel BOGGS] recorded 9 Nov 1808 in Book B, p. 420, conveyed by Ezekiel BOGGS to John MITCHELL by deed dated 11 Jul 1814, intended to be recorded; WIT: Joshua HATCHER, Jacob BRANSON, ack. 27 Jun 1815, Henry JOHNSTON, JP, receipt of $4,000, WIT: John MITCHELL, James SIMS.

E-252   Indenture, 8 Jun 1815, Fanney BARKHURST, BCO; Alexander McKETRICK, BCO; $15, part of S 32 T 6 R 3, NBR: mill known as Thomas SMITH's mill but now Alexander McKETRICK's, 2 acres 3 rods 15 poles, fee simple; her mark, WIT: Jesse BARCUS, Isaac MOORE (his mark), ack. George BARKHURST, JP, ent. 22 Aug 1815, rec. 23 same.

E-253   Know all men, Asaph BUTLER, Colerain twp., BCO, for $100 paid by James GREENELTCH, BCO; many of BUTLER's possessions, crops, livestock, WIT: George ATKINSON, John SMITH, ent. 22 Aug 1815, rec. 23 same.

E-254   Indenture, 22 Aug 1815, Obediah HARDESTY (wife Mary), BCO: Micheal AULT, BCO; $55, 15 acres 29 perches, part of the W 1/2 S 35 T 5 R 3, granted to Caleb DILLE by patent dated 9 Dec 1808, part on W side conveyed by DILLE to HARDESTY, NBR: Uriah HARDESTY; both mark, WIT: Henry JOHNSTON, Edward ROSSMAN, ack. Henry JOHNSTON, JP, ent. 22 Aug 1815, rec. 23 same.

E-256   Indenture, 22 Aug 1815, Micheal AULT (wife Christina), BCO; Uriah HARDESTY, BCO; $22, 7 1/4 acres [10] perches, part of SE 1/4 S 5 T 6 r 4, granted to AULT by patent dated 4 Aug 1814; his seal (looks germanic), her mark (name also looks germanic), WIT: Henry JOHNSTON, Edward ROSMAN, ack. (here their names are Michael and Catharine), Henry JOHNSTON, JP, ent. 22 Aug, rec. 24 same.

E-257   Indenture, 23 Aug 1815, Jonathan SUTTON (wife Hannah), BCO; John SUTTON, Westmoreland Co., Pennsylvania; $455, fee simple, NBR: William McFARLAND, William STRANCHAN, Jonathan SUTTON, 107 acres, conveyed to Jonathan SUTTON by patent dated 20 Apr 1812, part of S 32 T 6 R 3; his seal, her mark, WIT: Ezer ELLIS, John PATTERSON, ack. John PATTERSON, Assoc. Judge, ent. 23 Aug 1815, rec. 24 same.

E-258   James MADISON, President, know ye that Leonard HART, BCO, deposited in the treasury a certificate of the register of the land office at Steubenville, payment for SW 1/4 S 6 t 6 R 4, Steubenville district, sgn: at Washington, 19 Aug 1812, by Edward TIFFIN, Commissioner of the general land office, ent. 24 Aug 1815, rec. same.

E-259   Indenture, 7 Aug 1815, William CHAPLIN (wife Mary), Ohio Co., Virginia; Leonard HART, BCO; $20, lot #88 in Morristown as laid of by William CHAPLIN; WIT: Robert MORRISON, Richard FOSTER, ack. John EATON, JP, ent. 24 Aug 1815, rec. 24 Aug 1815, rec. 25 same.

E-260   Indenture, 1 Apr 1815, Sterling JOHNSTON, Esq., BCO; Robert THOMPSON, BCO; $1,334 owed to THOMPSON according to writing dated 7 Mar 1815, due by 1817, releases land: NBR: land formerly belonging to Bazel ISRAEL, 29 acres 35 perches, void if debt repaid, WIT: Henry JOHNSTON, John THOMPSON, Robert THOMPSON assigns interest to John THOMPSON on 21 Nov 1817, WIT: David JENNINGS, rec. Henry JOHNSTON, JP, ent. 31 Aug 1815, rec. same.

E-262   Indenture, 2 Jun 1815, John JARVIS (wife Ruth), BCO; Philip JARVIS, Junr., [no location]; $267.50, 71 acres, SE 1/2 NE 1/4 S 34 T 9 R 6 fee simple; his seal, her mark, WIT: Mead JARVIS, Phillip JARVIS, Snr. [his mark], ack. John N. SMITH, JP, ent. 31 Aug 1815, rec. 2 Sep same.

E-263   To all to whom these presents shall come, CCP at Dec term 1813 ordered Henry WEST, admr. of Jacob DURRANT, deceased to sell 73 acres 3 rods and 13 perches of land, part of S 27 T 4 R 2, to discharge debts, land exposed to sale on 4 Jun 1814, purchaser Timothy SPENCER for $152.18, land borders JCO/BCO line, sgn: 10 Oct 1814, WIT: Thos. MITCHELL, Harriet MITCHELL, ack. BCO, Peas twp., Thos. MITCHELL, JP, ent. 31 Aug 1815, rec. 2 Sep same.

E-265   Indenture, 10 Oct 1814, Timothy SPENCER, JCO; Henry WEST, JCO; $152.18, part of S 27 T 4 R 2, 73 acres 3 rods 13 perches; WIT: Thos. MITCHELL, Harriet, MITCHELL, ack. BCO, Peas twp., Thos. MITCHELL, JP, ent. 31 Aug 1815, rec. 4 Sep.

E-266   Indenture, 31 Aug 1815, Nicholas PUMPHREY (wife Elizabeth), Brook Co., Virginia; John PHILLIPS, BCO; $483, fee simple, part of S 33 T 6 R 3, NBR: BURRIS; WIT: William SHARPLESS, David VANCE, ack. Sterling JOHNSTON, JP, ent. 31 Aug 1815, rec. 5 Sep same.

E-268   Indenture, 31 Aug 1815, Nicholas PUMPHREY (wife Elizabeth), Brook Co., Virginia; Thomas FAWCET, BCO; $2,982, part S 33 T 6 R 3, NBR: William McFARLAND, John PHILLIPS, WIT: William SHARPLESS, David VANCE, ack. Sterling JOHNSTON, JP, ent. 31 Aug 1815, rec. 6 [Sep] same.

E-270   Plat of Town of Somerset in BCO, 33 3/4 acres 8 perches, part of SW 1/4 S 3 T 7 R 6, ack. 17 Aug 1815 by Borden STANTON, Jr., Samuel BERRY, JP, ent 7 Sep 1815, rec. 9 same.

E-271   Plat of Clarksburg, Kirkwood twp., BCO, surveyed by John CLARK, part of SW 1/4 S 23 T 9 R 6, ack. Jno. ISRAEL, John CLARK allows streets and alleys and lot #1 for public use, sgn: 7 Sep 1815; ack. Sterling JOHNSTON, JP, ent. 7 Sep 1815, rec. 9 same.

E-272   Indenture, 12 Nov 1814, Isaac SIMMONS (wife Mary), BCO; William RENNELS [RENNALS], St. Clairsville, BCO; $80, lot #122, as recorded in Book A, p. 31, conveyed from Nicholas BOWERS (and wife) to John MARTIN on 31 Mar [year not specified], from MARTIN (and wife) to John THOMPSON (and wife), from them to Magdaline PIPER on 21 Apr 1807, to RENNALS in fee simple; WIT: Wm. JOHNSTON, ack. Sterling JOHNSTON, JP, ent. 7 Sep 1815, rec. 12 same.

No.43   No.25   No.1   No.73
No.50   No.26   No.2   No.74
No.51   No.27   No.3   No.75
No.52   No.28   No.4   No.76

UNION ALLEY

No.53   No.29   No.5   No.77
No.54   No.30   No.6   No.78
No.55   No.31   No.7   No.79
No.56   No.32   No.8   No.80

STRAWBERRY ALLEY

No.57   No.33   No.9   No.81
No.58   No.34   No.10   No.82
No.59   No.35   No.11   No.83
No.60   No.36   No.12   No.84

BIRD STREET

No.61   No.37   No.13   No.85
No.62   No.38   No.14   No.86
No.63   No.39   No.15   No.87
No.64   No.40   No.16   No.88

TURKEY ALLEY

No.65   No.41   No.17   No.89
No.66   No.42   No.18   No.90
No.67   No.43   No.19   No.91
No.68   No.44   No.20   No.92

HAZEL ALLEY

No.69   No.45   No.21   No.93
No.70   No.46   No.22   No.94
No.71   No.47   No.23   No.95
No.72   No.48   No.24   No.96

WASHINGTON STREET

BACK   COMMONS   BACK   COMMONS   BACK

49.5

Plat of Somerset

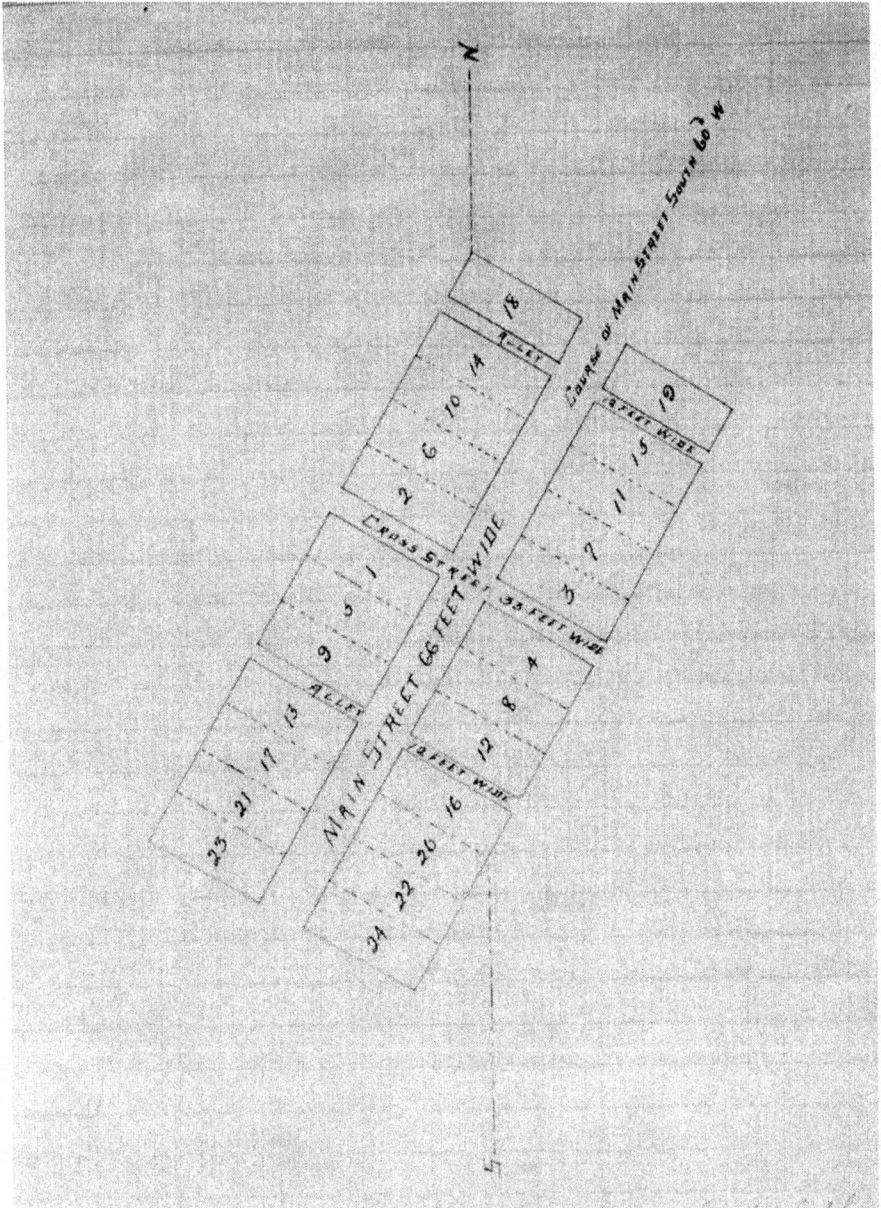

Plat of Clarksburg

E-273   Indenture, 18 Feb 1815, William REYNOLDS (wife Barbara [Barbary, Barbarah]), BCO; William BROWN, BCO; $50, lot #122 in St. Clairsville, conveyed to REYNOLDS from Isaac SIMMONS (wife Mary), on 12 Nov 1814; his seal [William B. REYNELS], her mark [Barbarah REYNOLDS], WIT: Israel BARNES, Sterling JOHNSTON, ack. Sterling JOHNSTON, JP, ent. 7 Sep 1815, rec. 12 same.

E-274   Indenture, 25 Aug 1815, George BARKHURST (wife Tamazin [Tamazen]), BCO; Zachariah BURRUS, BCO; $31, part of S 19 T 6 R 3, 12 acres 16 perches; his seal, her mark, WIT: Henry JOHNSTON, Jesse BARCUS, ack. Henry JOHNSTON, JP, ent. 9 Sep 1815, rec. 15 same.

E-275   Indenture, 18 Jul 1815, David KERR (wife Christina), of [Bart] twp., Lancaster Co., Pennsylvania, yeoman; David NEISWANGER, BCO; $1,580, land on waters of McMahan's creek, in state of Ohio, 79 acres, part of S 10 T 7 R 4, granted to Jacob BLACKWELL by patent dated 26 Jul 1789, from BLACKWELL to John CRAWFORD by deed dated 16 May 1796, conveyed frm CRAWFORD to Laban BROWNSON by deed dated 31 May 1796, from BROWNSON to Bazell WELLS by deed dated 8 Aug 1796, from WELLS to Allen STEWART by deed dated 18 Dec 1798, from STEWART to David KERR by deed dated 16 Nov 1805 as recorded in records of JCO and BCO; both mark, WIT: John FOWLER, Paul ZAUKINGER, ack. Lancaster Co., Pennsylvania, Walker FRANKLIN, pres. CCP in circuit consisting of York and Lancaster Cos.

E-277   Indenture, 1 Sep 1815, Thomas REAGH, BCO; Darling CONROW, BCO; $500, 104 acres in S 13 T 9 R 5, public lands, Steubenville district, 104 acres, fee simple; WIT: Thomas LOVE, John WILEY, ack. John WILEY, Assoc. Judge of CCP, ent. 11 Sep 1815, rec. 16 same.

E-278   Indenture, 3 May 1815, Vachel HALL, BCO; Edward ROSSMAN [ROSMAN], BCO; $700, fee simple, 100 acres, part of W 1/2 S 25 T 6 R 3, Steubenville district, NBR: Jeremiah BURRIS, Robert McCONNELL, Samuel CONNELL; WIT: David JENNINGS, Sterling JOHNSTON, ack. 4 May 1815, Sterling JOHNSTON, JP, ent. 11 Sep 1815, rec. 16.

E-279   Indenture, 8 Sep 1815, Noah ZANE (wife Mary), Ohio Co., Virginia; David LOCKWOOD, BCO; $400, SE 1/4 S 13 T 5 R 3; WIT: James CHAPLINE, Sarah [C.] CLARK, ack. Ohio Co., Virginia, Wm. CHAPLINE, Jr., C.O.C., ent. 11 Sep 1815, rec. 16 same.

E-280   Indenture, 25 Mar 1815, Thomas MARGUES (wife Joanna), BCO; William V. MARGUES, BCO; $320, SE 1/4 S 7 T9 R 5, granted to Thomas by patent dated 15 Nov 1807; WIT: John WILEY, Margaret WILEY, ack. John WILEY, Assoc. Judge, ent. 11 Sep 1815, rec. 16 same.

E-282   Indenture, 20 Jun 1805, John LYNCH and Jonathan HEWIT, overseers of the poor of Washington twp., Fayette Co., Pennsylvania, a poor black girl Melia BALL is bound to Mary FORSYTHE for the term of 14 years, Melia to serve, Mary to care for her and teach her to read, at end of term to give her two suits of apparel, one of them new, sgn: John LYNCH, Jonathan HEWITT, and Mary FORSYTHE, WIT: Joseph LYON, Isaac HASTINGS, ent. 11 Sep 1815, rec. 16 same.

E-283   Indenture, 1 d 6 m 1815, Adam KIRK, Union twp., BCO; Samuel PICKERING, same place; $480, S end SE 1/4 S 15, Steubenville district, granted to Benjamin KIRK by patent dated 22 Dec 1812, Benjamin and wife Elizabeth by indenture [without date] conveyed these 60 acres to Adam KIRK; WIT: Jesse FOULKE, Hanna FOULKE, ack. 2 Jun 1815, Robert LEE, JP, ent. 15 Sep 1815, rec. 18 same.

E-284   Indenture, 19 d 6 m 1815, George WALKER (wife Anna), BCO; Isaac JAMES, JCO; $600, 39 acres 109 perches, part of S 8 T 7 R 3, NBR: James RAILEY, Moses PIGGOT, section having been granted to Horton HOWARD by patent dated 10 d 9 m 1806, E 1/2 conveyed by HOWARD to Borden STANTON by deed dated 12 d 2 m 1809; WIT: Thomas MITCHELL, Levi WELLS, receipt of $600, ack. 19 Jun 1815, Thos. MITCHELL, JP, ent. 18 Sep 1815, rec. 20 same.

E-286   Indenture, 16 d 8 m 1815, Joseph GAMBLE (wife Elizabeth), BCO; Isaac JAMES, BCO; $20, part of S 8 T 7 R 3, conveyed to GAMBLE by Borden STANTON, NBR: George WALKER, Abner LAMBERT, Joseph GAMBLE, 1 1/2 acre; his seal, her mark, WIT: Thos. MITCHELL, Jemima MITCHELL, ack. Thos. MITCHELL, JP, ent. 18 Sep 1815, rec. 20 same.

E-287   Indenture, 28 d 8 m 1815, John MIDDLETON, (wife Mary), BCO; Henry BARNES, BCO; $520, 21 acres, part of NW 1/4 S 14 T 8 R 6; WIT: Edward THORNBROUGH, John BEVAN, ack. 28 Jun 1815, John BEVAN, JP, ent. 18 Sep 1815, rec. 20 same.

E-289   Indenture, 24 Oct 1814, Nathan SHEPHERD (wife Mary), BCO; Francis DUTTON, BCO; $600, NE 1/4 S 21 T 8 R 4, Steubenville district, granted to SHEPHERD by patent dated at Washington 25 Oct 1813, 60 acres; WIT: John CAMPBELL, Hannah DUTTON, ack. John CAMPBELL, JP, ent. 23 Sep 1815, rec. 27 same.

E-290   Indenture, 21 Aug 1815, William MEEK (wife Margaret), Washington Co., Pennsylvania; Richard IMES, of Ohio; $300, SE 1/4 S 36 T 5 R 3, 179 acres 64 perches, granted to MEEK, assignees of Richard MEEK of the U.S. by patent dated 15 May 1811, fee simple; WIT: Maria BOYLE, Maria GILLISPIE, ack. Washington Co., Pennsylvania, Zephaniah BEALL, JP, Alexander MURDOCK, Prothonotary of CCP, certifies BEALL on 22 Aug 1815, ent. 23 Sep 1815, rec. 27 same.

E-292   Indenture, 22 May 1815, James LUNDY [LUNDAY] (wife Anne), Green Co., Pennsylvania; William BELT [BELL], BCO; $555, part of NW 1/4 S 4 T 8 R 5, granted to Arthur MORRISON by Thos. JEFFERSON, president of U.S., by patent dated 13 Oct 1807, MORRISON conveyed to LUNDAY by deed dated 3 Apr 1812, this conveyed land 60 3/4 acres 17 perches, NBR: John BOYD, Samuel THOMPSON, Arthur MORRISON; his seal, her mark, WIT: Sterling JOHNSTON, John BERRY, ack. BCO, 22 Sep 1815, Sterling JOHNSTON, JP, ent. 23 Sep 1815, rec. 27.

E-293   Indenture, 20 [may be 28 because it was written only "twenty"] Sep 1815, John PRIOR (wife Margaret), BCO; Deborah WILSON, extx., and Nicholas WILSON, extr. of William WILSON, deceased, both BCO; $400, SE 1/4 S 35 T 6 R 4, Steubenville district, patent dated 16 Mar 1815, John PRIOR having made full payment for same, in trust for Nicholas WILSON, William WILSON, Ephrm. WILSON, and John WILSON, agreeable to LW&T of William WILSON, deceased; his seal [John PRIOR, Senior], her mark, WIT: John BERRY, Sterling JOHNSTON, ack. 28 Sep 1815, Sterling JOHNSTON, JP, ent. 28 Sep 1815, rec. 2 Oct same.

E-295   Indenture, 4 May 1815, James WATT (wife Sarah), BCO; James HASTINGS, BCO; $768, 88 acres 23 perches, part of NE and NW 1/4 S 30 T 7 R 4, granted to Joseph SHARP by patent dated 20 Jun 1809, SHARP granted to WATT 89 acres 4 perches by deed dated 26 Nov 1811, NBR: John STEWART, Samuel GRIGGS, Isaac FARMER; WIT: John STEWART, John McCLENAHAN, ack. David WALLACE, JP, ent. 30 Sep 1815, rec. 4 Oct same.

E-296   Indenture, 27 Apr 1815, Thomas LIGGET (wife Elizabeth), borough of Pittsburg, Allegheny Co., Pennsylvania; John OGILBEE, Washington Co., Pennsylvania; $960, land in BCO, SW 1/4 S 17 T 6 R 4, Steubenville district, 160 acres, same granted to LIGGET by patent dated 20 Apr 1812; WIT: L. STEWART, Robert GRAHAM, receipt of $960, WIT: L. STEWART, ack. Allegheny Co., Pennsylvania, 1 May 1815, L. STEWART, R. GRAHAM, JPs, ent. 30 Sep 1815, rec. 5 Oct same; Ephraim PENTLAND, prothonotary of CCP, certifies Lazarus STEWART and Robert GRAHAM, esqrs., 1 May 1815.

E-298   Indenture, 10 d 8 m 1815, Benjamin VAIL (wife Hannah), BCO; Thomas VANLAW, BCO; $1,300, part of S 36 T 6 R 4, NBR: Robert PRIOR, William WILSON, Richard TRUAX, Christian HARSHMAN, Jno. DUGAN, 100 acres, same that Caleb ENGLE (wife Mercy) by indenture dated 10 Jul 1813 granted to VAIL and Thomas VANLAW in fee, recorded Book D, p. 425; WIT: Jos. W. SATTERTHWAITE, Ann SATTERTHWAITE, ack. Union twp., BCO, John BOYD, JP, 17 Aug 1815, ent. 30 Sep 1815, rec. 5 Oct same.

E-300   Indenture, 20 Apr 1815, George FRUSH (wife Exey), BCO; Henry FRUSH, BCO; $300, 75 acres, part of SE 1/4 S 20 t 8 R 4, granted to George by James MADISON, president, by patent dated 15 Apr 1813, NBR: George FRUSH; both mark, WIT: David WALLACE, George ARMSTRONG, ack. David WALLACE, JP, ent. 5 Oct 1815, rec. 12 same.

E-301   Indenture, 6 d 5 m 1815, Benjamin GRIFFITH (wife Jane), BCO; Caleb ENGLE, BCO; $202, beginning at NW corner of SW 1/4 S 27 T 7 R 4, 41 acres, devised to GRIFFITH by LW&T of Abraham ENGLE dated 3 d 1 m 1814; WIT: Isaac GRIFFITH, Sterling JOHNSTON, ack. 6 May 1815, Sterling JOHNSTON, JP, ent. 5 Oct 1815, rec. 12 same.

E-302   Indenture, 19 d 5 m 1815, Samuel ENGLE (wife Elizabeth), BCO: Caleb ENGLE, BCO; $79.15, part of NW 1/4 S 21 T 7 R 4, NBR: John [HANESIS], 13 acres 31 poles, devised to Samuel in LW&T of his father Abraham ENGLE dated 3 d 1 m 1814; WIT: Jacob NAGLE, Sterling JOHNSTON, ack. 19 May 1815, Sterling JOHNSTON, JP, ent. 5 Oct 1815, rec. 12 same.

E-303   Indenture, 22 Apr 1815, David WALLACE (wife June or Jane), Wheeling twp., BCO; Jacob MYERS, Wheeling twp., BCO; $60, 10 acres in NE corner S 8 T 8 R 4, Steubenville district, granted by patent signed in Washington on 30 Dec 1807 to WALLACE; his seal, her mark, WIT: Henry DECKER, James CAMPBELL, ack. John CAMPBELL, JP, ent. 6 Oct 1815, rec. 12 same.

E-305   Indenture, 28 Apr 1815, Adam SEEBIRT [SEEBERT], Wheeling twp., BCO; Jacob MYERS, Wheeling twp., BCO; $640, 160 acres, SE 1/4 S 9 t 8 R 4, Steubenville district, granted to SEEBERT by patent dated at Washington 28 Dec 1807; his mark, WIT: George ARMSTRONG, Samuel ROBINSON, ack. David WALLACE, JP, ent. 6 Oct 1815, rec. 12 same.

E-306   Indenture, 29 Mar 1815, Alexander YOUNG (wife Jennie), BCO; Thomas KENNARD and Anthony KENNARD, BCO; $1,875, NBR: heirs of David BARTON, deceased, Martha JOHNSTON, land formerly belonging to Adam JOHNSTON, Samuel MUCHMORE, Abraham GANDY, 187 perches [acres?] 1 rod 38 perches, part of S 18 T 7 R 4, S granted to YOUNG by patent dated 10 Nov

1807 fee simple; her seal name is "Jean," WIT: Thomas SMITH, Sterling JOHNSTON, ack. Sterling JOHNSTON, JP, ent. 6 Oct 1815, rec. 13 same.

E-308   Know all men, James ST. CLAIR, late of BCO, deceased, contracted with Robert HOGE to sell 60 acres in S 34 T 7 R 4, BCO, NBR: Francis GEORGE, Matthew PATTERSON, and William ST. CLAIR, full purchase price received by ST. CLAIR but never made a deed, John COFFEE and Benjamin VEAL appointed extrs. by ST. CLAIR'S LW&T, extrs. set forth at March term of CCP the facts asking for an order to allow them to make the deed for land now bounded by NBR: George ST. CLAIR, Matthew PATTERSON, sgn: by John COFFEE and Benjamin VAIL on 10 Jul 1815, WIT: Joseph POSEY, Sterling JOHNSTON, ack. 11 Jul 1815, Sterling JOHNSTON, JP, ent. 10 Oct 1815, rec. 14 same.

E-309   Indenture, 5 Aug 1815, William CHAPLINE (wife Mary), Ohio Co., Virginia; John CARTER, BCO; $200, lot #24 in Morristown as laid of by William CHAPLINE; WIT: John MORRISON, [looks like a germanic name], ack. John EATON, JP, ent. 11 Oct 1815, rec. 16 same.

E-310   Indenture, 30 Sep 1815, Mary BARTON, BCO; Jacob MORGAN, BCO; $600, 61 1/2 acres, part of SW 1/4 S 14 T 8 R 4, granted to Jacob COON by patent dated 27 Aug 1805, COON conveyed to William CLARK by deed dated 8 Apr 1811, conveyed by CLARK (wife Christenah) to BARTON by deed dated 8 Mar 1812, NBR: Robert HAMMOND; her mark, WIT: David WALLACE, William WALLACE, ack. David WALLACE, JP, ent. 13 Oct 1815, rec. 17 same.

E-312   Indenture, 14 Sep 1815, John McCLURE (wife Mary), BCO; Joseph MOORE, BCO; $1,175, tract purchased jointly by Joseph MOORE and John McCLURE from Archibald WOODS of Ohio Co., Virginia, recorded in Book A, p. 337 on 21 Jun 1804, conveyed by MOORE to McCLURE by indenture dated 16 Feb 1808, recorded Book B, p. 340 on 23 Jun 1808, part of S 27 of fractional T 4 R 2, grant for said S issued 15 Nov 1797 by John ADAMS, president, NBR: Mr. HERVEY, Richard McKIBBON, Joseph MOORE, 47 acres 3 rods 4 perches; his seal, her mark, WIT: James ALEXANDER, Thomas COOPER, ack. James ALEXANDER, Assoc. Judge, ent. 16 Oct 1815, rec. 18 same.

End of Vol. E, certification by J. M. BECKETT, Recorder, that this is a true and correct copy, made by order of County Commissioners at their Spring Session 1889, sgn: 1 Apr 1890.

2 plats

Deed Abstracts, Belmont County, Ohio
Volume F (Oct 1815 - June 1817)

F-1   Belmont Manufacturing Company, 12 Oct 1815, since manufacturing is important to an inland country, form themselves into an associate company under above name; purpose is manufacturing flour, flaxseed oil, flax, and hempen linens webings "and any other business that we may from time to time think the most conductive to the interest of this association"; listing of 16 articles of business, founders: Joshua HUNT (30 shares), Seth HUNT (10 shares), Caleb EVANS (5 shares), Borden STANTON (5 shares), Robert YOST (5 shares), Elijah WOODS (10 shares), Ebenezer MARTIN (5 shares), Jonathan ZANE (10 shares), William BARNES (5 shares), $50 per share, ack. 19 Oct 1815, John CLARK, JP, ent. 19 Oct 1815, rec. same.

F-4   Indenture, 21 d 4 m 1815, John MITCHELL (wife Mary), BCO; William SMITH, BCO; $182.25, part of S 14 T 7 R 5, 81 acres, granted to John by patent from James Madison dated 17 Jun 1813, fee simple; WIT: Mahlon SMITH, John SPENCER, ack. 21 Apr 1815, Henry JOHNSTON, JP, ent. 19 Oct 1815, rec. 20 same.

F-5   Indenture, 22 Apr 1815, William BUNDY (wife Sarah), BCO; John WILLSON [WILSON], BCO; $55.68, 27 3/4 acres 14 perches, part of S 19 T 8 R 6, NBR: Richard EDGERTON; WIT: John BEVAN, Richard EDGERTON, his seal, her mark, ack. John BEVAN, JP.

F-6   Indenture, 21 d 4 m 1815, John MITCHELL (wife Mary), BCO; John SPENCER, BCO; $182.25, part of S 14 T 7 R 5, 81 acres, granted to MITCHELL by patent dated 17 Jun 1813, fee simple; WIT: George CLARK, Mahlon SMITH, ack. 1 Apr 1815, Henry JOHNSTON, JP, ent. 28 Oct 1815, rec. 30 same.

F-7   Indenture, 22 May 1815, Josiah HEDGES (wife Rebeckah), BCO; Joseph STUBBS, BCO; $800, NE 1/4 S 3 T 8 R 6, 160 acres, Steubenville district, granted to HEDGES by patent dated 21 Feb 1815, fee simple; his seal, her mark, WIT: Elzey HEDGES, Henry JOHNSTON, ack. Henry JOHNSTON, JP, ent. 30 Oct 1815, rec. same.

F-8   Indenture, 7 Jul 1813, James HUGHES (wife Mariah), BCO; Joseph MORRISON, BCO; $340, half lot in St. Clairsville, 1/8 acre, part of lot #28, conveyed to HUGHES by John CLELAND (wife Margaret) on 7 Jul 1812, fee simple; WIT: Sterling JOHNSTON, Zebulon WARNER, ack. 7 Jul 1813, Sterling JOHNSTON, JP, ent. 30 Oct 1815, rec. 31 same.

F-9   Indenture, 20 d 10 m 1815, Absalom BRODERICK (wife Nancy), BCO; Philip HUNT, late of Loudon County, Virginia; $362.50, beginning south boundary S 36 T 7 R 4, NBR: Wheeling Creek, 31 acres 3 rods 13 poles, sold to BRODERICKs on 18 d 10 m 1813, recorded Book D, p. 480; both mark, WIT: Wm. SINCLAIR, Samuel DANIEL, ack. 20 Oct 1815, William SINCLAIR, JP, ent. 1 Nov 1815, rec. same.

F-10   Indenture, 4 Nov 1815, Josiah HEDGES (wife Rebeckah), BCO; Jesse HARRIS, BCO; $1,200, SE 1/4 S 18 T 9 R 6, 168 acres, Steubenville district, deeded to Thomas WILSON by patent [no date], conveyed by WILSON (wife Nancy) to John THOMPSON, by THOMPSON (wife Sarah) to HEDGES by deed dated 6 Apr 1812, fee simple; WIT: Zachariah HAYS, Henry JOHNSTON, ack. Henry JOHNSTON, JP, ent. 4 Oct 1815, rec. 6 same.

F-11   Indenture, 21 d 7 m 1815, Horton HOWARD (wife Hannah), BCO; Samuel HOLLOWAY, Flushing, BCO; $30, lot #47 in Flushing; WIT: Rowse TAYLOR, Israel WILSON, ack. 21 Jul 1815, William DUNN, JP, ent. 6 Oct 1815, rec. same.

F-12   Know all men, Robert McFADEN of Peas twp, BCO, farmer, bound to William McKIM of state of Pennsylvania, carpenter, in sum of $650, sgn: 1 Nov 1815, void if McFADEN pays $325 on or before 1 Mar next; he signs Robert McFADDIN, WIT: William STRINGER, Malcom STRINGER, ent. 6 Oct 1815, rec. same.

F-12   Indenture, 7 Nov 1815, Michael CARREL [CARROLL] (wife Sally), BCO; Charles LOWENS, BCO; $1,000, 99 1/2 acres, part of S 12 T 7 R 4, granted to CARROLL by patent dated 8 May 1806; WIT: Isaac WILSON, Henry JOHNSTON, ack. Henry JOHNSTON, JP, ent. 7 Nov 1815, rec. same.

F-14   Plat of Burlington, BCO, between T 3 and 4, R 2, NBR: Sanibel ZANE, J. McELROY, Sr., ack. 24 Jan 1816 of Saith HUNT of Belmont Manufacturing Company, Sterling JOHNSTON, JP, ent. 25 Jan 1816, rec. 3 Feb same.

F-15   Indenture, 6 Apr 1815, Peter WIRICK (wife Catharine), BCO; Thomas LOVE, BCO; $926, NBR: George ARMSTRONG, Saml. STEEN, part of S 14 T 8 R 4, fee simple; his seal [germanic], her mark, WIT: David WALLACE, George ARMSTRONG, ack. Dd. WALLACE, JP, ent. 25 Nov 1815, rec. 8 same.

F-16   Indenture, 26 d 6 m 1815, Aron WOOD, BCO; John DAVIS, BCO; $250, part of SW 1/4 S 10 T 6 R 5, Marietta district, 51 3/4 acres 37 poles; he signs Aaron, wife Elizabeth WOOD also signs, WIT: Jesse WHITE, Samuel SMITH, ack. 26 Jun 1815, James WHITE, JP, ent. 25 Nov 1815, rec. 8 Dec same.

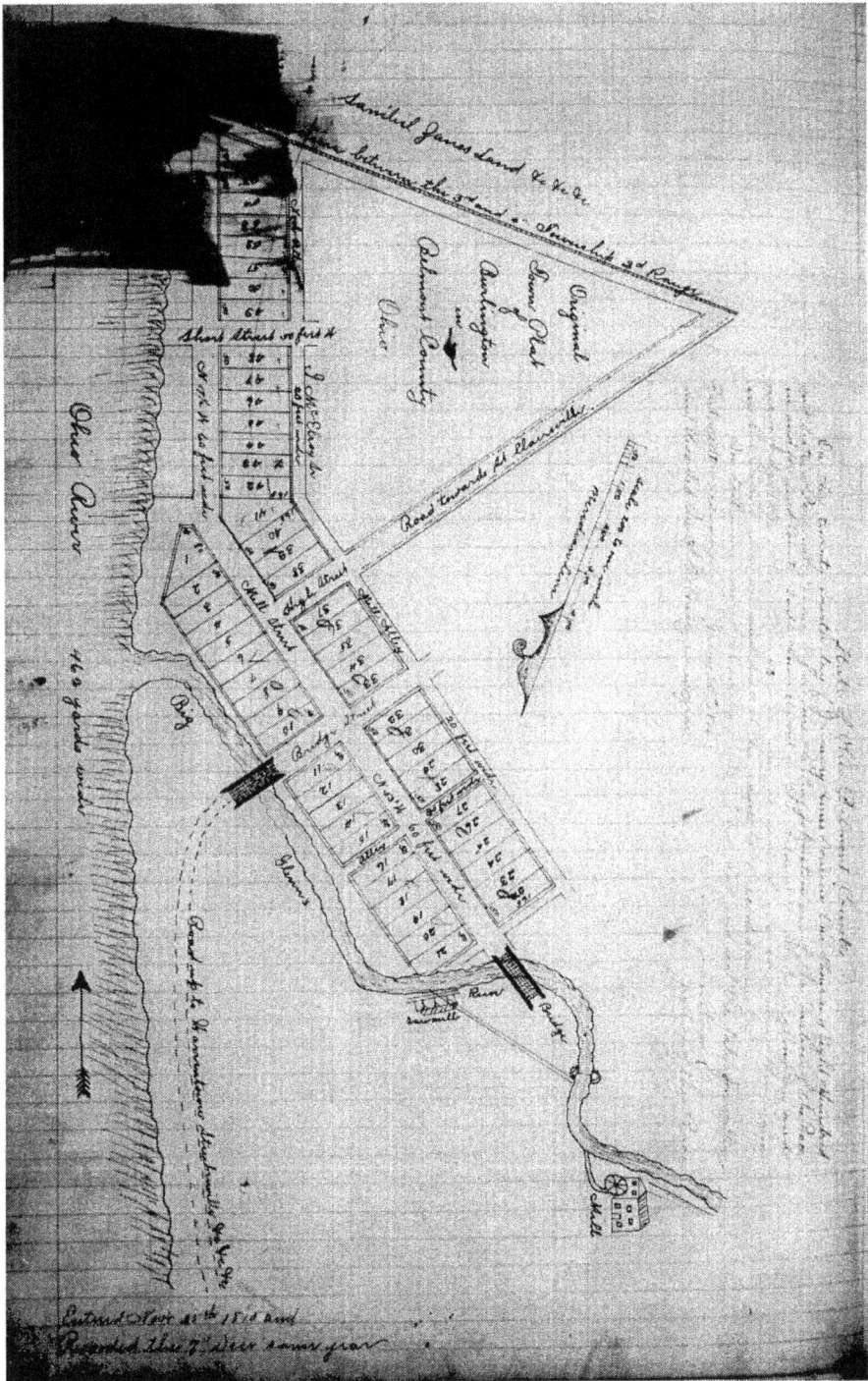

Plat of Burlington

F-17   James Madison, President of US, Know ye that William BROWN of St. Clairsville, Ohio, fully paid in Steubinville land office for SE 1/4 S 11 T 7 R 4, sgn: 22 May 1813, by Edward Tiffin, commissioner of the general Land office, ent. 25 Nov 1815, rec. 8 Dec same.

F-17   Indenture, 9 Nov 1815, William BROWN (wife Sarah), St. Clairsville, BCO; John PATTERSON, same town, county and state; $320, NE 1/2 of SW 1/4 S 11 T 7 R 4, part of 1/4 S conveyed to BROWN by patent dated 22 May 1813, fee simple; WIT: Robert ISRAEL, Sterling JOHNSTON, ack. 18 Nov 1815, Sterling JOHNSTON, JP, ent. 25 Nov 1815, rec. 8 Dec same.

F-18   Indenture, 13 Jul 1815, Daniel CAMPBELL (wife Barbara), BCO; John REYNOLDS [no location]; $70, lot #31 in addition to St. Clairsville laid out by William MATHERS, conveyed by Obediah JENNINGS (wife Ann) to William WOODBURN, from WOODBURN to CAMPBELL on 23 Feb 1814, fee simple; WIT: Jacob HAGLE, Sterling JOHNSTON, ack. Sterling JOHNSTON, JP, ent. 25 Nov 1815, rec. 8 Dec same.

F-19   Know all men, David MOORE, Sheriff of BCO, by virtue of an execution from CCP dated 4 Aug 1815, take from John REYNOLDS late of BCO $19.03, the amount of damage that David CAMPBELL recorded against REYNOLDS at July term last, plus $6.90 court costs, so MOORE levied on lot #31 on Ann Street in addition to St. Clairsville, property of REYNOLDS, after calling five good and lawful men as the law requires (as a jury), no improvement on lot, on 14 Oct last sold at public sale to John PATTERSON, Esqr., for $32.50 which satisfies judgment; sgn: 17 Nov 1815, David MOORE, Sheriff, BCO, WIT: David VANCE, Sterling JOHNSTON, ack. Sterling JOHNSTON, JP, ent. 25 Nov 1815, rec. 9 Dec same.

F-20   Indenture, 30 Sep 1815, John SMITH (wife Catharine), BCO; John WARNOCK, BCO; $131.25, 13 acres 28 perches, part of SE 1/4 S 17 T 6 r 4, granted to William SMITH, assignee of Da. MATHERS by patent dated 25 Oct 1813, SMITH to WARNOCK by deed dated 24 May 1814, NBR: McMahon's creek; WIT: Philip McGRAW, [Bueslah] McGRAW [her mark], ack. Philip McGRAW, JP, ent. 27 Nov 1815, rec. 9 Dec same.

F-21   Indenture, 13 Nov 1815, John LIST (wife Sarah), BCO; Jesse HARRIS, late of Montgomery County, Maryland; $1,000, NW corner of S 1/2 S 24 T 7 R 4, NBR: William McWILLIAMS and others [unnamed], 40 acres, same which Archibald McELROY (wife Sally) conveyed by deed dated 22 Jan 1805 recorded in Book A, p. 389, and another tract part of SE 1/4 S 30 T 7 R 4, granted by James Madison to Joseph SHARP by patent dated 20 Jun 1809, NBR: James McCOY,

John LIST, 10 acres; WIT: John PATTERSON, Ezer ELLIS, ack. 14 Nov 1815, Henry JOHNSTON, JP, ent. 27 Nov 1815, rec. 11 Dec same.

F-23   Indenture, 13 Nov 1815, John LIST, Junr., (wife Hannah), of Wheeling in Virginia; Jesse HARRIS, late of Montgomery County, Maryland; $1,000, part of SE 1/4 S 30 T 7 R 4, 20 acres, another in SW corner of S 1/2 S 24 T 7 R 4, 32 acres, totaling 52 acres, fee simple; WIT: James PEMBERTON (as to John LIST), Thomas LIST, ack. 14 Nov 1815, Ohio Co., Virginia, Archid. WOODS, [certified by] Joseph CALDWELL, ent. 27 Nov 1815, rec. 11 Dec same.

F-24   Indenture, 13 Nov 1815, Jesse HARRIS, late of Montgomery County, Maryland; John LIST, BCO, and John LIST, Junr., Wheeling, Ohio, Virginia; $1,500, land on NW corner of S 1/2 S 24 T 7 R 4, NBR: William McWILLIAMS and others [unnamed], 40 acres, same conveyed by Archibald McELROY (wife Sally) by indenture dated 22 Jan 1805 recorded in Book A, p. [389], plus another tract being part of SE 1/4 S 30 T 7 R 4, granted by James Madison to Joseph SHARP by patent dated 20 Jun 1809, NBR: James McCOY, Jesse HARRIS, 10 acres, another tract, part of SE 1/4 S 30 T 7 R 4, 20 acres, another tract in SW corner of S 1/2 S 24 T 7 R 4, 32 acres, total of 110 acres, void if HARRIS pays the LISTs four notes totaling $1,500; WIT: Jeremiah HAYS, Zachariah HAYS, ack. (BCO) __ Nov 1815, Henry JOHNSTON, ent. 27 Nov 1815, rec. 12 Dec same; mortgage satisfied [13] Dec 1825 by J. [W.] LIST, WIT: Wm. FARIS, Junr.

F-27   Know all men, Samuel DAVIS (wife Edith), Union twp., Fayette County, Penna.; George ARMSTRONG, Wheeling twp., Ohio; $880, 80 acres in NW corner S 30 T 7 R 4, fee simple; sgn: 1 Nov 1815, WIT: Nahl. MITCHELL, Silas BAILEY, ack. Fayette County, Pennsylvania, Silas BAILY, JP, confirmed by Richard William LANE, Prothondary signed as Richard Henry LANE same date at Union town, and a James LANE also signs.

F-28   Indenture, 10 Nov 1815, William HULCE (wife _____), BCO; John HULCE, BCO; $32, fee simple, part of Ss 28 and 34 T 6 R 3, NBR: William HULCE, 8 acres, purchased by William HULSE from Notley HAYS (wife Sarah) on 3 Sep 1807; WIT: David VANCE, Sterling JOHNSTON, ack. Sterling JOHNSTON, JP, ent. 29 Nov 1815, rec. 13 Dec same.

F-29   Indenture, 28 d 11 m 1814, Jesse FOULKE (one of the proprietors of town of Flushing) (wife Sarah); John NICHOLS [no location]; $26.50, lot #14 in Flushing; WIT: Robert LEE, Enos PICKERING [Bs.], ack. 28 Nov 1814, Robert LEE, JP, ent. 29 Nov 1815, rec. 13 Dec same.

F-30   Indenture, 10 d 10 m 1815, James LISLE, BCO; George HALL, BCO; $200, part of SE 1/4 S 10 T 6 R 5, 19 1/2 acres; Penninah [Penina] LISLE signs also, WIT: John DAVIS, Isaac MOORE, ack. Isaac MOORE, JP, ent. 29 Nov 1815, rec. 13 Dec same; receipt of money ack., WIT: John DAVIS.

F-31   Indenture, 13 Aug 1815, Zephaniah TISON (wife Margret), Washington Co., Ohio; Joel GILBERT, BCO; $450, NW 1/4 S 35 T 7 R 5, granted to TISON by patent, 142 acres; [Margaret's mark], WIT: Wm. SMITH, Abel GILBERT, ack. Wm. SMITH, JP, ent. 29 Nov 1815, rec. 14 Dec same.

F-32   Indenture, 28 Nov 1815, James BARNES (wife Nancy), BCO; Josiah PENNINGTON, BCO; $40, lots #8 (front) and #104 in Barnesville, each 1/4 acre; his seal, her mark, WIT: John BEVAN, Harriet BARNES, ack. John BEVAN, JP, ent. 1 Dec 1815, rec. 14 same.

F-33   Know ye that Esther HOLSE, BCO, having deposited a certificate of the register of the land office at Steubenville, made full payment for NE 1/4 S 5 T 6 R 4 of lands sold at Steubenville, sgn: 1 Nov 1811, James Madison by James Monroe, ent. 1 Dec 1815, rec. 13 same.

F-34   Indenture, 21 Nov 1815, Levi PICKERING (wife Susanna), BCO; Joel WILKINSON, BCO; $110, land in Richland twp, S 30 T 6 R 4, 11 acres 2 rods 14 perches, fee simple; WIT: Isaac WILSON, Henry JOHNSTON, ack. Henry JOHNSTON, JP, ent. 2 Dec 1815, rec. 15 same.

F-35   Indenture, 21 Nov 1815, Christian HARSHMAN (wife Elizabeth), BCO; Joel WILKINSON, BCO; $90, land in Richland twp, beginning S 36 T 6 R 4, NBR: Thomas VANLAW, 12 1/4 acres, same land that Caleb ENGLE (wife Mercy) conveyed to HARSHMAN by deed dated 10 Jul 1813, recorded in Book D, p. 375, fee simple; his seal, her mark, WIT: Levi PICKERING, Isaac WILSON, ack. Henry JOHNSTON, JP, ent. 2 Dec 1815, rec. [15] same.

F-36   Indenture, 29 Nov 1815, James BARNES (wife Nancy), BCO; Robert PRICE, BCO; $187, east half of lot #39 in Barnesville, 1/8 acre, plus all improvements except front room of the house on the front of said half lot; WIT: John BEVAN, Thomas SHANNON, receipt of money from Robert PRICE for use of James BEVAN ack. by John BEVAN, ack. John BEVAN, JP, ent. 4 Dec 1815, rec. 18 same.

F-37   Indenture, 29 Nov 1815, Josiah PENNINGTON (wife Deborah), BCO; Robert PRICE, BCO; $125, west 1/2 of front lot #8 (1/8 acre) and whole of back lot #104 (1/4 acre) in Barnesville; WIT: John BEVAN, Sally ALEXANDER, ack. John BEVAN, JP, ent. 9 Dec 1815, rec. 18 same.

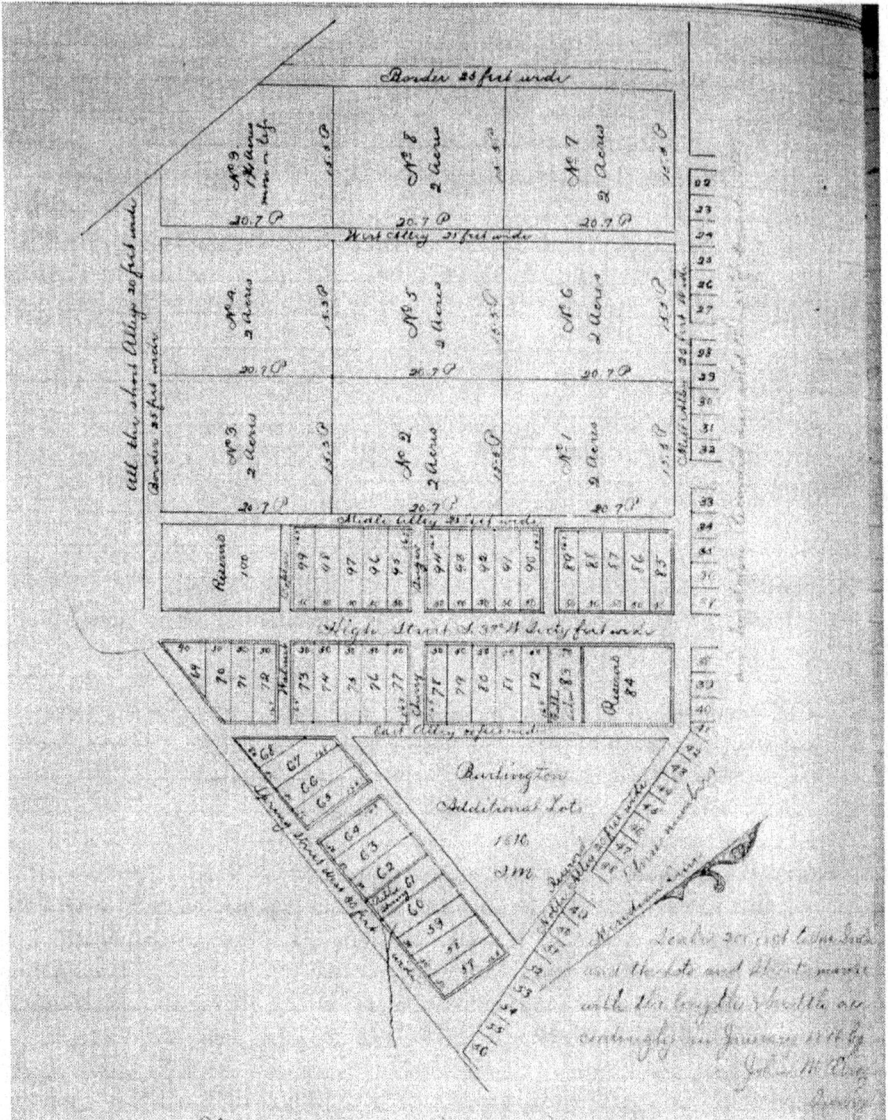

Plat of Additional Lots to Burlington

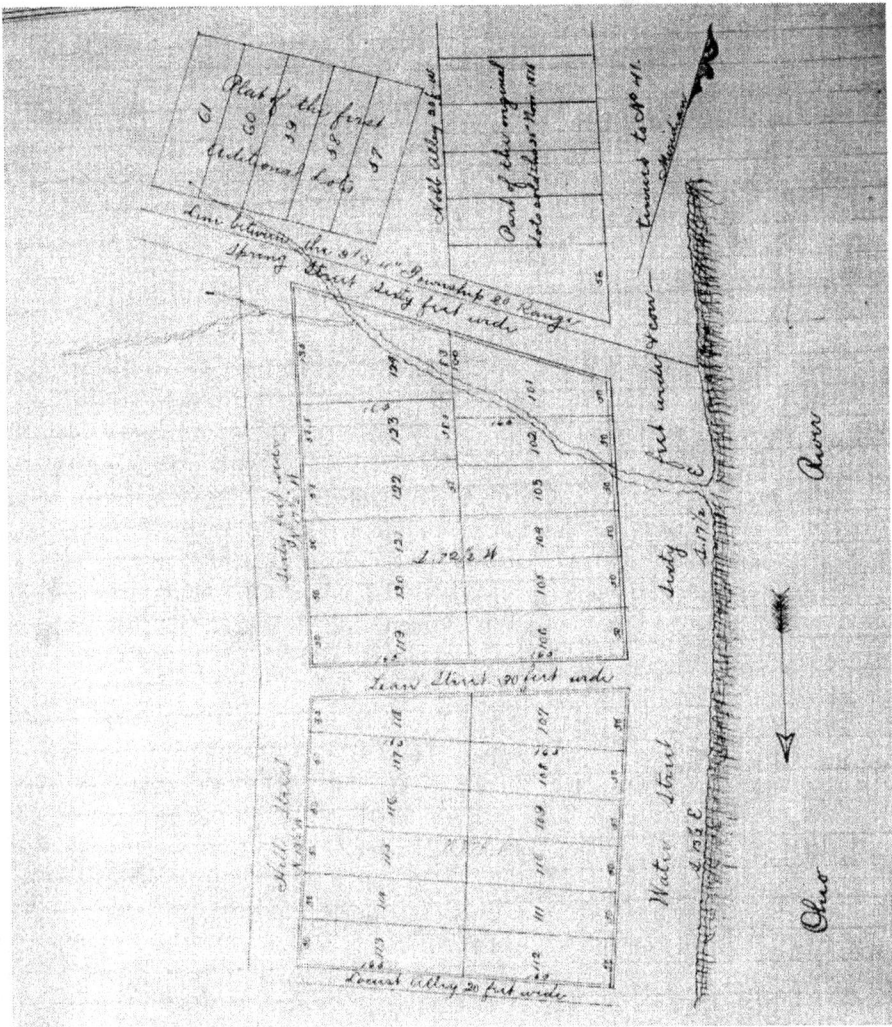

Plat of Another Addition to Burlington

E-38   Indenture, 1 Aug 1815, Joseph TILTON (wife Marcy), JCO; Jacob HAMBLER, BCO; $500, part of Ss 15 and 21 T 4 R 2 on Bigg run, NBR: Archibald WOOD(S?), Joseph TILTON, William STRINGER, 10 acres; his seal, her mark, WiT: [Euzander] TILTON (her mark), ack. JCO, Thomas MITCHELL, ent. 8 Dec 1815, rec. 18 same.

E-39   Indenture, 2 Dec 1815, Caleb ENGLE, BCO; George VANLAW, BCO; $180, part of NW 1/4 S 30 T 6 R 4, granted to ENGLE by patent dated 29 Dec 1808, NBR: Benjamin COMB(S), 78 acres 20 poles; WIT: David MOORE, Sterling JOHNSTON, ack. Sterling JOHNSTON, JP, ent. 8 Dec 1815, rec. 18 same.

E-40   Indenture, 14 d 10 m 1815, James WRIGHT (wife Hannah), BCO; Joseph DOUGLASS, Flushing, BCO; $500, land on [Truil] fork of big stillwater, SE 1/4 S 32 T 9 R 5, Steubenville district, 103 acres 80 perches except 51 acres 3 rods and 26 perches of west side deeded to Jacob VENPELT, same 1/4 S granted to WRIGHT by patent dated 15 Aug 1811, WIT: Robert LEE, William JONES, ack. 14 Oct 1815, Robert LEE, JP, ent. 12 Dec 1815, rec. 21 same.

E-41   Indenture, 1 Sep 1815, Frederick AULT (wife Nancy), Barnesville, BCO; John HINDS, St. Clairsville, BCO; $400, part of lot #93 of St. Clairsville, NBR: BENTLEY, Lewis SUTTON, fee simple; WIT: John BERRY, Sterling JOHNSTON, ack. of Frederick by Sterling JOHNSTON, JP, ack. 9 Dec 1815 of Nancy by John BEVAN, ent. 12 Dec 1815, rec. 21 same.

E-43   Indenture, 2 Oct 1815, James BARNES (wife Nancy), BCO; James B. FINLEY, BCO; $80, two front lots #26 and #27 and two back lots #122 and #123 in Barnesville, each 1/4 acre; his seal, her mark, WIT: John BEVAN, Harriet BARNES, ack. John BEVAN, JP, ent. 13 Dec 1815, rec. 23 same.

E-44   Indenture, 25 d 10 m 1815, William BELL (wife Mary), BCO; Samuel DANIEL, late of Loudon County, Virginia; $680.53, part of NW 1/4 S 4 T 8 R 5, NBR: John BOYED, Samuel THOMPSON, Arthur MORRISON, 60 3/4 acres 17 poles, same land sold by James LUNDY (wife Anne) of Green County, Pennsylvania, to William BELL on 22 May 1815 as recorded in Book E, p. 244; both mark, WIT: Wm. SINCLAIR, Eli NICKOLS, ack. 12 Dec 1815, Wm. SINCLAIR, JP, ent. 15 Dec 1815, rec. 25 same.

F-45   Indenture, 9 d 10 m 1815, Samuel EDGERTON (wife Elizabeth), BCO; James EDGERTON, BCO; $350, S 1/2 of NE 1/4 S 34 T 6 R 5, Marietta District; WIT: John BEVAN, Wm. FOULTON, ack. 9 Oct 1815, John BEVAN, ent. 19 Dec 1815, rec. 27 same.

Plat of Market Hill

F-46   Indenture, 9 Aug 1815, William CHAPLINE, Ohio County, Virginia; Duncan MORRISON, BCO; $130, land adjoining Morristown, 21 acres 2 rods 38 perches; WIT: John EATON, John STEWART, ack. John EATON, JP, ent. 22 Dec 1815, rec. 27 same.

F-47   Know all men, William WRIGHT, BCO, deceased, on 13 Jun 1806 purchased of Aaron HOLLIWAY (wife Rachel) of Stafford County, Virginia, the NW 1/4 S 32 T 9 R 5, Steubenville district, 147 20/100 acres, WRIGHT deceased before title could be made, now this indenture witnesses that for $586.80 paid by William WRIGHT and now conveyed to Joseph WRIGHT, John WRIGHT, William WRIGHT, Sarah WRIGHT, Elizabeth WRIGHT, and Rebeckah WRIGHT, heirs at law, as tenants in common, fee simple; sgn: 4 Jul 1815, WIT: John McCORMICK, Presley CORDELL, ack. Loudon County, Virginia, Rachel HOLLIWAY certifies that she still agrees with the transaction, by John McCORMICK, Presley CORDELL, Charles BINNS, clerk, acknowledges McCORMICK and CORDELL, Francis PEYTON, presiding justice of court of Loudon County, certifies BINNS's attestation, sgn: 29 Jul 1815, ent. 22 Dec 1815, rec. 27 same.

F-49   Plat of Markethill, in SE e1/4 S 10 T 5 R 3, Steubenville district, 40 in lots, done 20 Dec 1815, WIT: William JEFFERS, Proprietor, John DAUGHERTY, Surveyor, ent. 22 Dec 1815, rec. 27 same.

F-50   Indenture, 19 d 6 m 1815, Joseph NICHOLSON, BCO; Aaron WOOD, BCO; $182.25, part of S 14 T 7 R 5, 81 acres, fee simple; WIT: Jesse WHITE, Isreal WHITE, ack. James WHITE, JP, ent. 22 Dec 1815, rec. 29 same.

F-51   Indenture, 18 Apr 1815, James HUNTSMAN (wife Catharine), BCO; John McCLENAHAN, Washington County, Pennsylvania; $700, 100 acres, part of SE 1/4 S 14 T 8 R 4, granted to Jacob KEELIN by patent dated 27 Aug 1805, KEELIN conveyed E 1/2 to Peter WIRICK with a reserve of 50 acres in NE 1/4 S by deed dated 10 Feb 1808, WIRICK conveyed to HUNTSMAN by patent dated 25 Apr 1814; his seal, her mark, WIT: David WALLACE, James HASTINGS, ent. 22 Dec 1815, rec. 30 same, ack. <u>8</u> Apr 1815, David WALLACE, JP, [no ent. or rec. data].

F-52   Indenture, __ day of __ 1815, Stephen WORKMAN, BCO; John WORKMAN, BCO; $160, W 1/2 SE 1/4 S 4 T 5 R 3, granted to Stephen by James Madison by patent dated 15 Jan 1814, 80 acres; [no WIT], ack. 20 Dec 1815, John CUNNINGHAM, ent. 23 Dec 1815, rec. 30 same.

F-53   Indenture, 15 Nov 1811, Stephen MILLER, city, county and state of New York; George MILLER, Ohio Co., Virginia; $300, N portion S 36 T 1 R 2, NBR:

Samuel CARPENTER, Daniel McELHERON, deceased, 200 acres; [no WIT], ack. 15 Nov 1811, DeWitt CLINTON, Mayor of New York, ent. 30 Dec 1815, rec. 1 Jan 1816.

F-54   Indenture, 9 Sep 1815, James SINCLAIR (wife Mary), Barnesville, BCO; Isahel TOMPKINS, BCO; James SINCLAIR ([Senr.], deceased, by will dated 20 d 2 m 1806 bequeathed to James SINCLAIR above E end of SW 1/4 S 18 T 7 R 5, Steubenville district, 77 acres 2 rods 37 poles, recorded in Book ___ page ___, conveyed by James and Mary for $460 to Isahel TOMPKINS, fee simple; his seal, her mark, WIT: John BEVANS, Benjamin TOMPKINS, ack. John BEVAN, JP, ent. 4 Jan 1816, rec. same.

F-56   Indenture, 30 Aug 1815, Joseph WRIGHT (wife Eleanor), BCO; Mary TOMPKINS, BCO; $30, lot #80 in town of Belmont, 28 rods, plat recorded in Book B, p. 288; WIT: William SMITH, Benjamin TOMPKINS, ack. William SMITH, JP, ent. 4 Jan 1816, rec. 8 same.

F-57   Indenture, ____ of _____ 1815, Phebe YARNELL (widow of Mordecai YARNELL, late of Wheeling, Ohio Co., deceased) and his son Peter YARNELL, John YARNELL, Amos YARNELL, and Phebe his wife, Joseph CALDWELL and wife Mary, Aquila M. BOLTON and Elizabeth his wife, and Lucinda YARNELL, wife of Peter YARNELL, all now or late of Wheeling; John MAXWELL, Richland twp, BCO; $___ for land sold during Mordecai's lifetime, beginning SW corner S 29 T 6 R 3, NBR: George BEAM, 20 acres; WIT: John LIST, Joseph CALDWELL (and Mary CALDWELL), the witness of the last two dated 29 Dec 1815.

F-58   Indenture, 29 Nov 1815, James BARNES (wife Nancy), BCO; Benjamin BONEN, BCO; $180, one and a half lots in Barnesville, W 1/2 of front lot #39 and one back lot #71, front lot 1/8 acre, back lot 1/4 acre; his seal, her mark, WIT: John BEVAN, Thomas SHANNON, receipt of payment WIT: John BEVAN, ack. John BEVAN, JP, ent. 9 Jan 1816, rec. 10 same.

F-60   Indenture, 10 Jan 1816, Sterling JOHNSTON (wife Mary), BCO; George PAULL, BCO; $700, part of Ss 6 and 36 Rs 3 and 4, 131 1/4 acres 1 perch; another tract of land, NBR: George PAULL, 26 1/2 acres, part of S 6 T 7 R 4, fee simple; WIT: David MOORE, Henry JOHNSTON, ack. Henry JOHNSTON, JP, ent. 10 Jan 1816, rec. 12 same.

F-61   Indenture, 14 Dec 1815, John PIGGOTT, BCO; [Enos PICKERING, B.S.]; to secure debt and $1 paid by Enos PICKERING, B.S., 73 acres, NW 1/2 NW 1/4 S 26 T 9 R 5, BCO, where he now lives, void if PIGGOTT pays $200 plus interest in one year as well as a book account of $86, totaling $286; WIT: James GLEVE, John LIPPINCOTT, ack. 15 Dec 1815, John EATON, JP, ent. 17 Jan

1816, rec. same; satisfaction of mortgage received 25 Nov 1817 by Enos PICKERING, WIT: William FARIS, Junr., Recorder.

F-62   Indenture, 9 Aug 1815, William CHAPLINE (wife Mary), Ohio County, Virginia; John EATON, BCO; $77.50, out lot adjoining Morristown, NBR: Jno. C. HIERS, Samuel WILSON, 4 acres 1 rod 27 ps.; [Mary does not sign], WIT: A. GASTON, John MILLER, ack. Henry JOHNSTON, ent. 22 Jan 1815, rec. 23 same.

F-63   Indenture, 16 Nov 1815, William CONGLETON (wife Nancy) of Guirnsey County, Ohio; Daniel BRANGER [BRANINGER], of Pennsylvania; $125, four lots in St. Clairsville, #90, #82, #74, and #66; WIT: David DAUGHERTY, Peter UMSTOT, ack. Guernsey County, Ohio, Peter UMSTOT, JP, certified by Cyrus P. BEATTY, clerk, under seal of court at Cambridge, 27 Nov 1815, ent. 22 Jan 1816, rec. 24 same.

F-65   Indenture, 17 Nov 1815, Alexander YOUNG (wife Jane), Guernsey County, Ohio; William BOOKER, BCO; $60, lot #124 in St. Clairsville, 1/4 acre, plat recorded Book A, p. 31, conveyed from George MYERS (wife Mary) to Joseph MERRITT on 1 Feb 1807, [no statement about conveyance from MERRITT to YOUNG], fee simple; WIT: Robert ISRAEL, Sterling JOHNSTON, ack. 28 Dec 1815, Sterling JOHNSTON, JP, ent. 22 Jan 1816, rec. 26 same.

F-66   Indenture, 1 Dec 1815, Jacob WISE; John WISE, both BCO; $65.78, purchased one smith's anvil, one vice, one pair of smith's bellows, one sledge hammer and tongs which Jacob now possesses; WIT: Abm. WORKMAN, Samuel WISE, ack. 23 Dec 1815, Jacob DAVIS, JP, ent. 22 Jan 1816, rec. 26 same.

F-67   To all people, James EDGERTON (wife Sarah), George STARBUCK (wife Elizabeth), on 19 d 7 _____ 1809, execute deed poll to John BROWN, extr. of heirs of Francis TETER, land part of S 4 T 5 R 4, Marietta district, 50 acres, recorded Book C, p. 150; Caty TETER, one of heirs, for $35 paid by John BROWN conveys her quota and dividend of undivided land; her mark, WIT: [C. DENKIMS or DENHIMS], John WALTON, ack. Washington Co., Pa., [C. DENHIMS], ent. 23 Jan 1816, rec. 29 same.

F-68   Plat of additional lots to Burlington, by John McELROY, Surveyor, ack. 24 Jan 1816 of Saith HUNT, agent for the Belmont Manufacturing Company, Sterling JOHNSTON, (Senr.), JP, ent. 24 Jan 1816, rec. 30 same.

F-69   Plat of second additional lots to Burlington, laid off by Samuel LEAN, 23 Jan 1816, ack 23 Jan 1816 of Samuel LEAN, proprietor, part of fractional S 18 T 3 R 2, BCO, John CLARK, JP, ent. 24 Jan 1816, rec. 31 same.

F-70   Indenture, 29 Jan 1816, Robert ARMSTRONG (wife Margaret), BCO; William MOORE, Loudon County, Virginia; $2,300, land on Capteen creek, part of SW 1/4 S 21 T 4 R 3, Marietta district, NBR: Mc. MARTIN, Able BROWN, David RUBLE, 134 acres 1 rod, 6 poles; his seal, her mark [Margrit], WIT: Edw. BRYSON, Josiah DILLON, William DILLON, ack. Josiah DILLON, JP, ent. 30 Jan 1816, rec. 3 Feb same.

F-71   Indenture, 2 Dec 1815, David MOORE (wife Isabella), BCO; Isaac MOORE, BCO; $79.50, 39 3/4 acres, part of W 1/2 SW 1/4 S 26 T 6 R 3, 1/4 S granted to David MOORE by James Maddison, president, by patent dated 10 Oct 1815, NBR: William JOHNSTON; she signs "Isabella C. MOORE," WIT: Geo. PAULL, Sterling JOHNSTON, ack. Sterling JOHNSTON, JP, ent. 30 Jan 1816, rec. 5 Feb same.

F-72   Indenture, 17 Aug 1815, Artemus BAKER (wife ____), BCO; William CHAPLINE, Junr., Ohio County, Virginia; $1, lot in Canton as laid out by Ebenezer ZANE in fractional S 28, T 3 R 2, part of square #8 in town, ". . . nevertheless, that if the said Artemus BAKER does not pay off and satisfy a note this day drawn by the said Artemus BAKER, William HURKINS, and Moses W. CHAPLINE for the sum of ninety dollars payable to John WHITE &c. for the use of the Ohio Company in sixty days after the date thereof or does not pay off satisfy and finally discharge the said William HARKINS and Moses W. CHAPLINE from said note," William CHAPLINE can sell land to highest bidder, costs of advertising to be taken out, then paid to HARKINS and Moses W. CHAPLINE amount for which they are liable because of default of Artemus BAKER to pay to John WHITE for the use of the Ohio Company, if BAKER pays he gets to keep his land and William CHAPLINE, Junr., serves only as a trustee; wife's name at signing is Mehitable BAKER, WIT: Henry RHODES, James RICHARDS, ack. John CLARK, JP, ent. 3 Feb 1816, rec. 8 same.

F-74   Indenture, 25 Nov 1814, Joseph SHARP (wife Nancy), BCO; William SHARP, BCO; $320, 160 acres, part of W 1/2 S 32 T 8 R 4, granted to Joseph SHARP by patent dated 18 Feb 1806, NBR: William DIXON, Joseph SHARP; his seal, her mark, WIT: John CAMPBELL, Matthew McCALL, ack. 26 Nov 1814, John CAMPBELL, JP, ent. 5 Feb 1816, rec. 8 same.

F-75   Indenture, 11 Oct 1815, Philip LAURANCE (wife Lydia) of Short-creek twp, Harrison County, Ohio; Benjamin GRAY of Colerain twp, BCO; $450, 50 acres, same conveyed to LAURANCE from Christopher CARROTHERS by deed dated 30 Mar 1815, part of S 9 T 8 R 4; WIT: David WALLACE, Alexander SMILEY, ack. David WALLACE, JP, ent. 5 Feb 1816, rec. 9 same.

F-76   Indenture, 1 Mar 1815, Bazaleel WELLS and Elias VANARSDALE, two
of extrs. of Daniel McELHERAN, deceased, of Newark, Essex County, New
Jersey; John CUNNINGHAM, BCO; by McELHERAN's dated 25 May 1807
appointed William HILL (city of New York, New York), merchants Bazaleel
WELLS (Steubenville, JCO) and Elias VAN ARSDALE (Newark, Essex County,
New Jersey), counselor at law, extrs; $650, convey to CUNNINGHAM part of T
2 R 2, NBR: McMahon's creek, containing 224 acres 1 rod 22 perches; WIT for
VAN ARSDALE: A. DURAND, Archer GIFFORD, WIT for WELLS, Saml.
SALMON, J. G. HINING, ack. 28 Mar 1815, in Essex Co., New Jersey, Aaron
MUNN, MUNN certified by Silas WHITEHEAD, clerk of inferior court of
Common Pleas, ack. JCO, 26 Jul 1815, J. G. HINING, JP, ent. 6 Feb 1816, rec. 14
same.

F-78   Indenture, 31 Jan 1815, Peter LOFFER (wife Sarah, late Sarah PALMER),
Ohio County, Virginia; Artemus BAKER, Ohio County, Virginia; on 6 Aug 1809
Ebenezer ZANE (wife Elizabeth) sold to Sarah (wife of Peter LOFFER but then
Sarah PALMER), lot in Canton in fractional S 28 T 3 R 2, part of square #8, NBR:
Wheeling creek, now the LOFFERs for $130 convey same to Artemas BAKER;
she signs "Sally," WIT: Joseph CALDWELL, Jacob BURKITT, ack. Ohio Co.,
Virginia, 2 Feb 1815, Joseph CALDWELL and Jacob BURKITT, JPs, ent. 10 Feb
1816, rec. 17 same.

F-80   Indenture, 22 Dec 1815, James BARNES (wife Nancy), BCO; Alexander
LINTON, BCO; $40, lots #3 and 99 in Barnesville, each 1/4 acre; his seal, her
mark, WIT: John BEVAN, Thomas SHANNON, ack. John BEVAN, JP, ent. 10
Feb 1816, rec. 19 same.

F-80   Indenture, 25 d 12 m 1815, Jesse FOULKE, one of proprietors of town of
Flushing (wife Sarah), BCO; Jacob BRANSON, BCO; $30, lot #12 in Flushing;
WIT: James CROZER, Samuel CROSSBY], ack. 25 Dec 1815, Robert LEE, ent.
10 Feb 1816, rec. 19 same.

F-81   Indenture, 26 Dec 1815, William LUCAS, BCO; Precious [female]
LUCAS, BCO; $140, beginning SW corner NW 1/4 S 28 T 6 R 4, 35 acres, NBR:
Saml. LUCAS, Wm. LUCAS, Congress lands; sgn. William LUCAS and
Temperance LUCAS [her mark], WIT: Valentine SAURHEBER, Samuel LUCAS,
ack. 25 Dec 1815, Valentine SAUERHEBER, JP, ent. 12 Feb 1816, rec. 19 same.

F-83   Indenture, 12 Feb 1816, William REYNOLDS (wife Barbarah), BCO;
James PATTERSON, JCO; $150, part of lot #97 in St. Clairsville, conveyed to
REYNOLDS by Sterling JOHNSTON (wife Mary), 19 Jan 1814, fee simple; sgn:
William B. REYNOLDS, her mark, WIT: [Munrin TOUNGT] (possibly
germanic?), ack. Sterling JOHNSTON, JP, ent. 12 Feb 1816, rec. 19 same.

F-84   At a meeting of the Citizens of Barnesville and its vicinity, 4 Feb 1814, held at house of Samuel BARNES to consult upon measure for establishing a manufacturing company in Barnesville to manufacture woolen and cotton cloth, also a grist and saw mill, machinery propelled by steam, also a store; list of Articles of Association; commissioners: James BARNES, David SMITH, Richard EDGERTON, Joseph ALEXANDER, John SMITH, Samuel SHARPLESS, William PHILPOT; subscribers (places of residence): Jesse NEWPORT (Mount Pleasant), Isaac HALL, Junr. (Barnesville, now Bvl), James BARNES (Bvl), William PHILPOT (Bvl), Joseph COX (Bvl), Joseph ALEXANDER (Bvl), Saml. SHARPLESS (Bvl), John SMITH (Goshen), Jacob MEYERS (Bvl), Joel JUDKINS (Bvl), Jesse BAILEY (Bvl), Isaac HALL (Bvl), John HALL (Bvl), Isaac CLENDENON (Goshen), Henry HOWARD (Stillwater), Josiah PENINGTON (Bvl), George ADUDDELL (Bvl), David SMITH (Captina), Thomas SHANNON (Bvl), Richard EDGERTON (Bvl), John DOUDNA (Bvl), Nathan RILEY (Bvl), Wm. HAMILTON (Mount Pleasant), Robt. THOMPSON (St. Clairsville), Robert LYLE (Washington), Thos. PLUMMER (Bvl), Demsey BOSWELL (Bvl), William BUNDY (Bvl), Stephen HODGIN (Captina), Rachel MARIS [her mark] (Captina), Thomas WILLIAMS (Captina), Jas. M. ROUND (Bvl), David SNIDER (Bvl), Otho FRENCH (Bvl), Henry BARNES, Jr. (Bvl); ack. 15 Feb 1816, Jno. BEVAN, ent. 19 Feb 1816, rec. 21 same.

F-89   Indenture, 21 Feb 1816, Alexander GRAY, BCO; Richard TRAVES, BCO; $300, S 32 T 7 R 3, NBR: William FORGUSON, 60 acres 2 rods 11 perches; sgn: ___ Dec 1815, WIT: David JENNINGS, Josiah HEDGES, ack. Sterling JOHNSTON, JP, ent. 21 Feb 1816, rec. 23 same.

F-90   Indenture, 13 Dec 1815, Samuel HILTON, Montgomery County, Maryland; Vachel HALL, BCO; $200, lots #58/90, #59/91, total 1 acre in Barnesville; WIT: Abra. S. HAYS, Zadok LANHAM, ack. Montgomery County, 13 Dec 1815, Abram S. HAYS, Zadok LANHAM, Abraham S. HAYS and Zadok LANHAM certified by Upton BEALL, Clk., ent. 23 Feb 1816, rec. 24 same.

F-91   Indenture, 23 Nov 1815, Jacob BURKITT (wife Mary Ann), Burrough of Wheeling; Elijah WOODS, BCO; $1,000, fractional S 28 T 3 R 2, NBR: Ohio river, no right to construct a ferry or other transportation across the river; [no WIT], ack. Ohio County [Virginia], Geo. MILLER and Noah ZANE, JPs, ent. 26 Feb 1816, rec. same.

F-92   Indenture, ___ Jan 1816, Ezra WILLIAMS (wife Amelia), BCO; Joseph HARDEY, BCO; $500, land on which WILLIAMS now lives, NBR: CARTER and FREEMAN [doesn't seem to be an acreage total]; WIT: E. WOODS, John CLARK, ack. 11 Jan 1815, John CLARK, JP, ent. 26 [or 24] Feb 1816, rec. 27 same.

F-93   Indenture, 21 Feb 1816, David SNIDER (wife Margret [Margaret]), BCO; Jesse HATCHER, BCO; $441.80, part of front lot #11 and back lot #107 in Barnesville; WIT: Jno. BEVAN, William WEIR, ack. John BEVAN, JP, ent. 2 Mar 1816, rec. 5 same.

F-94   Indenture, 15 Dec 1815, Robert THOMPSON (wife Margaret), BCO; Andrew McKINDLEY, BCO; $300, lots #21 and #22 in addition to St. Clairsville as laid out by William MATHERS, conveyed by Samuel SULLIVAN (wife Mary) on 24 Sep 1811, fee simple; his seal, her mark, WIT: John COPELAND, Sterling JOHSTON, ack. 1 Mar 1816, Sterling JOHNSTON, JP, ent. 2 Mar 1816, rec. 5 same.

F-95   Indenture, 6 Oct 1815, Jacob WINDLE [WINDLAND] (wife Margaret), Monroe County, Ohio; Robert ARMSTRONG, BCO; $800, SW 1/4 S 21 T 4 R 3, Marietta district; both mark [as WINDLE], WIT: Levin OKEY, Mary PALMORE [her mark], ack. Monroe County, Ohio, Levin OKEY, one of associate judges, CCP, ent. 4 Mar 1816, rec. 7 same.

F-97   Indenture, 7 Aug 1815, William CHAPLINE, Ohio County, Virginia; John C. AYERS, BCO; $23, lot adjoining Morristown, BCO, beginning at SE corner of John C. AYERS' dwelling; WIT: Joseph LACOCK, David SNIDER, ack. John EATON, JP, ent. 4 Mar 1816, rec. 7 same.

F-98   Indenture, 2 Dec 1815, David MOORE (wife Isabella), BCO; William JOHNSTON, BCO; $160, 80 acres, E 1/2 SW 1/4 S 26 T 6 R 3, granted to MOORE by James Madison by patent dated 10 Oct 1815; WIT: Geo. PAULL, Sterling JOHNSTON, ack. Sterling JOHNSTON, JP, ent. 4 Mar 1816, rec. 7 same.

F-99   Indenture, 23 Jan 1816, Borden STANTON (wife Charlotte), BCO; Isahel BOOTH, Wheeling, Virginia; $1,000, part of Ss 1 and 7 T 7 R 3, NBR: James STEER, BERRY; WIT: John CLARKE, Nathan PIGGOTT, ack. John CLARKE, JP, receipt of money indicated, but no dates or witnesses, ack. 29 Feb 1816, Josiah HEDGES, clerk, CCP, stating Borden STANTON is a JP, ent. 4 Mar 1816, rec. 8 same.

F-101   Indenture, 6 Mar 1816, Robert WOODS (wife Elizabeth); Joseph ANDERSON [no locations given]; $385.50, in S 33 T 4 R 2, 128 acres 2 rods 32 perches, by John STEWART, county surveyor, WIT: James ALEXANDER, Simon BROWN, ack. James ALEXANDER, assoc. judge, ent. 8 Mar 1816, rec. [11] same.

F-102   Indenture, 9 Mar 1816, David MOORE, sheriff, BCO; Josiah HEDGES and Geo. PAULL, BCO; officers of Bank of Steubenville at July term 1815 obtained a judgment against Samuel ZANE for $367.09 damages, $11 costs; Samuel ROBINSON at same term obtained judgment against Samuel ZANE for $80._ _, $10 costs; two writs of fiere facious issued from CCP dated 4 Aug 1815 commanding MOORE to recover from ZANE's property enough to cover judgments, ROBINSON levied against a parcel of land owned by ZANE containing 100 acres, part of S 24 and fraction 18 T 3 R 2, W side of Ohio River, NBR: Ebenezer MARTIN, Samuel ZANE; MOORE sold at public sale on 2 Dec 1815 to Josiah HEDGES and George PAULL for $12 per acre; WIT: David JENNINGS, Joseph MORRISON, ack. 9 Mar 1816, Sterling JOHNSTON, JP, ent. 9 Mar 1816, rec. 12 same.

F-104   Indenture, 12 Sep 1815, Solomon COLES (wife Elizabeth), BCO; Thomas EMORY, BCO; $73, part of NW corner NW 1/2 S 21 T 8 R 6, Steubenville district, 2 acres 105 rods, fee simple; WIT: Robert MILLS, John BEVAN; receipt of money certified by COLES, same WIT, ack. John BEVAN, JP, ent. 12 Mar 1816, rec. same.

F-105   Indenture, 12 Sep 1815, James BARNES (wife Nancy), BCO; Thomas EMORY, BCO; $270, NW corner NE 1/4 S 21 T 8 R 6, Steubenville district, 10 acres 8 7/10 perches, fee simple; his seal, her mark, WIT: John BEVAN, Solomon COLES, ack. John BEVAN, JP, ent. 12 Mar 1812, rec. same.

F-106   Indenture, 12 d 2 m 1816, Rachel WOOLMAN, Goshen twp, Chester County, Pennsylvania, single woman; Evan GRIFFITH, same; $250, part of S 19 T 8 R 5, Steubenville district, granted to Samuel WOOLMAN, Junr., by patent dated 5 Apr 1806, Samuel and wife Rebeckah by indenture dated 12 d 10 m 1811, recorded in Book D, p. 207, conveyed to his father Samuel WOOLMAN, Senr., in fee; Samuel WOOLMAN, Senr., by LW&T dated 15 d 12 m 1814, since decease proven at CCP held at New Lisbon for Columbia County, Ohio, on 9 Mar 1815, part of NE 1/2 S 19 T 8 R 5, bounded on north by land devised to his son Aaron, on west by land devised to George WOOLMAN, on south by land devised to Elizabeth GRIFFITH, wife of Evan GRIFFITH, on east by other land; WIT: Joshua WEAVER, John GRAVES, ack. 12 Feb 1816, Chester County, Pennsylvania, John GRAVES, JP, receipt of money WIT: by Joshua WEAVER, GRAVES certified by Jesse JOHN, prothonotary of CCP at West Chester, ent. 13 Mar 1816, rec. 16 same.

F-108   Indenture, 11 Oct 1815, William BALLINGER, Frederick County, Maryland, extr. LW&T of Daniel BALLINGER, late of said county; Thomas SMITH, BCO; LW&T dated 20 Sep 1806 and recorded in office of the register of wills in Frederick County, Maryland, $800, 80 acres, W 1/2 NE 1/4 S 9 T 8 R 6, according to deed from Jonathan TAYLOR to Daniel BALLINGER; WIT: Jacob BARR, Michl. HOUSES, ack. Maryland, Jacob BARR, Michl. HOUSES, receipt of money acknowledged, BARR and HOUSES certified by John SCHOLEY, Clk., ent. 18 Mar 1816, rec. 19 same.

F-110   Indenture, 19 Dec 1815, John DELONG, Guernsey County, Ohio; Benjamin FISH, Ohio County, Virginia; $400, NE 1/4 S 11 T 5 R 3 and 7 acres of fractional S 5 T 5 R 3, NBR: David HARRAH; his seal, mark of Sarah DELONG, WIT: John BEVAN, Edward CARPENTER, ack. BCO, John BEVAN, JP, ent. 14 Mar 1816, rec. 19 same.

F-111   Indenture, 16 d 3 m 1816, Joel PATTERSON (wife Penninah [Peninah]), Warren twp, BCO; John PATTERSON, [Warren] twp, BCO; $160, 1/2 SW 1/4 S 17 T 7 R 6, 80 acres, fee simple; Jno. BEVAN, Thomas LAWSON, ack. 16 Mar 1816, John BEVAN, JP, ent. 18 Mar 1816, rec. 20 same.

F-112   Indenture, 23 Feb 1816, Joseph WRIGHT (wife Eleanor), BCO; Benjamin THOMPKINS, BCO; $50, lot #12 in town of Belmont, 28 rods, according to plat in Book B, p. 288; WIT: Ezer DILLON, Josh. TRIMBLE, ack. 28 Feb 1816, Wm. SMITH, JP, ent. 20 Mar 1816, rec. 25 same.

F-113   Indenture, 29 Dec 1815, Joseph WRIGHT (wife Eleanor), BCO; Joshua TRIMBLE, BCO; $150, lot #56 in town of Belmont, 28 rods, plat recorded in Book B, p. 288; WIT: Daniel [GINN], John BOYD, ack. 4 Jan 1816, Wm. SMITH, JP, ent. 20 Mar 1816, rec. 25 same.

F-114   Indenture, 20 Mar 1816, Joshua CLARK (wife Susannah), BCO; Isaac ELI [no location]; $570, NBR: Wheeling Creek, [Homes] WHITAKER, PATTON, formerly Richard TRUAX and Joshua CLARK, 60 acres 1 rod 7 perches, part of S 13 T 8 R 4, conveyed to CLARK by David BARTON (wife Nancy) on 26 May 1810, fee simple; both mark, WIT: John BAKER, Alexr. G. MAJOR, ack. Sterling JOHNSTON, JP, ent. 20 Mar 1816, rec. 26 same.

F-115   Indenture, 23 Mar 1816, Henry BILLMAN (wife Mary), BCO; William YATES, Philadelphia, Pennsylvania; $1,500, 104 acres, part of S 2 T 7 R 4, conveyed to BILLMAN by Leonard DIVEN by deed dated 15 Feb 1810, NBR: [Aban] ROBINSON, Thomas ROBINSON, William CHAMBERS, David MILLER; his seal, her mark, WIT: William FERGUSON, Henry JOHNSTON, ack. Henry JOHNSTON, JP, ent. 23 Mar 1816, rec. 26 same.

F-116   Indenture, 1 Mar 1815, Bazelial WELLS and Elias VAN ARSDALE, two of extrs. of LW&T of Daniel McELHERON of Newark, Essex County, New Jersey; Abraham WORKMAN, BCO; McELHERON's will dated 25 May 1807 authorizes sale of his land in fee simple, appointed William HILL (city of New York, New York), merchants Bazaleel WELLS (Steubenville, JCO) and Elias VAN

ARSDALE (Newark, Essex County, New Jersey), counselor at law, extrs; $160, conveyed SE 1/2 S 35 T 2 R 2, 160 acres, WIT for VAN ARSDALE: A. DURAND, Archie GIFFORD, WIT for WELLS: Samuel SALMON, J. G. HINING, ack. 28 Mar 1815, Essex County, Aaron MUNN, judge of inferior CCP, MUNN certified by Silas WHITEHEAD, clerk; ack. 26 Jul 1815, JCO, J. G. HINING, JP.

F-119   Indenture, 27 Feb 1816, James BARNES (wife Nancy), BCO; Thomas WEBSTER, BCO; $40, front lot #49 and back lot #81 in Barnesville, each 1/4 acre; his seal, her mark, WIT: Jno. BEVAN, Jacob MYERS, ack. John BEVAN, JP, ent. 25 Mar 1816, rec. 20 same.

F-120   Indenture, 28 Apr 1815, Jacob MYERS (wife Sarah), Wheeling twp, BCO; Reuben ALLEN, Cadiz twp, Harrison County, Ohio; $390, 14 acres 37 perches, part of Ss 8 and 9 in T 8 R 4, Steubenville district, Wheeling twp, the former to David WALLACE and the latter to Adam SEEBIRT who by their deeds dated 30 Dec 1807 conveyed lots to Jacob MYERS; his seal, her mark, WIT: David WALLACE, William [GUMMEURE], ack. David WALLACE, ent. 28 Mar 1816, rec. 3 Apr same.

F-121   Indenture, 2 Dec 1815, David MOORE (wife Isabella), BCO; Joseph LATSHAW, Washington County, Pennsylvania; $1,000, 40 1/4 acres, part of SW 1/4 S 26 T 6 R 3, granted to MOORE by patent dated 10 Oct 1815, NBR: Isaac MOORE, William JOHNSTON; WIT: Geo. PAULL, Sterling JOHNSTON, ack. Sterling JOHNSTON, JP, ent. 28 Mar 1816, rec. 3 Apr same.

F-123   Indenture, 2 Mar 1816, James BARNES (wife Nancy), BCO; Robert MILLS, BCO; $40, lots #12 and #108 in Barnesville, each 1/4 acre; his seal, her mark, WIT: Harriet BARNES, John BEVAN, ack. John BEVAN, JP, ent. 1 Apr 1816, rec. 5 same.

F-123   Indenture, 29 Mar 1816, Robert MILLS (wife Patience), BCO; Joseph KERR, Washington County, Pennsylvania; $325, lots #12 and 108 in Barnesville, each 1/4 acre; his seal, her mark; WIT: Jno. BEVAN, Josiah PENNINGTON, ack. John BEVAN, JP, ent. 1 Apr 1816, rec. 6 same.

F-124   Indenture, 5 d 2 m 1816, Joshua WOOD (one of proprietors of town of Flushing) (wife Hannah), BCO: Jesse FOULKE (also one of proprietors of Flushing); $8, part of lots #13, 65, and 66, NBR: Samuel CROSLEY, FOULKE; WIT: Horatio MURPHY, Thomas CROZIER, ack. 5 Feb 1816, Robert LEE, ent. 1 Apr 1816, rec. 6 same.

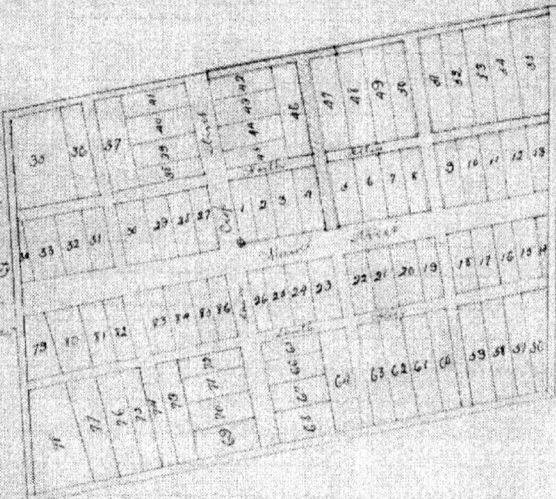

Plat of Farmington

F-125   Indenture, 1 Apr 1815, Caleb DILLE (wife Rebeckah), BCO; John MELOTT, BCO; $120, 30 acres 34 perches, part of S 35 T 5 R 3, granted to DILLE by patent dated 29 Dec 1808, NBR: McMahon's Creek, Obed. HARDESTY; his seal, her mark, WIT: Henry JOHNSTON, Phebe DILLE, ack. Henry JOHNSTON, JP, ent. 2 Apr 1816, rec. 6 same.

F-127   Indenture, 1 Apr 1815, Abner MURPHY (later wife Sarah), BCO; Peter WELLER, Guernsey County, Ohio; $150, lot adjoining Morristown, 34 perches, conveyed by Wm. W. GAULT on 1 Jun 1812; WIT: John MORRISON, Robert MORRISON, ack. D. MORRISON, JP, ent. 2 Apr 1816, rec. 9 same.

F-128   Plat of Town of Farmington, laid out by Daniel McPEAK (map upside down); sgn: 9 Apr 1816, his mark, WIT: Sterling JOHNSTON, Wm. [MORELY], ack. Sterling JOHNSTON, JP, rec. 10 Apr 1816.

F-129   Indenture, 20 Feb 1816, James BARNES (wife Nancy), BCO; David SNIDER, BCO; $40, lots #11 and #107 in Barnesville, each 1/4 acre; his seal, her mark, WIT: Jno. BEVAN, Harriet BARNES, ack. John BEVAN, JP, ent. 4 Apr 1816, rec. 10 same.

F-129   Whereas CCP in BCO at December term 1815 entered a rule of court authorizing William JOHNSTON and Sterling JOHNSTON, admrs. of Adam JOHNSTON, late of county deceased, to make to John FITZ a deed of conveyance for part of S 18 T 7 R 4, for $460, 76 acres 2 rods 39 perches, fee simple; WIT: Henry JOHNSTON, Margaret JOHNSTON, ack. 15 Dec 1815, Henry JOHNSTON, JP, ent. 4 Apr 1816, rec. 11 same.

F-131   Know all men, Thomas MARSHALL of Concord twp, Deleware County, Pennsylvania, appoint Zachar SCHOFIELD, BCO, his attorney, [refers to date "first written" but I don't see any such date]; WIT: Thomas SHANNON, Saml. SHARPLESS, ack. 18 Oct 1815, John BEVAN, JP, ent. 5 Apr 1816, rec. 11 same.

F-132   Indenture, 16 Mar 1816, Robert McBRIDE (wife Margaret), Wayne County, Ohio; Abner MOORE, Kirkwood twp, BCO; $340, part of SW 1/4 S 11 T 9 R 6, NBR: Stillwater, 90 acres, conveyed to McBRIDE by Reason PUMPHREY by deed dated 4 Apr 1814, recorded in Book D, p. 476, fee simple; WIT: Abner LAURENCE, Anna [CASE], ack. Wayne County, John LAWRENCE, JP, ent. 5 Apr 1816, rec. 12 same.

F-134   Indenture, 28 Mar 1816, Joseph LATSHAW (wife Mary), Washington County, Pennsylvania; Alexander McKITRICK, BCO; $2,000, 40 1/4 acres, part of SW 1/4 S 26 T 6 R 3, granted to David MOORE by patent dated 10 Oct 1815, NBR: Isaac MOORE, William JOHNSTON, fee simple; WIT: Christopher

HOLLINGSWORTH, Henry JOHNSTON, ack. Henry JOHNSTON, JP, ent. 6 Apr 1816, rec. 17 same.

F-135   Indenture, 23 Mar 1816, Leonard DIVAN (wife Abagail), BCO: David MILLER, BCO; $1,500, 85 1/4 acres 18 perches, part of S 2 T 7 R 4, conveyed by James CALDWELL to DIVAN by deed dated 16 Jun 1810, NBR: graveyard, a brook; both mark, WIT: Alban ROBINSON, Henry JOHNSTON, ack. Henry JOHNSTON, JP, ent. 8 Apr 1816, rec. 17.

F-136   Indenture, 9 Apr 1816, Mahlon SMITH (wife Mary), St. Clairsville, BCO; Daniel BRANNINGER, same place; $1,700, lots in St. Clairsville, #89 (conveyed by Abraham and Simon WOODROW to SMITH by deed dated 21 Apr 1807) and part of lot #105 (conveyed by David RUSSELL [wife Hannah] to SMITH by deed dated 27 Oct 1808); his seal, her mark, WIT: William [FROCTHE], Henry JOHNSTON, ack. Henry JOHNSTON, JP, ent. 8 Apr 1816, rec. 18 same.

F-138   Indenture, 12 Mar 1816, James BARNES (wife Nancy), BCO; Thomas EMORY, BCO; $40, lots #52 and #84 in Barnesville, each 1/4 acre, fee simple; his seal, her mark, WIT: John BEVAN, James STARR, ack. John BEVAN, JP, ent. 8 Apr 1816, rec. 18 same.

F-139   Indenture, 8 Dec 1815, Robert HENDERSON (wife Margaret), BCO; Elizabeth CRAIG and her son Joseph CRAIG, both Beaver County, Pennsylvania; $737, 86 3/4 acres 14 perches, part of SE 1/4 S 21 T 8 R 4, granted to David CAMPBELL by patent dated 9 Oct 1812, CAMPBELL conveyed to HENDERSON by deed dated 12 Apr 1814, NBR: Robert HENDERSON; his seal, her mark, WIT: John CAMPBELL, Samuel [GRAIG], ack. John CAMPBELL, JP, ent. 9 Apr 1816, rec. 23 same.

F-140   Indenture, 5 Jan 1816, Charles ACKLES (wife Mary), BCO: Solomon BENTLEY, BCO; $80, land near W end of St. Clairsville, conveyed to Robert McCOMBS "by James and Nancy his wife" [compiler's note: James BARNES, wife Nancy] by deed dated 13 May 1804, from McCOMBS by attorney Samuel SPRIGG on 13 May 1809 to Thomas IRELAND, by IRELAND (wife Sarah), to ACKLES, fee simple; sgn: and ack: ECKLES, WIT: Thomas LATIMER, Townsend W. FRASIER, ack. Thomas LATIMER, JP, ent. 10 Apr 1816, rec. 23 same.

F-141   Indenture, 28 Dec 1815, Samuel GREGG (wife Jane), BCO; Samuel WILSON, BCO; $120, NE corner of S 33 T 7 R 4, Steubenville district, NBR: Samuel ROBINSON, Samuel GREGG, part of land conveyed by Samuel GREGG, Senr. (wife Ann) by deed dated 16 Oct 1807 to this Samuel GREGG, fee simple;

WIT: Wm. SIN CLAIR, James GEORGE, ack. Wm. SINCLAIR, JP, ent. 16 Apr 1816, rec. 23 same.

F-143   Indenture, 5 d 2 m 1816, Jesse FOULKE (wife Sarah), one of proprietors of town of Flushing; Joseph DOUGLASS, same town; $30, lot #73 in Flushing; WIT: Samuel CROSSLY, David HOLLINGSWORTH, ack. 5 Feb 1816, Robert LEE, JP, ent. 16 Apr 1816, rec. 24 same.

F-143   Indenture, 16 d 3 m 1816, Joseph WRIGHT (wife Eleanor), BCO; Jacob GREGG, William EWERES [EWERS], William COFFEE, BCO; $16, parcel adjoining town of Belmont, NBR: Ezer DILLON, Joseph WRIGHT, in trust for members of society of friends, Goshen meeting; WIT: Allen BOND, James HOLLIWAY, John COFFEE, Junr., ack. 28 Mar 1816, Wm. SMITH, JP, ent. 1[6] Apr 1816, rec. 24 same.

F-145   Indenture, 30 Nov 1815, James BARNES (wife Nancy), BCO; Abraham PETERS, Junr., BCO; $30, lot #43 in Barnesville, 1/4 acre, fee simple; his seal, her mark, WIT. Thos. SHANNON, John BEVAN, ack. John BEVAN, JP, ent. 16 Apr 1816, rec. 29 same.

F-145   Whereas James RATIKIN, late of <u>Tuskeraway</u> County, Ohio, deceased, during life sold NW 1/4 S 24 T 7 R 5 to William SMITH of BCO for $497.33 to be paid by installments, RATIKIN died before completion of agreement, now Samuel BARBER of Harrison County and Isaac PARKER of Jefferson County, Ohio, extrs., SMITH having paid extrs. $146 and RATIKIN $333.33, by order of CCP at April term 1814, convey 1/4 S according to law, sgn: 17 Dec 1814, Samuel BARBER, Isaac PARKER, WIT: Joseph LACOCK, John MORRISON, ack: 27 May 1815, Duncan MORRISON, JP, ent. 18 Apr 1816, rec. 29 same.

F-147   Indenture, 28 Feb 1816, Robert ARMSTRONG (wife Margaret), BCO; Able BROWN, BCO; $50, 9 acres, part of S 21 T 4 R 3, NBR: David RUBLE, Captinia creek; his seal, her mark, WIT: Jno. CLINGAN, Joseph ARMSTRONG, ack. 29 Feb 1816, Micheal L. MARTIN, JP, ent. 16 Apr 1816, rec. 29 same.

F-148   Indenture, 22 Nov 1815, Joseph WRIGHT (wife Eleanor), BCO; William SMITH, BCO; $30, lot #49 in town of Belmont on plat recorded in Book B, p. 288, WIT: Joshua TREMBLE, Rachel DILLON, ack. James WHITE, JP, ent. 16 Apr 1816, rec. 30 same.

F-149   Indenture, 1 Apr 1816, Joseph HARDIE, Ohio County, Virginia; Elijah WOODS, BCO; $500, land on which Ezer WILLIAMS now lives, beginning at N corner of lot first <u>bot</u> by CARTER and FREEMAN and now occupied by Artemas BAKER; WIT: Sam. McCLURE, Cleaburn SIMMS, James SMITH, ack. Ohio

County, Geo. MILLER, Sam. McCLURE, two of the commonwealth's justices, justices certified by Wm. CHAPLINE, J.C.O.C., ent. 16 Apr 1816, rec. 30 same.

F-150   Indenture, 22 Mar 1816, Asa HOLLIWAY (wife Margaret), BCO; Eleazer EVANS, BCO; $500, SE 1/4 S 10 T 7 R 5, Steubenville district, patented 1 Nov 1811, Asa HOLLIWAY having made full payment; his seal, her mark, WIT: John NICHOLSON, Elizabeth HORSMAN, ack. John BOYD, JP, ent. 16 Apr 1816, rec. 30 same.

F-151   Indenture, 25 d 12 m 1815, Joshua WOOD, one of proprietors of town of Flushing, (wife Hannah); Samuel CROSSLEY, same town; $80, lot #62 in town of Flushing, 2 acres 4 perches; WIT: Jesse FOULKE, John KING, ack. 5 Feb 1816, Robert LEE, JP, ent. 17 Apr 1816, rec. 30 same.

F-152   Indenture, 12 Sep 1810, Allen BOND (wife Sarah), BCO; heirs of late Enos BROOMHALL, BCO; $9, land in S 13 T 8 R 5, Steubenville district, patented 21 Mar 1808, NBR: William EWERS, John [LAWIS], Allen BOND, &c.; WIT: John MORRISON, Michael ENLOW, ack. 20 Nov 1810, Duncan MORRISON, JP, ent. 17 Apr 1816, rec. 30 same.

F-154   Indenture, 14 Jan 1816, William RITCHIE, Wayne County, Ohio; Isaac HILL, BCO; $380, 31 acres 3 perches 13 perches, beginning NW corner S 1/2 S 36 T 7 R 4, patented to John EDWARDS on 7 Apr 1806, conveyed by EDWARDS to John PRICE on 28 May 1806, fee simple; WIT: Daniel BERRY, John LIST, ack. 15 Jan 1816, Henry JOHNSTON, JP, ent. 19 Apr 1816, recorded 6 May same.

F-155   Indenture, 5 d 9 m 1810, George STARBUCK (wife Elizabeth), Warren twp, BCO; Hezekiah STARBUCK, BCO; $100, land in NE 1/4 S 1 T 8 R 6, 50 acres, fee simple; William FLOOD [his mark], John GRIER, Senr., ack. 5 Sep 1810, John GRIER, JP, ent. 19 Apr 1816, rec. 6 May same.

F-156   Indenture, 28 d 11 m 1814, Jesse FOULKE, one of proprietors of town of Flushing) (wife Sarah), BCO; Ebenezer PIGGOTT, same town; $151, lots #23, #24, #25, #43, and #44 in town of Flushing; WIT: Robert LEE, Enos PICKERING, B.S., ack. 28 Nov 1814, Robert LEE, JP, ent. 19 Apr 1816, rec. 6 May same.

F-157   Indenture, 3 d 2 m 1816, Joseph STRAHL (wife Hannah), BCO; Owen HALE, BCO; $60, part of SW 1/4 S 27 T 7 R 5, 20 acres; WIT: Mary WHITE, James WHITE [both mark], ack. James WHITE, JP, ent. 29 Apr 1816, rec. 6 May same.

F-157   Indenture, 22 Apr 1816, Zachariah BURROWS [BURRIS, BURRUS] (wife Mary), BCO; John CARTER, BCO; $150, part of S 19 T 6 R 3, Steubenville district, 12 acres 16 perches; both mark, WIT: Jacob NAGLE, Wm. SHARPLESS, ack. Sterling JOHNSTON, JP, ent. 29 Apr 1816, rec. 6 May same.

F-158   Indenture, 25 d 12 m 1815, Jesse FOULKE (one of proprietors of town of Flushing) (wife Sarah), BCO; Nathan PIGGOTT, Concord, BCO; $50, lots #2 and #3, each 66 feet wide and 98 feet deep; WIT: Robert LEE, Hannah FOULKE, ack. 25 Dec 1815, Robert LEE, JP, ent. 1 May 1816, rec. 6 same.

F-159   Indenture, 7 d 6 m 1814, John PIGGOTT (wife Sarah), Union twp, BCO, Ebenezer PIGGOTT (wife Lydia), same; Nathan PIGGOTT, Peas twp, BCO; John PIGGOTT late of Loudon County, Virginia, deceased, died siezed of land in Ohio granted to him by the United States and disposed of the same by his LW&T to John PIGGOTT and Ebenezer PIGGOTT, each entitled to an equal fourth part of section, $100, to Nathan PIGGOTT NW 1/4 S 26 T 9 R 5, Steubenville district, patent dated 3 Aug 1810 and released by William PIGGOTT, son and heir of John PIGGOTT, deceased by indenture signed by William (wife Mary) dated 18 Mar 1814 unto Ebenezer PIGGOTT, 41 1/2 acres, but total amount conveyed seems to be 81 3/4 acres; John, Sarah, and Ebenezer seal, Lydia marks, WIT: Robert LEE, John VANPELT, ack. 8 Jun 1814, Robert LEE, JP, ent. 1 May 1816, rec. 6 same.

F-161   Indenture, 8 May 1816, William BROWN, Richland twp, BCO; Pell [Pall, Patt] GREGREGRY [GREGORGRY], same; $320, S 1/2 NW 1/4 S 7 T 7 R 4, 80 acres, granted to Sterling JOHNSTON by patent dated 8 Jun 1812, from JOHNSTON (wife Mary) to BROWN, fee simple; WIT: Wm. JOHNSTON, Sterling JOHNSTON, ack. 9 May 1816, Sterling JOHNSTON, JP, ent. 9 May 1816, rec. 13 same.

F-162   Indenture, 2 Jul 1814, David CHAMBERS (wife Prudence), Hamblon County, Ohio; Daniel PILLERS, Washington County, Pennsylvania; $30, lot #47 in Morristown as laid off by William CHAPLINE; his seal, her mark, WIT: Nathan SUTTON, Isaac O. FLINT, ack. 12 Aug 1814, Clermont County, Ohio, Nathan SUTTON, JP, ent. 9 May 1816, rec. 18 same.

F-162   Indenture, 13 May 1816, John SPENCER (wife Lydia), BCO; Aaron SPENCER (their son), BCO; natural love and affection, given NW 1/4 S 10 T 7 R 5, Steubenville district, granted to Elias HUGHES by patent dated 23 Mar 1810, from HUGHES to John SPENCER by indenture dated 10 Sep 1810, fee simple; WIT: John TRIGG, Henry JOHNSTON, ack. Henry JOHNSTON, JP, ent. 14 May 1816, rec. 18 same.

F-164   Indenture, 30 Sep 1812, Perigrine WATKINS (wife Henrietta), Brook County, Virginia; Providence [male] MOUNTS, Ohio County, Virginia; $550, NE 1/4 S 25 T 6 R 3, Steubenville district, granted to WATKINS by patent dated 8 Jun

1812; sgn: Pery WATKINS, WIT: John WATKINS, William MOUNTS, Racheal MOUNTS, ack. 7 May 1813, Jefferson County, Ohio, Robt. PATTERSON, JP, ent. 16 May 1816, rec. 18 same.

F-165   Indenture, 8 d 5 m 1816, James BARNES (wife Nancy), BCO; Joseph COX, BCO; $40, lots #44 and #76 in Barnesville; his seal, her mark, WIT: Isaac BARNES, John BEVAN, ack. 8 May 1816, Jno. BEVAN, JP, ent. 18 May 1816, rec. 20 same.

F-166   Indenture, 20 Nov 1815, Samuel GREGG (wife Ann), Knox County, Ohio, and George SINCLAIR, James SINCLAIR (wife Mary), Jacob GREGG (wife Mary), Traverse GEORGE (wife Esther), William SINCLAIR (wife Alice), BCO, and John SINCLAIR of Loudon County, Virginia, all heirs of James SINCLAIR, deceased, late of BCO; Thomas SMITH, BCO, who is also heir of James SINCLAIR, deceased; $180, undivided part of S 2 T 9 R 6, 60 acres, directed to be sold by LW&T of James SINCLAIR, deceased; WIT: William MITCHELL, [Gulielm] HARIS, John COFFEE, Benjamin VAIL, Joseph PANCOST, ack. 9 Dec 1815 Knox County, Ohio, Wm. SMITH, JP, 25 May 1816, rec. 27 same.

F-167   Indenture, 28 d 3 m 1816, Stephen BROOK [BROCK] (wife Ann), BCO; Amos GARRETSON, BCO; $413.50, land in Union twp, 50 acres, part of SW 1/4 S 20 T 9 R 5, Steubenville district, granted to Jonas PICKERING by patent dated 20 d 7 m 1808, conveyed by PICKERING (wife Ruth) by indenture dated 10 d 4 m 1810 to Samuel FAWCETT, conveyed by FAWCETT (wife Rachel) to BROOK by indenture dated 26 d 1 m 1813, BROOK (wife Ann) now to Amos GARRETSON; WIT: Nancy McWILLIAMS, William DUNN, receipt of money acknowledged, ack. 28 Mar 1816, William DUNN, JP, ent. 29 May 1816, rec. 30 same.

F-169   Indenture, 25 d 12 m 1815, Jesse FOULKE (one of proprietors of town of Flushing, BCO) (wife Sarah); John KING, same town; $600, lot #20 in Flushing; WIT: James CROZER, Samuel CROSSLEY, ack. Robert LEE, JP, ent. 30 May 1816, rec. 3 Jun same.

F-170   Indenture, 5 d 2 m 1816, Jesse FOULKE (one of proprietors of town of Flushing, BCO) (wife Sarah); John KING; $28, lot #__ in Flushing; WIT: Samuel CROSSLEY, David HOLLINGSWORTH, ack. 5 Feb 1816, Robert LEE, JP, ent. 30 May 1816, rec. 3 Jun same.

F-171   Whereas John KING of Flushing, BCO, bound by bond to John MURRAY, Junr., New York City, for $1,100 with interest, to secure payment and for $1 conveying to MURRAY lot #20 in Flushing, to be void if KING pays debt;

sgn: 9 d 5 m 1816, John KING, Mary R. KING, WIT: Hannah KING, Ann [TOWNLEY], ack. 27 May 1816, Robert LEE, JP, ent. 30 May 1816, rec. 3 Jun same.

F-172   Whereas Levi PITMAN, late of BCO, deceased, during his lifetime sold part of SW 1/4 S 9 T 8 R 5, Steubenville district, 30 acres, conveyed to PITMAN [PITTMAN] by Joshua HATCHER by deed dated 12 Aug 1806, sold to Jacob McKAY, now of BCO, PITTMAN died before completion of the agreement; now Joseph PANCOST, admr, and Elizabeth PITTMAN, admx, by order of CCP at April term 1816, convey to McKAY who had completed his obligation, fee simple; sgn: 27 d 5 m 1816, WIT: Benjamin ALLEN, Wm. SMITH, ack. 27 May 1816, Wm. SMITH, JP, ent. 3 Jun 1816, rec. 5 same.

F-173   Indenture, 27 d 5 m 1816, Jacob McKEAY [McKAY] (wife Rebeckah), BCO; Joseph PANCOST and Elizabeth PITTMAN, admrs, to estate of Levi PITTMAN [no location given]; $300, part of SE 1/4 S 15 T 8 R 5, Steubenville district, 81 acres 77 perches, fee simple; WIT: Benjamin ALLEN, Wm. SMITH, ack. [Jaycob McKAY], Wm. SMITH, JP, ent. 3 Jun 1816, rec. 5 same.

F-175   Indenture, 25 May 1816, John HOWELL (wife Ellenor [Elener]), BCO; John MERCER, BCO; $240, E 1/2 NW 1/4 S 30 T 8 R 5, Steubenville district, granted to HOWELL by patent dated 1 Nov 1811; WIT: Benjamin HOFF, William DUNN, ack. William DUNN, JP, ent. 4 Jun 1816, rec. 5 same.

F-176   Indenture, 3 d 6 m 1816, John PLUMMER (wife Ann), Warren twp, BCO; Thomas SMITH, Warren twp, BCO; $3,228, beginning on line of S 10 T 8 R 6, 269 acres; WIT: Jno. BEVAN, [Mynus] PEPPER, ack. 3 Jun 1816, John BEVAN, JP, ent. 4 Jun 1816, rec. 5 same.

F-177   Indenture, 1 Jun 1816, William GRIER, BCO; John PHILIPPS, BCO; $960, 1/4 S 28 T 8 R 6 (except 10 acres on W side), patent to Henry GRIER, deceased, conveyed by LW&T to William GRIER, fee simple; WIT: Jno BEVAN, Thos. PLUMMER, ack. Jno. BEVAN, JP, ent. 5 Jun 1816, rec. same.

F-178   Indenture, 25 May 1816, Arthur MORRISON (wife Grizel), BCO; John McCONNELL, BCO; $924, 103 acres, part of SE 1/4 S 5 t 8 R 5, granted to MORRISON by patent dated 13 Oct 1807; his seal, her mark, WIT: John STEWART, Robert MORRISON, ack. William DUNN, JP, ent. 5 Jun 1816, rec. 6 same.

F-179   A General Warranty Deed, indenture, 25 Apr 1816, Robert ARMSTRONG (wife Margaret), BCO; James PERRY, extr. for David RUBLE, deceased, Washington County, Pennsylvania; $44, beginning at SW corner S 21

T 4 R 3; his seal, her mark, WIT: Micheal L. MARTIN, Joseph ARMSTRONG, ack. 26 Apr 1816, Micheal L. MARTIN, JP, ent. 8 Jun 1816, rec. same.

F-181   Indenture, 26 May 1814, James BARNES (wife Nancy), BCO; Benoni BRYANT, BCO; $40, lots #13 and #109 in Barnesville, each 1/4 acre, fee simple; his seal, her mark, WIT: Thomas SHANNON, David SNIDER, ack. 27 May 1814, Thomas SHANNON, JP, ent. 8 Jun 1816, raec. 15 same.

F-182   Indenture, 29 d 12 m 1815, William PATTERSON [PATERSON] (wife Elizabeth), BCO; Isaac PATTEN, BCO; $15, [four] 1/2 acres, in E line of NW 1/4 S 32 T 7 R 5, NBR: Isaac PATTEN; his seal, her mark, WIT: John BEVAN, John DAVIES, ack. 29 Dec 1815, John BEVAN, JP, ent. 10 Jun 1816, rec. 15 same.

F-183   Indenture, 15 Dec 1815, Andrew McKINDLEY, BCO; Robert THOMPSON, BCO; three obligations dated same calling for $300 to be paid in installments ending 1 Aug 1818, to secure payment McKINDLEY conveys lots #21 and #22 in addition to St. Clairsville as laid out by William MATHERS, conveyed on same date by THOMPSON and wife Margaret to McKINDLEY, fee simple, void if McKINDLEY pays the $300; WIT: Jacob HOLLOWAY, ack. 16 Dec 1815, Henry JOHNSTON, JP, ent. 12 Jun 1816, rec. 15 same.

F-184   Indenture, 4 Apr 1816, James PARKE (wife Elizabeth), BCO; John NEEL [no location given]; $400, 20 acres in square 4 in NE corner of S 12 T 8 R 5, granted to Alexander HARAH by patent dated 13 Dec 1803; WIT: Joseph KINKEAD, John WILEY, ack. John WILEY, Associate Judge, ent. 25 Jun 1816, rec. same.

F-185   Indenture, 24 Feb 1816, Joseph WRIGHT (wife Eleanor), BCO; David WOOLFORD [WOLFORD], BCO; $45, lots #64 (28 rods), #63 (16 rods 24 links) and #93 (44 rods) in town of Belmont, plat in Book B, p. 288; WIT: John [FRED.], Joseph TRIMBLE, ack. 28 Feb 1816, Wm. SMITH, JP, ent. 25 Jun 1816, rec. 29 same.

F-187   Indenture, 1 Apr 1816, Samuel WILSON (wife Ann), BCO; William EATON, BCO; $1,200, part of S 20 TG 8 R 5, 60 acres, fee simple; WIT: Abraham McWILLIAMS, William DUNN, ack. William DUNN, JP, ent. 25 Jun 1816, rec. 29 same.

F-188   Indenture, 13 Feb 1816, Stephen WORKMAN, Senr., BCO; Jesse WORKMAN, BCO; $135, 40 acres, part of SE 1/4 S 4 T 5 R 3, granted to Stephen by patent dated 15 Jan 1814; WIT: John CUNNINGHAM, Hannah CUNNINGHAM, ack. John CUNNINGHAM, JP, engt. 27 Jun 1816, rec. 29 same.

F-189   Indenture, 13 Mar 1816, Jonathan SUTTON (wife Hannah), BCO; David MOORE, BCO; $300, NBR: William JOHNSTON, 44 acres, part of S 26 6 R 3, in SE 1/4, fee simple; his seal, her mark, WIT: Minoah SUTTON [his mark], Sterling JOHNSTON, ack. Sterling JOHNSTON, JP, ent. 29 Jun 1816, rec. same.

F-190   Indenture, 29 Jun 1816, Henry AMERINE (wife Mary), BCO; Joshua BERRY, BCO; $199, 49 3/4 acres 23 perches, part of NE 1/4 S 26 T 6 R 3, granted to AMERINE by patent dated 16 Mar 1814; both mark, WIT: John DAILY, Henry JOHNSTON, ack. Henry JOHNSTON, JP, ent. 29 Jun 1816, rec. 1 Jul same.

F-191   Indenture, 29 Jun 1816, Abraham AMERINE (wife Mary), BCO; Joshua BERRY, BCO, $40, 7 acres 2 rods 4 perches, part of 160 acres in S 27 GT 6 R 3 which was conveyed to AMERINE by Mordcia YARNELL (wife Pheobe) by deed dated 8 Mar 1809, NBR: Josiah UPDEGRAFF; both mark [she Mary M.], WIT: John DAILY, Henry JOHNSTON, ack. Henry JOHNSTON, JP, ent. 29 Jun 1816, rec. 6 Jul same.

F-192   Indenture, 29 Jun 1816, Henry H. EVANS (wife Hannah [Hannah M. in signature]), St. Clairsville, BCO; John WHITE, Wheeling, Ohio County, Virginia; $250, land on north side of St. Clairsville, NBR: land formerly belonging to James TAYLOR now the property of John THOMPSON, William BOGGS, 3 acres 37 perches, same lot conveyed from David NEWELL to Daniel CHURCH, from CHURCH to William WOODS, from WOODS to Robert THOMPSON, THOMPSON to EVANS, fee simple; WIT: Henry JOHNSTON, Wilmeth JONES, ack. Henry JOHNSTON, JP, ent. 1 Jul 1816, rec. 6 same.

F-194   Indenture, 16 Mar 1816, John PLUMMER (wife Ann), Warren twp, BCO; Samuel MEAD, Goshen twp, BCO; $1,320, beginning NE corner S 6 T 8 R 6, 165 acres; WIT: John BEVAN, George WOOTTEN, ack. John BEVAN, JP, ent. 2 Jul 1816, rec. 6 same.

F-195   Indenture, 23 d 7 m 1814, Daniel McPEAK (wife Elizabeth), BCO; Josiah POULTON, BCO; $65, part of S 19 T 7 R 3, part of tract conveyed by Bazelial WELLS (wife Sally) to McPEAK by deed dated 3 d 1 m 1811, NBR: Paul PRESTON, 11 acres 1 rod; only Daniel's mark, WIT: Thomas MAJOR, Wm. BOOKER, ack. 23 Jul 1814, Thomas MAJOR, JP, ent. 3 Jul 1816, rec. 6 same.

F-196   Indenture, 5 Apr 1816, Josiah POULTON (wife Mary), Colerain twp, BCO; Jesse [FELL], Short Creek twp, Harrison County, Ohio; $165, part of S 19 T 7 R 3, conveyed by Daniel McPEEK to POULTON by deed dated 23 Jul 1814, NBR: Paul PRESTON, 11 acres 1 rod; WIT: Thomas MAJOR, Paul PRESTON, ack. Thomas MAJOR, JP, ent. 3 Jul 1816, rec. 6 same.

F-197   Indenture, 1 Jun 1816, Thomas MILES, BCO; Frazey TAYLOR, BCO; $414, land in SW 1/4 S 32 T 5 R 3, granted by patent dated 10 Oct 1806; WIT: Josiah DILLON, Isaac DILLON, ack. 7 Jun 1816, Josiah DILLON, JP, ent. 4 Jul 1816, rec. 9 same.

F-198   Indenture, 6 Apr 1816, Abraham WORKMAN (wife Grace), BCO; William MOORE, Washington County, Pennsylvania; $320, in SE 1/4 S 35 T 2 R 2, NBR: Thomas McKEMMONS, Benjamin WORKMAN, 80 acres with exception of nursery of apple trees; his seal, her mark, WIT: Alexander DAVIS, Jacob DAVIS, Wm. WORKMAN, Junr., ack. Jacob DAVIS, JP for town of Poultney, ENT. 5 Jul 1816, rec. 9 same.

F-200   Indenture, 2 Jul 1816, William PHILPOT (wife Ruth), BCO; John WILSON, BCO; $750, 44 acres 142 2/10 perches, part of S 14 T 8 R 6; WIT: John BEVAN, Hugh WILSON, ack. John BEVAN, JP, ent. 8 Jul 1816, rec. 9 same.

F-201   Indenture, 7 May 1816, William PHILPOT (wife Ruth), BCO; Joseph ALEXANDER, BCO; $200, front lot #60 and back lot #92 in Barnesville; WIT: John BEVAN, Elisha MOORE [his mark], ack. John BEVAN, JP, ent. 13 Jul 1816, rec. 20 same.

F-202   Indenture, 7 Feb 1816, James BARNES (wife Nancy), BCO; George ADUDDLE, BCO; $30, lot #45 in Barnesville, 1/4 acre; his seal, her mark, WIT: John BEVAN, Morris HILTON, ack. John BEVAN, JP, ent. 13 Jul 1816, rec. 20 same.

F-203   Indenture, 27 Jun 1816, William CHAPLINE (wife Mary), Ohio County, Virginia; Duncan MORRISON, BCO; $160, outlot adjoining Morristown, 18 1/4 acres 15 perches; WIT: John STEWART, John C. AYERS, ack. John EATON, JP, ent. 17 Jul 1816, rec. 22 same.

F-204   Indenture, 1 Mar 1815, Bezelial WELLS and Elias VANARSDALE, two of extrs. of LW&T of Daniel McELHERAN, deceased, of Newark, Essex County, New Jersey; Thomas McKIMMON, BCO; will dated 25 May 1807, William HILL of New York City the other agent, $276, part of NE 1/4 S 35 T 2 R 2, NBR: McMahon's creek, 138 acres, WIT: A. DURAND, Archer GIFFORD [for VANARSDALE], Saml. SALMON, J. G. HINING [for WELLS]; ack. Essex County, New Jersey, 28 Mar 1815, Aaron MUNN, one of judges of Superior CCP, certified by Silas WHITEHEAD, clerk; ack. Jefferson County, Ohio, 26 Jul 1815, J. G. HINING, JP, ent. 20 Jul 1816, rec. 22 same.

F-206   Indenture, 29 Jun 1816, John GRIER (wife Rhoda), Guernsey County, Ohio; Thomas SMITH, BCO; $1,700, NW 1/4 S 9 T 8 R 6, sold to GRIER by

Jonathan TAILOR (wife Ann) by <u>patten</u> dated 18 d 3 m 1805, 160 acres; his seal, her mark, WIT: John BEVAN, David BUFKIN, ack. John BEVAN, JP, ent. 22 Jul 1816, rec. 23 same.

F-207   Indenture, 7 Aug 1815, William CHAPLINE (wife Mary), Ohio County, Virginia; John DOHERTY [DOUGHERTY], BCO; $10, lot #92 on plan of Morristown as laid off by William CHAPLINE; no WITs, ack. John EATON, JP, ent. 23 Jul 1816, rec. 24.

F-208   Indenture, 7 __ 1815, William CHAPLINE (wife Mary), Ohio County, Virginia; John DOHERTY, BCO; $10, lot #89 in Morristown laid off by William CHAPLINE; WIT: David SNIDER, Joseph HART, ack. BCO, John EATON, JP, ent. 23 Jul 1816, rec. 24 same.

F-208   Indenture, 25 Jul 1814, George SNIDER (assignee of Yasht LUKE) (wife Barbarah [Barbara]), BCO; James HILTON, BCO; SNIDER receive by patent dated 20 Mar 1813 the SW 1/4 S 26 T 7 R 4, Steubenville district, $515, NBR: Aaron SMITH, 98 acres 2 rods 1 pole, fee simple; his seal, her mark, WIT: Math. COLHAN, Henry JOHNSTON, ack. Henry JOHNSTON, JP, ent. 25 Jul 1816, rec. 1 Aug same.

F-210   Indenture, 25 Apr 1816, Samuel SPRIGG (wife Amelia), Ohio County, Virginia; Martha EVANS, BCO; $800, NW 1/4 S 26 T 6 r 3, Steubenville district, 160 acres, granted to SPRIGG by patent dated 29 Dec 1813; WIT: Josiah HEDGES, David MOORE, ack. Ohio County, Virginia, George MILLER, Saml. McCLURE, magistrates, Amelia can't travel to court, so MILLER and McCLURE given power to go Amelia to receive her acknowledgment, sgn: Wm. CHAPLINE, Jr., MILLER and McCLURE ack. same day, CHAPLINE confirms all same day, ent. 29 Jul 1816, rec. 1 Aug same.

F-212   Indenture, 24 Jul 1816, Robert GIFFEN (wife Hetty), Knox County, Ohio; Samuel FARIS, BCO; $396, 99 acres 13 perches, part of SW 1/4 S 9 T 6 R 3, granted to GIFFIN by patent dated 1 Oct 1806, NBR: Andrew PATTERSON, George GIFFIN; WIT: John GRIER, Mary GRIER, ack. Knox County, John GRIER, JP, ent. 29 Jul [1816], rec. 3 Aug same.

F-213   Indenture, 17 d 4 m 1816, Joseph STEER, JCO; Joseph WILEY, BCO; $320, part of S 12 T 5 R 3, NBR: Thomas LATTIMORE, 130 acres; Joseph and Grace seal, WIT: Jonathan TAYLOR, Jonah STEER, ack. 17 Apr 1816, Thomas LATIMER, JP, ent. 29 Jul 1816, rec. 3 Aug same.

F-214   Indenture, 27 Jul 1816, Eleazer EVANS (wife Mary), BCO; John RUSSELL, BCO; $900, S 1/2 NE 1/4 S 11 T 7 R 5, Steubenville district; WIT:

James WHITE, Benjamin CLENDENON, ack. James WHITE, JP, ent. 29 Jul 1816, rec. 5 Aug same.

F-215   Indenture, 24 Jul 1816, Robert GIFFIN [GIFFEN] (wife Hetty), Knox County, Ohio; George GIFFEN, BCO; $260, 65 acres 8 perches, part of S 9 T 6 R 3, granted to Robert by patent dated 1 Oct 1806, NBR: George GIFFIN, William SHARPLESS; WIT: John GRIER, Mary GRIER, ack. Knox County, John GRIER, JP, ent. 1 Aug 1816, rec. 5 same.

F-216   Indenture, 27 Oct 1813, David VANCE (wife Margaret), BCO; Sterling JOHNSTON, BCO; $1,600, part of S 36 T 6 R 3, and S 6 T 7 R 4, NBR: Robert HOPPER's heirs, Patrick NELLONS, 333 acres 1 rod 38 perches; his seal, her mark, WIT: Robert VANCE, Jacob NAGLE, ack. Robert VANCE, JP, ent. 1 Aug 1816, rec. 5 same.

F-218   Indenture, 10 Apr 1815, Robert THOMPSON (wife Margaret), BCO; Sterling JOHNSTON, BCO; $2,000, NBR: heirs of William GAMBLE, deceased, 29 acres 35 perches, part of S 4 T 7 R 4, conveyed to THOMPSON by David NEWALL (wife Sally) on 15 Apr 1803, fee simple; his seal, her mark, WIT: John THOMPSON, Henry JOHNSTON, ack. 19 Apr 1815, Henry JOHNSTON, JP, ent. 1 Aug 1816, rec. 5 same.

F-219   Indenture, 4 Mar 1816, James BARNES (wife Nancy), BCO; James M. ROUND, Jacob MYERS, John BEVAN, Archibald COLE, Henry HOSHIER, Joseph ALEXANDER, and Wm. PHILPOT, Trustees in trust for Methodist Society in Barnesville, BCO; $2, lot #4 adjoining town of Barnesville, NBR: Joseph TAYLOR; his seal, her mark, WIT: Harriet BARNES, John BEVAN, ack. John BEVAN, JP, ent. 1 Aug 1816, rec. 9 same.

F-220   Indenture, 3 d 6 m 1816, James BARNES (wife Nancy), BCO; Joel JUDKINS, BCO; $559, lots #15, #110, #77, #78, #79, 1/4 acre each; his seal, her mark, WIT: Jno. BEVAN, Robert MILLS, ack. 3 Jun 1816, John BEVAN, JP, ent. 6 Aug 1816, rec. 9 same.

F-221   Indenture, 31 Jul 1816, Ira ROBINSON (wife Judith), BCO; David JENNINGS, BCO; in consideration for uses and trusts afterwards mentioned and $5, E 1/2 lot #61 in St. Clairsville, 34 feet in front, on which Ira now lives, Ira has loan of $1,500 of Belmont Bank of St. Clairsville upon note payable at 60 days endorsed by Thomas ROBINSON and Alexander ARMSTRONG, JENNINGS to sell property if Ira ROBINSON fails to make payment on debt; WIT: Henry JOHNSTON, Robert ROBERTSON, ack. 6 Aug 1816, Henry JOHNSTON, JP, ent. 8 Aug 1816, rec. 15 same; payments completed 7 May 1827, ack. Stephen COLWELL, for the bank.

F-222   Indenture, 29 Jul 1816, Thomas ROBINSON, BCO; David JENNINGS, BCO; in consideration of trust and confidence in JENNINGS and for $5, part of S 2 T 7 R 4, NBR: Nicholas STONER, Jacob HOLTZ, 50 acres, security for Thomas's debt to Belmont Bank of St. Clairsville being one of endorsers for Ira ROBINSON's debt for $1,500; WIT: Henry JOHNSTON, John GIBSON, ack. Henry JOHNSTON, JP, ent. 8 Aug 1816, ent. 10 same; payment ack. 7 May 1817 by Stephen COLWELL, for Belmont Bank of St. Clairsville.

F-224   Indenture, 23 Dec 1814, Robert McBRIDE (wife Marget McBRIDE), Coshocton County, Ohio; Benjamin MURPHY, BCO; $385, part of SW 1/4 S 11 T 9 R 6, Steubenville district, NBR: Stillwater creek, 77 acres granted to Rasin PUMPHREY by patent dated 13 Jul 1813; she sgn. Margaret, WIT: W. BRADSHAW, John F. MORRISON, ack. [no date given] Duncan MORRISON, JP, ent. 9 Aug 1816, rec. 10 same.

F-226   Indenture, 6 Aug 1816, William BOOKER (wife Patience), St. Clairsville, BCO; Levi PICKERING, St. Clairsville, BCO; $180, lots #99 (conveyed by David BARNES [wife Elizabeth]), #107, #115, and #123 (last three conveyed by George ATKINSON [wife Elizabeth]) in St. Clairsville, fee simple; WIT: Henry JOHNSTON, James HUGHES, ack. Henry JOHNSTON, JP, [no ent. or rec. data].

F-227   Indenture, 13 Aug 1816, Levi PICKERING (wife Susanna), St. Clairsville, BCO; Reuben MILLER, Pittsburg, Pennsylvania; $185 lots #99, #107, #115, #123 in St. Clairsville, total of one acre, conveyed to PICKERING by William BOOKER (wife Patience) by deed dated 6 Aug 1816, fee simple; WIT: Isaac WILSON, Henry JOHNSTON, ack. Henry JOHNSTON, JP, ent. 13 Aug 1816, rec. same.

F-228   Indenture, 10 Aug 1816, Levi PICKERING (wife Susanna), BCO; John THOMPSON, BCO; $4,000, lot #61 in St. Clairsville, fee simple, conveyed to PICKERING by Peter YARNELL (wife Lucinda) on 8 Jul 1814, recorded Book D, p. 530; WIT: Jno. [BARNES], Sterling JOHNSTON, ack. Sterling JOHNSTON, JP [no ent. or rec. data].

F-230   Indenture, 13 Mar 1816, James BARNES (wife Nancy), BCO; Joseph ANDERSON, BCO; $229.33, part of NW 1/4 S 10 T 6 R 3, Steubenville district, 25 acres 1 rod 37 perches, NBR: John NICHOLS, David BAILEY, James BARNES, fee simple; his seal, her mark, WIT: Jno. BEVAN, Thomas BARNES, ack. 13 Aug 1816, Jno. BEVAN, JP, ent. 14 Aug 1816, rec. 17 same.

F-231   Indenture, 6 d 4 m 1816, Thomas MARSHALL (wife Margaret), Deleware County, Pennsylvania; Joseph COX, BCO; $1,250, E 1/2 S 33 T 6 R 5, Marietta district; WIT: Samuel MARSHALL, George W. JENKINS, ack. 8 Apr

1816 Deleware County, Pennsylvania, Thomas PEINE, JP, certified by Joseph ENGLE, recorder of deeds, ent. 16 Aug 1816, rec. 17 same.

F-232   Indenture, 29 Mar 1816, Nathaniel BELL (wife Catharine), BCO; Samuel WILSON, BCO; $600, part of NW 1/4 S 26 T 8 R 5, granted to Robert BELL by patent, NBR: Robert BELL, Nathaniel BELL, William WOODS, CALDWELL, 60 acres; both sgn BEAL, his seal, her mark, WIT: James DALLAS, William EATON, ack. (BELL) 1 Apr 1816, John EATON, JP, ent. 16 Aug 1816, rec. 17 same.

F-233   Indenture, [ptd], 29 Mar 1816, Nathaniel BELL (wife Catharine), BCO; Samuel WILSON (BCO); $400, part of NW 1/4 S 2 T 8 R 5, granted to Robert BELL, NBR: William WOODS, 40 acres 1 rod 30 perches; sgn. Nathaniel BEAL, Catharine BEAL [her mark], WIT: James DALLAS, John EATON, ack. 1 Apr 1816, John EATON, JP, ent. 16 Aujg 1816, rec. 20 same.

F-234   Indenture, 9 Jul 1816, Valentine AULT (wife Catharine), BCO; William SHARPLESS, BCO; $33, part of SE corner of S 4 T 7 R 4, conveyed to AULT by Bazaleel WELLS, JCO, on 25 Oct 1798, fee simple; his seal, her mark, WIT: Sterling JOHNSTON, George IRELAND, ack. Sterling JOHNSTON, JP, ent. 22 Aug 1816, rec. 30 same.

F-236   Indenture, 17 Aug 1816, William BOGGS (wife Elizabeth), BCO; William SHARPLESS, BCO; $400, part of NE 1/4 S 10 T 7 R 4, SE corner of lot upon which the Presbyterian Meeting House stands, 8 3/4 acres 19 perches; WIT: Andrew WHITE, Henry JOHNSTON, ack. Henry JOHNSTON, JP, ent. 22 Aug 1816, rec. 30 same.

F-237   Indenture, 20 Aug 1816, James CARROTHERS (wife Susannah), Monroe County, Ohio; Daniel BRANNINGER, BCO; $475, lot adjoining public commons of St. Clairsville on south and alley, NBR: John THOMPSON, Joseph MORRISON, Vachel HALL, 3 acres, fee simple; WIT: Levin OKEY, John CARTER, Amos B. JONES, ack. Monroe Co., Levin OKEY, Assoc. Judge, certified by Amos B. JONES, Clerk.

F-238   Indenture, 27 Jun 1807, James SINCLAIR, Senr. (wife Mary), BCO; Mathew PATTERSON, BCO; $300, 100 acres, part of NW 1/4 S 34 T 7 R 4, granted to James SINCLAIR, Senr., by patent dated 6 May 1806, sgn: James SINKLER, Mary SINKLER [her mark], WIT: Samuel GREGG, Junr., James SINCLAIR, Junr., ack. 27 Jun 1807, Arthur IRWIN, JP, ent. 23 Aug 1816, rec. 30 same.

F-239   Indenture, 26 Oct 1814, John VANPELT (wife Mary), BCO; Jacob SMITH, BCO; $1,438, 81 acres 2 rods 7 perches in S 13 T 9 R 5 or 3, NBR:

Darling CONROW, fee simple; his seal, her mark, WIT: Alexander HARAH, Peter TALLMAN, ack. William DUNN, JP, ent. 24 Aug 1816, rec. 30 same.

F-241   Indenture, 19 d 7 m 1816, James SINCLAIR (wife Mary), BCO; John HOLLINGSWORTH, Loudon County, Virginia; $400, 79 acres to W end of NW 1/4 S 18 T 7 R 5; [SINCLAIR here] his seal, her mark, WIT: Jno. BEVAN, S. HOLLOWAY, Levi HOLLINGSWORTH, ack. 19 Jul 1816, Jno. BEVAN, JP, ent. 24 Aug 1816, rec. 30 same.

F-242   Indenture, 3 Apr 1815, William GIFFEN (wife Betsey), BCO; Eleazer KINNEY, BCO; $765, part S 36 T 6 R 3, NBR: Wheeling creek, William DENHAM, 126 acres 2 rods 27 perches, [previously] conveyed 63 of above acres for $315; his seal, her mark, WIT: Sterling JOHNSTON, Charles McCARTY, ack. 5 Apr 1815, Sterling JOHNSTON, JP, ent. 28 Aug 1816, rec. 31 same.

F-243   Indenture, 23 Aug 1816, Eleazer KINNEY (wife Jemima), BCO; Samuel LOGAN, BCO; $1,700, part of S 36 T 6 R 3, NBR: Wheeling creek, William DENHAM, 126 acres 2 rods 26 perches; his seal, her mark, WIT: John McELROY, Henry JOHNSTON, ack. 26 Aug 1816, Henry JOHNSTON, JP, ent. 28 Aug 1816, rec. 31 same.

F-244   Indenture, 23 Aug 1816, Samuel LOGAN, BCO; Eleazer KINNEY, BCO; $1,000 owed to KINNEY by writing dated 13 Sep 1815 payable by installments, grants 126 acres 2 rods 27 perches [see above description], void if payments made; WIT: David JENNINGS, Henry JOHNSTON, ack. 26 Aug 1816, Henry JOHNSTON, JP, ent. 28 Aug 1816, rec. 31 same.

F-245   Indenture, 3 d 8 m 1816, Henry STANTON (wife Clary), BCO; Simeon TAYLOR, BCO; $210, S 1/2 NW 1/4 S 7 T 8 R 6, Steubenville district, 80 acres, fee simple; WIT: Richard EDGERTON, John BEVAN, ack. 3 Aug 1816, Jno. BEVAN, JP, ent. 31 Aug 1816, rec. same.

F-246   Indenture, 10 d 5 m 1816, Mathew [Matthew] WOOD (wife Margaret), BCO; Abram WOOD, son of Matthew, BCO; $240, beginning 40 rods N from SE corner of SW 1/4 S 19 T 7 R 5, 81 acres 2 rods; WIT: Isaac WOOD, James WHITE, ack. James WHITE, JP, ent. 31 Aug 1816, rec. same.

F-248   Indenture, 10 d 5 m 1816, Mathew WOOD (wife Margaret), BCO; Isaac WOOD, son of Mathew, BCO; $240, beginning 40 rods N from SW corner S 19 T 7 R 5, 81 acres 2 rods; WIT: James WHITE, Ann WOOD, ack. James WHITE, JP, ent. 31 Aug 1816, rec. 4 Sep same.

F-249   Indenture, 10 d 5 m 1816, Matthew WOOD (wife Margaret), BCO; Nathaniel MARIS, BCO; $120, beginning SW corner S 19 T 7 R 5, 40 acres 3 rods; WIT: James WHITE, Isaac WOOD, ack. James WHITE, JP, ent. 31 Aug 1816, rec. 4 Sep same.

F-250   Indenture, 18 d 11 m 1815, Thomas MARSHALL (wife Margaret), Deleware County, Pennsylvania; William BUNDY, BCO; $2,700, N 1/2 S 4 T 8 R 6, Steubenville district, 320 acres; WIT: Samuel MARSHALL, George W. JENKINS, ack. 8 Apr 1816, Deleware County, Pennsylvania, Thos. PEIRCE, JP, PEIRCE certified 10 Apr 1816 by Joseph ENGLE, recorder of deeds, ent. 31 Aug 1816, rec. 6 Sep same.

F-252   Indenture, 13 Mar 1816, William WELSH (wife Mary), BCO; James HUTCHINSON, BCO; $100, part of NW 1/4 S 18 T 8 R 6 in the SE corner thereof, 25 acres; WIT: John BEVAN, John P. BEVAN, ack. 30 Mar 1816, John BEVAN, JP, ent. 31 Aug 1816, rec. 7 Sep same.

F-253   Indenture, 30 d 3 m 1816, Joseph PATTERSON (wife Hannah), BCO; Richard EDGERTON and William THOMAS, trustees in behalf of the ridge meeting; $32, 4 acres in NW corner of my land beginning at NE corner of Richard EDGERTON's 1/4 S; his seal, her mark, WIT: William PATTERSON, Exum PATTERSON, ack. 30 Mar 1816, Jno. BEVAN, JP, ent. 31 Aug 1816, rec. 7 Sep same.

F-254   Indenture, 3 Sep 1816, William BOOKER (wife Patience), BCO; George CLARK, BCO; $1,000, fee simple, lot #100, NBR: Widow IRWIN's lot #108 in St. Clairsville, plat recorded in Book A, p. 31, conveyed from David BARNES (wife Elizabeth) to BOOKER; WIT: William FROST, Wm. FARIS, Jr., ack. Joseph ANDERSON, Assoc. Judge, CCP, ent. 4 Sep 1816, rec. 9 same.

F-255   Indenture, __ Jun 1816, John PURDY (wife Susan), BCO; Francis McCONNELL, BCO; $400, part of S 4 T 6 R 3, 40 acres; both mark, WIT: John CLARK, Joseph KIRKWOOD, ack. 15 Jun 1816, John CLARK, JP, ent. 7 Sep 1816, rec. 12 same.

F-256   Indenture, 26 Apr 1816, John BROWN, Junr. (wife Elizabeth), BCO; John TRIGG, BCO; $170, fee simple, lot #23 in addition to St. Clairsville as laid out by William MATHERS, conveyed by Obediah JENNINGS to William CONGLETON, by CONGLETON to Samuel HAWKINS, by HAWKINS to Jacob GRUBB, by GRUBB to William FARIS, Junr., by FARIS to John BROWN, Junr., fee simple; his seal, her mark, WIT: Henry JOHNSTON, Christopher HOLLINGSWORTH, ack. Henry JOHNSTON, JP, ent. 9 Sep 1816, rec. 14 same.

F-257   Indenture, 7 Jul 1815, William CHAPLINE (wife Mary), Ohio County, Virginia; John HART, BCO; $25, lot #91 in Morristown as laid off by William CHAPLINE; WIT: Jacob DOVENBERGER, Duncan MORRISON, ack. 7 Aug 1815, John EATON, JP, ent. 9 Sep 1816, rec. 14 same.

F-258   Indenture, 27 d 5 m 1816, Joel GILBERT, Goshen, BCO; Abraham ACKERSON, BCO; $350, N 1/2 NW 1/4 S 35 T 7 R 5, 73 acres 128 perches, fee simple; sgn: Joel GIBERT [suspected writing error], Elizabeth GILBERT [her mark], WIT: Garret ACKERSON, John ACKERSON, Wm. SMITH, ack. 27 May 18__, Wm. SMITH, JP, ent. 13 Sep 1816, rec. 18 same.

F-259   Indenture, 15 Nov 1815, John CONNELL (wife Eleanor), Brook County, Virginia; John RANKIN and Robt. SMITH, BCO; $840, land on waters of McMahon's creek, beginning corner to Samuel CONNELL, NBR: road leading from St. Clairsville to Marietta, 140 acres, part of NW 1/4 S 31 T 6 R 3, granted to John CONNELL, assignee of David TRINDLE, by patent dated 16 Feb 1809; no WITs, ack. 2 Jan 1816, JCO, John BARRETT, BARRETT certified 3 May 1816 by Thos. PATTON, Clerk of CCP, ent. 14 Sep 1816, rec. 23 same.

F-261   Indenture, 25 d 7 m 1815, Joseph W. SATTERTHWAITE (wife Ann), BCO; Horton HOWARD, BCO; $260, part of S 13 T 7 R 3, originally conveyed by deed dated 2 d 2 m 1816, recorded Book B, pp. 83 and 84, now correcting a mistake in the description of the 50 acres; WIT: William SINCLAIR, George BIGBY [his mark], ack. Wm. SINCLAIR, JP, ent. 16 Sep 1816, rec. 24 same.

F-262   Indenture, 26 d 7 m 1815, Horton HOWARD (wife Hannah), BCO; Isaac PARKER, JCO; $5,000, part of Ss 7 and 13 T 7 r 3, Steubenville district, part in S 7 granted to Borden STANTON by patent dated 27 d 8 m 1805, STANTON conveyed to HOWARD by deed dated 31 d 12 m 1806, part in S 13 granted to William SATTERTHWAITE by patent dated 9 d 3 m 1803, conveyed by LW&T of William SATTERTHWAITE to Joseph SATTERTHWAITE, conveyed by Joseph SATTERTHWAITE to HOWARD on 2 d 12 m 1806, 200 acres; WIT: William STANTON, Abner LAMBERT, ack. 26 Jul 1815, William DUNN, JP, ent. 16 Sep 1816, rec. 25 same.

F-263   Indenture, 26 Apr 1816, David NIESWANGER, BCO; Charles HAMMOND, BCO; for trust and confidence in him and $5, sell in trust 80 acres adjoining town of St. Clairsville, part of SE 1/4 S 4 T ___ R 4, whereas Notley HAYS, BCO, endorsed a note for Christopher NEISWANGER, son of David, in the Muskingum Bank at Zanesville for $1,000, this transfer to indemnify HAMMOND for possible risk, void if $1,000 paid; both sign, WIT: Geo. PAULL, Sterling JOHNSTON, ack. Sterling JOHNSTON, JP, ent. 16 Sep 1816, rec. 26 same.

F-265   Indenture, 18 Sep 1816, William ASKEW (wife Martha), BCO; William SHARPLESS, BCO; $330, remaining part of out lot #8 in plat of 15 out lots adjoining St. Clairsville as laid out by William MATHERS, acres on north side having been previously sold to George <u>ABAN</u> [ALBAN?], part of same lot conveyed to ASKEW by Samuel SULLIVAN (wife Mary) by deed dated 2 Jan 1810, 4 acres 11 perches; WIT: Isaac WILSON, Levi PICKERING, J. HOLLOWAY, ack. Henry JOHNSTON, JP, ent. 24 Sep 1816, rec. 26 same.

F-266   Indenture, 17 Sep 1816, John SHEPHERD (wife Leah), Brook County, Virginia; William SHARPLESS, BCO; $350, part of S 30 T 5 R 3, NBR: HARVEY, 100 acres; WIT: S. CONNELL, Ja. DADRIDGE, Robt. MARSHALL, ack. 20 Sep 1816, Brook County, Virginia, Robt. MARSHALL, Jas. <u>DOODRIDGE</u>, JP, John CONNELL certifies MARSHALL and DOODRIDGE, ent. 24 Sep 1816, rec. 26 same.

F-267   Indenture, 23 Sep 1816, William SHARPLESS (wife Ann), BCO; William IRWIN, Washington County, Pennsylvania; $480, part of S 30 T 5 R 3, NBR: HARVEY, 100 acres; WIT: Sterling JOHNSTON, Andw. WHITE, ack. Sterling JOHNSTON, JP, [no ent. or rec. data].

F-268   Indenture, 17 Aug 1816, Sterling JOHNSTON (wife Mary), BCO; David JENNINGS, BCO; $5, lot #17 in St. Clairsville with brick house, also tract of land JOHNSTON bought of Robert THOMPSON, 30 acres, where Sterling now lives, fee simple in trust to secure loan of $1,000 from Belmont Bank of St. Clairsville, endorsed by Charles HAMMOND and Valentine AULT, land to be sold in case of default, void if payment made; WIT: Josiah HEDGES, Wm. PERRINE, ack. 21 Aug 1816, Henry JOHNSTON, JP, ent. 24 Sep 1816, rec. 26 same.

F-270   Indenture, 28 Sep 1816, Thomas B. THOMPSON, BCO; Samuel FAIRHURST, BCO; $800, 99 acres 13 perches, part of SW 1/4 S 9 T 6 R 3, void if owed sums of money paid to FAIRHURST; WIT: Thomas THOMPSON, Sterling JOHNSTON, ack. Sterling JOHNSTON, JP, 28 Sep 1816, rec. same.

F-271   Indenture, 1 d 4 m 1816, Jesse FOULKE, Flushing, BCO; Joshua HATCHER, BCO, and Jane GREGG (late NICHOLS), BCO, extrs. of LW&T of Eli NICHOLS late of county deceased, FOULKE bound for $900 conditioned for payment of $450, to secure payment of $450 and $1 Jesse FOULKE (wife Sarah) convey to HATCHER and GREGG lot #7 in Flushing, same on which FOULKE now lives, void if FOULKE pays $450; WIT: Jane ROBERTS, Robert LEE, ack. 1 Apr 1816, Robert LEE, JP, ent. 28 Sep 1816, rec. same.

F-272   Indenture, 5 Jul 1816, Nathan DOD (wife Ruth), Warren twp, BCO; John WIER, BCO; $320, part of NE 1/4 S 20, 127 acres with buildings, received from

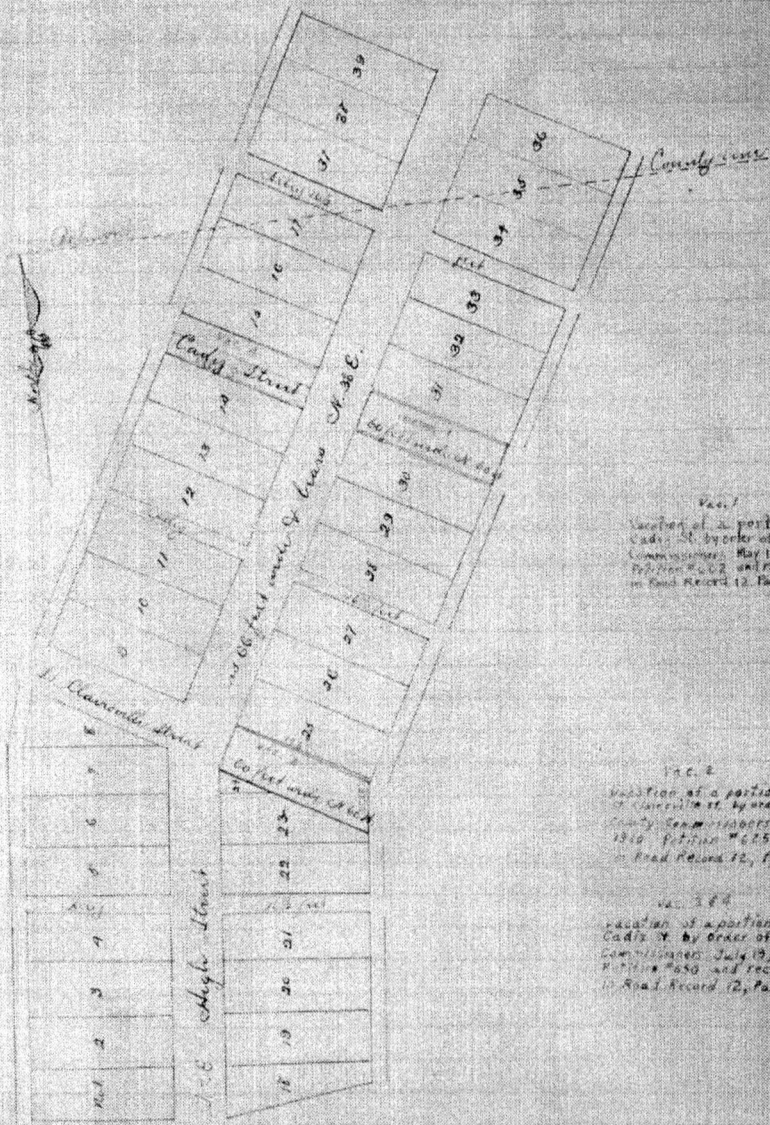

Plat of Shepherdstown

Nathan's father Aaron, 1/4 of said land at decease or marriage of Nathan's mother Rebecah; sgn: DODD, WIT: William CACELION, John BEVAN, William BARNES, receipt of money WIT: Wm. CONLION, ack. [13] Jul 1816, Jno. BEVAN, JP, ent. 28 Sep 1816, rec. same.

F-273   Plat of Shepherdstown, BCO; vacations (1) part of Cadiz Street, May 1958; (2) part of St. Clairsville Street, Sep 1960, (3 & 4), part of Cadiz Street, July 1963; Shepherds town on NE 1/4 S 21 T 8 R 4, Steubenville district, sgn: 23 Sep 1816, by Nathan SHEPHERD, ack. David WALLACE, JP, ent. 28 Sep 1816, rec. same.

F-275   Indenture, 1 Jun 1816, Robert MILLER (wife Margaret), BCO; John McKIBBONS, Robert LEE, and Charles RICHEY, trustees of the congregation of Crabapple; $39.69, part of SW 1/4 S 33 T 8 R 4, 5 2/4 acres 8 perches; WIT: John CAMPBELL, John LYLE, ack. John CAMPBELL, JP, ent. 28 Sep 1816, rec. same.

F-276   Indenture, 4 Sep 1816, George CLARK (wife Mary), BCO; David JENNINGS, BCO; $5, lot #100 in St. Clairsville, same on which George now lives, George obtained a loan of $1,000 at Belmont Bank of St. Clairsville, endorsed by Joseph ANDERSON and John WARNOCK, note to secure loan, void if loan repaid; WIT: Wm. FARIS, Junr., Wm. BOOKER, ack. Joseph ANDERSON, Assoc. Judge, ent. 28 Sep 1826, rec. same.

F-277   Indenture, 28 Sep 1816, Samuel FAIRHURST (wife Anne), BCO; Thomas B. THOMPSON, BCO; $800, 99 acres 13 perches, part of SW 1/4 S 9 T 6 R 3; both mark, WIT: Thos. THOMPSON, Sterling JOHNSTON, ack. Sterling JOHNSTON, JP, ent. 28 Sep 1816, rec. 4 Oct same.

F-278   Indenture, 24 May 1816, John BROWN (wife Nancy), BCO; William BROWN, BCO; $67, E 1/2 SW 1/4 S 24 T 8 R 6, 67 acres; sgn: John BROWN and Agnes BROWN, WIT: Jno. BEVAN, John BROWN, Junr., ack. Jno. BEVAN, JP, ent. 28 Sep 1816, rec. 4 Sep same.

F-279   Indenture, 1 d 10 m 1814, Horton HOWARD (wife Hannah), BCO; John DOUGHERTY, BCO; $125, part of NW 1/4 S 18 T 8 R 6, granted to HOWARD by patent dated 1 d 6 m 1807, this portion 50 acres; WIT: Thos. MITCHELL, James [MELAY] his mark, ack. Thos. MITCHELL, justice, receipt of money ack. 1 d 10 m 1814, ent. 5 Oct 1816, rec. 14 same.

F-280   Indenture, 7 Jun 1816, Andrew PATTERSON (wife Lydia), BCO; Andrew HENDERSON, BCO; $7,680, S 2 T 8 R 4, 640 acres, granted to PATTERSON by patent dated 16 Dec 1806, Steubenville district, fee simple; WIT:

Sterling JOHNSTON, Alexander McCONNELL, ack. Sterling JOHNSTON, JP, ent. 5 Oct 1816, rec. 14 same.

F-281   Indenture, 6 Jul 1816, Henry DOUDNA (wife Martha), BCO; Archibald COLE, BCO; $600, front lot #24 and back lot #120 in Barnesville, each 1/4 acre; his seal, her mark, WIT: Jno. BEVAN, Jacob MYERS, ack. John BEVAN, JP, ent. 11 Oct 1816, rec. 16 same.

F-282   Indenture, 8 Apr 1816, James B. FINLEY (wife Hannah), JCO; [Archibald COLE, BCO]; $200, lots #27 and #123 in Barnesville, each 1/4 acre; his seal, her mark, WIT: Jas. M. ROUND, Jacob MYERS, ack. John BEVAN, JP, ent. 11 Oct 1816, rec. 16 same.

F-283   Indenture, 26 Mar 1816, Robert GRIFFITH (wife Sarah), BCO; Solomon BENTLEY, BCO; $36, lot #155 in St. Clairsville, according to plat recorded in Book B, p. 31, fee simple; his seal, her mark, WIT: Jacob ELERICK, John GRIFFITH, ack. 7 Oct 1816, John EATON, JP, ent. 12 Oct 1816, rec. 18 same.

F-284   Indenture, 17 Sep 1816, Christian BLAZER, BCO; Christopher HOOVER, BCO; $60, NBR: Samuel CRAWFORD, 1/8 acre near W end of St. Clairsville, W 1/2, sold to HOOVER by Jeremiah BURRIS (wife Rachel) as recorded in Book D, p. 281, fee simple; WIT: Isaac WILSON, Barnard ELERICK, ack. 12 Oct 1816, Henry JOHNSTON, JP, ent. 12 Oct 1816, rec. 21 same.

F-286   Indenture, 12 Oct 1816, Christopher HOOVER (wife Rachel), BCO; David McCREY, BCO; $80, lot near W end of St. Clairsville, NBR: Samuel CRAWFORD, 1/8 acre, W 1/2 of lot conveyed to HOOVER by Christian BLAZER by deed dated 17 Sep 1816, fee simple; WIT: Henry JOHNSTON, James TAGGART, ack. Henry JOHNSTON, JP, ent. 12 Oct 1816, rec. 21 same.

F-287   Indenture, 22 Jun 1816, Robert GRIFFITH (wife Sarah), Union twp, BCO; Patrick NELLONS, Richland twp, BCO; $300, lot #140 in St. Clairsville, plat recorded in Book A, p. 31, 1/4 acre, fee simple; WiT: John EATON, Benjamin EATON, ack. John EATON, JP, ent. 19 Oct 1816, rec. 24 same.

F-288   Indenture, 22 Jun 1816, Robert GRIFFITH (wife Sarah), Union twp, BCO; Patrick NELLONS, Richland twp, BCO; $50, lot #139 in St. Clairsville, 1/4 acre, fee simple; WIT: John EATON, Benjamin EATON, ack. John EATON, JP, ent. 19 Oct 1816, rec. 24 same.

F-289   Indenture, 19 Oct 1816, Francis BARKURST [BARKHURST] [female], BCO; Patrick NELLONS, BCO; $66, 5 1/2 acres 8 perches, part of tract on which BARKHURST lives, part of S 32 T 6 R 3, NBR: NELLONS, Johnathan SUTTEN,

Nathan HEATON; her mark, WIT: Sterling JOHNSTON, Thos. HEANEY, ack. Sterling JOHNSTON, JP, ent. 19 Oct 1816, rec. 25 same.

F-291 Indenture, 15 Oct 1816, Joseph WRIGHT (wife Eleanor), BCO; Andrew THOMPSON, BCO; $30, lot #34 in town of Belmont, 20 rods; WIT: Robt. GRIFFITH, [Nick] GASSAWAY, ack. 16 Oct 1816, John EATON, JP, ent. 21 Oct 1816, rec. 26 same.

F-292 Indenture, 15 Oct 1816, Andrew THOMPSON (wife Lydia), Belmont, BCO; Joshua TRIMBLE, BCO; $292, lot #34 in town of Belmont, 20 rods; his seal, her mark, WIT: John EATON, Josh. WRIGHT, ack. 16 Oct 1816, John EATON, JP, ent. 21 Oct 1816, rec. 28 same.

F-293 Indenture, 24 Aug 1816, William C. ANDERSON (wife Agnes), BCO; Humphrey ANDERSON, BCO; $600, NW 1/4 S 34 T 8 R 6, Steubenville district, patented to William C. [no date]; his seal, her mark, WIT: Jno. BEVAN, Jno. BARKER [his mark], ack. Jno. BEVAN, JP, ent. 24 Oct 1816, rec. 28 same.

F-294 Indenture, 2 Sep 1816, Thomas EMERY (wife Rebecca), BCO; Henry HOSHIER, BCO; $250, back lot #84 in Barnesville; sgn: EMORY, she Rebeckah, WIT: Jno. BEVAN, Rebecca DODD [her mark], ack. (EMRY), John BEVAN, JP, ent. 28 Oct 1816, rec. same.

F-295 Indenture, 29 Oct 1816, Samuel ISRAEL (wife Mary), JCO; William LIGHTFOOT, JCO; $300, lot #29 in addition to St. Clairsville; his seal, her mark, WIT: John WATSON, William HATHORN, ack. JCO, 30 Oct 1816, John WATSON, JP, ent. 8 Nov 1816, rec. 25 same.

F-296 Indenture, 7 Nov 1816, Robert WINTERS (wife Sarah), St. Clairsville, BCO; William LIGHTFOOT, St. Clairsville, BCO; $1,400, lots #84 (conveyed to WINTERS by Isaac VORE and wife Eleanor on 14 Jan 1811) and #91 (conveyed to WINTERS by Isaac VORE and wife Eleanor on 14 Jan 1811), each 1/4 acre, fee simple; his seal, her mark, WIT: Henry [McGREYRUKEN], Henry JOHNSTON, ack. Henry JOHNSTON, JP, ent. 18 Nov 1816, rec. 25 same.

F-297 Know all men, William RIDDLE (wife Isabel) of BCO for $300 paid to husband and $1 paid to wife by Obediah JENNINGS, attorney at law of Washington County, Pennsylvania, she relinquishes all rights to lots #109, #100, #111, #32, #63, and #2 in Morristown, sgn: 21 Jul 1814, his seal, her mark, WIT: John BROWN, D. MORRISON, ack. [29] Jul 1814, D. MORRISON, JP, ent. 18 Nov 1816, rec. 25 same.

F-298   Indenture, 24 Oct 1816, C. D. HAMPTON, Harrison County, Ohio; Paul PRESTON, same; $500, 84 acres in BCO, conveyed to PRESTON by Joseph MATSON by deed dated 23 Apr 1814, void if $500 paid with interest; WIT: Thos. MAJOR, John TARBET, ack. Thomas MAJOR, JP, ent. 18 Nov 1816, rec. 26 same.

F-300   Indenture, 27 Jun 1816, William CHAPLINE (wife Mary), Ohio County, Virginia; Dunkan [Dunken, Dunkin] MORRISON and Joseph BELL, BCO; $10, lot #64 in Morristown as laid off by CHAPLINE; WIT: John C. AYERS, John STEWART, ack. John EATON, JP, ent. 19 Nov 1816, rec. 26 same.

F-301   Indenture, 6 Nov 1816, Vachel HALL (wife Susana HALL), BCO; Daniell BRANINGER, BCO; $200, NBR: Joseph MORRISON, Daniel BRANINGER, NE corner of lot, 1 acre 3 rods 39 perches; WIT: John DENT, Henry JOHNSTON, ack. 7 Nov 1816, Henry JOHNSTON, JP, ent. 19 Nov 1816, rec. 26 same.

F-302   Indenture, 23 d 9 m 1816, James MOORE, Loudon County, Virginia; Abner MOORE, St. Clairsville, BCO; $1,000, W half of lot #68 in St. Clairsville, 1/8 acre, purchased by James MOORE from Maylon SMITH and Isaac VORE, now in possession of Abner MOORE; WIT: Saml. HOUGH ["Wm." written to the right], Wm. WRIGHT, Caldwell WRIGHT [his mark], ack. 8 Oct 1816, BCO, of Samuel HOUGH, Wm. WRIGHT, and Caldwell WRIGHT, by Sterling JOHNSTON, JP, ent. 19 Nov 1816, rec. 27 same.

F-303   Indenture, 31 d 5 m 1816, Thomas MARSHALL (wife Margaret), Concord twp, Deleware County, Pennsylvania; Joseph COX, BCO; $1,500, NW 1/4 S 29 (except for five acres, deeded to James EDGERTON made by COX in T 6 R 5, Marietta district; WIT: Saml. MARSHALL, William WILSON, ack. 31 May 1816, Delaware County, Thos. PEIRCE, JP, certified by Joseph ENGLE, recorder of deeds, 3 Jun 1816, ent. 19 Nov 1816, rec. 27 same.

F-304   James Madison, President of the United States, James TARBET, BCO, full payment for NE 1/4 S 31 T 3 R 2, Steubenville district; sgn: city of Washington, 12 May 1815, Josiah MEIGS, Commissioner of the General Trust Office, ent. 19 Nov 1816, rec. 29 same.

F-305   Indenture, 28 d 11 m 1814, Jesse FOULKE, one of proprietors of town of Flushing, (wife Sarah); Enos PICKERING, same town; $75, two lots in Flushing, #10 and #11 and an out lot #2, NBR: Mary FAWCETT, [10] acres 11 perches; Robert LEE, Rees BRANSON, ack. 28 Nov 1814, Robert LEE, JP, ent 20 Nov 1816, rec. 28 same.

F-306   Indenture, 27 Mar 1816, Bazil RIDGEWAY (wife Ammaney), BCO; David SHAY, BCO; $150, part of NW 1/4 S 29 T 9 R 6, 50 acres, fee simple; both mark, WIT: James SMITH, John N. SMITH, ack. John N. SMITH, JP, ent. 20 Nov 1816, rec. 28 same.

F-307   Indenture, 10 d 2 m 1816, Jesse FOULKE (wife Sarah), Union twp, BCO; Joshua WOOD, same twp; $130, part of S 20 T 9 R 5 (south of town of Flushing), NBR: Joseph FAWCETT, 12 acres 35 perches; another lot joining thereto, NBR: land sold to FOULKE by Thomas BUFKIN, land owned by Joshua WOOD, 4 acres; WIT: Horatio MURPHY, Thomas CROZER, ack. 12 Feb 1816, Robert LEE, JP, ent. 20 Nov 1816, rec. 28 same.

F-308   Indenture, 1 d 8 m 1816, Horton HOWARD (wife Hannah), BCO; Abraham KENNEY, BCO; $400, NW 1/4 S 20 T 9 R 6, granted to HOWARD by patent dated 10 d 5 m 1807; WIT: John HOWARD, Joshua KENNARD, ack. 1 Aug 1816, Thos. MITCHELL, JP, ent. 21 Nov 1816, rec. 29 same.

F-309   Indenture, 16 Nov 1816, Keziah TIPTON, BCO; Joseph ROGERS, BCO; $1,600, fee simple, on McMahan's creek, part of S 9 T 7 R 4, NBR: Eli PLUMMER, Alexander BOGGS, Benjamin RUGGLES (and others), part of a tract conveyed by deed dated 13 Nov 1798 from Bazaleel WELLS to Thomas TIPTON, Senior (now deceased), to Keziah by will dated 20 Apr 1815, 50 acres; her mark, WIT: John ANDERSON, Alexander BOGGS, ack. Henry JOHNSTON, JP, ent. 21 Nov 1816, rec. 29 same.

F-310   Indenture, 9 May 1816, Samuel B. MARTIN (wife Ann), Baltimore, Maryland; president and directors of Belmont Bank of St. Clairsville and successors; $1,200, lot #20 in St. Clairsville, 1/4 acre, conveyed by John B. MARTIN (wife Ann [though it later appears to be Elizabeth]) of Baltimore on 6 Oct 1813, recorded in Book D, p. 413 and 414, from deed from John MARTIN (wife Elizabeth), St. Clairsville, to John B. MARTIN (wife Elizabeth), Baltimore, Maryland, on 26 Aug 1806, recorded in Book A, p. 686 and 687, another deed from Jesse McGEE, of St. Clairsville, to John MARTIN dated 22 Mar 1806, recorded in Book A, p. 639; WIT: S. [Samuel] H. GATCHELL, Nathl. KNIGHT, ack. Baltimore County, Maryland, S. H. GATCHELL, Nathl. KNIGHT, JPs, certified 14 May 1816 by Wm. GIBSON, Clerk, Baltimore, ent. 22 Nov 1816, rec. 2 Dec same.

F-312   Indenture, 16 Nov 1816, Noah ZANE (wife Mary L. ZANE), Wheeling, Virginia; Mary Ann KNOUGH [{KNOW}], BCO; $500, NW 1/4 S 13 T 5 R 3; [no WITs], ack. Virginia, Ohio County, William CHAPLINE, Clerk, ent. 22 Nov 1816, rec. 2 Dec same.

F-313   Indenture, 13 Oct 1816, James McKIRK, BCO; John KING (wife Mary), Samuel WORLEY (wife Nancy), Robert ALEXANDER (wife Jenney), William MYERS (wife Margaret), George MYERS (wife Hannah), George ELERICK (wife Elizabeth), Thos. ALEXANDER (wife Rachel), Rebecca DIXON, Susanna DIXON, and Mosey DIXON, the heirs and legal representatives of Andrew DIXON, deceased, all of BCO; $100, part of S 7 T 6 R 3, 270 acres, NBR: James McKIRK, Samuel WORLEY; WIT: John STEWART, James ALEXANDER, ack. James ALEXANDER, Assoc. Judge, ent. 22 Nov 1816, rec. 2 Dec same.

F-314   Indenture, 16 Nov 1816, Samuel DUNN (wife Mary), BCO; Henry GRIGREY [GREGREY], BCO; $65, beginning center S 28 T 9 R 6, 20 acres; both mark, WIT: John N. SMITH, Francis PENN, ack. John N. SMITH, JP, ent. 22 Nov 1816, rec. 2 Dec same.

F-315   Indenture, 20 Aug 1816, Richard WILLIAMS (wife Sarah), Starke County, Ohio; Ezekial SMITH, BCO; $320, NE 1/4 S 14 T 7 R 5, conveyed by WILLIAMS by patent dated 12 May 1815; WIT: Francis SMITH, Mary SMITH, ack. Stark County, Ohio, Francis SMITH, JP, certified 21 Aug 1816 by Wm. RAYNOLD, Clk., ent. 23 Nov 1816, rec. 2 Dec same.

F-316   Indenture, 24 d 10 m 1816, Paul PRESTON (wife Sarah), Harrison County, Ohio; Charles D. HAMPTON, same; $1,000, part S 19 T 7 R 3, NBR: Thomas BLACKLEDGE, conveyed to PRESTON from Joseph WALTON by deed dated 23 Apr 1814; WIT: Thomas MAJOR, John TARBOT, ack. 24 Oct 1816, Thomas MAJOR, JP, ent. 23 Nov 1816, 3 Dec same.

F-317   Indenture, 23 Nov 1816, C. D. HAMPTON, Harrison County, Ohio; Jonathan TAYLOR and George KINSEY, same; $250, 84 acres, same conveyed to HAMPTON from Paul PRESTON and wife by deed dated 24 d 10 m 1816, void if HAMPTON pays $250 with interest to parties of second part; WIT: Paul PRESTON, Sarah PRESTON, ack. BCO, Thomas MAJOR, JP, ent. 23 Nov 1816, rec. 3 Dec same.

F-319   Indenture, 27 May 1816, Abraham ACKERSON (wife Darkee), Warren twp, BCO; Rebecca TODD and Robert TODD [no relationship given], same; $350, S 1/2 of SW 1/4 S 35 T 7 R 5, granted to ACKERSON by U.S., 70 acres and 61 perches; his seal, her mark, WIT: Richard FAWCETT, Thomas ACKERSON, Wm. SMITH, ack. Wm. SMITH, JP, ent. 25 Nov 1816, rec. 4 Dec same.

F-320   Indenture, 14 Nov 1816, Henry BARNES, Junr., (wife Marium), BCO; James BARNES, same; $900, 21 acres, part of NW 1/4 S 14 T 8 R 6; his seal, her mark [looks like Marion here], WIT: Jno. BEVAN, Peter BARNES, ack. Jno. BEVAN, JP, ent. 27 Nov 1816, rec. 4 Dec same.

F-321   Indenture, 9 Nov 1816, James CALDWELL (wife Ann), BCO; John CARTER, BCO; whereas W 1/2 S 25 T 6 R 3, Steubenville district, was patented to CALDWELL as assignee of Jeremiah BURRIS, whereas SW 1/4 S 19 T 6 R 3, Steubenville district, was patented to CALDWELL as assignee of George BARKHURST, received patents and title to lands in trust for Jeremiah BURRIS to be conveyed to BURRIS upon payment of money due and owing from Jeremiah BURRIS to James CALDWELL, whereas all interest of Jeremiah BURRIS has been seized by a suit of Josiah HEDGES against Jeremiah and sold to John CARTER, whereas CARTER has paid and satisfied to CALDWELL all money owed by Jeremiah BURRIS, so by these presents James CALDWELL (wife Ann) convey to John CARTER W 1/2 S 25 T 6 R 3, except land CALDWELL had previously sold to Vachal HALL with assent of Jeremiah BURRIS, also all right CALDWELL has to SW 1/4 S 19 T 6 R 3; WIT: Wm. BROWN, Junr., Sterling JOHNSTON, ack. Sterling JOHNSTON, JP, ent. 29 Nov 1816, rec. 5 Dec same.

F-322   Indenture, 10 Jun 1816, Yate PLUMMER, Frederick County, Maryland; Joshua SCOTT, BCO; $523, SW 1/4 S 33 T 7 R 5; WIT: Abm. SHREVER, (also WIT receipt of money), ack. Frederick County, Maryland, Abm. SHREVER, Assoc. Judge of fifth judicial district of Maryland, certified by John SCHLEY, Clerk, ent. 30 Nov 1816, rec. 5 Dec same.

F-323   Indenture, 5 Nov 1816, Jacob MORGAN (wife Mary), BCO; Andrew McFARLAND, BCO; $840, 61 1/2 acres, part of SW 1/4 S 14 T 8 R 4, granted to Jacob COON by Thomas Jefferson, President, by patent dated 27 Aug 1805, conveyed to COON by Wm. CLARKE (B-47 [probable page on which it was recorded]) by deed dated 8 Apr 1811, CLARKE (wife Christenah) conveyed to Mary BARTON (C-223) by deed dated 28 Mar 1812, BARTON conveyed to MORGAN (E-310) by deed dated 13 Sep 1815; WIT: Thos. LOVE, Joseph LYON, ack. John CAMPBELL, JP, ent. 2 Dec 1816, rec. 9 same.

F-325   Indenture, 25 d 12 m 1815, Jesse FOULKE, one of proprietors of town of Flushing, BCO; Robert GUTHRIE, Virginia; $35, lot #16 in Flushing, 66 feet in front and rear and 198 feet in length; sgn: Jesse FOULKE, Sarah FOULKE, WIT: James CROZIER, Samuel CROSSLEY, ack. BCO, Robert LEE, JP, ent. 4 Dec 1816, rec. 9 same.

F-325   James Madison, President, John PERRY, assignee of Matilda WAY, deposited in general land office a certificate of the register of land office at Steubenville, payment made for NW 1/4 S 23 T 8 R 6, sgn: 27 Oct 1815, ent. 6 Dec 1816, rec. 9 same, Josiah MEIGGS, Commissioner of the General Land Office.

F-326   Indenture, 23 Nov 1816, David MOORE, Sheriff of BCO; Samuel HOUGH, BCO; in CCP in chancery sitting George PAULL and James

CALDWELL, decree of court against John BROWN, Junr., April term 1816, debt of $190.42 and $6.72 damages,$11.99 for costs of suit; also John LONG for use of James CALDWELL obtained a judgment of court against John BROWN, Junr., April term, debt of $72.57 plus $2.51 damages plus $12.42 costs of suit, secured 102 pieces of lots in St. Clairsville and in BCO, sold two of said lots and obtained $375 to pay debts, sold to Samuel HOUGH as highest bidder, part of lots #160 and #159, conveyed to BROWN by John LONG (wife Catherine) on 26 Apr 1808 (B-304); WIT: Sterling JOHNSTON, ack. 27 Nov 1816, Sterling JOHNSTON, JP, ent. 7 Dec 1816, rec. 10 same.

F-328	Indenture, 1 Aug 1816, John MELOTT (wife Mary), BCO; Jesse PENROSE, BCO; $517, two tracts, one 64 acres, part of S 34 T 5 R 3, granted to Caleb DILLE by patent dated 29 Dec 1808, conveyed to MELOTT by deed dated 26 Apr 1809, NBR: Obediah HARDESTY, second containing 33 acres, part of same section, conveyed by DILLE to MELOTT by deed same date as this indenture, NBR: McMahon's creek, Obediah HARDESTY; his seal, her mark, WIT: Amos WORKMAN, William MELOTT, ack. 31 Aug 1816, John CUNNINGHAM, JP, ent. 7 Dec 1816, rec. 10 same.

F-329	Indenture, 3 Dec 1816, John LARKIN, Senr., Frederick County, Maryland, George WINROD, BCO; $500, NE 1/4 S 14 T 10 R 6, Steubenville district, conveyed to LARKIN by WINROD by deed dated 8 Oct 1813, rec. Book D, p. 406, fee simple; WIT: Abm. SHRIVER, ack. Frederick County, Maryland, Abm. SHRIVER, Assoc. Judge, 5th judicial district of Maryland, certified by John SCHLEY, Clerk, ent. 9 Dec 1816, rec. 10 same.

F-331	Indenture, 7 Jun 1816, George MILLER, Wheeling, Ohio County, Virginia; John McLURE, same place; $700, land in S 36 T 1 R 2, NBR: Samuel CARPENTER, estate of Daniel McELHERAN, deceased; WIT: Jos. McRAY, Jonathan NESBIT, ack. Ohio County, Virginia, Wm. CHAPLINE, Jr., COC, ent. 10 Dec 1816, rec. 20 same.

F-332	Indenture, 30 Nov 1816, Valentine AULT, BCO; George PAULL, BCO; PAULL stands as security for Valentine AULT in bank of the Ohio Company at Wheeling, Virginia, for $280, bond given to John WHITE for use of said company dated 7 Nov 1816, to indemnify PAULL plus for $.01 paid by PAULL conveys part of S 4 T 7 R 4, 94 acres, land on which AULT and his son Andrew AULT now live, conveyed to AULT by Bazaleel WELLS (wife Sally), void if AULT keeps PAULL clear of the debt; WIT: David MOORE, Sterling JOHNSTON, ack. Sterling JOHNSTON, JP, ent. 15 Nov 1816, rec. 20 same.

F-333	Indenture, 10 d 8 m 1816, Jesse FOULKE (wife Sarah), town of Flushing, BCO; Samuel CROSLEY, same town; $30, lot #35 measuring 66 feet wide and 198 feet deep; WIT: Thos. FAWCETT, Jacob BRUNSON, ack. 10 Aug 1816, Robert LEE, ent. 12 Dec 1816, rec. 24 same.

F-333   Indenture, 6 Dec 1816, Jacob JENKINS, BCO, George KINSEY and Sarah JENKINS, JCO, administrators of estate of Mishael JENKINS, deceased; John FULTON and Andrew FULTON, "both of the state and county aforesaid"; $1,100, 110 acres, part of SE and SW 1/4 S 20 T 8 R 4, granted to Mishael JENKINS by patent dated 10 Oct 1806, NBR: John LOVE; WIT: John CAMPBELL, John LOVE, ack. John CAMPBELL, ent. 12 Dec 1816, rec. 24 same.

F-335   Indenture, 30 Oct 1816, John and Mary KING, his wife, Samuel and Nancy WORLEY, his wife, Robert and Jenney [Jane] ALEXANDER, his wife, William MYERS and Margaret [Peggy] his wife, George MYERS and Hannah his wife, George ELERICK and Elizabeth [Betsey] his wife, Thomas ALEXANDER and Rachel his wife, Rebeccah DIXON, Susanah DIXON, and Mosey DIXON (heirs of Andrew DIXON, deceased as mentioned in his LW&T), all BCO; James McKIRK, BCO; $100, 265 acres, part of S 7 T 6 R 3, NBR: Samuel WORLEY; all mark except John KING and Robert ALEXANDER, [Jane ALEXANDER's looks like there could be a mark but they simply forgot to identify it], WIT: John STEWART, James ALEXANDER, Alexander GREENLEE, James DIXON, ack. James ALEXANDER, Assoc. Judge, ent. 12 Dec 1816, rec. 25 same.

F-336   Indenture, 31 d 5 m 1816, Thomas MARSHALL (wife Margaret), Concord twp, Delaware County, Pennsylvania; William ANSLEY [AUSLEY], BCO; $1,120, NW 1/4 S 22 T 8 R 6, same patented to MARSHALL on 28 Feb 1816; WIT: Saml. MARSHALL, William WILSON, receipt of money ack., ack. 31 May 1816 Deleware County, Thomas PEIRCE, JP, certified by Joseph ENGLE, recorder of deeds, ent. 16 Dec 1816, rec. 26 same.

F-338   Indenture, 17 Sep 1816, Abram BLAUVELT (wife Sarah), Warren twp, BCO; Caleb OGBORN, Frederick County, Maryland; $400, 50 acres beginning at SE corner S 5 T 8 R 6; WIT: John ACKERSON, Jno. BEVAN, ack. John BEVAN, JP, ent. 16 Dec 1816, rec. 26 same.

F-339   Indenture, 12 Nov 1816, John HART (wife Susanna), BCO; Lenard [Leonard] HART, BCO; $25, lot #91 in Morristown as laid off by William CHAPLINE, conveyed by CHAPLINE to John HART by deed dated 7 Jul 1815; both mark, WIT: John C. AYERS, Daniel BOGGS, ack. John EATON, JP, ent. 16 Dec 1816, rec. 26 same.

F-340   Indenture, 25 Jun 1816, William CHAPLINE (wife Mary), Ohio County, Virginia; Henry SMITH, BCO; $10, lot #4 in Morristown as laid off by CHAPLINE; [only William signs], WIT: John STEWART, John EATON, ack. 28

Jun 1816, John EATON; on 20 Aug 1816 Henry SMITH signs over all title to deed to Joshua TRASEY, WIT: Richard BAGGER, ent. 20 Dec 1816, rec. 26 same.

F-341   Indenture, 23 Aug 1816, Henry SMITH (wife Sally), BCO; Joshua TRAICY, BCO; $70, lot #4 in Morristown as laid off by William CHAPLINE; WIT: John EATON, Joseph LACOCK, ack. John EATON, JP, ent. 20 Dec 1816, rec. 26 same.

F-342   Indenture, 12 May 1816, William LINGO (wife Patience), BCO; Andrew Mc[VEIN], BCO; $204, part of NW 1/4 S 34 T 7 R 5, 83 acres 2 rods 11 poles, NBR: Isaac STRAHL, D. THORNBURGH; his seal, her mark, WIT: Joseph ALEXANDER, Isaac STRAHL, ack. 24 Jul 1816, Wm. SMITH, JP, ent. 26 Jun 1816, rec. 27 same.

F-343   James Madison, Josiah DILLON, BCO, deposited certificate of the register of land office at Marietta, full payment for NE 1/4 S 36 T 4 R 3, sgn: 10 Dec 1816, Josiah MEIGS, Commissioner of General Land Office, ent. 1 Jan 1817, rec. same.

F-343   Indenture, 30 Aug 1816, Henry GREGRY (wife Betsey), BCP; Thomas MILLER, BCO; $112.50, part of NE 1/4 S 28 T 9 R 6, 45 acres; both mark, WIT: Mead JARVIS, Daniel CONNER, ack. John N. SMITH, JP, ent. 1 Jan 1817, rec. 6 same.

F-344   Indenture, 30 Aug 1816, Henry GRIGRY (wife Betsey), BCO; Edmond SPENCER, BCO; $125, land in Kirkwood twp, part of S 28 T 9 R 6 (NE 1/4), NBR: David LONG, 50 acres; both mark, WIT: Mead JARVIS, Daniel CONNER, ack. John N. SMITH, JP, ent. 1 Jan 1817, rec. 6 same.

F-345   Know all men, Artemas BAKER, town of Canton, BCO, for $200 paid by William YOUNG, BCO, convey track of land bought of Peter LOFFER (wife Sarah), which Sarah LOFFER (then Sarah PALMER) bought of Ebenezer ZANE (wife Elizabeth) by deed dated 6 Aug 1809 and recorded in Book C, p. 137, fee simple in trust, deed of trust in favor of Moses CHAPLINE and William HARKINS to secure them for being his sureties in a note to the Ohio Company, only $70 remains unpaid, indebted to John McLURE of Wheeling, Ohio County, Virginia, this deed void if payment made, Mehalabel BAKER [Mehatabel?] is Artemas's wife, sgn: 5 Mar 1816 by all three, WIT: John BAKER, David L. [PEIRCE], BAKER retains possession for a year from date of deed, ack. John CLARK, JP, ent. 4 Jan 1817, rec. 6 same.

F-347   Indenture, 1 Feb 1816, Peter KREMER (wife Margaret), Frederick County, Maryland; Daniel BRANNINGER, Washington County, Pennsylvania;

$525, lot #81 in St. Clairsville, 1/4 acre; his seal, her mark, [no WITs], ack. 5 Feb 1816, Corporation of Winchester [Sct], Virginia, George REED, mayor, ent. 4 Jan 1816, rec. 10 same.

F-348   Indenture, 16 Nov 1816, James FERGUSON, BCO; David JENNINGS, BCO; for uses and trusts and $4, part of NE 1/4 S 29 T 7 R 4, same patented to David DRAKE by James Madison on 19 Aug 1812, deeded to FERGUSON, NBR: Wheeling creek, 139 1/4 acre 7 perches, James FERGUSON indebted to Joseph MORRISON for $800 by promissory note dated 27 Nov 1815 payable before 1 Mar with legal interest, John PATTERSON security, debt to be paid before 1 Jan 1817 with all interest, if not land to be sold; WIT: John CARTER, Sterling JOHNSTON, ack. Sterling JOHNSTON, JP, ent. 4 Jan 1817, rec. 10 same; release recorded Book H, p. 320.

F-351   Indenture, 7 Nov 1816, William LIGHTFOOT, St. Clairsville, BCO; Robert WINTERS, St. Clairsville, BCO; $400, lots #84 and #91 in St. Clairsville, each 1/4 acre, void if $400 paid to WINTERS; WIT: Henry McCRAKEN, Henry JOHNSTON, ack. Henry JOHNSTON, JP, ent. 9 Jan 1817, rec. 16 same.

F-352   Indenture, 11 Dec 1816, William LYON (wife Mary), BCO; John FORST, JCO; $200, part of S 19 T 8 R 4, Steubenville district, 20 acres, part of land granted to LYON and wife Mary by John WITNTER, BCO, dated 6 Mar 1806, granted to WINTERS by patent dated 11 Feb 1806, fee simple; his seal, her mark, WIT: John LYON, Henry GADDIS, ack. Dd. WALLACE, JP, ent. 16 Jan 1817, rec. 23 same.

F-354   Indenture, 11 Dec 1816, Joseph LYON (wife Ann), BCO; John FORST, JCO; $300, land in S 19 T 8 R 4, Steubenville district, 30 acres, part of land granted to John WINTERS, BCO, by patent dated 11 Feb 1806, conveyed by WINTER to LYON on 28 Mar 1806, fee simple; WIT: David WALLACE, William LYON, ack. David WALLACE, JP, ent. 16 Jan 1817, rec. 23 same.

F-355   Indenture, 15 Aug 1816, Jacob DAVIS, BCO; John CUNINGHAM, BCO; $413, land beginning at SW corner S 29 T 2 R 2, NBR: BUCHANAN, 43 acres 1 rod 36 perches; WIT: Wm. WORKMAN, Jr., David WORKMAN, ack. 6 Sep 1816, Thos. [WORTON], JP, ent. 23 Jan 1816 [probably 1817], ent. 3 Feb same.

F-356   Indenture, 6 d 11 m 1816, John NICHOLS (wife Mary), BCO; Phebe WILKINSON, Flushing, BCO; $125, house and lot in Flushing #14; WIT: Saml. HOLLOWAY, Robert LEE, ack. 6 Nov 1816, Robert LEE, JP, ent. 23 Jan 1817, rec. 3 Feb same.

F-357   Indenture, 30 Mar 1816, Benjamin VANFASSEN [VANFOSSEN] (wife Polly), Union twp, BCO; John NICHOLS, Peas twp, BCO; $960, SW 1/4 S 25 T

8 R 5, granted to John NICHOL and conveyed by John NICHOL (wife Ann) to Benjamin VANFOSSEN, fee simple; his seal, her mark, WIT: John EATON, William SCOTT, ack. 8 Apr 1816, John EATON, JP, ent. 1 Feb 1817, rec. 5 same.

F-358   Know all men, Robert GIFFEN, Knox Co., Ohio, for $100 paid by John NICHOL of BCO, land in S 9 T 6 R 3, NBR: Wheeling creek, 5 acres, sgn: 24 Jul 1816, Robert and Hetty GIFFEN, WIT: John GRIER, Mary GRIER, ack. Knox County, Ohio, John GRIER, JP, ent. 1 Feb 1817, rec. 7 same.

F-359   Indenture, 24 Jan 1817, Thomas THOMPSON (wife Elizabeth), BCO; Thomas B. THOMPSON, BCO; $50, lot #7 of Morristown as laid off by William CHAPLINE, WIT: John CLARKE, Martha THOMPSON, ack. John CLARKE, JP, ent 3 Feb 1817, rec. 5 same.

F-360   Indenture, 8 Jan 1817, John PERRY, Senr. (wife Jean [Jane]), BCO; Alexander MORRISON, BCO; $1,850, S 15 T 7 R 4, 100 acres, on S side of SE 1/4 S; WIT: A. GASTON, Joshua C. ANDERSON, ack. John EATON, JP, ent. 4 Feb 1817, rec. 6 same.

F-361   Indenture, 1 Nov 1815, John MITCHELL (wife Sarah), BCO; Stephen VANVORHIS, BCO; $100, lot #1 in Morristown as laid off by William CHAPLINE, conveyed by him and wife Mary to Leonart HART by deed dated 25 Jun 1808, conveyed to John MITCHELL by conveyance dated 6 Oct 1814; both mark, WIT: John EATON, Alexander HARRAH, ack. John EATON, JP, ent. 6 Feb 1817, rec. 7 same.

F-362   Indenture, 28 Jan 1817, Samuel DUNN (wife Mary), BCO; [Mariam] PENN, Baltimore County, Maryland; $615, land beginning at SW corner of S 28 T 9 R 6, 146 acres; both mark, WIT: Nicholas FLAHARTY, Mead JARVIS, William BRATTON, ack. Nicholas FLAHARTY, JP, ent. 6 Feb 1817, rec. 10 same.

F-363   Indenture, 28 Jan 1817, Mead JARVIS (wife Nancy), BCO; John BARRETT, BCO; $107, land beginning centre of N line of S 26 T 9 R 6, 30 acres 100 perches; his seal, her mark, WIT: Nicholas FLAHARTY, Samuel DUNN [his mark], ack. Nicholas FLAHARTY, JP, ent. 6 Feb 1817, rec. 10 same.

F-364   Indenture, 9 Jan 1817, Joseph TAYLOR (wife Mary), BCO; Charles COLES, BCO; $80, lots #56 and 88 in Barnesville, each 1/4 acre; WIT: Jno BEVAN, Thomas SHANNON, ack. 8 Jan 1817, John BEVAN, JP, ent. 10 Feb 1817, rec. 11 same.

F-365   Indenture, 30 Aug 1816, Edmond SPENCER, BCO; Robert ROBINSON, BCO; $50, land in Kirkwood twp, part of NE 1/4 S 28 T 9 R 6, NBR: Henry GRIGRY, SPENCER, 14 acres; his seal, her mark (Mary SPENCER), WIT: Mead JARVES, David CONNER, ack. John N. SMITH, JP, ent. 10 Feb 1817, rec. 13 same.

F-366   Indenture, 20 Jan 1817, Peter YARNELL, Ohio County, Virginia, attorney in fact for Mordecai YARNELL, late of same county and commonwealth under a deed of trust executed by Mordecai during his lifetime; George IRELAND, BCO; $180, 60 acres 38 perches, part of NW 1/4 S 29 T 6 R 3, NBR: John MAXWELL; WIT: John LIST, Junr., ack. Ohio County, Virginia, Joseph CALDWELL, ack. BCO, 27 Jan 1817, John CLARK, JP [no ent. or rec. data].

F-367   Indenture, 15 d 8 m 1816, Hezekiah STARBUCK, BCO; Nathan PUSEY, Washington County, Pennsylvania; $824.78, NE 1/4 31 T 7 R 5, Steubenville district, void if $824.78 paid in installments; Ann STARBUCK also signs, WIT: Joseph COX, Elizabeth COX, ack. 16 Sep 1816, James WHITE, JP, ent. 13 Feb 1817, rec. 14 same.

F-369   Indenture, 11 Feb 1817, Jonathan ELLIS (wife Lydia), BCO; David GADD, Ohio County, Virginia; $50, lot #145 in St. Clairsville, 1/4 acre, conveyed to Lydia ELLIS, wife of Jonathan, by David NEWELL (wife Sally), fee simple; WIT: Abel ROBERTS, Robert LEE, ack. 12 Feb 1817, Robert LEE, JP, ent. 14 Feb 1817, rec. 17 same.

F-370   Indenture, 11 Feb 1816, Jonathan ELLIS (wife Lydia), BCO; David GADD, Ohio County, Virginia; $50, lot #146 in St. Clairsville, same conveyed to Lydia by David NEWELL (wife Sally) by deed dated 27 Feb 1802, fee simple; WIT: Abel ROBERTS, Robert LEE, ack. Robert LEE, JP, ent. 14 Feb 1817, rec. 17 same.

F-371   Indenture, 12 Feb 1817, Mathew SCOTT (wife Elizabeth), BCO; Alexander THOMPSON, Allegheny County, Pennsylvania; $2,500, land beginning at S corner CUSTER and FREEMAN lot; WIT: William ROGERS, Jas. WALLACE, Mary SCOTT, ack. Jacob DAVIS, JP, ent. 17 Feb 1817, rec. 18 same.

F-372   Indenture, 31 d 1 m 1817, Samuel CROSLEY (wife Phebe), Flushing, BCO; Jacob HOLLOWAY, BCO; $325, lot #62 in Flushing (66 feet wide 165 feet long), one out lot adjoining S border of that lot containing 1 acre 2 perches; sgn: CROSSLEY, WIT: Robert LEE, James LIKES, ack. 31 Jan 1817, Robert LEE, JP, ent. 18 Feb 1817, rec. 19 same.

F-373   Indenture, 5 d 12 m 1816, Horton HOWARD (wife Hannah), St. Clairsville, BCO; Jacob HOLLOWAY, BCO; $3,000, NW 1/4 S 15 T 9 R 5, BCO, granted to HOWARD by patent [no date given]; WIT: M. SMITH, William ASKEY, money received same date, ack. 14 Feb 1817, Henry JOHNSTON, JP, ent. 18 Feb 1817, rec. 24 same.

F-374   Indenture, 10 d 9 m (Sep) 1816, Matthew McCALL (wife Nancy), BCO; John DAVIS, BCO; $200, S 18 T 8 R 5, granted to McCALL by patent dated 20 May 1806, 15 acres; his seal, her mark, WIT: William DUNN, Joseph [SHUIEN], ack. William DUNN, JP, ent. 22 Feb 1817, rec. 27 same.

F-375   Indenture, 23 Aug 1816, Borden STANTON, BCO; Thomas MITCHELL and Alexander McWILLIAMS, BCO; $1,000, E 1/2 of his land in SE corner S 25 T 4 R 2, void if $1,000 paid by STANTON; his seal and Charlotte STANTON's seal, WIT: John McWILLIAMS, William TORBET, ack. James ALEXANDER, acting judge, ent. 27 Feb 18<u>16</u> [probably 1817], rec. 3 Mar same.

F-377   Payment made by Joseph ANDERSON, BCO, for NW 1/4 S 11 T 7 R 4, Steubenville district, granted to him on 1 Feb 1816 by James MADISON and Josiah MEIGS, ent. 27 Feb 1817, rec. 3 Mar same.

F-378   Indenture, 30 Jan 1817, Patrick NELLONS (wife Action), BCO; Abner MOORE, BCO; $165, house and lot #140 in St. Clairsville; WIT: Sterling JOHNSTON, Steel SMITH, ack. Sterling JOHNSTON, JP, ent. 28 Feb 1817, rec. 4 Mar same.

F-379   Indenture, 11 Feb 1817, James BARNES (wife Nancy), BCO; Thomas SHANNON, BCO; $1,200, lots #16 and #112 in Barnesville, fee simple; his seal, her mark, WIT: Jno. BEVAN, William G. SHANKLAND, ack. John BEVAN, JP, ent. 28 Feb 1817, rec. 4 Mar same.

F-380   Indenture, 13 Jan 1817, Humphrey ANDERSON (wife Lavina), BCO; Dorcas WAY, BCO; $450, part of S 34 T 8 R 6, 100 3/4 acres 26 perches; his seal, her mark, WIT: Asa ANDERSON, Thomas SHANNON, ack. Jno. BEVAN, JP, ent. 28 Feb 1817, rec. 8 Mar same.

F-381   Indenture, 11 Sep 1816, Benjamin MURPHY (wife Eleanor), BCO; Joseph MEDDLEY, George WADDELL, Abner MOORE, William GREEN, and James WADDELL, trustees, BCO; $.06, part of NW 1/4 S 10 T 9 R 6, Steubenville district, granted to MURPHY by deed dated 1 Jun 1810, 1 acre, place of worship for use of Methodist Episcopal Church, instructions to maintain nine trustees; both mark, WIT: Edward [CONDEN, CONDON?], William MOORE, ack. Abner MOORE, JP, [no ent. or rec. data].

F-383   Indenture, 10 Dec 1816, John HURDLE (wife Susanna), BCO; Benjamin GALLOWAY and Nancy HAWES, BCO; $200, part of SW 1/4 S 29 T 7 R 5, Steubenville district, NBR: Timothy HESKIT, 53 1/4 acres, granted to HURDLE by patent dated 10 Aug 1815; his mark, her seal, ack. Wm. SMITH, JP, ent. 8 Mar 1817, rec. 12 same.

F-385   Indenture, 26 Feb 1817, James FERGUSON, BCO; Thomas WHITE, BCO; $1,800, part of NE 1/4 S 29 T 7 R 4, same 1/4 granted to David DRAKE by patent dated 19 Aug 1812, NBR: Wheeling Creek, 139 1/4 acres 7 perches; WIT: Sterling JOHNSTON, Eli NICHOLS, ack. Sterling JOHNSTON, JP, ent. 10 Mar 1817, rec. 12 same.

F-386   Indenture, 21 Oct 1815, David NICHOLS (wife Lear [Leah]), Loudon County, Virginia; Eli NICHOLS, BCO; $1, 1/10 part of S to which David became entitled as one of the heirs and representatives of George NICHOLS, late of Loudon, Virginia, dec'd.; WIT: Thomas WHITE, Thomas SMITH, John WHITE, ack. Loudon County, Lewis ELLZEY and Joshua OSBURN, magistrates, BINNS' certification of 1 Jun 1816 approved by Benjamin GRAYSON, presiding justice of County Court of Loudon, GRAYSON certified 1 Jun 1816 by Charles BINNS, Clerk of County Court of Loudon, ent. 10 Mar 1817, rec. 12 same.

F-388   Indenture, 8 Aug 1815, William CHAPLINE (wife Mary), Ohio County, Virginia; Jacob DOVENBARGER, BCO; $10, lot #71 in Morristown as laid off by William CHAPLINE; WIT: Duncan MORRISON, John MILLER, ack. 11 Aug 1816, John EATON, JP, ent. 10 Mar 1817, rec. 12 same.

F-389   Indenture, 8 Aug 1815, William CHAPLINE (wife Mary), Ohio County, Virginia; Jacob DOVENBARGER, BCO; $10, lot #44 in Morristown, as laid off by William CHAPLINE; WIT: Duncan MORRISON, John MILLER, ack. 11 Jul 1816, John EATON, JP, ent. 10 Mar 1817, rec. 13 same.

F-390   Indenture, 8 Aug 1815, William CHAPLINE (wife Mary), Ohio County, Virginia; Jacob DOVENBARGER, BCO; $10, lot #45 in Morristown as laid out by William CHAPLINE; WIT: Duncan MORRISON, John MILLER, ack. 11 Jul 1816, John EATON, JP, ent. 10 Mar 1817, rec. 13 same.

F-391   Indenture, 7 Nov 1816, Abner MOORE (wife Mary MOORE), BCO; John INSKEEP, BCO; $650, half lot #68 in St. Clairsville, adjoining INSKEEP, deeded to MOORE by James MOORE by indenture dated 23 Sep 1816; his seal, her mark, wit; Wm. MOSELEY, Jacob HOLLOWAY, ack. Henry JOHNSTON, JP, ent. 10 Mar 1817, rec. 13 same.

F-392   Indenture, 27 d 2 m 1817, John PIGGOTT (wife Sarah), BCO; Joseph WRIGHT, John WRIGHT, William WRIGHT, Sarah HOGE, Elizabeth WRIGHT, and Rebecca WRIGHT, BCO; $75.31, 30 acres 20 perches in NE corner of SE 1/4 S 2 T 10 R 6; WIT: Jesse FOULKE, Enos PICKERING, ack. 27 Feb 1817, Robert LEE, JP, ent. 11 Mr 1817, rec. 13 same.

F-393   Indenture, 20 May 1816, John PIGGOTT (wife Sarah), BCO; Josiah WICKERSHAM, BCO; $315, 135 acres 3 rods 20 perches, part of SE 1/4 S 2 T 10 R 6, granted to PIGGOTT by patent dated 18 Jul 1812, NBR: William WRIGHT; WIT: Ebenezer PIGGOTT, William DUNN, ack. William DUNN, JP, ent. 11 Mar 1817, rec. 13 same.

F-395   Indenture, 27 d 2 m 1817, John PIGGOTT (wife Sarah), BCO; Jesse FOULKE, Flushing, BCO; $584, 1/2 NW 1/4 S 26 T 9 R 5, Steubenville district, 83 acres, 1/2 of the 1/4 S granted to John PIGGOTT, father of the above named, by patent dated 3 Aug 1810, who died without disposing of the same and the heirs at law by deed dated 7 d 6 m 1814 conveyed said 1/4 to John PIGGOTT, recorded in the office in BCO 12 Dec 1814, Book E, page 61; WIT: Enos PICKERING, B.S., Joseph WRIGHT, ack. 27 Feb 1817, Robert LEE, JP, ent. 11 Mar 1817, rec. 13 same.

F-396   Indenture, 25 Nov 1816, James ALEXANDER, BCO; John SIMPSON, BCO; $_____, 181 1/2 acres in S 6 T 5 R 3, NBR: [Mr.] KINKEAD, McMACKON's creek, Robert MERRITT; WIT: Robert GRAY, James ALEXANDER, Jr., ack. of James ALEXANDER, Senr., by James ALEXANDER, Associate Judge, ent. 12 Mar 1817, rec. 14 same.

F-397   Indenture, 24 Oct 1816, Thomas CAVEN (wife Hannah), BCO; Joseph PARKER, JCO; $600, land bounded by Robert FINNEY and others in S 31 T 4 R 2, NBR: little fork of Glenn's run, 61 1/2 acres, sold to CAVEN by George BROKAW (wife Jane) on 20 Feb 1807, recorded 1 May 1807 in Book B, p. 102; WIT: Thos. MITCHELL, James CARVEN, ack. Thos. MITCHELL, JP, ent. 12 Mar 1817, rec. 14 same.

F-399   Indenture, 25 Nov 1817, William CHAPLINE (wife Mary); George KNOX, all of Ohio County, Virginia; to secure to David JONES of Pennsylvania payment of debts, two promissory notes each for $533 and a third of $1 drawn by William CHAPLINE and Moses CHAPLINE dated 26 Aug 1802 and payable to Joseph TOMLINSON by whom they were assigned to David JONES, also one other note from William CHAPLINE to David JONES bearing current date payable 1 May 1819 for $785, $1 paid to William CHAPLINE by George KNOX, S 20 T 8 R 5, granted to William by patent dated 7 Jan 1808, void if payment made; WIT:

Arch. McCLEAN, George SNIDER, Morgan JONES, ack. William PALMER, JP, ent. 12 Mar 1817, rec. 14 same.

F-400   Agreement between James McCUNE, Huntington County, Morris twp, farmer; Samuel McCUNE, same place; Samuel entered a section of land in Steubenville district, S 8 T 9 R 5, Samuel will transfer James's portion as soon as he gets the deed for the payment of the whole purchase money, Samuel acknowledges owing half according to agreement dated 28 Nov 1803, land to be divided in half equally, Samuel to have his choice of the shares, sgn: 28 Nov 1803, Samuel McCUNE and Jas. McCUNE, Junr., WIT: James McCUNE, Senr., George REYNOLDS, ent. 12 Mar 1817, rec. 14 same.

F-401   Indenture, Richard POWELL (wife Sarah), BCO; Benjamin RING, BCO; $200, NBR: Capteen Creek, 30 acres 16 1/2 perches, part of survey of 100 acres surveyed to Jacob WINDELIN by James EDGERTON out of S 4 T 4 R 4, from WINDELIN to POWELL; sgn: 15 Jan 1817, both mark, WIT: Josiah DILLON, John SHEPHERD, ack. Josiah DILLON, JP, ent. 13 Mar 1817, rec. 14 same.

F-402   Indenture, 25 d 2 m 1817, Thomas WILLIAMS (wife Prudence), BCO; Matthew BAILEY, BCO; $900, part of SW 1/4 S 2 T 8 R 6, Steubenville district, 118 acres; his seal, her mark, WIT: James WHITE, George WILLIAMS, ack. James WHITE, JP, ent. 13 Mar 1817, rec. 14 same.

F-403   Indenture, 15 Apr 1811, Knonis DOUDNA (wife Hannah), BCO; John DOUDNA, Senr., BCO; $144 W 1/2 of SW 1/4 S 3 T 8 R 6; WIT: John GRIER, Senr., John DOUDNA, ack. John GRIER, JP, ent. 13 Mar 1817, rec. 17 same.

F-404   Indenture, 17 Sep 1816, Andrew DOWNING, BCO; Joshua LOYD, BCO; $300, part of S 14 T 7 R 3, NBR: Josiah BUNDY, Robt. McBRATNEY, 69 acres 3 rods 13 perches, void if DOWNING pays LOYD $300 plus interest out of bank of Mt. Pleasant on 17 Mar 1817; WIT: John WATSON, Abner MOORE, ack. JCO, John WATSON, JP, ent. 14 Mar 1817, rec. 17 same; "see page 428 for release of this mortgage."

F-405   Indenture, 21 d 1 m 1817, James BARNES (wife Nancy), BCO; Horton HOWARD, St. Clairsville, BCO; $1,800, lots #37, #38, #45, and #46 in St. Clairsville, NBR: Robert WINTERS, lots #37 and #38 conveyed by Jacob HOLTZ (wife Peggy), to James WILKINS, by James WILKINS (wife Lydia) to James BARNES by deed dated 29 Jun 1809, other lots conveyed to BARNES by Robert JOHNSTON by deed dated 18 Sep 1807; his seal, her mark, WIT: Jno. BEVAN, Wm. G. SHANKLAND, ack. 23 Jan 1817, John BEVAN, JP, ent. 25 Mar 1817, rec. 17 same.

F-407   Indenture, 21 Jan 1817, James BARNES (wife Nancy), BCO; Horton HOWARD, BCO; $1,000, front lot #42 and back lot #74 in Barnesville, BCO, each 1/4 acre; his seal, her mark, WIT: Jno. BEVAN, Wm. G. SHANKLAND, ack. 23 Jan 1817, John BEVAN, JP, ent. 15 Jan 1817, rec. 17 same.

F-408   Indenture, 25 d 1 m 1817, Joseph GILL (wife Nancy), Mt. Pleasant, JCO; Horton HOWARD, BCO; $3,000, lot #21 in St. Clairsville, BCO, purchased of Samuel SULLIVAN by indenture dated 22 Apr 1809, recorded in St. Clairsville on 11 May 1809 in Book C, page 30; WIT: Jacob HOLLOWAY, George ATKINSON, receipt of money ack., ack. 25 Jan 1817, George ATKINSON, JP, ent. 15 Mar 1817, rec. 17 same.

F-409   Indenture, 25 d 1 m 1817, Joseph GILL, Mount Pleasant town, JCO; Horton HOWARD, St. Clairsville town, BCO; $300, out lot #6, 4 acres 3 rods 37 perches in plan of 15 out lots laid out by Bazaleel WELLS adjoining addition to St. Clairsville, recorded in Book A, page 429, conveyed to GILL by Samuel SULLIVAN by deed dated 22 Apr 1809; WIT: Jacob HOLLOWAY, George ATKINSON, receipt of money ack., ack. George ATKINSON, JP, [no ent. or rec. data].

F-410   Indenture, 25 d 1 m 1817, Joseph GILL (wife Nancy), Mount Pleasant, JCO; Horton HOWARD, St. Clairsville, BCO; Josiah HEDGES, Sheriff of BCO, conveyed to Samuel SULLIVAN (of St. Clairsville) by deed dated 19 Apr 1805, lot #22, taken as property of William MATHERS as result of a judgment in CCP and supream court of BCO wherein James ROSS and James BOND, trading as Ross and Bond, for use of Thomas FOULKE were plaintiffs and William MATHERS, Joseph SHARP, and Andrew MARSHALL were defendants, SULLIVAN conveyed to Joseph GILL by indenture dated 22 Apr 1809, recorded on 12 May 1809, recorded in Book C, page 32, and now from GILL to Horton HOWARD for $200; WIT: Jacob HOLLIWAY, George ATKINSON, ack. of payment, ack. George ATKINSON, JP, ent. 15 Mar 1817, rec. 18 same.

F-411   Indenture, 6 Mar 1817, John KING (wife Mary), Samuel WORLEY (wife Nancy), William MYERS and George MYERS (wife Hannah), George ELRICK (wife Elizabeth), Thomas ALEXANDER (wife Rachel), Rebecca DIXON, Susanna DIXON, and Massey DIXON[female], all heirs and legal representatives of Andrew DIXON, deceased; Robert ALEXANDER, all of BCO; $3,085.25, part of S 7 T 6 R 3, 275 acres 39 perches, NBR: James McKIRK, Samuel WORLEY, Jos. McKIRK, except one acre for a public burying ground; all marks except for John KING, George ELRICK, and Thomas ALEXANDER, WIT: Jacob DAVIS, Peter ALEXANDER, Archibald CAMPBELL, Bernard McKEY, Conrad FORNEG [his mark], ack. BCO, of John KING (wife Mary), Samuel WORLEY (wife Nancy), William MYERS (wife Margaret), George MYERS (wife Hannah), George

ELERICK (wife Elizabeth), and Rebecca DIXON, Jacob DAVIS, JP; ack. 8 Mar 1817, BCO, Thomas ALEXANDER (wife Rachel), Susanna DIXON, and Massy DIXON, James ALEXANDER, Associate Judge, ent. 15 Mar 1817, rec. 28 same.

F-414   Indenture, 28 Sep 1816, John THOMPSON (wife Sally), BCO; George ROUSE, Alligania County, Pennsylvania; $10,500, 238 1/4 acres, all of S 29 and part of S 35 T 1 R 2, NBR; Ohio River, land sold by John DILLE to David LANE [could it be ZANE?], land conveyed by Absolom MARTIN to John DILLE on 16 Sep 1796, plus another piece of land beginning at stake on Ohio River, NBR: David LOCKWOOD and others, 440 acres, surplus after deducting [ten or two?] hundred acres on south side of section conveyed to George MILLER by Stephen MILLER by deed dated 15 Nov 1811 shall belong to George ROUSE, last mentioned tract of land conveyed to John THOMPSON by John DILLE (wife Margaret) on 12 Dec 1814, also land belonging to John THOMPSON in fractional S 36 T 1 R 2 containing 61 1/2 acres, fee simple; his seal, her mark, WIT: Sterling JOHNSTON, Townsend W. FRAZIER, ack. Sterling JOHNSTON, JP, ent. 17 Mar 1817, rec. 24 same.

F-416   To all to whom these presents may come, Jacob MOORE, BCO for $1 paid him grants Richard TRUAX right to erect and maintain a mill dam across Captina Creek no more than 100 yards above the mouth of the Cove run, both bind themselves in the penal sum of $1,000, TRUAX binds himself that he will $20 for every acre that the dam might cause to be drowned or otherwise rendered unfit for use; both sign on 18 Dec 1816, WIT: David KIRKBRIDE, ack. 12 Mar 1817, Isaac MOORE, JP, ent. 20 Mar 1817, rec. 25 same.

F-417   Indenture, 6 Mar 1817, William BOOKER (wife Patience) of the borough of St. Clairsville, BCO; John MITCHELL, same place; BOOKER by an indenture from Alexander YOUNG (wife Jane) became seized in fee simple of lot #116 in St. Clairsville dated 17 Nov 1815, recorded in Book F, page 59, now for $35 paid by MITCHELL they convey W 1/2 of lot #116; WIT: Thomas SHARPLESS, William SHARPLESS, Augt. M. GROVE, Thomas SHARPLESS WIT for receipt of money, ack. Henry JOHNSTON, JP, ent. [26] Mar 1817, rec. 28 same.

F-418   Know all men, David BARNES, BCO, owes to Richard TRUAX $2,200 to be paid in installments up through Apr 1825 by nine written obligations dated 11 Dec 1816, for better securing of payments now sells to TRUAX part of S 36 T 6 R 4, 100 acres, 50 acres conveyed to Joseph SILLS, 1/2 acre for meeting or school house, second tract 148 acres 1 rod 9 poles, same that TRUAX (wife Mary) conveyed to David BARNES on 25 Jan 1817, land held in fee simple, void if obligations paid; WIT: Isaac MERRITT, Sterling JOHNSTON, ack. 25 Jan 1817, Sterling JOHNSTON, JP, ent. 25 Mar 1817, rec. 28 same.

F-420   Plat of Mount Aiery in BCO in SE 1/4 S 15 T 10 R 6, plat dated 18 Mar 1817, surveyed by John STEWART, County Surveyor for Mr. Thomas MORROW, ack. 28 Mar 1817, Henry JOHNSON, JP, ent. 28 Mar 1817, rec. 31 same.

F-421   Indenture, 1 Oct 1816, Absalom RIDGELEY (wife Drusilla), Ohio County, Virginia; Morras KELLY, BCO; $400, NW 1/4 S 4 T 6 R 4, same granted to RIDGELEY by patent dated 15 Jan 1814; [her name signed as Drusylla], WIT: Henry McCRECKIN, John WATSON, ack. 2 Oct 1816, JCO, John WATSON, JP, ent. 28 Mar 1817, rec. 3 Apr same.

F-422   Indenture, 28 Mar 1817, Ira ROBINSON, admr. of John HINDS, dec'd., BCO; John BROWN, Junr., BCO; John HINDS in his lifetime sold to John BROWN, Junr., part of lot #93 in St. Clairsville, NBR: Solomon BENTLEY, Lewis SUTTON, agreement not completed before HINDS' death, ordered issued out of CCP for BCO dated 26 Mar 1817 to Ira ROBINSON, admr., to convey premises to BROWN, so for $400 conveys in fee simple; WIT: Wm. FARIS, Junr., Joseph ANDERSON, ack. Joseph ANDERSON, Assoc. Judge, ent. 28 Mar 1817, rec. 3 Apr same.

F-423   Indenture, 28 Mar 1817, John BROWN, Junr., BCO; Ira ROBINSON, admr. of John HINDS, late of BCO; $300, for use of heirs of John HINDS, lot #93 in St. Clairsville, NBR: Solomon BENTLEY, Lewis SUTTON, same conveyed by ROBINSON to BROWN on same date, fee simple, void if BROWN pays $300; WIT: Wm. FARIS, Jr., Joseph ANDERSON, ack. Joseph ANDERSON, Assoc. Judge, ent. 28 Mar 1817, rec. 3 Apr same.

F-425   Indenture, 1 Apr 1817, Samuel SHARPLESS (wife Rebecca), St. Clairsville, BCO; David BOGGS, Ohio County, Virginia; SHARPLESS seized in fee of two tracts, for the first beginning SW corner S 17 T 6 R 3, NBR: John BELL, 164 acres, for the second beginning at white oak in Aaron NEWPORT's line, 33 acres, as in indenture dated 18 Apr 1815, recorded Book E, p. 145, for $2,000; WIT: Andr. WHITE, ack. 3 Apr 1817, Sterling JOHNSTON, JP, ent. 3 Apr 1817, rec. 4 same.

F-427   Indenture, 22 Nov 1815, Daniel MERRITT (wife Nancy), BCO; Caleb DILWORTH, JCO; $491.75, 65 3/4 acres 10 perches, part of S 31 T 8 R 4, granted to MERRITT by patent dated 27 Aug 1805; WIT: John CAMPBELL, William DIXON, ack. John CAMPBELL, JP, ent. 3 Apr 1817, rec. 5 same.

F-428   Indenture, 31 Mar 1817, William SHARP, BCO; Abraham DILWORTH, JCO; $[2],000, 160 acres, part of W 1/2 S 32 T 8 R 4, granted to Joseph SHARP by patent dated [18] Feb 1806, NBR: Wm. DIXON; WIT: Isaac AGNEW, John W. SMITH, ack. John CAMPBELL, JP, ent. 3 Apr 1817, rec. 5 same.

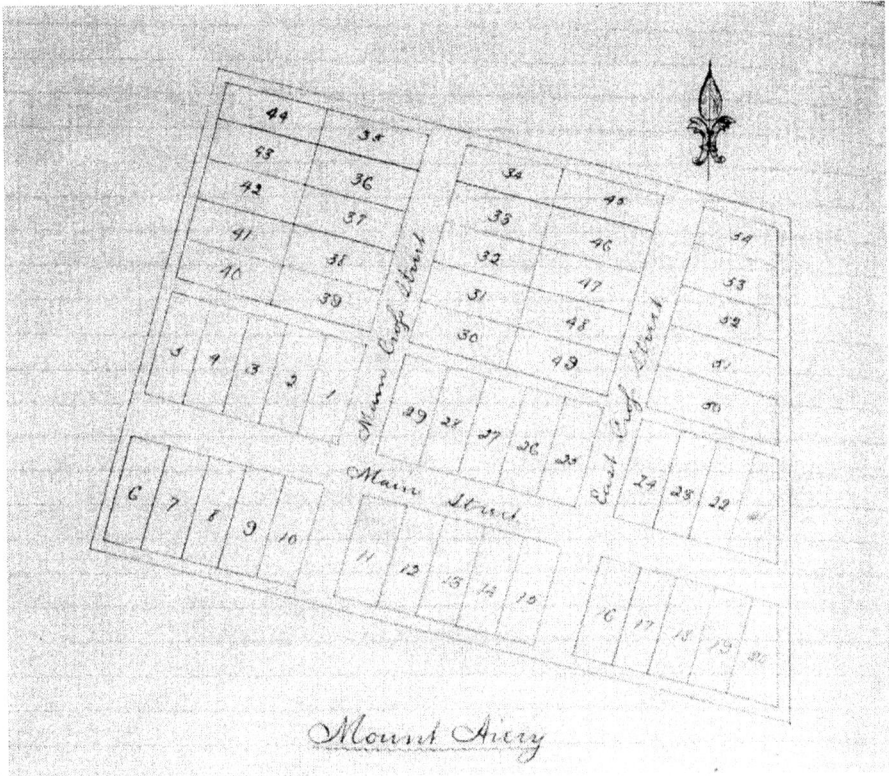

Plat of Mount Aiery

F-429   Indenture, 28 Mar 1817, John EATON (wife Catherine), BCO; Margret [Margrett, Margaret] HAZLETT, BCO; $1,280, N 1/2 S 14 T 8 R 5, granted to Joseph EATON by patent dated 14 Aug 1807, conveyed to John EATON; WIT: Thomas McWILLIAMS, William DUNN, ack. 29 Mar 1817, William DUNN, JP, ent. 3 Apr 1817, rec. 5 same.

F-430   Indenture, 16 d 12 m 1817, Jesse FOULKE, one of proprietors of town of Flushing, (wife Sarah) BCO; Benj. BROCK, BCO; $55, lots #13 and #65 in Flushing; WIT: Mary SAMUELS, Robert LEE, ack. 16 Jan 1817, Robert LEE, JP, ent. 4 Apr 1817, rec. 5 same.

F-431   Indenture, 1 d 4 m 1817, John SCHOOLEY and Daniel STONE, extrs of estate of William HOUGH, deceased, late of Loudon County, Virginia; Joseph RODGERS, BCO; $1,600, land, saw-mill and grist-mill, part of S 30 T 6 R 3, NBR: Wheeling Creek, 133 3/4 acres 24 perches; WIT: Henry JOHNSTON, George LOVE, ack. 4 Apr 1817, Henry JOHNSTON, JP, ent. 4 Apr 1817, rec. 7 same.

F-433   Indenture, 1 Apr 1817, Joseph RODGERS, BCO; John SCHOOLEY and Daniel STONE, extrs. of estate of William HOUGH of Loudon County, Virginia, deceased; indebtedness of $2,133.33, conditioned for payment of $1,066.66, to secure payment and for $.50, [description as in preceding indenture], void if RODGERS pays $1,066.66; WIT: Henry JOHNSTON, George LOVE, ack. 4 Apr 1817, Henry JOHNSTON, JP, ent. 4 Apr 1817, rec. 8 same.

F-435   Indenture, 21 Mar 1817, Joseph WRIGHT (wife Eleanor), BCO; William NICKOLS, BCO; $40, lot # 10 in town of Belmont; WIT: Joseph PANCOST, Wm. SMITH, ack. 31 Mar 1817, Wm. SMITH, JP, ent. 4 Apr 1817, rec. 8 same.

F-436   Indenture, 25 Feb 1817, Richard TRUAX (wife Mary), BCO; David BARNES, BCO; $2,500, first tract beginning at NW corner S 36 T 6 R 4, 100 acres, second tract beginning at NE corner S 36 T 6 R 4, 148 acres 1 rod 9 poles, 50 acres excepted which was conveyed to Joseph SCILLS by TRUAX and wife Mary on __ Feb 1817, beginning at NW corner of S 36 T 6 R 4, also 1/2 acre which TRUAX promised for the use of public buildings such as a meeting house and school house adjoining 50 acres, all land conveyed to Richard TRUAX by Caleb ENGLE (wife Mercy), fee simple; his seal, her mark, WIT: John BIGELEY, Zadock COLLINS, ack. [22 or 23] Mar 1817, Sterling JOHNSTON, JP, ent. 5 Apr 1817, rec. 8 same.

F-438   Indenture, 27 Mar 1817, Abel SWEZEY (wife Mary), BCO; Robert IRWIN, BCO; $275, fee simple, part of SE 1/4 S 11 T 6 R 4, 1/4 S granted to SWEZEY by patent dated 3 Oct 1816, 95 acres; his seal, her mark, WIT:

Chrawford WELSH, Martha PORTERFIELD [her mark], ack. Chrawford WELSH, JP, ent. 7 Apr 181<u>6</u> [suspect 1817], rec. 8 same.

F-439   Indenture, 9 Jan 1817, Joseph TILTON (wife Marcy), Warren twp, JCO; Zacheus TILTON, same place; $1,450, part of Ss 21 and 22 t 4 R 2, part in BCO and part in JCO, NBR: Samuel BEGGER, 145 acres 2 rods 30 perches, TILTON reserves to himself right of cutting timber for his own place for term of natural life; his seal, her mark, WIT: John RAMSEY, Jesse MARTIN, ack. 10 Jan 1817, JCO, Jesse MARTIN, JP, ent. 14 Apr 1817, rec. 21 same.

F-441   Indenture, 19 Oct 1816, Frances BARKHURST [female], BCO; Patrick NELLONS, BCO; $37, part of S 32 T 6 R 3, NBR: Mr. HEATON, BARKHURST's old tract, Jonathan SUTTON, NELLONS, 3 acres 20 perches; her mark, WIT: John SUTTON, Sterling JOHNSTON, ack. 19 Apr 1817, Sterling JOHNSTON, JP, ent. 19 Apr 1817, rec. 23 same.

F-442   Indenture, 22 Apr 1817, William COULSON (wife Lydia), BCO; Joel ELLIOTT, Frederick County, Maryland; $750, front lot # 41 and back lot #73 in town of Barnesville, BCO, each 1/4 acre; WIT: J. BEVAN, Archibald COLE, ack. John BEVAN, JP, ent. 23 Apr 1817, rec. same.

F-443   Indenture, 22 Apr 1817, James BARNES (wife Nancy), BCO; William COULSON, BCO; $80, front lots #41 and #38 and back lots #70 and #73 in town of Barnesville, BCO, each 1/4 acre; both indicated as sealing, WIT: Thos. PLUMMER, J. BEVAN, ack. J. BEVAN, JP, ent. 23 Apr 1817, rec. 29 same.

F-444   Indenture, 22 Apr 1817, <u>Micheal</u> CARROLL (wife Sarah) of Richland twp, BCO; William GRIMES, same twp, BCO; $320, land in Richland twp, part of S 12 T 7 R 4, 91 acres 1 rod 16 perches, fee simple; she signs "Sally," WIT: Wm. GILL, Sterling JOHNSTON, ack. Sterling JOHNSTON, JP, ent. 26 Apr 1817, rec. 29 same.

F-445   Indenture, 1 Apr 1817, William FROST, St. Clairsville, BCO; Daniel BRANINGER, same place; $2,200 owed to BRANINGER by a writing obligatory dated 15 Nov 1816, payments to be made in leather and cash, convey lots #89 and part of lot #81 in St. Clairsville, void if payments made; WIT: Henry JOHNSTON, John McELROY, ack. 21 Apr 1817, Henry JOHNSTON, JP, ent. 26 Apr 1817, rec. 29 same; satisfaction of mortgage recorded 10 Feb 1823 by Daniel BRANINGER, WIT: Wm. FARIS, Jr., Recorder.

F-446   Indenture, 1 Apr 1817, Eleazer KINNEY, St. Clairsville, BCO; Daniel BRANINGER, BCO; $800, KINNEY indebted to BRANINGER by a writing obligatory dated 11 Nov 1816, payable in payments, conveyed to BRANINGER

W part of lot #81 in St. Clairsville, void if payments made; WIT: Henry JOHNSTON, John McELROY, ack. 21 Apr 1817, Henry JOHNSTON, JP, ent. 26 Apr 1817, rec. 30 same; satisfaction of mortgage recorded 15 Jan 1821 by Daniel BRANINGER, WIT: Wm. FARIS, Jr., Recorder.

F-448   Indenture, 21 Mar 1817, William HENDERSON, Junr., (wife Arabella), BCO; Enos BROWNFIELD, BCO; $500, part of NE 1/4 S 24 T 7 R 4, 60 acres, NBR: George KELLAR, Joseph IRWIN, conveyed to John HOPKINS by Samuel OSGOOD and Walter LIVINGSTON, commissioners of the board of treasury of the U.S. by instrument of writing dated 3 Mar 1789; his seal, her mark, WIT: John BEVAN, George ADDUDDELL, ack. John BEVAN, JP, ent. 1 May 1817, rec. 8 same.

F-449   Indenture, 21 Mar 1817, William HENDERSON, Jr. (wife Arabella), BCO; Enos BROWNFIELD, BCO; $500, in S 23 T 7 R 4, NBR: George KELLAR, 60 acres, conveyed to John HOPKINS by Samuel OSGOOD and Walter LIVINGSTON, commissioners of the board of treasure of the U.S. by instrument of writing dated 3 Mar 1789; his seal, her mark, WIT: Jno. BEVAN, George ADUDDELL, ack. J. BEVAN, JP, ent. 1 May 1817, rec. 8 same.

F-450   Indenture, 30 Jan 1816, Mathew SCOTT and William WORKMAN, both BCO; WORKMAN for $253, 63 1/4 acres, land which he purchased 50 acres of Absalom MARTIN dec'd. in his life time and which 50 acres begins W corner S [13] T 6 R 3, 50 acres and the residue of 63 1/4 acres, the 9 1/4 acres William bought of Haddock WARREN, 4 acres William bought of George WILLIAMS, 13 1/4 acres joins above 53 acres which William bought of Absalom MARTIN, dec'd, 9 1/4 acres he purchased of Haddock WARREN as follows: NBR: Haddock WARREN; WIT: John CUNINGHAM, Hannah CUNINGHAM, ack. 10 Feb 1816, John CUNINGHAM, JP, ent. 7 May 1816, rec. 10 same.

F-451   Indenture, 8 Mar 1816, Robert THOMPSON (wife Mary), BCO; Matthew SCOTT, BCO; $1,400, lot of ground which Artemas BAKER and Robert THOMPSON reside, in town of Canton, Peas twp, BCO, fee simple; WIT: Thos. THOMPSON, David NEISWANGER, ack. 20 Aug 1816, John CLARK, JP for Peas twp, ent. 7 May 1816 [probably 1817?], rec. 10 same.

F-453   Indenture, 12 Feb 1817, Alexander THOMPSON, Allegheny County, Pennsylvania; Mathew SCOTT, BCO; $2,096, land formerly conveyed by Thomas THOMPSON (wife Elizabeth) to Robert THOMPSON and by Robert to Mathew SCOTT, by Mathew SCOTT to Alexander THOMPSON and now in possession and occupancy of Mathew SCOTT, if Alexander THOMPSON pays Mathew SCOTT $100 the premises are to go to him, further $96 payable in a wagon or horses delivered at the town of Wheeling, THOMPSON further acknowledges indebtedness of $1,900, void if Alexander THOMPSON pays full amount; WIT: Wm. RODGERS, Mary SCOTT, Jos. WALLACE, ack. BCO, Jacob DAVIS, JP, ent. 7 May 1817, rec. 12 same.

F-454   Indenture, 25 Nov 1815, Moses MILIGAN [MILLIGAN] (wife Mary), BCO; John JEAKS [JEAKES, JAKES], BCO; $15, lot #94 in Morristown as laid off by William CHAPLINE; his seal, her mark, WIT: John EATON, Stephen VOORHES, ack. 19 Jan 1816, John EATON, JP, ent. 8 May 1817, rec. 12 same.

F-455   Indenture, 22 Mar 1817, John JACQUES (wife Eleanor), BCO; John MILLER, BCO; $150, lot #94 in Morristown; both mark, WIT: William RIDDLE [BIDDLE?], John EATON, ack. John EATON, JP, ent. 8 May 1817, rec. 12 same.

F-456   Indenture, 14 Apr 1817, John MILLER (wife Barbery), BCO; Edward THOMAS, BCO; $150, lot #94 in Morristown; his seal, her mark, WIT: John EATON, Andrew THOMPSON, ack. John EATON, JP, ent. 8 May 1817, rec. 12 same.

F-457   Indenture, 20 d 5 m ("called May") 1812, James EDGERTON (wife Sarah) and George STARBUCK (wife Elizabeth), BCO; Daniel THOMAS, BCO; $600, part S 4 T 5 R 4, Marietta district, 106 acres; WIT: David SMITH, Hugh WILSON, ack. David SMITH, JP, ent. 9 May 1817, rec. 13 same.

F-458   Indenture, 25 d 4 m 1817, Mathew WOOD (wife Margret [Margaret]), BCO; James EDGERTON, Senr., Joseph COX, and Peter SEARS, BCO; $10, S side of Captina Creek, part of NW 1/4 S 23 T 6 R 5, 3 acres for the use of the Captina preparative meeting of the society of friends for a friends meeting house; WIT: James WHITE, Stephen HODGIN, ack. James WHITE, JP, ent. 9 May 1817, rec. 13 same.

F-460   Indenture, 19 Aug 1816, James DALLAS (wife Fanny), BCO; Samuel CASEY, BCO; $100, beginning at corner of Robert BEALL, his land part of W side of 1/4 S 27 T 8 R 5, 60 acres, fee simple; WIT: Joseph EATON, John EATON, ack. John EATON, JP, ent. 10 May 1817, rec. 13 same.

F-461   Indenture, 21 Sep 1816, Amos PENNINGTON (wife Elizabeth), BCO; James HUTCHESON, BCO; $37, part of NE corner of SW 1/4 S 8 T 8 R 6, 15 acres; his seal, her mark, WIT: Jno. BEVAN, Mymes PEPPEN, ack. Jno. BEVAN, JP, ent. 14 May 1817, rec. 17 same.

F-462   Indenture, 25 Nov 1815, William HUTCHERSON (wife Jane), BCO; Margaret CALDERHEAD, BCO; $90, part of SW 1/4 S 3 T 8 R 4, granted to William HUTCHISON by patent dated 20 Jan 1812, 19 3/4 acres 8 perches, NBR:

Joseph HENRY, Humphrey ALEXANDER; his seal, her mark, WIT: David WALLACE, Humphery ALEXANDER, ack. David WALLACE, JP, ent. 15 May 1817, rec. 17 same.

F-463   Indenture, 22 Feb 1817, Jacob MYERS (wife Sarah), BCO; David WALLACE, BCO; $1,240, 155.85 acres, the chief part of SE 1/4 S 9 T 8 R 4, granted to Adam SEEBERT by patent dated 28 Dec 1807, conveyed by SEEBERT to MYERS "by patent" dated 28 Apr 1815; his seal, her mark, WIT: John CAMPBELL, Nathaniel COLEMAN, ack. John CAMPBELL, JP, ent. 15 May 1817, rec. 17 same.

F-465   Indenture, 11 Mar 1817, Joseph MERRITT (wife Mary), JCO; John BARNES, BCO; $900, lot on S side of St. Clairsville adjoining commons, NBR: Benj. RUGGLES, land Joseph SATTERTHWAIT purchased of MERRITT, 3 acres 3 rods 24 poles; WIT: Sterling JOHNSTON, George PAULL, ack. Sterling JOHNSTON, JP, ent. 17 May 1817, rec. 24 same.

F-466   Indenture, 16 May 1817, John BARNES (wife Ann), BCO; Samuel HOUGH, BCO; $1,500, S side of town of St. Clairsville adjoining commons, beginning at NW corner of commons, NBR: Benjamin RUGGLES, Joseph SATTERTHWAIT which he purchased of MERRITT, 3 acres 3 rods 24 poles; WIT: Notley HAYS, Henry JOHNSTON, ack. Henry JOHNSTON, JP, ent. 17 May 1816, rec. 24 same.

F-467   Indenture, 13 Jan 1817, Humphrey ANDERSON (wife Lavinia), BCO; John BARKER, BCO; $172, S 34 T 8 R 6, NBR: Dorcas WAY, 69 3/4 acres 12 poles; his seal, her mark, WIT: Asa ANDERSON, Thomas SHANNON, ack. Jno. BEVAN, JP, ent. 17 May 1817, rec. 24 same.

F-468   Indenture, 23 Oct 1816, Daniel McPEEK (wife Elizabeth), Guernsey County, Ohio; James MORTON, BCO; $772.005, 36 acres 17 perches, the N part of tract conveyed to Daniel by Baz. WELLS (wife Sally), 8 Dec 1809, part of S 18 T 6 R 3, NBR: Jesse FINCH, post on N side of commons of Farmington, Hugh PARKS; both mark, WIT: Levi WILLIAMS, William MOORE [p. 469 is blank], ack. Guernsey County, Christopher BURNWORTH, JP, certified by Zacheus A. BEATTY, Clerk pro tempore of CCP, at Cambridge on 25 Oct 1816, ent. 20 May 1817, rec. 24 same.

F-470   Indenture, 3 Apr 1817, Wm. STRANAHAM (wife Jenny), BCO; John CARTER, St. Clairsville, BCO; $400, on waters of McMahon's creek, part of S 33 T 6 R 3, Steubenville district, NBR: William McFARLAND, Thomas FAWCETT, Jonathan SUTTON, 33 acres, fee simple; both mark, WIT: Sterling JOHNSTON,

William SHEPHERD, ack. 3 Mar 1817, Sterling JOHNSTON, JP, ent. 21 May 1817, rec. 24 same.

F-471   Indenture, 18 Apr 1815, David WALLACE (wife Jane) and James HASTINGS (wife Agnes), BCO; James GALASPE, Washington County, Pennsylvania; $1,030, 90 acres, part of NE 1/4 S 15 T 8 R 4, NE 1/4 granted to David WALLACE and Agnes WALLACE, tenants in common and not as joint tenants, Agnes WALLACE now the lawful wife of James HASTINGS, patent dated 15 Jan 1814, NBR: William LOVE; Jane WALLACE does not sign, the rest do, WIT: John CAMPBELL, George LOVE, ack. John CAMPBELL, JP [Jane was present there], ent. 22 May 1814, rec. 24 same.

F-472   W. P. LANS, Register of land office at Marietta, on 30 Jul 1816 granted a certificate to James BERRITT, BCO, for NW 1/4 S 6 T 4 R 4, Marietta district, James BROWN able to petition for title of said 1/4 S, conveying for $150, quit claim, sgn: 26 Apr 1817, WIT: Samuel MARTIN, Micheal L. MARTIN, ack. William PALMER, JP, ent. 24 May 1817, rec. 26 same.

F-473   Indenture, 8 Apr 1817, Nathan FIDLER (wife Hannah), Knox County, Ohio; Frederick AULT, BCO; $1,000, the SW 1/4 S 5 T 6 R 4, Steubenville district, patented to FIDLER on 1 Sep 1808; his seal, her mark, WIT: Wm. W. FARQUHAR, Jas MARTIN, ack. Wm. W. FARQUHAR, ent. 24 May 1817, rec. 26 same.

F-474   Indenture, 7 Apr 1817, Robert WATSON (wife Rachel), Hartford County, Maryland; Joseph TROUT, Hopewell twp, York County, Pennsylvania; $321, S 1/2 SW 1/4 S 21 T 8 R 6, Steubenville district, 83 acres 4 perches, part of land WATSON obtained by patent dated 15 Jan 1814; WIT: John MOFFATT, Alexr. WALLACE, [Jamno] PAYNE, receipt of money WIT by Alexr. WALLACE, ack. of Robert WATSON, York County, Alexr. WALLACE, JP, certified by Jacob BARNITS, Recorder, ent. 26 May 1817, rec. same day.

F-475   Indenture, 16 May 1817, Samuel HOUGH, BCO; John BARNES, BCO; $1,500, fee simple, beginning on the commons at S side of St. Clairsville, NBR: Benjm. RUGGLES, Joseph SATTERTHWAIT (purchased of Joseph MERRITT), 4 acres, HOUGH indebted to BARNES for $1,500, payments with interest beginning 1 Dec 1816, void if payments made; WIT: Henry JOHNSTON, Noley [Notley] HAYS, ack. Henry JOHNSTON, JP, ent. 26 May 1817, rec. 28 same.

F-476   Indenture, 24 d 5 m 1817, Isaac PARKER (wife Sarah), JCO; David HIRST [HURST], BCO; $6,000, part of Ss 7 and 13 T 7 R 3, Steubenville district, granted by patent dated 27 d 8 m 1805 to Borden STANTON, part in this indenture was conveyed by STANTON to Horton HOWARD by deed dated 31 d 12 m 1806,

Horton conveyed to Isaac PARKER by deed dated 26 d 7 m 1815, S 13 granted by patent to William SATTERTHWAITE on 9 d 3 m 1808, part in this indenture given by LW&T to his son Joseph SATTERTHWAITE and conveyed to Horton the 2 d 12 m 1806, and conveyed by HOWARD to Isaac PARKER by deed dated 26 d 7 m 1815, both pieces of land conveyed by PARKER to HURST, together 200 acres; WIT: John ALEXANDER, J. WATSON, ack. 24 May 1817, J. WATSON, JP, ent. 30 May 1817, rec. 2 Jun same.

F-478   Indenture, 28 d 3 m 1817, James BARNES (wife Nancy), BCO; Caleb ENGLE, BCO; $150, lots # 37 and 69 in Barnesville, each 1/4 acre; his seal, her mark, WIT: Wm. G. SHANKLAND, Isaac BRANSON, ack. John BEVAN, JP, ent. 30 May 1817, rec. 9 Jun same.

F-479   Indenture, 29 Aug 1814, James CALDWELL (wife Nancy), BCO; Benjamin RUGGLES, BCO; $813, part of SW 1/4 S 4 T 7 R 4, S 4 purchased by James NEWALL of Bazaleel WELLS of JCO, conveyed by him to CALDWELL, NBR: Moses MOREHEAD, reservation made by James E. NEWALL in his deed to William MATHERS (recorded Book A, p. 404); WIT: William BROWN, John PATTERSON, ack. John PATTERSON, Assoc. Judge, ent. 3 Jun 1817, rec. 9 same.

F-480   Indenture, 7 Apr 1817, Jonathan WINTER (wife Nancy), Stark County, Ohio; Benjamin RUGGLES, BCO; $600, part of SE 1/4 S 9 T 7 R 4, 1/4 S conveyed to Thomas TIPTON by Bazaleel WELLS by deed dated 13 Nov 1798, part of above land received by WINTER by deed dated 16 Jan 1812 and recorded 17 Jan in Book D, p. 161, NBR: Joseph PARISH, Eli PLUMMER, Alexander BOGGS, 50 acres with incumbrance of a mill race on land as reserved by Thomas TIPTON in the deed made by him to WINTER to convey this land; his seal, her mark, WIT: Francis SMITH, Catharine WINTER, ack. 17 Apr 1817, Francis SMITH, JP, ent. 3 Jun 1817, rec. 10 same.

F-481   Indenture, 19 Apr 1817, Andrew DOWNING, JCO; Robert BLAIR, BCO; $1,000, part S 14 T 7 R 3, NBR: Josiah BUNDY, Robt. McBRATNEY, 69 acres 3 rods 13 perches; WIT: Joshua LOYD, John WATSON, ack. JCO, 22 Apr 1817, John WATSON, JP, ent. 9 Jun 1817, rec. 10 same.

F-482   Indenture, 24 Aug 1816, Abraham KENNEY (wife Marget), BCO, Kirkwood twp; William MITCHELL, Guernsey County, Ohio; $200, part of E side of NW 1/4 S 20 T 9 R 6, granted to Horton HOWARD by patent dated 1 Aug 1816, 40 acres; his seal, her mark, WIT: Abner MOORE, George MILLER, ack. 13 Sep 1816, Abner MOORE, JP, ent. 10 May 1817, rec. same.

F-483   George POOL [POLL?] of BCO, deposited certificate in land office full payment for NW 1/4 S 26 T 3 R 2, Steubenville district, sgn: 20 Jan 1817, Josiah MEIGS, Commissioner of the General Land Office, ent. 13 Jun 1817, rec. same.

F-484   Indenture, 14 Jun 1817, Abraham KENNEY, BCO; John H. GILBERT and William BRATTON, BCO; GILBERT and BRATTON securities as endorsers for KENNEY to Belmont Bank in St. Clairsville for $300 and for $2 granted part of NW 1/4 S 20 T 9 R 6, fee simple, void if KENNEY pays $300 to bank; WIT: John CUNNINGHAM, Wm. W. GAULT, ack. Licking County, Ohio, John CUNNINGHAM, JP, ent. 17 Jun 1817, rec. 20 same.

F-485   Know all men, Abraham KINNEY now of Licking Co., Ohio, John H. GILBERT power of attorney to prosecute a suit in chancery now pending in Belmont CCP, KINNEY plaintiff and Jacob REILEY and John LIPPINCOTT defendants, sgn: 14 Jun 1817, WIT: John CUNNINGHAM, Wm. W. GAULT, ack. Licking County, Ohio, John CUNNINGHAM, JP, ent. 17 Jun 1817, rec. 20 same.

F-485   Indenture, 4 Jun 1817, William WOODS (wife Mary), BCO; John BELL, BCO; $784, 56 acres 2 perches in SW corner S 36 T 7 R 4, granted to John EDWARD [EDWARDS], Senr., by patent dated 7 Apr 1806, 56 acres 2 perches conveyed by EDWARDS to dau Mary LAPPEN (now Mary WOODS) by deed dated 4 Feb 1809, NBR: Wheeling Creek, John WILKINSON; WIT: John SMITH, William DUNN, ack. William DUNN, JP, ent. 18 Jun 1817, rec. 20 same.

F-487   Indenture, 17 Jun 1817, James BARNES (wife Nancy), BCO; Joshua LOYD and William STANTON, JCO; $1,500, front lots #54 and #55 and part of lot #53 in Barnesville, each 1/4 acre; his seal, her mark, WIT: John BEVAN, George WOOTEN, ack. John BEVAN, JP, ent. 18 Jun 1817, rec. 20 same.

F-488   Indenture, 21 Jun 1817, John CARTER, St. Clairsville, BCO; Titus BENNET and Joseph WALTON, stationers of the city of Philadelphia trading under the firm of Bennet and Walton; $903.26, land in Union twp on the headwaters of Wheeling Creek, part of SW 1/2 S 15 T 8 R 5, Steubenville district, 90 1/4 acres 12 poles; WIT: David JENNINGS, Ira ROBINSON, ack. Henry JOHNSTON, JP, ent. 21 Jun 1817, rec. same.

F-489   Indenture, 21 Mar 1816, Nathan SHEPHERD (wife Polly), BCO; Robert HENDERSON, BCO; $60, 6 acres, part of NW 1/4 S 21 T 8 R 4, granted to SHEPHERD by patent dated 16 Nov 1812; WIT: Andrew HENDERSON, John CAMPBELL, ack. John CAMPBELL, JP, ent. 5 Jun 1817, rec. 10 same.

F-490   Know all men, a written indenture of bargain and sale dated 17 Sep 1816 between Andrew DOWNING, BCO, Joshua LOYD, BCO, $300, conveys part of

S 14 T 7 R 3, NBR: Josiah BUNDAY, Robert McBRATNEY, 69 acres 3 rods 13 perches "contained a proviso that the same should be on the sum of three hundred dollars . . . with bank interest on the same and all other banking expenses that might accrue from draining the sd. sum of three hundred dollars, out of the bank of Mount Pleasant on the seventeenth day of March one thousand eight hundred and seventeen," LOYD acknowledges receiving payment, [no signing date given]; WIT: John WATSON, Samuel PENNINGTON, ack, JCO, 22 Apr 1817, John WATSON, JP, ent. 9 Jun 1817, rec. 10 same month.

F-491   Indenture, 1 Jan 1817, Garret ACKERSON (wife Mary ACKERSON); Amos VERNOR (wife Cathrine VERNAS [VERNOR?]), all of Goshen twp, BCO; exchange land on the great road leading from Morristown to Barnesville, for piece from ACKERSON to VERNOR beginning at SE corner of NE 1/4 S 34 T 7 R 5, 3 acres 114 perches; his seal, her mark, WIT: James WHITE, John SMITH, ack. James WHITE, JP, ent. 23 Jun 1817, rec. same day.

F-492   To all to whom, Richard COX (wife Elizabeth), of Wayne County, North Carolina, for $320 paid by Joseph HALL of Ohio, NE 1/4 S 3 T 7 R 6, 150 acres, sgn: 17 d 4 m 1811, WIT: Thomas KENNEDY; Wayne County, Nov. term 1812, deed from Richard COX (wife Elizabeth) to Joseph HALL, on oath of John TAYLOR, Junr., ordered to be registered, att: John McKINNELL, No. Carolina, Wayne County registers Office, 19 Feb 1813, recorded in Liber [I], No. 617, J. HANDLY, Regtr., certified in Wayne County, North Carolina, 14 Jul 1814 by John C. PINDER, chairman of the county court, and also certifies HANLY as register same date, ent. 23 Jun 1817, rec. same.

F-493   Indenture, 11 Mar 1817, George PAULL, BCO, for the use of Mary MERRITT, JCO; John BARNES, BCO; John BARNES indebted to PAULL for the use of MERRITT and her children for $500, to be paid by 1817, to secure debt and for $.01 convey land on S side of St. Clairsville adjoining commons, NBR: Benjamin RUGGLES, Joseph SATTERTHWAIT (purchased of Joseph MERRITT), 3 acres 3 rods 24 poles, WIT: Sterling JOHNSTON, ack. Sterling JOHNSTON, JP, ent. 23 Jun 1817, rec. same.

F-494   Indenture, 10 Mar 1817, David NEISWANGER, BCO; President, directors, and company of Bank of Marietta; NEISWANGER indebted by endorsing a note for Christopher NEISWANGER to President, directors and company of the bank of Marietta for $2,600 dated 1 Nov 1815, already $1,000 paid, to secure conveying 80 acres in S 10 T 7 R 4 conveyed to David NEISWANGER by David HARR, void if debt is paid; WIT: Chrisr. NEISWANGER, Geo. PAULL, ack. Henry JOHNSTON, JP, ent. 23 Jun 1817, rec. same.

F-495   Indenture, 10 Apr 1817, Samuel ZANE, BCO; Josiah HEDGES and Geo. PAULL, BCO; $550, part of S 24 T 3 R 2, 100 acres sold by sheriff of BCO, NBR: Stubbs field; WIT: John CLARK, William ROGERS, ack. John CLARK, JP, ent. 23 Jun 1817, rec. 28 same.

F-497   Indenture, 11 Mar 1817, Joseph MERRITT (wife Mary), JCO; Joseph SATTERTHWAIT, BCO; $240, land adjoining commons of St. Clairsville, NBR: John BARNES, 1 acre 1 rod 34 poles; WIT: Sterling JOHNSTON, George PAULL, ack. Sterling JOHNSTON, JP, ent. 23 Jun 1817, rec. 28 same.

F-498   Indenture, 6 d 1 m 1816, Thomas MARSHALL (wife Margaret), Delaware County, Pennsylvania; Joseph COX (wife Elizabeth), BCO; $40, lots #4 and #100 in Barnesville; WIT: Daniel WILSON, Saml. MARSHALL, ack. 8 Apr 1816, Delaware County, Pennsylvania, Thos. PEINE, JP, 8 Apr 1816, certified 10 Apr 1816, by Joseph ENGLE, Recorder of Deeds, ent. 16 Aug 1816, rec. 17 same.

F-499   Plat of Jacobsburg, laid off by John STEWART, County Surveyor for BCO, submitted by Jacob CALVERT on 20 Nov 1815, located on S 2 T 6 R 4 on S 1/2 NE 1/4, ack. Henry JOHNSTON, JP, ent. 27 Nov 1815, rec. 12 Dec same.

F-500   J. M. BECKETT certifies copy of Deed Book Vol. F, BCO, Record of Deeds, made by order of the County Commissioners at Spring Session 1889, sgn: 1 Apr 1890, J. M. BECKETT, Recorder.

Plat of Jacobsburg

INDEX OF NAMES

BRUNSON
   Jacob 167
BRYANT
   Benoni 76, 148
BRYSON
   Edward . . . 10, 11, 13, 18, 42, 49,
            53, 59, 72, 134
BUCARTUS
   Barney 70
BUCHANAN 169
   John 5
BUFKIN
   David 151
   Ruth 38
   Thomas 38, 71, 163
BUNDY (BUNDAY)
   Benjamin 68
   Josiah 37, 44, 68, 110, 175, 185, 187
   Sarah 10, 16, 56, 109, 113, 116, 125
   William . . . 2, 10, 16, 56, 109, 111,
          113, 116, 125, 136, 156
BUNTING
   James 38
BURK
   Thomas 13
BURKITT
   Jacob 135, 136
   Mary Ann 136
BURNERS
   John M. 105
BURNET
   Robert 66
BURNWORTH
   Christopher 183
BURRIS (BURRISS) 118
   Abner 85
   Enerly, Emrly, Euerly 64
   Jeremiah 42, 47, 57, 86, 107,
           119, 160, 165
   Margaret 85
   Rachel 42, 57, 160
BURROW
   Abner 85
   Margaret 85
BURROWS (BURRUS)
   Mary 144
   Zachariah 119, 144
BUSCARTUS
   Barney 70

BUSKIRK
   Isaac 79
BUTLER
   Asaph 116
BYERS
   Andrew 35
CACELION
   William 159
CAFFEE (see also COFFEE)
   Amos H. 49
CAHEY
   John 19
CAHOON
   Mary 82
CALDERHEAD
   Margaret 182
CALDWELL 154
   Ann 165
   James . 2, 27, 28, 41, 45, 78, 84-86,
        88, 97, 98, 101, 107, 142,
          165, 166, 185
   Joseph . 77, 108, 128, 132, 135, 171
   Mary 132
   Nancy 45, 78, 88, 107, 185
CALHOON 92
CALVERT
   Jacob 300
CAMPBELL (CAMPBEL, CAMPBLE)
   Ann 73
   Anne 73, 77
   Archibald 176
   Barbara 127
   Charles 41
   Daniel 127
   David 73, 77, 105, 127, 142
   James 75, 105, 122
   John 12, 14, 15, 20, 25, 28, 31, 32,
     36, 45, 55, 56, 61, 73, 77, 79, 89,
    103, 105, 113, 120, 122, 134, 142,
       142, 159, 165, 167, 178,
          183, 184, 186
   Mary 14, 15, 45, 79
   Moses 44
   Ruth 75
   William 14, 104, 105
CANARY
   James 41, 42
CARLIN
   Edward G. 12

CLENDENON
Benjamin 152
Hannah 54
Isaac 50, 54, 136
CLEVENGER
Catharin 69
Isaac 69
CLINGAN
John 143
CLINTON
DeWitt 132
CLITHERS
John 115
CLOYD
Alice 91, 92, 96
James 91, 96, 97
COCHRAN 40, 112
COEN
Elisabeth 89
Sarah 104
William 104
COFFEE (see also CAFFEE)
John 123, 146
John, Junr. 143
William 143
COGHRON
Rebeckah 33
Robert 33
COLE
Archibald 152, 160, 180
COLEMAN
Nathaniel 183
COLES
Charles 170
Elizabeth 138
Solomon 102, 138
COLHAN
Math. 151
COLLINS
Henry 107
James 11, 107
John, Senr. 107
Samuel 107
Zadock 179
COLVILLE
James 6
COLWELL 81
Stephen 152, 153

COLYAR
John 17
Rhoda 17
COMBS
Benjamin 8, 130
CONDIT
Silas 9, 50
CONDON (CONDEN)
Edward 172
CONGLETON
Nancy 4, 5, 15, 86, 133
William 4, 5, 15, 24, 68, 86,
114, 133, 156
CONLION
William 159
CONNELL (CONNEL)
Eleanor (Elenor) 26, 29, 32, 36, 157
John 7, 26, 29, 32, 36, 75, 157, 158
S. 29, 158
Samuel 29, 157
CONNER
Daniel 85, 168
David 171
CONROW
Darling 96, 119, 155
COOK
Jeremiah 82
COON
Barbara (Barbary) 4, 7, 11, 13
George 4, 11
Jacob . . . 4, 7, 11, 13, 19, 30, 33,
83, 123, 165
John 7, 11, 13, 19
Susanah 19
William 71
COOPER
Francis 68
Thomas 123
COPE
George 105
COPELAND
John 137
COPLEN
Richard 74
COPPOCK
Isaac 2, 16, 50
Mary 2, 16
CORDELL
Presley 131

ELI
  Isaac 139
ELLIOTT (ELLIOT)
  Joel 46, 180
  John 24, 31, 33, 50, 83
  Rachel 50
ELLIS
  Ezer 68, 69, 79, 81, 117, 128
  Jonathan 10, 14, 15, 18, 25,
                              31, 92, 171
  Lydia 10, 14, 15, 25, 92, 171
ELLZEY
  Lewis 173
ELRICK (see ELERICK)
EMORY (EMERY)
  Rebecca 161
  Thomas 138, 142, 161
ENDLY (ENDLEY)
  Jacob 1, 27, 63
  Mary 1
ENGLE
  Abraham 10, 81, 91, 122
  Abram 24
  Caleb   8, 10, 31, 52, 53, 56, 67, 82,
              122, 129, 130, 179, 185
  Elizabeth 122
  Job 24
  Joseph 154, 156, 162, 167, 188
  Mercy 8, 31, 53, 56, 67, 82,
                        122, 129, 179
  Patience 10
  Samuel 10, 122
  Sarah 24
ENGLISH
  Richard 10
ENLOW
  Michael 144
ERWIN (see IRWIN)
EVANS
  Caleb 125
  Calwalder 108
  Eleazer 14, 144, 151
  Hannah 149
  Henry H. 79, 80, 86, 149
  James 6
  Martha 151
  Mary 151
  Thomas 106

EWERS (EWARS)
  Amy 20, 25
  William 20, 25, 80, 143, 144
FAIRHURST
  Anne 159
  Jeremiah   10, 13, 14, 20, 27, 57, 77
  Samuel 158, 159
FAQUHAR (see FARQUHAR)
FARIS
  Samuel 151
  William 3, 14
  William, Junr.   3, 8, 15, 19, 22, 24,
      36, 43, 58, 62, 64-66, 70, 75, 92,
      95, 96, 98, 102, 111, 114, 128,
      133, 156, 159, 178, 180, 181
  William, Senr. . 24, 36, 71, 87, 92
FARMER
  Isaac 20, 28, 75, 121
  Mary 75
FARNLEY
  Hannah 17
FARQUHAR (FAQUHAR, FORQUHAR))
  Allen 91, 92
  Amos 87, 91, 92
  Benjamin 87, 91, 92
  Elisabeth 92
  Eliza 6
  Esther 6
  George 28, 40
  James 91, 92
  Jonah 91, 92
  Mary 92
  Rachel 92
  Sarah 87
  William 49, 87, 91, 92
  William W. 4, 6, 184
  William Z. 66
FAWCETT (FAUCETT, FAWCET)
  David 17
  Jacob 50
  John 15
  Jonathan 44, 50
  Joseph 163
  Mary 50, 92, 93, 162
  Rachel 49, 82, 146
  Richard 164
  Samuel 49, 50, 82, 146
  Thomas 118, 167, 183

FRED.
    John 148
FREEMAN 26, 136, 143, 171
    Margery 1
    Richard 1
FRENCH
    Israel 46
    Otho 136
FRITCH
    John 3, 24, 42
FROCTHE
    William 142
FROST
    Nancy 49, 107
    William 49, 107, 156, 180
FRUSH
    Exey 122
    George 122
    Henry 30, 122
FRYMAN
    Charles 90
    Mary 90
FRYUNNGER
    Nicolous 10
FULTON
    Andrew 167
    David 86
    John 167
FURGUSON (see FERGUSON)
FURNAN
    Michael 112
GADD
    David 171
GADDIS
    Henry 169
GAITZE
    George 72
GALASPE (see GILLESPIE)
GALLOWAY
    Benjamin 173
    James 72, 80
GALT
    Dominick 45
GAMBLE
    Elizabeth 120
    Joseph 76, 120
    William 37, 152
GANDY
    Abraham 122

GARRET (see GARRETT)
GARRETSON
    Amos 146
GARRETT (GARRET)
    Andrew 41, 82
    James 10
GASKIEL
    David 31
GASSAWAY
    Ann 57
    Benjamin 23, 57
    Nick 161
GASTON
    A. 133, 170
    Alexander . . . 46, 47, 49, 108, 109
    Robert 81, 82
GATCHELL
    Samuel H. 163
GATTON
    William 7
GAULT
    Sarah 23, 35, 57
    William G. 141, 186
    William W. 3, 36, 57, 60
    William Weir 23, 35
GEAGE
    James 100
GEITZE
    Sevile 53
GEORGE
    Esther 15, 146
    Francis 123
    James 143
    John 17, 21
    Traverse 12, 15, 21, 146
GETTINGER (GETINGER, GITTINGER)
    Henry 19
GIBBONS (GIBBENS, GIBBINS, GIBBON)
    Joseph 38, 39, 90, 103
    Peter (Petter) 28, 38, 39
GIBSON
    John 78, 87, 153
    William 41, 63, 76, 163
GIFFEN (GIFFIN)
    Elizabeth (Betsey) 35, 71, 155
    George 151, 152
    Hetty 151, 152, 170
    Robert 99, 151, 152, 170
    William . . 22, 34, 35, 71, 100, 155

GREGG (GRAIG, GREG) (continued)
Samuel 9, 20, 37-40, 78,
142, 146
Samuel, Junr. 12, 100, 154
Samuel, Senr. 12, 100, 142
GREGREGRY
Patt (or Pell) 145
GREGREY/GRY, GRIGREY/RY)
Betsey 168
Henry 164, 168, 171
GRIER
Henry 147
John . . 2, 7, 10, 11, 16, 17, 44, 62,
150-152, 170, 175
John, Senr. 10, 11, 144, 175
Mary 151, 152, 170
Rhoda 150
Robert 11, 77
William 147
GRIFFITH
Benjamin 122
Elizabeth 138
Evan 138
Isaac 122
Jane 122
John 160
Joseph 1, 19, 74, 100
Robert 2, 3, 5, 11, 13, 15, 19, 22-25,
29, 55, 56, 60, 102, 116, 160, 161
Sarah 160
Thomas, W. 41
GRIGGS
Samuel 121
GRIGREY/GRIGRY (see GREGREY)
GRIMES
Arthur 51
Arthur, Junr. 52
Arthur, Senr. 52
Elisabeth (Elizabeth) 37, 39
Is 92
James 51
John 5
Joseph 18, 37, 39
Mathew (Matthew) 47, 49
Nelly 51
William 180
GROVE
Augt. M. 177

GROVES
Elisabeth 97
Michael 76, 84, 86, 97
William 58, 85
GRUBB
Elizabeth 24, 72
Jacob . . . 24, 49, 58, 72, 114, 156
GUMMEURE
William 140
GUTHRIE
Robert 165
HAFLING
John 108
HAGIN
John, Junr. 29
HAGLE
Jacob 127
HAILFORD
G. 70
HAINES
Eli 6
HAINS
John 24
Samuel 103
HALE
Owen 144
HALL
Benjamin 103
Dinah 20
Francis 53, 96
George 30, 128
Isaac . . 10, 17, 20, 39, 41, 48, 136
Isaac, Junr. 136
Jf. 115
John 48, 136
Joseph 187
Mary 39, 48
Robert 76
Sarah 42
Susana 162
Vachel (-al) 119, 136, 154, 162, 165
HAMBLER
Jacob 130
HAMBLETON (see HAMILTON)
HAMERLIN (see HAMMERLY)
HAMILTON (HAMBLETON)
John G. 5
Nancy 5
William 50, 82, 136

KEELIN
    Jacob 131
KELLAR (KELLER)
    George 3, 91, 181
KELLY
    Morras 178
KELSEY
    James 9, 16
KELVY
    James 88
KENNARD (KENARD, KERMARD) (see
    also KINNARD)
    Anthony 111, 122
    Catharine 111
    Eli (Ely) 19, 45, 90, 111
    Joseph 111
    Joshua 163
    Katharine 111
    Levi 90
    Thomas 111, 122
    William 111
KENNEDY 92
    John 100
    Moses W. 14
    Thomas 187
KENNEY (KENNY)
    Abraham . 74, 98, 99, 163, 185, 186
    Eleazer . . . 1, 11, 35, 60, 155, 180
    Jemima (Jamima) 60, 155
    John 105
    Marget 185
    Richard 108, 109
KERR (see also CARR)
    Christina 119
    David 119
    George 78, 83
    Joseph 140
KERRICK
    Edw. 45
KIMBERLY
    Mary 68, 72, 89
KIMMEL
    Gabriel 4
    Jacob 4
    John 4
KING
    Hannah 147
    John . 144, 146, 147, 164, 167, 176
    Mary (R.) 147, 164, 167, 176

KINKEAD (KINKADE)
    David 5, 6, 47
    Elizabeth 6
    Joseph 148
    Mr. 174
KINNARD (see also KENNARD)
    Mary Ann 100
    William 111
KINNEY, KINNY (see KENNEY)
KINSEY
    George 164, 167
    Stephen 28
KINSY
    John 54
KIRK
    Adam 79, 120
    Benjamin 79, 120
    Elizabeth 79, 120
    William 110
KIRKBRIDE
    David 107, 177
KIRKPATRICK
    David 74
KIRKWOOD
    Joseph 156
KNIGHT
    James 25
    Mary 25
    Nathl. 163
KNOUGH
    Mary Ann 163
KNOWLS
    James 24
    Mary 24
KNOX
    Charles D. 108
    George 174
KOON
    George 82
KRAMER (KREMER) (see also
    CREAMER)
    Margaret 168
    Peter 86, 168
KRATZER
    Samuel 66, 94
KUHN
    Conroe 4
    Jacob 4, 100

MEAD
    Samuel 149
MEADLEY (MEDDLEY)
    Joseph 73, 172
MECHEM
    John 100
    Sally 100
MEDCALF
    Abigail 41
    Mavers 110
    Moses 90
    William M. 41
MEDDLEY (see MEADLEY)
MEEK
    Margaret 121
    Richard 121
    William 121
MEEKS
    Samuel 47
MEIGS (MEIGGS)
    Josiah 162, 165, 168, 172, 186
MELAY
    James 159
MELOTT
    John 141, 166
    Mary 166
    William 166
MELTON 105
MERADAY
    William 102
MERCER (MERCIER)
    Elizabeth 12, 33
    John   16, 33, 34, 38, 39, 43, 49, 50,
          60, 63, 67, 74, 82, 96, 147
    John D. 12, 23, 33, 60, 99
    Richard 82
MERIDITH
    Benjamin 32
MERRITT (MERIT, MERRET, MERRIT)
    Daniel 6, 15, 88, 113, 178
    Isaac 81, 91, 99, 177
    Joseph 6, 23, 38, 87, 133, 183,
                184, 187, 188
    Mary 23, 183, 187, 188
    Moses 6, 88
    Nancy 6, 15
    Polly 6, 88
    Robert 174

MEYER
    Anthony 72
MEYERS (see MYERS)
MICHEM (MICHENS)
    John 84
MIDDLETON
    John 50, 120
    Joseph 50
    Mary 120
MIERS (see MYERS)
MILES
    Thomas 150
MILHOUS (MILHOUSE, MILLHOUSE)
    Hannah 37
    John 81
    Robert 101
    Sarah 101
    William 13, 37, 42, 76, 92
    William, Junr. 77
MILIGAN (see MILLIGAN)
MILLER 12
    Barbery 182
    David 139, 142
    George . 77, 91, 95, 131, 136, 144,
             151, 166, 177, 185
    George, Junr. 96
    George, Senr. 96
    Hannah 96
    John 47, 133, 173, 182
    Jonathan (Johnathan) 91
    Margaret 159
    Reuben 153
    Robert 42, 159
    Sarah 91
    Stephen 3, 91, 95, 131, 177
    Thomas 96, 168
MILLHORNE (probably MILHOUS)
MILLHOUSE (see MILHOUS)
MILLIGAN (MILIGAN)
    Mary 63, 182
    Moses 63, 85, 182
MILLS
    Nathan 16
    Patience 140
    Robert 104, 138, 140, 152
    Samuel 61, 73, 78, 89
MILNER
    Edward 29
    Jane 29

MOTT
　　William 73
MOUNTS
　　Providence 145
　　Racheal 146
　　William 146
MUCHMORE
　　Samuel 122
MULLAN
　　William 60
MULLINSON
　　J. 29
MUNN
　　Aaron 135, 140, 150
MURDOCK
　　Alexander 5, 23, 121
MURPHY (MURPHEY)
　　Abner 36, 98, 99, 103, 141
　　Benjamin 64, 115, 153, 172
　　Eleanor 172
　　Horatio 140, 163
　　Sarah 103, 141
MURRAY
　　John, Junr. 146
MUSSARD
　　Ami 104, 113
MYERS (MEYERS, MIERS) (see also
　　MAYERS)
　　George . 2, 107, 133, 164, 167, 176
　　Hannah 164, 167, 176
　　Jacob . . . 16, 27, 39, 41, 122, 136,
　　　　　　　　　140, 152, 160, 183
　　Margaret 164, 167, 176
　　Mary 133
　　Peggy 167
　　Sarah 140, 183
　　William 164, 167, 176
NAGLE (NAGAL)
　　Jacob 5, 32, 42, 52, 107, 109,
　　　　　　　　　110, 122, 145, 152
NEAL (see also NEIL, NEILL)
　　John R. 25
NEEL
　　John 148
NEFF
　　Barbary 64
　　Conrad 90, 98
　　Elisabeth (Elizabeth) 90, 98
　　Henry 21, 64

　　Henry, Junr. 64
　　Jacob 90, 98
　　John 21
　　Margaret 98
　　Peter 21
　　Sarah 21
NEIL (see also NEAL, NEEL)
　　Abigail 70
　　Hannah 70
　　Moses 70
NEILL (NEILE)
　　Lewis 94, 102
NEISWANGER
　　Christopher 157, 187
　　David 67, 68, 84, 86, 103,
　　　　　　　　　119, 157, 181, 187
　　Mary 103
NELLONS (NELANS, NELLANS,
　　NELONS) 180
　　Alexander 113
　　Action 172
　　Patrick 55, 67, 73, 76, 152,
　　　　　　　　　160, 172, 180
NESBIT
　　Jonathan 166
NEWALL (NEWELL)
　　Anne 74
　　Benjamin 74
　　David 24, 56, 74, 77, 80, 97,
　　　　　　　　　98, 149, 152, 171
　　Elisabeth (Elizabeth) 97
　　J. E. 105
　　James 185
　　James E. 97, 185
　　Sally . . 24, 56, 74, 77, 97, 152, 171
NEWPORT
　　Aaron 54, 107, 178
　　Jesse 136
　　Joseph 39
NEWSOME
　　Charles 22
NIBLOCK
　　John 7
NICHOL
　　Ann 10, 170
　　John 10, 14, 99, 170
　　William 14

POWELL (continued)
Sarah 175
William 59
POWER
John N. 72
PRESTON
Paul 66, 115, 149, 162, 164
Sarah 164
PRICE
Betsy 54
Elizabeth 18
George 40, 112
John . . . 3, 18, 34, 54, 73, 89, 144
Phineas 31
Robert 129
PRIOR (PRYOR)
Jemima 88
John 16, 67, 121
John, Senr. 88, 121
Margaret 121
Robert 56, 88, 122
PROCTER
Izak 23
Sarah 23
PROSSER
James 51
PRYAN
Stephen 27
PRYOR (see PRIOR)
PUL
Moses 86
PUMPHREY
Ann 72, 73
Elizabeth 73, 75, 118
Joseph 47
Nicholas 57, 118
Reason (Rasin, Reasin) 72, 73, 141,
153
William 73, 75
PURDY
John 156
Susan 156
PURVIANCE
W. Y. 62
PURVIES
John 101
PUSEY
Nathan 80, 105, 171

PYLE
Jesse 51, 99
RALEY (RAILEY)
James 13, 53, 120
RALSTON
Catharine 108
John 109
RAMSEY
John 180
RANDAL
Ananias 52
RANDALL
David 67
RANKIN
John 157
RATIKIN
James 114, 143
RAVEN
James M. 103
RAYNOLD
William 164
REAGH
Thomas 119
REED
George 169
REEVES
Elizabeth 70
Josiah 70
Vanmeter 62
REILY (REILEY)
Jacob 72, 186
Sarah 72
REPLOGAL (REPROGAL)
Elizabeth 42
Jacob 42, 80, 87, 93
REYNOLDS (RENNALS, RENNELS,
REYNELS)
Alexander 103
Barbara (Barbarah) 119, 135
George 175
Henry B. 103
John 127
William 70, 78, 118, 119, 135
William B. 71, 119, 135
RHODES
Henry 134
RICHARDS
James 134
Mikel 22

SMITH (continued)
Samuel 60, 96, 126
Steel 78, 172
Thomas . . 14, 15, 18, 25, 101, 111,
116, 123, 138, 146, 147, 150, 173
William . . 6, 10, 12, 14, 18, 19, 21,
30, 37, 40, 49, 54, 58, 61, 72, 79,
80, 96, 105, 108, 114, 125, 127,
129, 132, 139, 143, 146-148,
157, 164, 168, 173, 179
William, Senr. 35
SNEDEKER (SNEDACRE, SNEDACREE,
SNEDAKER, SNEDIKER)
Eleanor 79
Garret 22, 69, 71
Jacob 22, 61, 79, 87, 105
John 69, 71
Mary 69, 71
Nicholas 71
Peter 78, 83
SNIDER (SNYDER)
Abraham 99
Barbara (Barbarah) 82, 151
Catherine 27
David 27, 83, 136, 137, 141,
148, 151
George 82, 151, 175
Margaret (Margret) 137
Peter 23, 27
SNODGRASS
John 64, 115
Rebeckah 115
SNYDER (see SNIDER)
SPANGLER
Christian 18
SPARKS
Jesse 54
SPENCER
Aaron 145
Edmond 60, 168, 171
John 12, 17, 37, 38, 125, 145
Lydia 17, 145
Mary 171
Sarah 8, 46
Timothy 118
William 8, 46, 52
SPRIGG (SPRIGGS)
Amelia 47, 60, 99, 151
James 12, 42

Samuel . 11, 12, 22, 28, 33, 37, 47,
49, 60, 94, 95, 99, 113, 142, 151
Zac 12
SPROAT
Earl 29
ST. CLAIR (see also SINCLAIR)
George 123
James 123
John 123
William 123
STALEY
Christian 29
STANLEY (STANLY)
Elizabeth 30, 82
John 30, 82
STANTON
Benjamin 48
Borden . . . 53, 105, 106, 120, 125,
137, 157, 172, 184
Borden, Junr. 53, 118
Charlotte 53, 106, 172
Clary 110, 155
Henry 110, 155
William 157, 186
STARBUCK
Ann 171
Elizabeth 114, 133, 144, 182
George . . . 16, 114, 133, 144, 182
Hezekiah 144, 171
STARR
James 142
Merrick 45, 92
STEEL
Thomas 45
STEEN
Samuel 106, 126
STEER
Grace 151
James 105, 106, 137
Jonah 151
Joseph 151
Ruth 106
STEPHENSON
William 33
STEWART
Allen . . 36, 55, 69, 71, 84-86, 119
Henry 9, 63, 64, 109
Jacob 5
Jennet 64

WADDELL
George 88, 172
James 88, 172
Lydia 88
WAGGONER
Ann 81
John 59
William 59, 60, 81
WAGNER
William 49
WALKER
Andrew 15, 25
Anna 120
George 120
WALLACE
Agnes 184
Alexander 101, 184
Andrew 101
David . 4, 7, 11, 14, 19, 30, 33, 83,
100, 104, 106, 121-123, 126, 131,
134, 140, 159, 169, 183, 184
Dd. 169
Jane 122, 184
Jas. 171
John 8, 9, 26
Jos. 182
June 122
Margaret 26
William 101, 123
WALTON
John 133
Joseph 45, 56, 115, 164, 186
WARD
Jane 59
Thomas 9, 50
WARDELL
Solomon 3, 4, 11
WARNER
Zebulon 6, 8, 10, 11, 13, 14, 16, 18,
24, 25, 28, 36, 42, 64, 78, 125
WARNOCK
John 127, 159
WARREN
Haddick, Haddock 101, 181
WATKINS
Benjamin 16
Henrietta 145
John 146
Perigrine (Pery.) 145, 146

WATSON
J. 185
John . 11, 43, 48, 72, 92, 102, 115,
161, 175, 178, 185, 187
Rachel 101, 184
Robert 11, 101, 184
WATT
James 28, 36, 78, 93, 121
Sarah 78, 121
WATTS
James 20
William 99
WAY
Dorcas 172, 183
Matilda 165
WEAVER
Joshua 138
WEBB
William 88
WEBSTER 12
John S. 42
Jon 87
Thomas 140
WEILL
Lewis 102
WEIR
William 137
WELCH
William 88
WELLER
Peter 141
WELLS
Bazaleel, Bazalel, Bazeleel, Bazelial,
Bazeliel, Bazell, Bezaleel, Bezeleel,
Bezelial, Bezeliel . 2, 8, 10, 18, 19,
22, 24, 26, 45, 50, 53, 56, 57, 61,
68, 79, 85, 90, 97, 99, 106, 110,
111, 119, 135, 139, 149, 150, 154,
154, 163, 166, 176, 183, 185
Levi 13, 42, 120
Margaret 13
Sally . 2, 19, 22, 26, 45, 53, 56, 57,
68, 90, 99, 110, 111, 149, 166, 183
WELMAN
Rudolf 71
WELSH
Crawford (Chrawford) . 14, 64, 180
Mary 156
William 156

WILSON (WILLSON) (continued)
  Samuel 26, 57, 59, 133, 142,
                        148, 154
  Stephen 98
  Thomas 18, 26, 42, 126
  William 7, 56, 88, 121, 122,
                        162, 167
WINCHEL
  Silas 98, 99
WINDLAND (WINDELIN) (see also
        WINLIN)
  Jacob 137, 175
  Margaret 137
WINDLE
  Jacob 137
  Phillip 70
WINLIN (see also WINDLAND)
  Margaret 11
WINROD
  George 166
WINTER (see also WITNTER)
  Catharine 185
  Christopher 44
  John . . . 24, 25, 43, 44, 55, 56, 61,
                  65, 75, 98, 106, 115
  Jonathan 24, 185
  Nancy 185
  Robert 1, 106
WINTERS
  John 169
  Robert 161, 169, 175
  Sarah 161
WIRICK (see WYRICK)
WISE
  George 63
  Jacob 133
  Jane 63
  John 63, 133
  Samuel 133
WITCHELL
  John 72, 73, 80, 81
  John, Junr. 68, 72, 81
  Mary 72, 73, 80
WITNTER (see also WINTER)
  John 169
WOLF
  John 21
WOLFORD (WOOLFORD)
  Catherine 19

  David 148
  John 19
WOLGAMOTE
  Henry 85
WOOD (see also WOODS)
  Aaron (Aron) 20, 28, 126, 130, 131
  Abram 155
  Ann 155
  Archibald 130
  Elizabeth 126
  Hannah 71, 140, 144
  Isaac 155, 156
  Joshua . . 60, 71, 72, 140, 144, 163
  Margaret (Margret) . 155, 156, 182
  Mathew (Matthew) . . 38, 39, 155,
                        156, 182
  William 81
WOODBURN
  John 19
  William 127
WOODRAM (probably WOODROW)
WOODROW
  Abraham 142
  Joshua, Junr. 31, 92
  Nancy 31
  Simon 142
WOODS (see also WOOD)
  Ann (Anne) 36, 77
  Archibald 10, 12, 32, 36, 75, 77, 123
  Archid. 128
  E. 136
  Elijah 125, 136, 143
  Elizabeth 53, 137
  Joshua 72
  Mary 186
  Mr. 75
  Moses 85
  Robert 35, 53, 137
  William 6, 80, 154, 186
WOODYEAR
  Edward 62
WOOLFORD (see WOLFORD)
WOOLMAN
  Aaron 138
  Aaron A. 67
  George 67, 138
  Jane 67
  Joel 67
  Rachel 138

www.ingramcontent.com/pod-product-compliance
Lightning Source LLC
Chambersburg PA
CBHW061722270326

41928CB00011B/2080